RELIGION AND MORALITY

Religion and Morality addresses central issues arising from religion's relation to morality. Part I offers a sympathetic but critical appraisal of the claim that features of morality provide evidence for the truth of religious belief. Part II examines divine command theories, objections to them, and positive arguments in their support. Part III explores tensions between human morality, as ordinarily understood, and religious requirements by discussing such issues as the conflict between Buddhist and Christian pacifism and requirements of justice, whether "virtue" without a love of God is really a vice, whether the God of the Abrahamic religions could require us to do something that seems clearly immoral, and the ambiguous relations between religious mysticism and moral behavior.

Covering a broad range of topics, this book draws on both historical and contemporary literature, and explores afresh central issues of morality and religion offering new insights for students, academics and the general reader interested in philosophy and religion.

ASHGATE PHILOSOPHY OF RELIGION SERIES

Series Editors

Paul Helm, King's College, University of London, UK
Jerome Gellman, Ben-Gurion University, Beer-Sheva, Israel
Linda Zagzebski, University of Oklahoma, USA

Due to the work of Plantinga, Alston, Swinburne and others, the philosophy of religion is now becoming recognized once again as a mainstream philosophical discipline in which metaphysical, epistemological and moral concepts and arguments are applied to issues of religious belief. The *Ashgate Philosophy of Religion Series* fosters this resurgence of interest by presenting a number of high profile titles spanning many critical debates, and presenting new directions and new perspectives in contemporary research and study. This new series presents books by leading international scholars in the field, providing a platform for their own particular research focus to be presented within a wider contextual framework. Offering accessible, stimulating new contributions to each topic, this series will prove of particular value and interest to academics, graduate, postgraduate and upper-level undergraduate readers world-wide focusing on philosophy, religious studies and theology, sociology or other related fields.

Titles in the series include:

Mystical Experience of God
A Philosophical Inquiry
Jerome Gellman

Religious Diversity
A Philosophical Assessment
David Basinger

Rationality and Religious Theism
Joshua L. Golding

God and Realism
Peter Byrne

God and the Nature of Time
Garrett J. DeWeese

Religion and Morality

WILLIAM J. WAINWRIGHT
University of Wisconsin-Milwaukee, USA

ASHGATE

Published by
Ashgate Publishing Limited
Gower House
Croft Road
Aldershot
Hants GU11 3HR
England

Ashgate Publishing Company
Suite 420
101 Cherry Street
Burlington, VT 05401-4405
USA

Ashgate website: http://www.ashgate.com

British Library Cataloguing in Publication Data

Wainwright, William J.
  Religion and morality. - (Ashgate philosophy of religion
  series)
  1. Divine commands (Ethics) 2. God - Proof, Moral 3. Religious
  ethics
  I. Title
  205

Library of Congress Cataloging-in-Publication Data
Wainwright, William J.
  Religion and morality / William J. Wainwright.— 1st ed.
    p. cm. -- (Ashgate philosophy of religion series)
  Includes bibliographical references and index.
  ISBN 0-7546-1631-2 (hardcover : alk. paper) -- ISBN 0-7546-1632-0 (pbk. : alk. paper)
1. Religion and ethics. I. Title. II. Series.

  BJ47.W35 2005
  205--dc22

                                    2004013979

ISBN 0 7546 1631 2 (Hbk); 0 7546 1632 0 (Pbk)

Typeset by Manton Typesetters, Louth, Lincolnshire, UK.
Printed and bound in Great Britain by MPG Books Ltd, Bodmin, Cornwall.

For Mimi, Rebecca, Sarah, Chantal, Nicholas, and Alan

Contents

Preface

Most twentieth- and early-twenty-first-century work on moral philosophy has had little or nothing to say about religion. When its authors do speak of it, they tend to be dismissive or patronizing, and almost inevitably brief. Similarly, most analytic philosophers of religion have had little of substance to say about morality. Alleged moral truths are of course sometimes appealed to. (Discussions of the problem of evil are the most obvious example.) But the implications of morality *as such* for religion, and religion's implications for it, have been largely neglected.

This book is about these issues. It is divided into three parts. The four chapters of Part I examine three moral arguments for God's existence—Immanuel Kant's contention that a belief in God and immortality is a necessary postulate of moral reason, J. H. Newman's insistence that human conscience attests to a divine lawgiver and judge, and the claim made by W. R. Sorley and others that God (or something like God) is needed to explain the apparent objectivity of moral value. After critically discussing contemporary critiques of the three arguments, I conclude that, when suitably qualified, versions of each of them are sound.

Part II discusses the most hotly contested theistic account of moral obligation—divine command theory. Chapter 5 surveys medieval and early modern divine command theories and their critics. In Chapter 6 I turn to the two most important recent versions of divine command ethics—those of Philip L. Quinn and Robert M. Adams. Chapters 7 and 8 of this section examine the major linguistic, logical, and ethical objections to divine command theory, and the positive case that can be made for it. I argue that the objections to divine command theory can be met, but that the positive case for it isn't conclusive since other theistic accounts of moral obligation, and in particular Linda Zagzebski's divine motivation theory, may be equally compelling.

It is typically assumed that the *moral* requirements of religion and secular moral requirements are essentially the same. Part III questions this assumption by examining three areas in which religious requirements come into apparent conflict with the requirements of ordinary human morality. Chapter 9 argues for two claims: first, the absolute pacifism of the Buddha and Jesus can only be viewed as irrational by human moral reason, and, second, a strong case can be made for the contention that what we ordinarily regard as virtues aren't real virtues when they are divorced from the love of God—a claim equally offensive to ordinary moral reason. Chapter 10 examines the implications of God's command to Abraham to sacrifice his son Isaac. It argues that attempts to water the story down, or soften its message, are ultimately unsuccessful. God's goodness and human moral goodness may not be fully compatible. The book's final chapter explores the ambiguous relations between mysticism and morality. The issue is important because the mystical strand plays a significant role in all of the major religious traditions, and a decisive role in some. While I disagree with those who think that mysticism and morality are incompatible, I shall show that the relations between them are much less straight-forward than is often supposed.

The general thrust of the book as a whole is that moral philosophy and philosophy of religion have very important bearings on each other. Philosophers of religion and moral philosophers can't afford to ignore each other as they too often do. The cost of doing so is an impoverishment of both disciplines.

Finally, I would like to thank Sallie B. King and C. Stephen Evans for their kind permission to quote from unpublished manuscripts in Chapters 9 and 10 respectively. I would also note that Chapter 11 is a significantly revised version of material that first appeared in chapter 5 of my *Mysticism: A Study of its Nature, Cognitive Value and Moral Implications* (Madison: University of Wisconsin Press, 1981). Thank you too to Oxford University Press for allowing me to quote material by Robert Adams—from *Finite and Infinite Goods: A Framework for Ethics* by Robert Merrihew Adams, © 1999 Robert Merrihew Adams. Used by permission of Oxford University Press, Inc.

PART I
MORAL ARGUMENTS FOR THE EXISTENCE OF GOD

CHAPTER 1

The Nineteenth-Century Background

Classical arguments for God's existence came under increasing fire in the seventeenth and eighteenth centuries, culminating in David Hume's scathing attack on design and cosmological arguments and in Immanuel Kant's critiques of *all* attempts to establish God's existence by "theoretical" or speculative reason. Yet Kant also thought that a belief in God and immortality were necessary postulates of "practical" (that is, moral) reason. It is important to realize how innovative Kant's move was. Many had previously offered religious *interpretations* of morality, or claimed that sincere religious belief was a necessary *causal condition* of moral behavior. But Kant was the first to clearly argue that morality provided *rational support* for belief in God and an afterlife.

Kant's move proved especially attractive to nineteenth- and early twentieth-century thinkers who, while unimpressed by the classical proofs and radically skeptical of traditional religion and orthodox dogmas, were deeply sympathetic to the sentiments and moral teachings which they believed underlie them. George Eliot and Matthew Arnold were typical of many thoughtful people of this period.

F. W. H. Myers records a conversation he had with George Eliot in 1873:

> I remember how, at Cambridge, I walked with her once in the Fellows' Garden of Trinity, on an evening of rainy May; and she, stirred somewhat beyond her wont, and taking as her text the three words which have been used so often as the inspiring trumpet-calls of men,—the words, *God, Immortality, Duty*,—pronounced, with terrible earnestness, how inconceivable was the *first*, how unbelievable the *second*, and yet how peremptory and absolute the *third*. Never, perhaps, have sterner accents affirmed the sovereignty of impersonal and unrecompensing Law. I listened, and night fell; her grave, majestic countenance turned towards me like a Sibyl's in the gloom; it was as though she withdrew from my grasp, one by one, the two scrolls of promise, and left me the third scroll only, awful with inevitable fates. And when we stood at length and parted, amid that columnar circuit of the forest-trees, beneath the last twilight of starless skies, I seemed to be gazing like Titus at Jerusalem, on vacant seats and empty halls,—on a sanctuary with no Presence to hallow it, and heaven left lonely of a God.[1]

Or consider Matthew Arnold, who argued that "Israel did not find out God by reasoning or by inference; he 'felt and experienced' what was revealed to him," namely, "that 'Righteousness tendeth to life,' that 'to righteousness belongs happi-

---

1   Quoted in Basil Wiley, *Nineteenth Century Studies: Coleridge to Matthew Arnold*. New York: Columbia University Press, 1949, p. 204.

ness' . . . The essential faith of the Old Testament . . . , for Arnold, is belief in 'the Eternal not ourselves that makes for righteousness'." Religion, in short, "is founded upon moral experience."[2]

There is a variety of moral arguments. Some claim that religious belief is necessary for moral motivation. Others contend that if religion is false, morality loses its point or ceases to be fully intelligible. These arguments are similar but distinct. William James, for example, employs both. Kant employs the second but self-consciously rejects the first. Still others claim that something like God or the Platonic forms are needed to explain morality's objectivity or the reliability of conscience. Thus, W. R. Sorley and Hastings Rashdall make the first claim, and John Henry Newman the second. Arguments like Sorley's and Newman's presuppose that morality is in fact objective and that conscience is in order. Others clearly assume that only a *belief* in morality's objectivity or in the reliability of conscience is needed for successful moral practice. Kant is sometimes thought to be an example of the latter. These matters need careful sorting out, however, and will be the subject of the next three chapters.

Interest in the moral arguments sharply declined in the middle years of the last century. William Lad Sessions has suggested that there were four reasons for this. The first is that the arguments "had nearly always been presented in Idealistic idiom." It is not surprising, then, that the repudiation of the philosophical idealism which had dominated nineteenth-century thought led to decreased interest in any argument for God's existence couched in its terms. A second reason was the "eclipse of speculative metaphysics." Since moral arguments for religious conclusions presuppose general pictures of the cosmos and our place in it, skepticism about speculative metaphysics cannot help but adversely affect our attitudes towards them. The third is the rise of ethical noncognitivism, the doctrine that moral assertions neither state facts nor express necessary truths. If they don't, then morality isn't objective, and arguments like Sorley's or Rashdall's can't get off the ground. The fourth reason is a general indifference "to religious interests," "a commitment to science as the one rationally acceptable human [intellectual] activity."[3]

These reasons aren't equally basic. Sessions's fourth reason, for example, helps explain indifference to religious apologetics in general but doesn't explain why moral arguments have been more neglected that ontological, or design, or cosmological arguments. His first reason accounts for the comparative neglect of arguments like Sorley's but doesn't account for the neglect of arguments like Newman's which aren't expressed in the language of idealism. As for Sessions's second reason, speculative metaphysics is once again in fashion (at least among theistic philosophers) but has not, for the most part, led to renewed interest in the moral arguments. Richard Swinburne, for example, offers many arguments for

---

2   Ibid., p. 269.
3   W. L. Sessions, "A New Look at Moral Arguments for Theism," *International Journal for Philosophy of Religion* 18 (1985), pp. 51–67.

God's existence but "find[s] 'the moral law within' considerably less good testimony to God than 'the starry heavens above'."[4]

Sessions's third reason for the eclipse of the moral arguments is, I suspect, the most fundamental. Whether they are ethical noncognitivists or not, few philosophers today think that moral values have the kind of objectivity that many eighteenth- and nineteenth-century thinkers attributed to them, or share Eliot's and Arnold's sense of the peremptoriness or absoluteness of moral duty. In a climate of this sort, moral arguments are even less likely to be apologetically effective than arguments from the existence of contingent being, say, or the fine tuning of the universe. In so far as theistic philosophers have themselves been infected by this climate, they are also less likely to find moral arguments for religious beliefs persuasive. The upshot, as Robert Adams said in 1979, is that "moral arguments . . . have become one of philosophy's abandoned farms."[5] He added, however, that "the fields are still fertile," and proceeded to discuss and defend several attempts to justify religious belief by appeals to moral convictions. Interest in the moral arguments has recently resurfaced in other philosophers as well. The following three chapters will examine some of the most important of these arguments. I shall argue that, subject to certain qualifications, the arguments we will discuss are successful.

---

4 Richard Swinburne, *The Existence of God*. Oxford: Clarendon Press, 1979, p. 175.
5 "Moral Arguments for Theistic Belief," reprinted in Robert M. Adams, *The Virtue of Faith and Other Essays in Philosophical Theology*. New York: Oxford University Press, 1987, p. 144.

CHAPTER 2

Kant, God, and Immortality

Kant's Ethical Position

Kant thought that a wholehearted commitment to morality is rational only if God exists and we are immortal. What does a wholehearted commitment to morality involve? The key is found in his concept of a morally good will. One's will is good when one acts from duty, when the maxims on which one acts are morally lawful, and when one acts out of respect for the moral law. The three conditions are equivalent in the sense that if any one of them is met, so are the two others. But how are they to be understood?

Acting *from* duty must be distinguished from merely acting in *accordance* with it. In the latter case, one does *what* duty prescribes but doesn't do it *because* duty prescribes it; one does it because of desire or inclination. Suppose, for example, that I help an acquaintance out of a tight spot because I am a tender-hearted person who is easily moved by people's difficulties, and I sympathize with his distress. The act I perform may be the act duty prescribes. The *spring* of my action, however, is sympathy or benevolence. I help my acquaintance because I feel sorry for him, not because I see that it is my duty to do so. Kant is not denying that my action has worth. But he *is* denying that it has *moral* worth.

To see why, let us briefly consider his distinction between hypothetical and categorical imperatives. Hypothetical imperatives prescribe actions as means to desired ends. Their standard form is "If you want x, do y." They are of two sorts. Imperatives of "skill" prescribe actions as means to desired ends which may or may not be endorsed by any given individual. An example is "If you want to be a social success, cultivate the right people." Imperatives of "prudence," on the other hand, prescribe actions as means to happiness, and happiness is an end of *every* rational being with inclinations. But in both cases the end depends on our desires. Social success is an end for me only if I want it. And since happiness is the *sum* of what we desire, its content will vary from one person to another depending on what he or she wants. As a result, actions prescribed by hypothetical imperatives are binding only in so far as the person to whom they are addressed *has* the desires, and thus *seeks* the ends, on which the hypothetical imperatives rest. One thus escapes the obligations they impose if one lacks the relevant desires. For example, if I have no desire for social success, the fact that cultivating the right people can help me achieve it provides me with no reason for cultivating them. Similarly, if I don't count health as part of my happiness, the injunction to promote my happiness by caring for my health gives me no reason to exercise, be careful of my diet, and the like.

Categorical imperatives, on the other hand, prescribe actions unconditionally, not as mere means to desired ends, and thus hold regardless of what we desire. As a consequence, the obligations these imperatives impose can't be escaped by modifying or relinquishing our desires. Since *moral* principles are binding on all (possible) rational beings, they must be categorical. If moral principles were merely hypothetical, they would rest on specific desires and wants, and would thus not be binding on rational beings whose desires were different.

The trouble with acting solely on the basis of natural incentives like sympathy is therefore this. The maxims which are guiding our actions are derived from desires which aren't shared by all (possible) rational beings, and thus can't be regarded as expressions of pure moral reason.

Why does Kant adopt this position? A person's emotions, feelings, and inclinations are part of his or her biological inheritance. However admirable they may be, acts that are *only* expressions of feeling and inclination are acts of *human animals*, of beings caught up in the web of nature, locked into the system of natural causes and effects. When we act because we see that something is right, however, our behavior is an expression of our *reason* and *will*, of those aspects of ourselves which *transcend* nature.

Two "worlds" or realities must be distinguished. The phenomenal world or world of appearances discloses itself in sense perception and is investigated by science. It includes observable substances, qualities, and events, and theoretical entities like subatomic particles which science postulates to explain them. "Behind" the world of appearances lies the noumenal world—reality as it is in itself, and not as it manifests itself *to us*. This world is inaccessible to theoretical reason and is therefore, in the strict sense, unknowable.[1] But human beings belong to both worlds. As parts of nature, we are members of the phenomenal world, and our behavior can be explained in terms of natural causality. As free and rational beings, we are members of the noumenal world, and our actions are self-determined.

Kant's second answer to the question "When is a will good?" is that one's will is good when its conduct is governed by morally lawful maxims. What maxims are lawful? Kant provides three tests which are equivalent in the sense that their application yields the same results. We will briefly consider two of them.

The first test is consistency: one should "act only according to that maxim which [one] can at the same time will should become a universal law." Consider the maxim "Deceive others when it is advantageous to do so." The universalized maxim is "*Everyone* deceives others when they find it useful to do so." Can I coherently will that this be a universal law? No, because the very possibility of

---

1   *Knowledge*, or "cognition," for Kant, involves matching concepts and intuitions. We know that concepts like causality or motion aren't empty because they can be applied to sensory intuitions. But while we can *think* the noumenal (form concepts of it) we have no intuitions of it, and thus don't *know* that these concepts apply to anything. (Kant does think, however, that it is reasonable to *believe* that they do.)

deception rests on trust. I can't deceive *you*, for example, if you don't trust *me*. And, in general, I can't successfully govern my conduct by a maxim of deceit unless (at least some) others don't. The maxim can't be universalized, then, because it is impossible for everyone to successfully act on it. For similar reasons, I can't universalize maxims of controlling or enslaving others, since those who are enslaved or controlled *lose their autonomy* and are consequently incapable of guiding their lives by *any* freely chosen maxims—including those of controlling or enslaving others. Maxims of controlling or enslaving others thus can't be freely endorsed by everyone.[2]

Other maxims are unlawful because the attempt to universalize them involves a contradiction in the *will*.[3] Am I entitled to govern my conduct by a maxim of nonbeneficence, for example? That is, is it permissible for me not to aid others as long as I don't positively harm them? The universalized maxim ("No one aids others") isn't incoherent. But willing the maxim *is* inconsistent with something else that I necessarily will as a rational being with inclinations, namely, my own happiness. Why is this the case? Willing an end (as distinguished from simply wishing for it) necessarily involves willing the means needed to achieve it. If *nobody* helps others when they need it, however, no one will help *me* when *I* need it. So I can't rationally will that a maxim of nonbeneficence be a universal law. And, in general, agents who aren't self-sufficient, and therefore can't ensure that they won't at some time need to draw on the resources of others to achieve their ends, can't rationally will things (such as a universalized maxim of non-beneficence) that would deprive them of those resources.[4]

Kant's second test for distinguishing morally lawful from unlawful maxims is this: act only on maxims which are such that in following them one treats people as ends and not as means only. Maxims of deceiving or controlling others are unlawful because acting on them involves treating others as mere means or instruments subordinated to our own purposes. Treating others as ends requires more than simply not using them, however. To function autonomously, agents need the resources to accomplish the ends which they necessarily have as rational beings with inclinations. I am therefore obligated to provide help when I can do so and others need my help. So maxims of nonbeneficence, too, are incompatible with the respect I owe others, that is, with a recognition of their intrinsic worth or dignity.[5]

---

2   I owe this point to Onora O'Neill, *Constructions of Reason: Explorations of Kant's Practical Philosophy*. Cambridge: Cambridge University Press, 1989, pp. 156–7.
3   As distinguished from a contradiction in the universalized maxim itself.
4   O'Neill, *Constructions of Reason*, pp. 98–101.
5   Kant's third test yields the same results. Onora O'Neill suggests that the first test adopts the perspective of an agent who is selecting a maxim to govern her action, and asks whether everyone can successfully follow the proposed guideline. The second adopts the perspective of an agent who is potentially affected by another's action, and asks whether those who are acted upon will "retain the capacities for agency that would permit them" to act "on the proposed guidelines." (That is, not only whether

Kant's discussion of the second test has an important implication. Human beings must be treated as ends. This not only implies that I should not treat myself or others as mere means; it also implies that I should further the ends which I and others necessarily have as rational beings with inclinations. What are those ends?

Virtue, the perfect conformity of one's behavior to the requirements of "practical" (moral) reason, is an end reason necessarily sets for itself. But this does "not imply that virtue is the entire and perfect good as the object of the faculty of desire of rational finite beings. For this, happiness is also required." The second end is subordinate to the first, however, because "virtue (as the worthiness to be happy) is the supreme condition of whatever [else] appears to us to be desirable and thus of all our pursuit of happiness;" other ends have moral legitimacy only if their pursuit is constrained by the requirements of morality.[6]

The highest good, then, is the systematic union of worthiness to be happy and happiness. "For to be in need of happiness and also worthy of it and yet not to partake of it could not be in accordance with the complete volition of an omnipotent rational being, if we assume such only for the sake of argument." (*CP* 114–15) In furthering the ends which I and others necessarily have as rational beings with inclinations, I am therefore obligated to make the highest good my end, and do whatever lies in my power to achieve it.[7]

---

their agency won't be undercut or destroyed by being treated as a mere means, but also whether they will be provided with the "positive support from others" they need "to remain agents.") The third test combines the two perspectives and asks whether a set of maxims could be adopted in a "systematic union of rational beings under common objective laws—that is, a *Kingdom*." (Kant, *Groundwork for the Metaphysics of Morals* IV, 433) In other words, the third test asks us to "consider ourselves both as acting (as hypothetical universal legislators) and as acted upon (as hypothetical subjects to those laws . . .)," and thus doesn't add anything to the content of the first two. It does, however, map them "onto the heritage of religious and political metaphors in which an ideal 'Kingdom' or 'realm' is the symbol of" a longed-for but as yet unrealized community. (O'Neill, *Constructions of Reason*, pp. 139–43)

6   Immanuel Kant, *Critique of Practical Reason*, trans. Lewis White Beck. New York: The Liberal Arts Press, 1956, p. 114. Henceforth *CP*.

7   Kant seems to think that the most effective way of discharging this obligation is by cultivating one's *own* moral nature and promoting the (morally legitimate) happiness *of others*. While I can and should indirectly contribute to the moral growth of others by providing encouragement, offering moral instruction, fostering an environment in which conscience is neither stunted nor warped, and the like, each individual is ultimately responsible for her own moral development. Only she can make herself moral. And while I have a duty to make the (morally legitimate) happiness of others my end, I do not have a duty to make my own happiness my end. (Kant's idea appears to be this. I necessarily take an interest in my own happiness [though not in the happiness of others]. Since I am not obligated to do what I can't help doing, I have no obligation to make my own happiness my end. [However, I surely do sometimes have a duty to do those things which will *further* or *promote* my own happiness since I don't automatically do *them*.]) On these points see Kant's *The Metaphysics of Morals, Part II: The Doctrine of Virtue*, trans. Mary J. Gregor, henceforth *MM*. New York: Harper Torchbooks, 1964, pp. 44–7.

Kant's third (and last) answer to the question "What is a good will?" is that a will is good when it acts out of respect for the moral law.

Respect shouldn't be confused with natural feelings, emotions, and inclinations. The objects of the latter—food, drink, making someone smile, another person's ruin—are parts of nature, the phenomenal world. The object of respect, however, is the moral law and the moral law *transcends* nature.[8] Furthermore, the objects of our natural feelings and inclinations are only valuable because we desire them. Wealth, freedom from pain, another's prosperity or ruin, have worth or value only because people want them. Their value consists in their being desired or in the fact that they would satisfy desire if one were to obtain them. If there were no desires, then, these things would be worthless. The moral law, on the other hand, is good (has worth or dignity) whether or not it is cherished by anyone. Its goodness isn't created by respect in the way in which the goodness of objects of desire is created by desire.

What sort of "feeling" or "emotion" is respect for the moral law? At the end of *The Critique of Practical Reason*, Kant compares it with the "admiration and awe" aroused by contemplating "the starry heavens above me." The latter "begins at the place I occupy in the external world of sense, and it broadens the connection in which I stand into an unbounded magnitude of worlds beyond worlds and systems of systems . . . ," annihilating, "as it were, my importance as an animal creature . . . " The former "begins at my invisible self, my personality," and connects me to a world "comprehensible only to the understanding," infinitely raising "my worth as that of an intelligence by my personality, in which the moral law reveals a life independent of all animality and even of the whole world of sense . . . " (*CP* 166)

The *Critique of Judgment* associates respect or reverence for the moral law with the sense of the "dynamical sublime," a feeling excited by "bold, overhanging, and as it were threatening rocks, thunderclouds piling up in the sky and moving about accompanied by lightning and thunderclaps, volcanoes with all their destructive power, hurricanes with all the devastation they leave behind, the boundless ocean heaved up," and the like—things which are fearful in the sense that if we wanted to resist them our resistance would be futile, yet are also attractive because they arouse a feeling of the mind's superiority to that which could crush it.

What does the mind's superiority consist of? The power of nature can destroy anything in us which is merely natural, that is, part of nature, including our minds in so far as they, too, are mere phenomena. (A blow on the head can lead to a loss of mental functioning, for instance.) A feeling of the mind's superiority to nature must therefore be a feeling that the mind is not only part of nature but transcends it—that some part or aspect of the mind belongs to the supersensible (noumenal) world. Objects are experienced as dynamically sublime, then, when they cause the mind "to feel its own sublimity, which lies in its vocation [to act on moral principles] and

---

8   Persons are also objects of respect, but they are objects of respect because they are both authors of, and subject to, the moral law, i.e., they are objects of respect in so far as they too transcend nature.

elevates it even above nature." For it "calls forth our strength (which does not belong to nature) . . . to regard as small the [objects] of our [natural] concerns: property, health, and life," and as something we "should [not] have to bow to . . . if our highest principles were at stake and we had to choose between upholding or abandoning them."[9]

Respect or reverence for the moral law is akin to this. It is an emotion in which one feels "at once humbled and [yet] also uplifted or exalted,"[10] and is connected with the fact that we apprehend the moral law as a *command* or *imperative*. A rational being's will would be perfectly good or "holy" if and only if each of its actions were fully determined by practical (that is, moral) reason. Now Kant appears to think it impossible for a limited or dependent being not to have wants or inclinations. He also seems to think it impossible for the will of a being with inclinations to be perfectly good or holy (since our desire for happiness will constantly tempt us to subordinate moral incentives to incentives of self-love). An independent and unlimited being alone, then, could possess a holy will. Such a being would "love" the law rather than reverence it. But to rational beings like us, who often find it difficult to do what the law prescribes, the moral law appears as a command or imperative. It is the unconditional character of the law's demand for moral purity which arouses respect or reverence.[11]

We are now in a position to turn to our main question. Why does a wholehearted commitment to morality implicitly commit one to a belief in God and immortality?

---

9 Kant, *Critique of Judgment*, trans. Werner S. Pluhar. Indianapolis: Hackett, 1987, pp. 119–21.

10 H. J. Paton, *The Categorical Imperative: A Study in Kant's Moral Philosophy*. New York: Harper Torchbooks, 1967, p. 64.

11 Kant's claim that we should act out of respect for the moral law is often understood in this way. We first recognize the law as an *objective* principle (the principle we ought to follow). This arouses a feeling of respect which, in turn, induces us to make the law the *subjective* principle or maxim of our conduct. On this interpretation, the feeling of respect is "the connecting link between our recognition of the law as an objective principle and our adopting it as a subjective principle or maxim." The problem with this interpretation is that Kant frequently insists that "the moral law must determine the will *immediately* [i.e., directly] without the intervention of feeling of any kind." That is, the *law itself*, and not feeling or emotion, must be the sufficient determining ground of our behavior. The contradiction is more apparent than real, however, for the feeling of respect isn't *distinct* from our recognition that something is our duty; it is its "emotional side," that is, the form that recognition takes in a being with inclinations. Respect or reverence for the moral law isn't a discrete psychological state which is *caused* by the recognition that something is our duty but, rather, an *aspect* of it, namely, its emotional resonance in a rational being with inclinations. (Paton, *Categorical Imperative*, pp. 66–8. This interpretation is confirmed by Kant's discussion in the *Critique of Judgment*, Division I, Book I, #12.)

The Postulate of Immortality

In his *Critique of Practical Reason*, Kant argues that "complete fitness of the will to the moral law is holiness." Now holiness "is a perfection of which no rational being in the world of sense is at anytime capable. But since it is required as practically [that is, morally] necessary it can be found only in an endless progress to that complete fitness. . . . This infinite progress is possible, however, only under the presupposition of an infinitely enduring existence and personality of the same rational being." (*CP* 126–7) Kant's argument is roughly this:

1   We are morally obligated to perfect conformity to the moral law.
2   No one is morally obligated to do something she can't do.
3   Moral perfection is thus possible. (From 1 and 2.) But
4   Moral perfection isn't possible in this life. The solicitations of pleasure and pain, the pull of desire, and our bias towards our own happiness make failure inevitable.
5   The moral self must therefore survive death; moral reason requires us to postulate an eternity in which the self can endlessly progress toward perfection. (From 4 and 5.)

Those who doubt the argument's conclusion will be tempted to run it in reverse: if we can't achieve moral perfection in this life, and *don't* survive death, then moral perfection is impossible. Given that we aren't obligated to do what we *can't* do, we aren't obligated to be morally perfect. While we may have a duty to *strive* towards perfection, we have no duty to *attain* it.

Some of Kant's remarks seem to lend credence to this charge. In *The Doctrine of Virtue*, for example, Kant says that while I have a "narrow" or "perfect" duty to strive for moral perfection, I have only a "wide" or "imperfect" duty to attain it. I am thus not strictly required "to achieve it [moral perfection] (in this life)." (*MM* 113) Kant's thought, however, appears to be this.

Perfect duties prescribe specific actions. An example is our duty to keep promises we have made. Imperfect duties prescribe goals or ends without specifying precisely how they are to be realized.[12] We have an imperfect duty to further the happiness of others, for instance. But the maxim "Promote the happiness of others" doesn't tell us whether we should promote human happiness by contributing to hunger relief or by assisting in the education of underprivileged children or in some other way. Nor does it tell us how much we should contribute to hunger relief or how much time we should devote to the education of underprivileged children. Unlike our duty to keep our promises, our duty to promote the happiness of others is comparatively indeterminate.

---

12   Though they do strictly prescribe that the maxims governing our actions must be *consistent* with the pursuit of those ends. (Cf. *MM* 48f.)

Now moral perfection includes both an "objective" and a "subjective" component. One must not only perform "all one's duties," one's motives must be pure "without any admixture of purposes derived from sensuous inclinations" (the desire for one's own happiness). Because "the depths of the human heart are unfathomable," however, one can never be sure that one's motives are pure. We can therefore never be sure whether or to what degree we have succeeded in realizing the goal of moral perfection, and so cannot be sure of precisely what still remains to be done, that is, of just what, at this point in our lives, we should do. Our duty to perfect ourselves is thus "imperfect." But our duty to make moral perfection our *goal*, that is, to *strive* to attain it, is not. (Making the attainment of moral perfection our goal is comparatively determinate.) I can't rationally make the attainment of something my goal, however, *unless I believe that its attainment is (really) possible.*[13] Note, too, that while, given "the *frailty (fragilitas)* of human nature," I can't attain, and so have no duty to attain, moral perfection "*in this life*" (my emphasis), Kant does *not* deny that I have a duty to attain it *sans phrase.* (*MM* 113)

And indeed, that we have a duty to be morally perfect is difficult to deny. "Perfect truthfulness is a duty" seems equivalent to "We ought always to speak the truth." Similarly, "Perfect justice is a duty" seems equivalent to "We ought always to act justly." By parity of reasoning, then, "Moral perfection is a duty" would appear to be equivalent to "We ought always to act morally." Since the latter is surely true, so is the former. Moral perfection thus does seem to be a duty.

But why think that moral perfection can't be attained in this life? If I am raised in a society that is careless of the truth, and find it easy to lie, I will undoubtedly lie upon occasion. Perfect truthfulness is overwhelmingly improbable. But it isn't *impossible.* It *would* be impossible if my upbringing and natural dispositions *causally determined* my behavior or if I couldn't control my inclinations by exerting my will. A strong bias toward dishonesty doesn't imply that I *can't* make the necessary effort, however, and speak the truth. Nor does Kant think that it does. Similarly, a bias towards evil may make moral perfection difficult or improbable but it doesn't make it impossible.

The force of this objection is uncertain since it depends on the *strength* of our bias toward evil. Kant thought it was very powerful. He sometimes identifies it with the pull of our inclinations, which can make doing the right thing very difficult. My desire for promotion, for example, may induce me to silently acquiesce in the illegal and socially harmful acts of the company for which I work. Kant's consid-

---

13 Can't I strive towards a goal whose attainment I believe is impossible? In a sense I can do so. For example, I can strive towards the realization of a perfectly egalitarian society even though I believe that a perfectly egalitarian society is impossible. But, strictly speaking, my goal in this case isn't the attainment of a perfectly egalitarian society but, rather, the realization of the most perfect possible *approximation* of that society, and that goal is, by hypothesis, not impossible.

ered view, however, is that the problem lies deeper than our recalcitrant inclinations. For it fundamentally consists in a "propensity to evil," a settled tendency to subordinate moral incentives to the incentives of self-love, a more or less willing policy of only acting on moral maxims when doing so seems consistent with the pursuit of our own happiness. A consequence of these considerations is that while I may be able to exert my will and control my inclinations on any *particular* occasion, I can't maintain this control permanently.

But if a person is able to control her inclinations on *any* occasion, why can't she control them on *all* occasions (and thus always act morally)? Consider an analogy. I am driving while over-tired. At any moment, I can pull myself together and focus my attention on the road. Nevertheless, I can't *keep* my attention on it. My mind wanders and I must again pull myself together. Similarly, a strong bias towards evil could necessitate our failing at some time or other even though it does not necessitate our failing on any given occasion.[14] If it does necessitate our failing at some time or other, moral perfection can't be attained in the present life; the most we can hope for in this life is a *progress towards* moral perfection in which the obstacles posed by our bias towards evil are gradually overcome. But to actually *meet* the demand for moral perfection, our progress must be *unending*.

Yet even if it is, there is another difficulty. If our actions are to have moral worth, then our choice of maxims must be guided by a policy of subordinating the incentives of self-love to moral incentives. But in view of our "propensity to evil," our settled policy of subordinating the latter to the former, how is this possible? Since any choice we make would appear to be an expression of that policy, all of our choices are tainted at their source. The problem, then, is this: how can we choose good if we are *already evil*?

Kant's answer in *Religion Within the Limits of Reason Alone* is that in order to think this possibility we must introduce the notion of "a supernatural accession to our moral . . . capacity" which makes possible the conversion from an evil policy to a good policy. Kant admits that it is hard to reconcile the idea of divine assistance with the conviction that "that which is to be accredited to us as morally good conduct must take place . . . solely through the best possible use of our own powers." But he thinks that because our freedom itself is "just as incomprehensible

---

14   R. Dennis Potter ("Moral Dilemmas and Inevitable Sin," *Faith and Philosophy* 20 [2003], pp. 63–71) has recently argued that a doctrine of inevitable sin is incoherent. For consider the set, A1, A2, A3, . . . An, consisting of all the actions I ought to perform. For each action in the set, it is true that I ought to perform it. Thus, I ought to perform A1, I ought to perform A2, and so on, through An. But if I ought to perform A1, I ought to perform A2, . . . , and I ought to perform An, then, by the "agglomeration" principle, I ought to perform (A1 and A2 and A3 . . . and An). Now "ought" implies "can." So if I *ought* to bring about the conjunction, I *can* bring it about, and thus always do what I have an obligation to do. This argument is flawed, however, because the agglomeration principle is probably false. (See Chapter 10, page 202)

to us[15] as is the supernatural factor which we would like to regard as a supplement to [our] spontaneous but deficient" exercise of freedom, we aren't justified in denying that this combination of divine assistance and freedom is possible.[16]

The upshot is therefore this. Since we are obligated to moral perfection, we must assume that our obligation can be met. The only way of meeting it, however, is by reversing our policy of subordinating moral incentives to the incentives of self-love, and then implementing our new policy by engaging in an unending struggle against any obstacle that might tend to subvert it. But for this to be possible two things are necessary—a "supernatural accession to our moral . . . capacity," and an assurance that death won't cut short our struggle towards perfection.

How should we evaluate Kant's argument? Peter Byrne argues that "the claim that we should feel guilty . . . for some primal fault" over and above "individual infractions of the moral law" will seem plausible only to those who already "use religious categories"—that God commands us to imitate his own perfection, for example, or that humanity is fallen and trapped in sin.[17] But this isn't clearly true. Kant conceives of our primal fault as a more or less willful policy of subordinating moral incentives to incentives of self-love. It is by no means obvious that we *aren't* guilty of this fault, and the fact that we act morally on "frequent occasions" is no evidence to the contrary. (The immoral policy in question does not dictate that we never, or even infrequently, do *what* duty prescribes. It only dictates that we privilege happiness over duty when the two seem clearly to conflict.) Nor is it obvious that our fault as Kant conceives it implicitly employs religious categories. Yet if Kant *is* right about our propensity to evil, it is difficult to see how we *can* discharge our obligation to reverse our policy of subordinating moral incentives to incentives of self-love without some kind of supernatural assistance.

What, though, about Kant's claim that endless progress toward virtue is needed as well as "conversion"? The first difficulty is that the self which endures is presumably our *noumenal* self, and it isn't clear what "endless progress" could *mean* when applied to a noumenal world that is timeless. Kant's only response to this difficulty occurs in a late essay in which he says that the notion of "eternal duration" is "a purely negative one . . . because where there is no time also *no end* is possible."[18] But this doesn't really help because, "where there is no time," no *progress* is possible either.

---

15 Our free acts are acts of our *noumenal* selves, and we have no theoretical understanding of the noumenal realm. We are entitled to believe *that* we are free since morality presupposes it but just *how* we can be free is "incomprehensible" to theoretical reason.

16 Kant, *Religion Within the Limits of Reason Alone*, trans. Theodore M. Greene and Hoyt H. Hudson. New York: Harper Torchbooks, 1960, p. 179. Henceforth *Religion*.

17 Peter Byrne, *The Moral Interpretation of Religion*. Grand Rapids, MI: William B. Eerdmanns, 1998, p. 83.

18 "The End of All Things" (1794). Quoted in Allen W. Wood, *Kant's Moral Religion* (Ithaca: Cornell University Press, 1970), p. 123.

Suppose we set this difficulty aside, however, and assume that death needn't end the self's progress toward virtue. Does the possibility of endless progress solve our problem by showing that our obligation to moral perfection can be met? On the face of it, it does not for, as C. D. Broad points out, that we can only *asymptotically approach* moral perfection through endless progress towards it entails that we can never actually *achieve* it and, in that case, our obligation to attain moral perfection can never be met.[19]

In responding to this criticism, Stephan Körner notes that "mathematicians . . . [hold] that an infinite sequence [of the right sort] can be regarded as completed in a sense which is quite compatible with its having no last member."[20] Thus the sequence 1/2, 1/2 + 1/4, 1/2 + 1/4 + 1/8, 1/2 + 1/4 + 1/8 + 1/16 . . . 1, can be regarded or counted as 1. That Kant had something like this in mind is at least suggested by his claim that "the Infinite Being, to whom the temporal condition is nothing, sees in this series, which for us is without end, a whole conformable to the moral law." (*CP* 127)

What God's "single intellectual intuition" comprehends, however, is not just the series in its "progress from the worse to the morally better" but "the immutability of intention" which lies behind it. (*CP* 127–8) Or, as Kant puts it in *Religion*, the revolution in our dispositions whereby we freely decide to subordinate our inclination to happiness to moral incentives works itself out in time as "a continual *progress* from bad to better," but "for Him who penetrates to the intelligible ground of the heart (the ground of all maxims of the will) and for whom this unending progress is a unity, i.e., for God, this amounts to his actually being a good man (pleasing to Him)." (*Religion* 43)

So Kant's position appears to be this: God's timeless intellectual vision of the moral agent's closer and closer approximation to perfection "in the infinity of his [the agent's] duration" (*CP* 128), together with the immutable intention to shape his life by the moral law which underlies the agent's progress, *counts as*, or is viewed by God as *virtually equivalent to*, moral perfection. Whether endless progress toward moral perfection, plus the "immutable" intention which underlies it, really *is* virtually equivalent to, or as good as, the actual attainment of moral perfection is debatable, however, although, in my opinion, that it is is not clearly unreasonable. But suppose we set aside any doubts we might have on this score. Then a new problem confronts us.

If the revolution in the ground of our maxims (our freely chosen commitment to henceforth subordinate the incentives of self-love to those of morality), and the consequent progress in time from bad to morally better, is sufficient for God to regard or count us as morally good, then why is immortality *also* needed? Why, in other words, must our progress be *unending*? The answer cannot be "Because the

---

19   C. D. Broad, *Five Types of Ethical Theory*. Paterson, NJ: Littlefield, Adams, and Co., 1959, p. 140.
20   S. Körner, *Kant*. Harmondsworth, Middlesex: Penguin Books, 1955, p. 166.

process by which we progress from bad to better can be completed if we are immortal while it cannot be if we are not," for an endless process can't be completed either. And if God can take our "immutability of intention" and continued progress toward the morally better for the deed (the attainment of perfection) when the process is unending, why can't he do so when it isn't?[21] Presumably because an asymptotic approximation or approach to an infinitely remote terminus can be identified with it in a way in which an aborted approach or approximation to it cannot. Thus, while it may be reasonable to identify the series 1/2, 1/2 + 1/4, 1/2 + 1/4 + 1/8 . . . 1 with 1, it is not reasonable to identify 1 with 1/2 or with (1/2, 1/2 + 1/4). Similarly here. If our progress toward the goal of moral perfection is cut short by death, it is unreasonable to regard our inadequate (although progressively more successful) efforts toward it as somehow equivalent to, or as good as, the real thing.

This does not put all questions to rest, however, for Kant's primary stress is on the *inner revolution in the will*,[22] and while death is a threat to endless *progress*, it isn't so obviously a threat to our new immutable intention. For the latter is a free decision of our *noumenal* selves, and our noumenal selves *aren't in time*. Why, then, isn't the immutable intention sufficient for God to regard us as good even if we *aren't* immortal—especially given that the immutable intention *would* be sufficient to ensure continual progress if (contrary to what we are now supposing) our lives *were* to extend beyond the grave?

It is not entirely clear, then, that immortality is needed for it to be possible for us to discharge our obligation to moral perfection, and thus isn't clear that Kant's argument for immortality is successful.

But notice that this criticism of Kant's argument still leaves us with an argument *for God*. For if the only way in which our obligation can be discharged is if *God regards* our immutable intention and (finite or infinite) progress from bad to better as equivalent to the actual achievement of perfection, then God must exist if compliance with the demand for moral perfection is to be possible.[23]

---

21 Kant himself seems to suggest in *Religion* that he can. A person's "life-conduct" is "judged by Him who knows the heart, through a purely intellectual intuition, as a completed whole, because of" his "*disposition*, supersensible in its nature [because noumenal], from which this progress itself is derived. Thus may man, notwithstanding his permanent deficiency, yet expect to be *essentially* well-pleasing to God, *at whatever instant his existence be terminated.*" (*Religion* 60f., last emphasis mine)

22 Though this revolution in the will must work itself out in practice "as a continual progress from bad to better."

23 Would it be sufficient if it were true that God *would* regard them as equivalent if (contrary to fact) God *were* to exist? That is, would a merely hypothetical divine intuition be sufficient? Not clearly. A merely *hypothetical* "atonement" seems insufficient for it to be possible for us to *actually*, and not merely hypothetically, discharge our obligation.

The Postulate of God's Existence

Kant thinks that God as well as immortality is a necessary postulate of practical reason. Why does he think this? Roughly, for this reason:

1　Pure practical (moral) reason has an end, namely, the "highest good," a situation in which each person is happy in proportion to his or her moral worthiness. Furthermore,

2　Worthiness to be happy and happiness aren't merely conjoined in the highest good; they are systematically connected, related as "ground and consequence." The connection "is predicated upon virtue's producing happiness . . . as a cause produces an effect." (*CP* 115)

3　One can't rationally pursue ends whose realization one believes to be either logically or factually impossible.

4　Pure practical reason must therefore affirm the real possibility of the systematic connection of virtue and happiness. (From 1, 2, and 3.)

5　If we restrict our attention to the phenomenal world, however, a connection of this sort appears fantastic. All of our observational evidence is against it. (Happiness and unhappiness appear to be randomly distributed among the morally good and the morally bad alike.) And the laws of nature take no account of a person's moral worthiness or lack of it. If science tells us the whole story, the highest good is a chimera, and a belief in its possibility is a product of wishful thinking.

6　If the highest good is to be (really) possible, then, science *can't* have the last word. (From 5.)

7　Moral reason must therefore postulate an "intelligible ground" which transcends nature, and systematically connects happiness and worthiness to be happy. God's existence is thus a necessary postulate of pure practical reason.[24] (From 4 and 6.)

Kant's argument raises a number of questions of which we will consider two especially important ones. (1) Why must the intelligible ground of the systematic connection of happiness and worthiness to be happy be *God*? (2) Why must moral reason aim at the highest good rather than the closest (empirically) possible approximation to it?

24　We do not have a *duty* to affirm God's existence, however. A commitment to morality requires only that we affirm that morality's end (the highest good) *is* possible. It does not require us to affirm some account of *how* the end is possible (e.g., that God systematically connects happiness and worthiness to be happy). Religious belief is a "*need*" of moral reason since it alone can make the possibility of the highest good "comprehensible," and as such can be called a "pure *rational* faith." But a failure to believe is not a failure of *duty*. (*CP* 130)

1 The "Intelligible Ground"

Peter Byrne argues that Kant is at most entitled to the postulate that there is an intelligible ground of moral order. Given the absence of (empirical) "traces or perceptions of the activity or the character" of this ground, however, and Kant's professed agnosticism about the nature or constitution of the intelligible world, he is *not* entitled to claim that the intelligible ground of the world's moral order is *God*. Anthropomorphic conceptions of God (that is, ideas of God as a person) are imaginative constructs which we have no reason to believe resemble their alleged referent.[25]

But this misrepresents Kant. Kant *does* insist that we have no theoretical understanding of the intelligible world; that is, we have no substantive knowledge of the intelligible referents of our ideas of God, freedom, and immortality. But we do have some grasp of what is *analytically entailed* by these concepts. In particular, Kant seems to think that the ideas of omniscience, omnipotence, and moral righteousness (and thus personality) are analytically connected with the idea of an intelligible ground of the systematic connection of happiness and worthiness to be happy.

Only the "cause of the whole of nature, itself distinct from nature," would have sufficient control of nature to systematically adjust people's happiness to their worthiness to be happy. Furthermore, because the "supreme cause . . . contains the ground of the agreement of nature not merely with actions moral in their form but also . . . with their moral intention," we must suppose that this cause is cognizant of these intentions and is hence intelligent. Finally, since the aim of its activity is the instantiation of the highest good, we must ascribe righteousness to it. (*CP* 129–30) In short, "this Being must be omniscient, in order to be able to know my conduct even to the most intimate parts of my intention in all possible cases and in the entire future. In order to allot fitting consequences to it, He must be omnipotent, and similarly omnipresent, eternal, etc." (*CP* 145) He must also be all good since "we can hope for the highest good . . . only from a morally perfect (holy and benefi-cent)," as well as "omnipotent, will." (*CP* 134) "Thus the moral law, by the concept of the highest good as the object of a pure practical reason, defines the concept of the First Being as that of a Supreme Being." (*CP* 145)

Allen Wood puts it this way: "We are attempting to conceive the practical possibility of a systematic causal connection between worthiness and happiness, where this connection itself is regarded as the object of purposive volition and action." But since "merely human purposiveness" isn't sufficient to establish the connection, we must postulate an intelligible purposiveness which does have the power to do so, or as Kant puts it, "a supreme cause of nature which has a causality corresponding to the moral intention." (*CP* 130)[26]

---

25 Byrne, *Moral Interpretation of Religion*, p. 60.
26 Wood, *Kant's Moral Religion*, pp. 132–3.

But whether the notion of purposiveness really is analytically connected with the idea of an intelligible ground of moral order is another matter. For why must the connection be represented as an *object of volition*? Why isn't it sufficient that moral agents enjoy happiness or misery *because* they have the appropriate moral quality (worthiness or unworthiness to be happy)? Why, in other words, isn't it enough that the connection not be *accidental*? Why, for instance, wouldn't something like the impersonal law of karma, according to which people's fortunes are the more or less automatic consequence of their good or evil deeds, be sufficient? Of course, by postulating something like the law of karma, we merely postulate that the connection is *not* accidental without shedding any light on how it *could be* non-accidental. Postulating an intelligible purposiveness, on the other hand, does shed some light on this, and that it does so may be a reason for preferring the latter hypothesis to the former. Whether this reason is available to Kant, however, is doubtful since, for him, the constitution of the intelligible world is a mystery.

The problem, in short is this: moral reason must postulate an intelligible ground of a systematic (and hence non-accidental) connection between happiness and worthiness to be happy. Kant thinks that the idea of such a cause analytically implies the notions of omnipotence, omniscience, and perfect goodness, that is, it implies the notion of God. It does not, however, since something like the impersonal law of karma would ensure that the connection is non-accidental. One must therefore find other reasons for asserting that the intelligible ground is God. Given Kant's professed agnosticism about the nature of the intelligible world, it is difficult to see how he could come up with any.

In *Religion Within the Limits of Reason Alone* Kant offers another argument for postulating God's existence which may ease the difficulty. "Passions" such as "lust for power, greed, and the malignant inclinations bound up with these," are the inevitable product of our association with others. (*Religion* 85) As a result, it is difficult and, indeed, for all practical purposes, impossible to maintain the sovereignty of the "good principle" (a firm commitment to the good) without support from like-minded men and women. We therefore have a duty to work toward an "ethical commonwealth"—"a universal republic based on laws of virtue." This duty is distinct from our other duties, however, for while the latter "concern what we know to lie in our own power," the former does not. Hence, "this duty will require the presupposition of another idea, namely, that of a higher moral Being through whose universal dispensation the forces of separate individuals, insufficient in themselves, are united for a common end."[27] (*Religion* 89)

Why, though, must this higher power be *personal*; that is, why must it be *God*? Because the very idea of an ethical commonwealth implies it. The notion of a

---

27   It is only by proceeding "as though everything depended upon *him*," however, "that man ... dare ... hope that higher wisdom will grant the completion of his well-intentioned endeavors." (*Religion* 92, my emphasis)

commonwealth includes that of a "public legislation;" "all laws which bind" its members "must be capable of being regarded as commands of a common law-giver." Human laws "are directed only toward the legality of actions," however, and not toward their "inner" morality. The legislator of an *ethical* commonwealth, whose only laws are the laws of virtue, cannot, then, be thought of as human. (*Religion* 90) Now the idea of a commonwealth includes that of executive and judicial, as well as legislative, power. Hence the idea of an *ethical* commonwealth not only includes the idea of a "*holy* legislator," it also includes the idea of a "*benevolent* ruler and moral guardian" through whose "cooperation" and "management" alone the "goal [of an ethical commonwealth] can be reached," and the idea of a "*righteous* judge who "bring[s] it about that each receives whatever his actions are worth." (*Religion* 130–31, 91)

Legislators, rulers, and judges are obviously *persons*. Furthermore, the person who heads the ethical commonwealth must have all the attributes needed to perform its role. For example, as ruler and judge, it must have the attributes ("unchangeableness, omniscience, omnipotence, etc.") which are needed to ensure that our struggles to bring about the ethical commonwealth aren't abortive, and to see "the innermost parts of the disposition of each individual," apportioning happiness according to his or her worthiness to be happy. But the concept of such a being, of course, "is the concept of God as moral ruler of the world."[28] (*Religion* 130, 90–91, my emphasis)

---

28 Are the arguments offered for postulating God's existence in the *Religion* and in the second *Critique* really distinct? On the face of it, they appear to be. In the *Critique* we are to aim at our own perfection and at the highest good, and God is postulated to ensure the real possibility of both. In the *Religion*, we are to aim at a "*social* good," namely the moral perfection of the human *race*, and God is postulated to ensure the real possibility of *the universal sovereignty of the "good principle."* These aims may not be wholly distinct, however. John Hare has argued that Kant has *two* concepts of the highest good—a "less ambitious sense" in which it refers to a state of affairs in which happiness is proportional to virtue, and a "more ambitious sense" in which it refers to a state of affairs in which everyone is virtuous and everyone is happy. (The second entails the first but not vice versa.) (*The Moral Gap* [Oxford: Clarendon Press, 1996], pp. 72–95) One could argue that aiming at the highest good in the more ambitious sense includes aiming at universal moral perfection (the perfection of the human race). If so, the aim of the second *Critique* (when taken in the more ambitious sense) *includes* the aim of the *Religion*. Moreover, because universal perfection includes my *own* perfection, and because the divine ruler and judge of the ethical commonwealth apportions happiness in accordance with moral worth, aiming at an ethical commonwealth includes aiming my own perfection and at a state of affairs which incorporates the realization of the highest good in both its more and less ambitious sense. As a result, the aim of the *Religion* includes that of the second *Critique*.

2   *Moral Reason and the Highest Good*

C. D. Broad thinks that Kant's argument is vitiated by a confusion between "two different senses of ought . . . If I say: 'You ought to do so and so,'" I imply that what you ought to do is *factually* or empirically, and not merely logically, possible. "But if I say: 'So and so ought to exist,' I imply only that it would involve no logical contradiction, and that any being who could bring it about ought to do so." If we keep this distinction in mind, it is clear that "Kant is entitled only to the hypothetical proposition: 'If a perfect God existed he would order the course of nature so that virtue would receive its appropriate reward in happiness.'" He is not entitled to the categorical proposition that there really is a God who does so.[29]

But this misses Kant's point, namely that the highest good is not just something that ought to exist but a goal that we are *morally obligated to pursue*. And, by Broad's own admission, this does imply that its attainment is factually, and not merely logically, possible.

Or does it? What we are obligated to do is to *pursue* the highest good. It does not follow that we are obligated to *attain* it. One might therefore argue that we are only obligated to work for the closest (factually) possible *approximation* to the highest good.

But this is to substitute *another* goal for Kant's—a substitution that is reasonable only if we know or have good reason to believe that the latter is *not* factually possible. The highest good is not factually possible, however, only if God does not exist. So to make approximation to the highest good, rather than the highest good itself, our end is reasonable only if we know or have good reason to believe that God doesn't exist. And, if Kant is correct, this is something we do *not* know.

Still, why must moral reason make the highest good its end? John Hare argues that "if we are to endorse wholeheartedly the long-term shape of our lives, we have to see this shape as consistent with our own happiness." To wholeheartedly commit ourselves to morality we must therefore "believe that there is in operation a system in which my virtue is [really, and not merely logically] consistent with my happiness even if other people fail to be virtuous."[30]

This argument doesn't show that a commitment to morality commits me to a belief that the highest good is factually possible, however. That virtue is (really) *consistent* with my happiness, that is, that nothing *systematically precludes* their conjunction, doesn't entail that I will actually *be* happy if I am virtuous. That is, it doesn't entail that virtue and happiness are *systematically connected*. Hare may be right in thinking that, if I am wholeheartedly to commit myself to morality, I have to believe that such things as martyrdom and self-sacrifice don't make my happiness impossible. Why, though, must I believe (and not merely hope) that if I am virtuous I really *will* be happy? Why, in other words, must I commit myself to

---

29   Broad, *Five Types of Ethical Theory*, pp. 141–2.
30   Hare, *Moral Gap*, p. 88.

either the reality or the real possibility of the highest good? It would seem that I must do so only if the falsity of "Happiness and worthiness to be happy are systematically connected" entails "Worthiness to be happy systematically precludes happiness (or makes its achievement highly unlikely)," and it doesn't.

So, once again, why *must* we make the highest good our end? Allen Wood's explanation is more promising. Since all action must have an end,[31] one can't will *anything* without forming the representation of an end. In so far as I am a *moral* being, however, my ends are constrained by moral requirements, and ends constrained by moral requirements essentially consist in my own virtuous disposition "and that of others," and "happiness proportioned to worthiness to be happy, for myself and for others." Now the highest good is simply the "complete and total attainment of both these components."[32] So to prize obedience to the moral law is to implicitly prize the attainment of the highest good.

Does it follow that attempting to implement the former by obeying the moral law involves trying to *implement* the latter (and thus believing that the latter is really possible)? It at least follows that one can't act to implement the former and be "indifferent to the ... attainment" of the latter;[33] if nothing else, one must have a moral interest in it. But one can't have a moral interest in impossibilia. It follows that one can't consistently regard the highest good as impossible and wholeheartedly commit oneself to morality.

General Objections to Kant's Moral Arguments

How convincing are Kant's moral arguments? Peter Byrne contends that they are based on *substantive* moral claims. Because these claims are controversial, they can't be regarded as demands of moral reason *per se*. Hence, even if Kant's arguments are valid, they will only persuade those who are antecedently convinced of the truth of his ethical system. Kant's arguments depend, for example, on the existence of obligations to be morally perfect and to treat others as ends in themselves whose moral agency must be respected and happiness furthered in proportion to their worthiness to be happy. But not all rational ethical systems share these values. Utilitarianism prizes happiness *wherever* it is found, including the unworthy. And contractarian approaches like Thomas Hobbes's and David Gauthiers's are only concerned to construct "principles designed to grant the maximum liberty to each, compatible with leaving the liberty of others undisturbed," that is, to maximize people's freedom to pursue "their own private preferences."[34]

---

31   An action's end may be internal to it. Dancing, for example, may be performed for its own sake.
32   Wood, *Kant's Moral Religion*, p. 92.
33   Ibid., p. 94.
34   Byrne, *Moral Interpretation of Religion*, p. 86.

It isn't clear that this objection is compelling. In the first place, *no* interesting philosophical argument is universally persuasive. In the second, Byrne assumes that unless a moral requirement is included in every rational moral system, it isn't a demand of moral reason *as such*. "Rational moral system" is ambiguous, however, since it can either refer to the product of any conscientious attempt to derive an adequate set of rational moral principles *or* to the product of *successful* attempts to do so, that is, to correct or sound accounts of morality. That D is a demand of moral reason entails only that D is implicated in any *sound* moral system. It does not entail that it is implicated in every moral system which good philosophers have endorsed. So the fact that Kant's moral principles are controversial doesn't show that they are not in fact requirements of moral reason.

Finally, the only moral claims that Kant's arguments seem to *require* are these: "One ought to be morally perfect" and "One ought to aim at a state of affairs in which people are happy in proportion to their worthiness to be happy." While the first is often rejected, I have argued that it is a simple consequence of the self-evident "One ought always to do one's duty." The second claim really *is* controversial. But anyone will find it persuasive who shares Kant's intuitions that moral worth has great intrinsic value, and that (while the legitimate happiness of others should be furthered) the conjunction of *vice* and happiness is intrinsically bad.

A more powerful objection is that Kant is arguing from "a need of pure practical reason" to the existence of God and immortality, and arguments "from a need to the objective reality of the object of the need" are illegitimate. (*CP* 148–9) The fact that I wish or want or need something to be so is no reason for thinking that it really is so.

A possible response is that this way of formulating Kant's argument misconstrues it. Kant's conclusion (or so one might argue) is not that God and immortality *exist*, but that there is a practical need (a need of moral reason) to *believe* that they do. Moral need, in other words, justifies the *believing*—not the *content* of the belief.

This won't do, however, since, for the committed moral agent, this distinction is without a difference. For from the first-person point of view, whatever justifies one's believing p, justifies p. ("I believe that p but p is false"[35] expresses a pragmatic contradiction. The distinction between believing p and the truth of p can only be made from a third-person perspective.[36]) So, if a committed moral agent finds that her practical need to believe in God and immortality justifies her in believing in God and immortality, then, from her point of view, it also justifies her asserting that God and immortality are objectively real.

Now Kant thinks that this need is an essential feature of moral reason itself. It follows that anyone who adopts the moral point of view, and understands its implications, must postulate the objective reality of God and immortality.

---

35   Or "I believe that p but the (epistemic) probability of p is equal to or less than 0.5."
36   I can, of course, adopt a third-person point of view on my past and future beliefs. "I believed p but p is false" or "I will believe p but p is false" are perfectly coherent.

But aren't arguments from need to fact unavoidably circular? Kant argues from our need to make moral sense of the world to the conclusion that the world is friendly to our moral ideals. However, a universal *need to believe* that the world supports our moral endeavors raises the probability that it really *does* support them only if the world is "such as to meet our deepest needs and allow human reason [including *moral* reason] to flourish in it." And this is precisely the question at issue: the argument from need presupposes its own conclusion.[37]

Yet this underestimates the force of Kant's argument. Kant concedes that we have no "right to argue from a need to the objective reality of the object of the need" in cases in which "the need is based on [mere] inclination." The need, in question, however, "has its ground objectively in the character of things as they must be universally judged by pure reason and is not based on inclination . . . " Reason *must* judge that we have obligations to be morally perfect and to pursue the highest good. It *must* therefore assume that moral perfection and the highest good are possible, and so must assume whatever conditions are "necessary" to their "objective possibility." As a result, these assumptions are "as necessary as the moral law, in relation to which alone [they are] valid." (*CP* 148–9) Or as Allen Wood puts it: "we do not believe the highest good [or moral perfection] to be possible because we *want* it to be possible; we believe it to be possible because we *must* do so if we are rationally to continue our pursuit of it."[38]

If we concede that the need to believe in God and an afterlife (or that the world supports our moral endeavors and aspirations) really is a need of reason, then Kant's argument is persuasive. The charge is that arguments from need are irrational. And this may be true where the need is based on inclination; wishing that something is so doesn't make it so. But a need *of reason* can't be *opposed* to reason unless reason can be opposed to itself, and the assumption that reason *can't* be opposed to itself is presupposed in every use of it. (It is important to remember that, as Kant says, there is only *one* reason "which judges a priori by principles, whether for theoretical or for practical purposes." [*CP* 125] Theoretical reason and practical reason aren't two distinct faculties which might come into conflict.)

There is also a pragmatic reason for allowing our thought to be shaped by the promptings of these needs and interests. If we trust reason, we will accede to its demands, and therefore affirm the objective reality of God and an afterlife (or, at the very least, that the world is friendly to our moral ideals and aspirations). But trust in reason is *itself* a need of reason. Hence, other things being equal, trust in reason is rationally more satisfying that distrust. In the absence of compelling reasons for *mis*trusting reason, then, we should trust it. For what is the alternative? *Not* to trust reason until we have a convincing noncircular proof of its reliability?

---

37 Byrne, *Moral Interpretation of Religion*, pp. 65–8.
38 Wood, *Kant's Moral Religion*, p. 187.

Any such proof would *presuppose* the reliability of reason, however, and thus be unconvincing to those who don't *already* trust it.

Finally, the argument from need is self-certifying in the sense that if its conclusion were true, it would probably be cogent. Toward the end of the second *Critique*, Kant argues that it is good that our knowledge of God is practical (moral), and not speculative or theoretical, since a speculative or theoretical knowledge of God would actually *corrupt* morals. If the objective reality of the object of rational faith could be proved, "God and eternity in their awful majesty would stand unceasingly before our eyes (for that which we can completely prove is as certain as that which we can ascertain by sight)." But, in that case, our desire for happiness would prompt us to obey the moral law to secure happiness and avoid misery. "Thus most actions conforming to the law would be done from fear, few would be done from hope, none from duty. The *moral* worth of actions, on which alone the worth of the person and even of the world depends in the eyes of supreme wisdom, would not exist at all." Since our "view of the future" is "very obscure and ambiguous," however, and "the Governor of the world allows us only to conjecture his existence and majesty, not to behold or clearly prove them," reason "need[s] to endeavor to gather its strength to resist the inclinations by a vivid idea of the dignity of the [moral] law." Only thus "can there be a truly moral character dedicated directly to the law . . . " (*CP* 152–3, my emphasis)

The situation, in other words, is this. If a moral ruler of the world exists, we would expect him to deny us any knowledge of his reality that would corrupt morals. The argument from moral need is the only argument for God and immortality which protects the purity of morals since (in contrast to compelling speculative proofs) it will convince only those who are antecedently committed to morality's unconditional demand for a morally good will and are wholeheartedly commited to pursuing the highest good. It is thus just the sort of argument we would expect to be probative if its conclusion were true.

Appendix

Kant thinks that while rational faith is not *commanded* (see note 24), the *denial* of God or immortality implies that one is either irrational or a scoundrel. Why? Allen Wood explains it this way. If I deny the existence of God or a future life, I implicitly deny the possibility of the highest good since I am denying the only conditions under which I can conceive their real possibility. Denying their real possibility, however, presupposes or implies "that I will not pursue the highest good, or [that I] commit myself not to pursue it" (for in pursuing an end I presuppose that its attainment really is possible). But that amounts to a decision not to obey the moral law, in which case I am a "scoundrel [*Bösewicht*]." If, on the other hand, I deny the existence of God and immortality but commit myself to obeying the moral law anyway, "I am acting 'irrationally'" since "according to my own beliefs I *should* (in a logical, but not a moral sense of 'should') give up my pursuit of the highest good and my obedience to the moral law and *become a Bösewicht.*"[39]

Is this convincing, though? One *could* argue that certain aspirations or hopes (for an ethical commonwealth, for example, or the highest good) are a necessary feature of moral goodness, and that (rational) aspiration or hope involves a minimal theoretical commitment, namely, that the object of one's aspiration or hope isn't impossible or overwhelmingly improbable.

It isn't clear, however, that the absence of these aspirations and hopes really is a sign that one is a bad (*böse*) person. Suppose that Mary neither aspires to, nor hopes for, the highest good because she regards its realization as overwhelmingly improbable. She nevertheless fervently *wishes* that it could be realized and deeply regrets that there is no real possibility of its realization. Is she a scoundrel? Surely not if her wish is heartfelt and her regret sincere, and if she does everything in her power to promote the goal whose full realization she believes to be impossible. Compare Mary with John, who believes that a perfectly just society is a chimera but fervently wishes for a perfectly just community, deeply regrets its impossibility, and does all he can to make existing society more just. If we wouldn't fault John (and we surely would not), why should we fault Mary? It isn't clear, then, that the hopes or aspirations we are discussing are necessary for moral goodness.

However, this objection assumes that a lack of belief in the real possibility of the highest good or perfect social justice is compatible with a wholehearted attempt to promote these goods, and this may be doubted. Toward the end of the *Critique of Pure Reason*, Kant admits that a merely "*negative* belief," that is, a belief that there is no "*certainty* that there is *no* such being and *no* such life," may be sufficient to provide "a powerful check upon the outbreak of evil sentiments," but then argues that this is only "an *analogon*" of "morality and good sentiments"—not the genuine article.[40] While a merely "negative belief" may be "morally tolerable,"[41] it does not comport well with our duty "to promote [the highest good] with all [our] strength." (*CP* 148) For, as Kant says, while we may not have a *duty* to postulate God and immortality, we (morally) *need* to do so. For they alone make the possibility of moral perfection and the highest good intelligible to us, and a sense of their intelligibility "is conducive to morality."[42] (*CP* 151)

---

39 Ibid., pp. 29–30.
40 Kant, *Critique of Pure Reason*, trans. Norman Kemp Smith. London: Macmillan, 1956, A830.
41 As Wood, *Kant's Moral Religion*, puts it on page 31.
42 But why, then, isn't the *cultivation* of rational faith, if not rational faith itself, commanded? If I have a duty to cultivate good moral sentiments (though not to *have* them since sentiments, as distinguished from their cultivation, can't be commanded), and a belief in God and immortality are necessary to that end, don't I have a duty to cultivate belief in God and an afterlife?

CHAPTER 3

Newman and the
Argument from Conscience

In *An Essay in Aid of a Grammar of Assent*, John Henry Newman claimed that nature furnishes three "main channels" for acquiring knowledge of God—"the course of the world," "the voice of mankind," and "our own minds," that is, conscience. The last is "the most authoritative," however.[1] For the argument from conscience "is a proof common to all, to high and low, from earliest infancy. It is carried about in a compact form in every soul. It is ever available—it requires no learning . . . "[2] Newman's argument from conscience is, in essence, this.

1   Conscience points to a "Supreme Governor, a Judge, holy, just, powerful, all-seeing, retributive." (*Grammar* 101)
2   Conscience is a natural faculty, like reason or memory.
3   It is reasonable to trust our natural faculties in the absence of compelling reasons for doubting them.
4   It is thus reasonable to trust conscience, and consequently believe that there really *is* a "Master" or "Judge."

The present chapter examines this argument.

Preliminary Observations

Before examining Newman's argument in detail, two preliminary observations are in order. First, Newman's argument from conscience is an argument *from experience*, not from the meaning of terms like "claim," "obligation," and the like. As Newman himself says, his "proof" is not an "abstract argument from the force of the terms, (e.g. 'A law implies a lawgiver') but from the peculiarity of that feeling

---

1   John Henry Newman, *An Essay in Aid of a Grammar of Assent*. Notre Dame, IN: University of Notre Dame Press, 1979, p. 303. Henceforth *Grammar*.
2   Newman, "Proof of Theism" (1859), in Adrian J. Boekraad and Henry Tristram, *The Argument from Conscience to the Existence of God According to J. H. Newman*. Louvain: Editions Nauwelaerts, 1961, p. 121f. Henceforth Proof. Newman's "Proof" is also found in *The Philosophical Notebooks of John Henry Newman*, vol. ii, ed. Edward Sillem and revised by A. J. Boekraad (Louvain: Editions Nauwelaerts, 1970), pp. 30–77. It was unpublished in Newman's lifetime.

to which I give the name of conscience." (Proof 117) In other words, Newman's argument is based on the *phenomenology* of conscience, that is, on conscience *as consciously experienced*, and not on conceptual analysis.

It is important to distinguish the two since they are often conflated. Thus H. P. Owen writes: "When we call an action right . . . we mean that it is required by a moral claim. Now a claim is something that confronts us. But how can it confront us unless it has real existence? . . . The very word 'obligation' stands for that which, coming from without, constrains and binds us. Through their obligatory character claims exert a pressure that is as real as any which is exerted by objects in the material world."[3] Again, "Claims . . . are not self-explanatory. . . . We feel their 'pressure;' we are aware of being 'constrained' by them . . . [Moreover,] words like 'obligation,' 'duty,' 'claim' always imply a *personal* constraint . . . "[4] And so on. Note how Owen weaves conceptual and phenomenological claims together ("we mean . . . ," "we feel their 'pressure' . . . ").

Arguments like Newman's are frequently attacked on the grounds that our everyday use of expressions like "claim" and "law" can't bear the weight that theists sometimes place on them. Thus W. G. Maclagan argues that "law" and "claim" are only metaphors in moral discourse. We therefore can't infer a divine lawgiver or claimant from the existence of moral laws and claims.[5] Even if this is true, it is irrelevant to Newman's argument since his "proof" isn't based on linguistic considerations.

The second preliminary observation is this. Newman thinks that there is an analogy between the way in which we form beliefs about material objects and the way in which we form beliefs about God on the basis of the experienced effects of conscience. Just as we instinctively (and correctly) form notions of the existence and character of an external world from the impressions of the senses, so we instinctively (and correctly) form notions of the existence and character of "a Supreme Ruler and Judge" from "the intimations of conscience." (*Grammar* 97)

S. A. Grave believes that there are problems with this analogy, however. In the first place, Newman seems to think that the transition from the phenomena of conscience to the existence of God involves implicit reasoning; it is psychologically but not logically immediate.[6] The transition from sense impressions to a belief in the reality of independently existing material objects, on the other hand, is logically, and not merely psychologically, immediate; no inference is involved. (Newman thinks that animals take themselves to be in contact with independently

---

3   H. P. Owen, *The Moral Argument for Christian Theism.* London: George Allen and Unwin, 1965, p. 26f.

4   Ibid., p. 49.

5   W. G. Maclagan, *The Theological Frontier of Ethics.* New York: Macmillan, 1961, pp. 72–9.

6   That is, an inference is involved but the mind isn't consciously aware of the movement from premises to conclusion.

existing objects, and animals, in Newman's view, don't reason.) In the second place, Newman sometimes professes agnosticism about the real nature of material objects but he is not agnostic about the nature of the "voice" that speaks to us in conscience. In his opinion, the phenomena of conscience provide materials for forming a true picture of God.[7]

Grave's second disanalogy seems to me real but the first, and more significant, is problematic. Newman does sometimes speak as if the transition from the phenomena of conscience to a belief in God involves implicit reasoning. But he also speaks of the transition as direct and instinctive. (See *Grammar* 102.) Is Newman inconsistent? I suggest that he isn't—that he thought that the move from conscience to a belief in a "higher sanction" or "transcendent voice" is both psychologically *and* logically immediate, but that the belief that this "voice" is the voice *of God* is based on (implicit) reasoning.[8]

With these preliminaries out of the way, let us now examine Newman's premises.

Newman's Phenomenology of Conscience

The first premise of Newman's argument is that conscience points to a "Supreme Governor, a Judge, holy, just, powerful, all-seeing, retributive." What does Newman think conscience is like, and why does he think that it points to God?

Newman believes that "the feeling of conscience . . . is twofold:—it is a moral sense, and a sense of duty; a judgment of the reason and a magisterial dictate." While the act of conscience is "indivisible," conscience's "critical" and "judicial office[s]" are distinct. I can lose my sense of the "moral deformity" of dishonesty, for example, without losing my sense that it is "forbidden to me." Or I can lose "my sense of the obligation which I lie under to abstain from acts of dishonesty" without losing my sense of their moral deformity.[9] (*Grammar* 98) Conscience's judicial office is the source of religion.

---

7   S. A. Grave, *Conscience in Newman's Thought*. Oxford: Clarendon Press, 1989, pp. 68–74.

8   Grave also notes another potential disanalogy. A passage in the "Proof of Theism" contrasts the impressions of sense and the impressions of conscience. The testimony of conscience is somehow self-certifying because the object to which it witnesses is internal. The testimony of the senses is not because the object of the senses is external. As Grave points out, "it is likely that Newman himself came to repudiate" this position because "there is no trace of it in the *Grammar of Assent,* where, on the contrary, the phenomena of conscience and the impressions of the senses are placed entirely on a level as regards their witness to what lies beyond them." The object is "external" in both cases, and neither form of testimony is self-certifying (although both may be entirely convincing). (Grave, *Conscience in Newman's Thought*, p. 82n.)

9   Why say, then, that acts of conscience are "indivisible"? Presumably, because the two aspects of conscience are normally united in one complex act of consciousness. A comparison may be helpful. I can attend to a conjunction of two propositions in a

The difference between conscience's critical and judicial office can be brought out by contrasting conscience with our sense of beauty. Aesthetic "taste is its own evidence, appealing to nothing beyond its own sense of the beautiful or the ugly ... " In its critical aspect, our moral sense is like our sense of beauty. Conscience as a whole, however, "does not repose on itself, but vaguely reaches forward to something beyond self, and dimly discerns a sanction higher than the self for its decisions, as is evidenced in that keen sense of obligation and responsibility which informs them. And hence it is that we are accustomed to speak of conscience as a voice ... and moreover a voice, or the echo of a voice, imperative and constraining, like no other dictate in the whole of our experience." (*Grammar* 99) Or as Newman had put it earlier, the stirrings of conscience are "attended by ... *sanction*," "hope or fear," "a misgiving of the future," and the like, feelings which "*carry the mind out of and beyond itself*," vaguely implying "a tribunal in the future." (Proof 118–19) These conclusions are instinctive and noninferential, both psychologically and logically immediate.

But we can go further. The magisterial aspect of conscience "has an intimate bearing on our affections and emotions, leading us to reverence and awe, hope and fear, especially fear, a feeling which is foreign for the most part ... to the Moral Sense." Transgression of duty leads to "a lively sense of responsibility and guilt, though the act be no offense against society,—of distress and apprehension, even though it may be of present service to" the transgressor—"of compunction and regret, though in itself it be most pleasurable,—of confusion of face, though it may have no witnesses." (*Grammar* 100) Now emotions like these are "correlative with persons."[10] That "we feel responsibility, are ashamed, are frightened, at transgressing the voice of conscience" therefore "implies that there is One to whom we are responsible, before whom we are ashamed, whose claims upon us we fear[11] ...

---

single act of awareness. It is nevertheless possible for me to attend to the first conjunct without attending to the second, or to the second without attending to the first. Similarly, I can attend to the forbiddenness of dishonesty without attending to its moral deformity, and I can attend to its moral deformity without attending to its forbiddenness.

10   What Newman actually *says* is that emotions and affections (as distinguished from admiration and dislike, pain and pleasure, and the like) are *in general* correlative with persons. Be this as it may, it is doubtful that persons alone can arouse our affections. Arguably, though, nonpersonal objects arouse our affections only when they are either anthropomorphized or are associated with persons. We needn't settle this issue here, however, since all Newman needs is the plausible claim that the emotions *associated with conscience* are *typically* directed toward persons.

11   Are moral obligations grounded in claims persons make on us, as Newman seems to imply? Kant, at least, thought not. Our moral obligations to others aren't grounded in the claims they make upon us but in the moral law which obligates us to respect those claims. The moral law is prior to personal claims in the order of explanation. In Kant's view, our respect for persons is derivative from our respect for the moral law. Persons are objects of respect only in so far as they can or do embody the laws of pure practical reason. (Cf. Maclagan, *Theological Frontier of Ethics*, p. 80)

These feelings in us are such as to require for their exciting cause an intelligent being: we are not affectionate towards a stone, nor do we feel shame before a horse or a dog; we have no remorse or compunction on breaking mere human law[12] . . . If the cause of these emotions does not belong to the visible world, the Object to which" conscience " is directed must [therefore] be Supernatural and Divine; and thus the phenomena of Conscience, as a dictate, avail to impress the imagination with a picture [and a conviction of the living reality] of a Supreme Governor, Judge, holy, just, powerful, all-seeing, retributive." (*Grammar* 101)

The move from a "voice" to a "Supreme Governor" appears to be at least implicitly inferential. Thus, after saying that the feeling of conscience "is analogous or similar to that which we feel in human matters towards a *person* whom we have offended" ("a tenderness almost tearful on going wrong, and a grateful cheerfulness when we go right which is just what we feel in pleasing or displeasing a father or revered superior"), Newman adds that *"contemplating and revolving on this feeling, the mind will reasonably conclude* that it is an unseen father who is the object of this feeling. And that this father necessarily has some of those special attributes which belong to the notion of God. He is invisible—He is the searcher of hearts—He is omniscient so far as man is concerned—He is (to our notions) omnipotent, if he can after so many ages at length hold the judgment, when all sin shall be punished and virtue rewarded." Again, Newman claims that "conscience or the sense of an imperative coercive law . . . (*when analyzed, i.e.*) *reflected on*, involves an inchoate recognition of a Divine Being." (Proof 118–19, last two emphases mine)

But if reason is involved in the transition from the intimations of conscience to a belief in God, just what sort of argument are we dealing with? The first quotation in the preceding paragraph suggests that it is an argument by analogy. Since the feelings of conscience are "analogous or similar to" those that we "feel in human matters towards" persons, we are justified in concluding that they too are directed toward a person.[13]

There is another way of construing Newman's argument, however (although it seems to me less likely that he had this in mind). Consider his claim that guilt or shame over wrongdoing "implies that there is One to whom we are responsible, before whom we are ashamed." (*Grammar* 101) Feelings of guilt or shame typi-

---

12　That is, I take it, human law which lacks any moral authority.

13　Is this compatible with Newman's claim in the *Grammar* "that in the dictate of conscience, without previous experiences *or analogical reasoning*," the child "is able gradually to perceive the voice, or the echoes of a voice, of a Master, living, personal, and sovereign"? (*Grammar* 102, my emphasis) It is, if what the child *non-inferentially* perceives is the "voice, or the echoes of a voice," and not that this voice is God's. And note that even if the child's coming to believe that the voice he perceives is the voice of a living, personal, and sovereign master *is* based on inference, the inference can be spontaneous, natural, and psychologically (although not logically) immediate, "singularly congenial to his mind, if not connatural with its initial action." (*Grammar* 103)

cally incorporate beliefs about persons. Guilt, for example, incorporates a belief that one has offended someone. Shame incorporates a belief in the existence of someone's (actual or potential) scorn or contempt. If the feelings are appropriate, then the beliefs incorporated in them must be true. Now the guilt and shame associated with conscience often lacks the right sort of *human* target. If these feelings are nonetheless appropriate, they must therefore have a *non*human one.

Yet why must the incorporated propositional attitude be *belief*? Why isn't it sufficient to simply *entertain* the relevant proposition? For example, in discussing the internalization of shame in Greek culture, Bernard Williams suggests that the shame of an agent who has committed a base action incorporates a *fictive* other before whom he or she is ashamed. Belief in the other's real existence isn't necessary.[14] But will the feelings so construed have the *weight* of these feelings as ordinarily experienced? No doubt one can feel guilty or ashamed even when one is convinced that there is no one whom one has offended or before whom one is ashamed. And no doubt this can be explained by saying that one's attitudes incorporate a fictive other. But cases like these can also, and more accurately,[15] be described by saying that one believes that the *belief* incorporated in one's feelings of guilt or shame is false, and that one's feelings are therefore irrational.

Compare these feelings with another. My daughter's fear of flying incorporates false *beliefs* about the dangers of flying. When she experiences momentary terror as the plane is about to take off, my daughter isn't merely *entertaining* what she believes to be false propositions about the fragility of aircraft, the high incidence of crashes, and the like. (Her affective and conative responses are significantly different from her responses to an airplane disaster movie.) At the same time, my daughter believes that the beliefs incorporated in her attitudes are false, and that her fears are therefore irrational and inappropriate.

The point, of course, is this. If the feelings we are discussing (guilt, shame, or a fear of flying) are to have the weight they typically have, they must incorporate beliefs about the existence of the relevant objects. If the feelings are to be rational or appropriate, these beliefs must also be *true*. It follows that if (as Newman thinks) guilt and shame take persons as their objects, and if the guilt and shame associated with conscience sometimes lack a *human* object, and if these feelings are nonetheless *rational or appropriate*, then there must be a supernatural person whom one has offended and before whom one is ashamed.

How should we evaluate Newman's description of conscience? John Mackie argues that if conscience is indeed "legitimate or authoritative," as Newman claims, then it does *not* point beyond itself.

---

14   Bernard Williams, *Shame and Necessity*. Berkeley and Los Angeles: University of California Press, 1993, pp. 81–4.

15   More accurately because it better accounts for the felt weight of the feelings of guilt and shame. Responses to fictive objects don't have the same moral weight as responses to what one at some level believes to be real objects.

> If we take conscience at its face value . . . we must say that there is a rational
> prescriptivity about certain kinds of action in their own right; that they are of
> this or that kind is in itself a reason for doing them or refraining from them.
> There is a to-be-done-ness or a not-to-be-done-ness involved *in that kind of*
> *action itself.* If so, there is no need to look beyond this [to a higher sanction or
> authoritative person]. Equally, the regret, guilt, shame, and fear associated
> with consciousness of doing wrong, although normally such feelings arise only
> in relations with persons, are in this special case natural and appropriate; what
> conscience, taken at its face value, tells us is that this is how one should feel
> about a wrong action simply in itself.[16]

Newman has therefore misdescribed the phenomenology of conscience: it does not
point beyond itself.

Newman would insist, however, that it is Mackie, and not he, who has misdescribed the phenomena of conscience. In the first place, Mackie focuses too heavily
on conscience's "critical" function and not enough on its "judicial office." The
"moral sense" does not point beyond itself. But conscience's "magisterial dictate"
does. In the second place, while conscience may tell us that a to-be-done-ness or
not-to-be-done-ness is involved in actions of "this or that kind," it does *not* tell us
that they are involved in this or that kind of action *in itself.* Similarly, while
conscience tells us that we should feel shame or guilt about a wrong action, it
doesn't tell us that "this is how we should feel about" it "*simply in itself.*" (My
emphasis) (Conscience *may* tell us that lying, say, is not-to-be-done, and that
shame or guilt are appropriate reactions to it regardless of lying's connections with
things extrinsically related to its wrongness [societal approval or disapproval, for
example, or its utility or disutility]. But conscience surely doesn't tell us that
lying's relation to the prohibitions of a "higher sanction" or a "divine person" is
extrinsic to its wrongness.[17])

So for all Mackie has shown to the contrary, Newman's phenomenology of
conscience is accurate. When taken at face value, the phenomena of conscience
point beyond themselves. They include an immediate perception of a "voice, or the
echoes of a voice," and spontaneously suggest an inference to a supreme governor
or judge.

Taking Conscience at Face Value

Yet *should* we take the phenomena of conscience at face value? Suppose that
Newman *has* correctly described conscience's phenomenology. Couldn't con-

---

16   J. L. Mackie, *The Miracle of Theism.* Oxford: Clarendon Press, 1982, pp. 104–5.
17   *Nor* does it tell us that the relation is intrinsic. Conscience may point to a higher
     sanction but surely tells us nothing about whether the relation between an action's
     rightness or wrongness and the dictates of a judge or authoritative person are extrinsic
     or intrinsic to it.

science nonetheless be an artifact of a prior belief in God, in which case it would appear to have no independent epistemic force? Don't the "sense of a unique constraint and the presence of foreboding" which are internal to conscience "both presuppose theistic belief rather than, as Newman held, enabling it to be engendered?" Grave answers his own question in the negative, since "many people who have lost belief in God" continue to "experience the phenomena" of conscience. He immediately qualifies his answer, however, by adding that, even so, "past belief may be necessary," though conceivably the past need not be one's own. "The phenomenon could exist as a sort of cultural deposit preserved in ways of speaking about conscience that linger on." Or perhaps, a belief that God *might* exist is all that is needed.[18]

Whether these claims, if true, would undermine the authority of conscience is another matter. It isn't immediately clear, for example, why a dependence of the phenomena of conscience on one's own or others' past belief, or on a belief that God might exist, would destroy its evidential value. (This case can be usefully compared with another. Arguably, ordinary perceptual experiences[19] depend on our own and others' past beliefs in the reality or real possibility of physical objects—without these background beliefs these experiences wouldn't occur. It doesn't follow that our perceptual experiences provide no backing for the belief that physical objects exist.[20]) What *might* undermine conscience's epistemic authority, however, would be a convincing explanation of the features of conscience to which Newman has drawn our attention which contain no reference to God.

For example, one might argue that our sense that conscience has a transcendent dimension or points beyond itself is no more than a sense that the standards it imposes hold independently of our desires (or our desires of the moment). If moral standards are expressions of our reason, and we identify ourselves with our desires, then moral claims will be experienced as coming from "without." Of course we might identify ourselves with our reason rather than our desires (as in our better moments we sometimes do). But even so, conscience's demands may still be experienced as transcendent. For if Kant is right, the reason in question is *pure practical reason*, an expression of our *noumenal* selves; it has a transcendent dimension. (Whether this explanation of the externality of conscience's demands avoids all reference to God is unclear, however, given Kant's discussion of the postulates of pure practical reason. [See Chapter 2.])

---

18   Grave, *Conscience in Newman's Thought*, pp. 184–5.
19   As distinguished from simply experiencing *sensa* (being appeared to redly, for example, or experiencing an auditory sensation).
20   The point could be put this way. Ordinary perceptual beliefs like "There is a red chair in front of me" seem to presuppose that a functioning public object language is already in place. I wouldn't have the experience of perceiving a *red chair* (as distinct from simply being the subject of certain familiar visual sensations) if I lacked the concepts of chair and red, and these concepts wouldn't be available to me if people didn't sometimes make judgments like "There is a red chair in front of me."

A convincing naturalistic explanation of conscience might create more serious difficulties for Newman. For example, J. L. Mackie thinks that Newman's account of conscience is undermined by persuasive "naturalistic, psychological account[s] of the origin of conscience." If instead of taking "conscience at its face value," we attempt to understand how it "has come into existence and has come to work as it does, then we do indeed find persons in the background, but human persons, not a divine one." Conscience is best understood as the "introjection into each individual of demands that come from other people"—perhaps most immediately from one's "parents and immediate associates, but ultimately" from society at large.[21]

Perhaps the best-known example of such an account is Sigmund Freud's. Freud's final map of the mind divides it into three regions: instinctual libidinous and aggressive impulses (the "id"), the rational prudential self (or "ego"), and the conscience or "superego." The superego is an aspect of the ego, or actual individual self, which is created when parental demands that the child repress or restrain its instinctive drives are internalized. Conscience is a much more severe taskmaster than one's parents, however. "Originally . . . renunciation is the consequence of a dread of external authority; one gives up pleasures so as not to lose its love" and protection. "But with the dread of the super-ego the case is different. Renunciation of gratification does not suffice here, for the wish persists and is not capable of being hidden from the super-ego" as it is from one's parents. The result is a persistent sense of guilt.[22]

Moreover, conscience's severity is intensified by feelings of aggression. The child naturally resents the demands placed upon it. But these feelings of aggression toward the source of these demands must themselves be renounced or repressed. They are therefore redirected by being incorporated in the superego, and turned against the ego.

> Conscience is a function we ascribe . . . to the super-ego; it consists of watching over and judging the actions and intentions of the ego, exercising the functions of a censor. The sense of guilt, the severity of the super-ego, is therefore the same thing as the rigour of conscience; it is the perception the ego has that it is watched in this way, the ego's appreciation of the tension between its strivings and the standards of the super-ego; and the anxiety that lies behind all these relations, the dread of [conscience, expresses itself in a fear of and] need for punishment.[23]

---

21 Mackie, *Miracle of Theism*, pp. 105–6.
22 Sigmund Freud, *Civilization and its Discontents*. Garden City, NY: Doubleday Anchor Books, 1958, p. 82.
23 Ibid., p. 93. One's need for punishment is "an instinctual manifestation on the part of the ego which has become masochistic under the influence of the sadistic super-ego." The child not only fears its parents; it loves them and craves their protection. As a surrogate for the parents, the superego is an object of "erotic attachment" as well as dread. (Ibid.)

Note that Freud's explanation, if true, provides a *non*supernatural account of the phenomena of conscience to which Newman has called our attention—the sense of a magisterial dictate, of a searcher of hearts, of a transcendent judge, of heart-rending guilt, fear of punishment, and the like.

Freud and Newman thus provide competing pictures of the same phenomena. Why should we prefer Freud's? It isn't clear that independent evidence[24] supports it, and Newman's account is more natural since it takes the phenomena of conscience at face value (describes conscience as it is consciously experienced). Furthermore, it isn't clear that descriptions like Freud's do justice to conscience's sense that what is required of us can't be equated with parental or societal norms.[25] Note too that when coupled with a recognition that our parents' and society's claims on us can't be absolute, conscious acceptance of an account like Freud's undercuts conscience's authority.[26] If so, we are forced to choose between accepting Freud's account, and thus regarding the authority of conscience as spurious, or acquiescing in conscience's demands and rejecting it. In the absence of compelling non-question-begging reasons for endorsing Freud's picture of conscience, it is pardonable if many of us choose to reject it.

But suppose we grant that Newman has done a better job of describing the *phenomenology* of conscience, and conscience does point to a "Supreme Ruler and judge," rather than obscurely pointing to our parents or society. Still, are its intimations of transcendence *reliable*? Wouldn't a naturalistic account like Freud's—*even if phenomenologically less accurate*— nevertheless undermine conscience's *epistemic value*? We will explore this issue more fully in the next section.

The Reliability of Conscience

In his book on Newman, S. A. Grave calls our attention to the prominence of developmental accounts during the period in which Newman was writing. (Darwin's *Origin of Species* and Newman's own account of the growth of Christian doctrine are examples.) It is therefore surprising that Newman made no attempt to undercut potential naturalistic rivals to his account of conscience.[27] Grave's surprise is misplaced.

Part of the reason for Newman's apparent obliviousness to alternatives is that well-developed naturalistic theories of conscience like Freud's were still in the

---

24   That is, evidence that is independent of the phenomena of conscience themselves.

25   Not even idealized ones?

26   Indeed, this appears to have been one of the aims of early psychoanalysis. Freud thought that conscience was often excessively severe and unreasonable. "Consequently in our therapy we often find ourselves obliged to do battle with the super-ego and work to moderate its demands." (Freud, *Civilization and its Discontents*, p. 102)

27   Grave, *Conscience in Newman's Thought*, pp. 80–81.

offing. But a more important reason emerges when we examine his argument more closely.

Both Grave and Mackie believe that Newman's argument is best understood as an inference to the best explanation. On this interpretation, the phenomena of conscience are regarded as standing in need of explanation. That the "voice" of conscience is the voice of God explains them. If no other equally good explanatory hypothesis is available, we can reasonably infer that conscience probably is God's voice. The strength of arguments of this sort, however, depends on the absence of equally plausible alternative explanations. Arguments undercutting rival hypotheses are thus crucially important. So if Newman's argument *is* an inference to the best explanation, the absence of any attempt to undercut naturalistic accounts is as surprising as Grave thinks it is.[28]

But this is not the best way to construe Newman's argument. To see why, consider his third premise: it is reasonable to trust[29] our natural faculties in the absence of compelling reasons for doubting them.

In Newman's view, conscience is a natural faculty like our powers of reasoning or memory. Opinions about the rightness or wrongness of particular actions vary from culture to culture, and from age to age. But the *fact* of conscience, the "feeling . . . of right and wrong *under a special sanction*," the sense that some actions are enjoined on me and others prohibited, "remains one and the same in all men." (Proof 111–12) An ordinary "child of five or six," for example, "whose reason is at length fully awake," displays the reactions and draws the inferences that Newman has described. (*Grammar* 103) The minds of those who believe "in God and in a future judgment" are thus "in the normal condition of human nature." (*Grammar* 379) Conscience is part of our natural noetic equipment and (when it has not been blunted) clearly witnesses to God.

Yet how do we know that a sensitive conscience is natural and proper? And, more generally, how do we know when the mind is functioning as it should? Newman's answer appears to be: by determining what uses of our powers contribute to human flourishing. A thing's natural powers are "suitable to it, and subserve its existence." Each species finds its "good in the use" of its "particular nature." (*Grammar* 273) If it does, then our faculties are functioning as they should when they contribute to our well-being. Because a developed conscience is essential to human flourishing, a belief in God and a future judgment (which are natural effects of conscience) are expressions of properly functioning epistemic capacities.

But granted that these capacities are natural, why regard them as *reliable*? For three reasons. The first is "necessity:" "Our being, with its faculties . . . is a fact not admitting of question, all things being of necessity referred to it, not it to other things." Indeed, there is no middle ground "between using my faculties, as I have

---

28   Or, at the very least, its absence is a serious lacuna in Newman's argument.
29   For the appropriateness of the word "trust" see the appendix to this chapter.

them, and flinging myself upon the external world according to the random impulse of the moment." (*Grammar* 272) Just as we must rely on reasoning, memory, and sense perception in forming judgments about the course of natural events, so we must fall back on conscience in moral matters. It is reasonable to trust conscience and our other faculties because we have no real alternative.

The second reason is "interest." "It is a general law that, whatever is found as a function or attribute of any class of beings, or is natural to it, is in its substance suitable to it and subserves its existence." Each species thus finds its "good in the use of [its] particular nature." (*Grammar* 273) Because conscience is natural to us, its proper deployment subserves our existence and contributes to our good. If conscience systematically misled us, however, it is doubtful that its proper deployment would do so.

The third reason is providence. "The laws of the mind are the expression, not of a mere constituted order, but of His will." (*Grammar* 275) "A Good Providence watches over us" and "blesses such means of argument as it has pleased Him to give us ... if we use them duly for those ends for which He has given them." (*Grammar* 320–21) Confident in the divine providence, "we may securely take them as they are, and use them as we find them." (*Grammar* 275)

None of these arguments is conclusive. While I have no alternative but to rely on my reason, senses, and memory, there are alternatives to conscience. I can regulate my conduct exclusively by counsels of prudence, for example, asking only what would benefit or injure me. And sociopaths function without conscience. Nor should one be too quick to admit that conscience is necessary for human flourishing or contributes to human good. Freud, for instance, has called our attention to the (alleged) harmful effects of an overactive conscience. Finally, Newman's last argument seems circular. How do I *know* that my noetic capacities (including conscience) are gifts of providence? Only by deploying them. "Since one of their very functions is to tell me of Him, they throw a reflex light upon themselves." (*Grammar* 275) By employing my faculties, I learn of God's providence and thus acquire a reason for trusting them. But there is an obvious circularity in this argument; my justification employs the very capacities whose credentials are in question.

Newman's arguments should not be dismissed too quickly, however. For while one can perhaps effectively pursue one's own narrow interests without conscience, it is less clear that one can dispense with it in moral matters. It is unclear, for example, that either what Newman calls a "moral sense" or abstract moral reasoning provide an adequate guide or incentive to moral conduct. If we take morality seriously, must we not sometimes fall back on the call of conscience, saying with Luther, "Here I stand, I can do no other"? Again, while conscience can undoubtedly be perverted, it is hardly obvious that humanity would be happier or better if conscience were blunted or eliminated. Finally, if we restrict our attention to conscience, the circle in Newman's third argument is less glaring. For conscience is only one (though the principal) "channel" that "Nature furnishes" for acquiring "a knowledge of God." (*Grammar* 303) (The other two are the course of nature and the testimony of humankind.) In so far as our belief in divine providence is grounded in the operation of our other faculties (reason, memory, the senses, our disposition to rely on the testimony of others), we can appeal to it to establish the epistemic credentials of conscience without obvious circularity.

The upshot of these considerations is that while Newman's case for the claim that we should trust our faculties (including conscience) in the absence of compelling reasons for doubting them is not beyond question, it is by no means unreasonable. But this has an important bearing on the contention that Newman's position is undermined by the existence of more or less plausible naturalistic explanations of conscience. For the contention assumes that we are dealing with two rival *explanations* of the phenomena of conscience whereas we are in fact dealing with a (natural) explanation *and a rule*.

Now if it were merely two rival explanations which were at stake, then neither Freud, say, nor Newman would bear any special burden of proof; each would be in the same epistemic position in relation to the other. It would be incumbent on Freud to show that his explanation is as good as or better than Newman's, and it would be incumbent on Newman to show that his explanation is as good as or better than Freud's. If what is at stake is an explanation and Newman's rule, however, the epistemic situation is different. For the rule is that our natural faculties, and therefore conscience, should be trusted, and their deliverances accepted, in the absence of compelling reasons to the contrary. If we accept this rule,[30] then the burden of proof is squarely on critics like Freud who would undercut conscience's authority.

Can the burden be met? Perhaps it can, but it is important to see how difficult it would be to do so. There are two possibilities to consider.

The first is that the mechanisms postulated in the "naturalistic, psychological" explanation of conscience are known to be unreliable; that is, that like psychosis or wish fulfillment, they systematically produce delusive experiences and false beliefs. If the phenomena of conscience are caused by *this* sort of mechanism, we should indeed discount its dictates and intimations.

If this line of attack is to be effective, however, a critic like Freud must do three things: first, provide good empirical evidence that the mechanisms he postulates (such as the introjection of the father's image) are actually *operating*; second, provide good empirical evidence that these mechanisms are not only operating but actually *produce* the phenomena of conscience; finally, offer good reasons for thinking that the dictates and intimations of conscience, and other beliefs and perceptions produced by this mechanism, are *false* (since, if they aren't, it isn't clear why we should think that the mechanism is unreliable). This burden would be hard to discharge. Not only are the empirical credentials of Freud's theory controversial;[31] it is unclear how

---

30   And it is difficult to see how one could reasonably reject it.
31   See especially Adolf Grunbaum's attacks on Freud's theory in particular, and on psychoanalysis in general.

Freud could show that the dictates and intimations of conscience are false without begging the question against theism. In the absence of compelling reasons for thinking that there is no God or judgment, or that conscience systematically errs in moral matters, it is difficult to see why we should think that the mechanism underlying conscience is unreliable.

Suppose, however, that critics like Freud drop the charge of unreliability. (This is the second possibility.) Many philosophers think that an experience of x is veridical only if x is one of its causes. For example, a visual experience of my desk is a perception of my desk only if the desk causes my experience. So if critics like Freud have correctly identified the natural causes underlying the phenomena of conscience, doesn't it follow that God isn't their cause or, at least, that there is no reason for *thinking* that he is, and thus that either the so-called voice of conscience isn't veridical or we don't know that it is? This would *not* follow.

Classical theists believe that scientifically adequate explanations can be provided for most natural phenomena. But they also believe that these phenomena are immediately grounded in God's causal activity. Hence an adequate scientific explanation of the phenomena of conscience would not show that God isn't their cause. Nor would it show that God's causal activity isn't *necessary* for their occurrence.

Why is this the case? There are two senses of "x is a causally sufficient condition of y." In a broad sense, x is a causally sufficient condition of y if and only if x, in conjunction with certain background conditions, produces y. In this sense, striking a match is a causally sufficient condition of its bursting into flame. But in a stronger sense, x is a causally sufficient condition of y if and only if x *alone* (in the absence of other conditions) produces y. Striking a match isn't a causally sufficient condition of the match's ignition, in this sense, for many other conditions are necessary. (The match can't be wet, oxygen must be present, and so on.) In short, "x is a causally sufficient condition of y in the strong sense" entails that nothing else is necessary for its occurrence. However, "x is a causally sufficient condition of y in the broad sense" does not.

If this is correct, scientifically adequate explanations of conscience won't imply that God's causal activity isn't necessary for its occurrence unless the causal mechanisms cited in the explanation are causally sufficient in the strong sense— unless, that is, they are capable of producing the phenomena of conscience even if God doesn't exist or is causally inactive. But how could one show that a natural cause is sufficient in this sense? Only by showing that the relevant mechanisms would produce the phenomena of conscience in situations in which God doesn't exist or is causally inactive. It is difficult to see how one could do this without establishing God's nonexistence.

Thus, an adequate scientific explanation of the phenomena of conscience wouldn't show that God wasn't their cause. But would it show that there is no justification for *thinking* that God is their cause or that the dictates and intimations of conscience are veridical? There is a reason why one might think so.

If we have an adequate scientific explanation of the phenomena of conscience, we can explain them without appealing to the causal activity of a transcendent source. But if so, we have no reason for thinking that a transcendent reality is their cause and thus no reason to believe that conscience's dictates and intimations are veridical.

This argument is unsound, however. For one thing, we might have *independent* reasons for thinking that God's causal activity is the immediate cause of *all* natural phenomena including conscience. Yet suppose we don't. Are claims like Newman's therefore baseless? It is not clear that they are. If the existence of a "higher sanction," standing under a judgment which can't be evaded and the like, and the scientific account of conscience were rival *explanations* of the phenomena of conscience, then the claims that Newman believes are built into the experience of conscience might be superfluous. If natural mechanisms are sufficient for the occurrence of the phenomena of conscience, no other explanation seems necessary. If Newman is correct, however, a person who takes these phenomena at face value *is not offering an explanation* but (implicitly) *following a rule*, namely, that our natural faculties are to be trusted in the absence of compelling reasons for not doing so—a rule, moreover, which is not only intrinsically plausible but can be supported by appeals to necessity, the contribution these faculties make to human flourishing, and the like.

We aren't, then, dealing with rival explanations but with a causal explanation and the *application of a rule*. Since natural causes don't preclude God's causal activity, and the rule is reasonable, why shouldn't the claims of conscience be accepted at face value? The discovery of an adequate scientific explanation of the phenomena of conscience might justify concluding that there are no grounds for thinking that a transcendent reality is their cause *if* there were no other reasons for doing so. But there are—the reasonableness of the rule that is being appealed to, the appropriateness of its application to the phenomena of conscience, and the deliverances of conscience themselves.

It isn't clear, then, that the existence of "naturalistic, psychological" accounts of conscience pose a significant threat to Newman's argument. What would threaten it are good reasons for believing that Newman is wrong in thinking that conscience is a natural faculty.[32]

Is Conscience a Natural Faculty?

Recall Grave's claim that one's own or others' past belief in God, or a belief that God might exist, might be needed for the development of conscience. I argued

---

32 Note that developmental accounts of conscience like Freud's have no tendency to show that conscience isn't "natural." Our reasoning powers and social instincts, too, require a long and sometimes convoluted process of development. They are perfectly natural, however.

earlier that even if these claims are true, it isn't immediately obvious that they undermine Newman's account of conscience. They *do* present us with a difficulty, however. For if conscience's formation depends on the existence of theistic beliefs, *is* conscience truly universal (and hence natural) as Newman believes? At one point, Newman himself suggests that there might be a problem here. A note added to his "Proof of Theism" on April 26, 1860 reads: "It is to be considered whether this feeling of Conscience, as involving a personal Governor is peculiar: e.g. to the Anglo-Saxon? [Or, we might add to Victorian Anglo-Saxons of the nineteenth century.] Have the Germans it? Have the Chinese?" (Proof 117) Newman doesn't pursue the question, however, and his settled view clearly is that the phenomena of conscience are universal.

Conscience is as indubitable a fact as thought, reasoning, or memory. We can doubt particular *deliverances* of these faculties (that I had pancakes for breakfast last Saturday, for instance) but we can't doubt *that* we think, reason, and remember. Similarly, while we can doubt our "judgment in the *particular* case about what is right and wrong" (whether it was right for me to quit my job without notice, for example), we cannot doubt the *fact* of conscience, that is, our "feeling . . . of right and wrong *under a special sanction.*" The contents of our ethical judgments vary, but the sense of standing under "a special sanction" does not: it "remains one and the same in all men." (Proof 111–12) Conscience is inescapable. "The man himself has no power over it . . . ; he did not make it, he cannot destroy it. He may silence it in particular cases or directions; he may distort its enunciations; but he cannot, or it is quite the exception if he can, he cannot emancipate himself from it."[33] (Proof 114) As a consequence of these facts, the proof from conscience is "common to all, to high and low, from earliest infancy. It is carried about in a compact form in every soul. It is ever available—it requires no learning. . . . " (Proof 121f)

Newman's discussion here and elsewhere tends to conflate distinct notions— indubitability, inescapability, universality, and naturalness. They are not the same. My aversions to beets and to smoked calves' tongue are indubitable. (I can't doubt that I have them.) They are also inescapable. (I have tried to overcome these aversions on various occasions since childhood but without success.) And while my aversion to tongue is acquired (I liked it until I was about six), my distaste for beets appears to be a natural rather then an acquired aversion. It is not universal, though. Musical gifts like Mozart's or Schoenberg's are also natural,[34] but they too aren't universal. Or again, on an orthodox Christian view like Newman's, sin is universal and inescapable (by purely human effort). But it is not indubitable (since many people doubt their own sinfulness). And it is not natural (since it is the result of the Fall).

---

33 Newman is quoting from his own *Occasional Sermons*, v.
34 Can their possessors doubt that they have them, or without special effort and rarely, if then, emancipate themselves from them? If not, they are also indubitable and inescap-able.

What Newman wants and needs is that conscience is *natural*. For the key premise in his argument from conscience is that it is reasonable to trust faculties that are part of our *natural* noetic equipment. The indubitability, inescapability, and even universality of conscience are at most fallible *signs* of its naturalness. Its is nonetheless true that the universality of an epistemic faculty provides some evidence that the faculty is part of our natural cognitive endowment. If it can be found in all cultures and all ages, there is reason to believe that it isn't merely a cultural artifact.

Is conscience universal, then, as Newman thinks? Proponents of the claim that conscience is conventional, a product of culture, typically point to its variable content. Huck Finn's conscience tells him not to abet the slave Jim's escape. (Though, to Huck's credit, he decides to act against his "conscience.") The conscience of a dedicated Abolitionist like William Lloyd Garrison would direct him to do the opposite. Homosexual acts are against the consciences of some people but not others. Strict honor codes form part of the conscience of military castes but not part of the conscience of monastic celibates. But all this is irrelevant to Newman's thesis. For, as we have seen, what is invariable in conscience, in Newman's view, is its "sense of standing under a special sanction," not its contents.

The trouble is that Newman himself clearly thinks that countless thousands lack this sense. In his view many modern men and women have a highly developed moral sense but little or no sense of a magisterial dictate or higher sanction. Does this falsify Newman's claim that conscience is part of our natural endowment? His explanation of this apparent counter-example is instructive. Modern "civilization" overemphasizes the intellectual aspects of human nature while neglecting the others. It thus tends to erase the "judicial" or "magisterial" aspect of conscience, leaving only the "critical." (*Grammar* 308) Furthermore, Newman admits that in *any* period of civilization, conscience can be not only "strengthened and improved" but "dimmed, distorted, or obliterated" by "neglect," "the temptations of life," "bad companions," "the urgency of secular occupations," and the like. (*Grammar* 105)

Newman thus has ready-made explanations of most apparent counter-examples. Conscience is indeed part of our natural noetic equipment but it can be lost through neglect or by being placed in unfavorable environments. It is thus unclear what, if anything, would falsify the thesis that conscience is natural.

The suspicion that nothing would is reinforced by a discussion in the *Grammar*. At one point, Newman concedes that the sense of a moral ruler or judge (which is a natural expression of conscience) may presuppose some prior religious instruction or familiarity with the relevant notions (of judge, moral governor, and so on). He insists, however, that the mind of the child is naturally and spontaneously receptive to them. They are "singularly congenial" to the child's soul. "His mind reaches forward with a strong presentiment to the thought of a Moral Governor, sovereign over him, mindful, and just. It comes to him like an impulse of nature to entertain it." (*Grammar* 103) These remarks suggest that what is universal is not conscience as such but its "rudiments," the disposition to respond to the ideas of a moral governor or judge in the appropriate way once they have been presented. Suppose that Grave is right and that one's own or others' prior theistic belief is presupposed by at least some of the phenomena of conscience; conscience as Newman describes it is then a product of (historically) theistic or quasi-theistic cultures. It would not follow, however, that the *rudiments* of conscience, a natural disposition on the part of a child to respond to the relevant ideas in the way Newman describes, isn't universal (and natural) as Newman believes.

Should we conclude that Newman's claim that conscience is natural is unfalsifiable and therefore empirically empty? It is not clear that we should. Note first that Newman's explanations of apparent counter-examples (the sense of a magisterial dictate withers in cultures that overemphasize the intellectual side of human nature while neglecting others, the various ways in which conscience can be stunted or extinguished and, perhaps, the fact that what is universal and natural is only the susceptibility to the phenomena of conscience) are not *ad hoc* additions to his interpretation of conscience but integral parts of it. The second and more important point, however, is this. The phenomena of conscience are widely distributed across times and cultures. That conscience is natural can be regarded as the best explanation of this fact.[35] And *this* thesis could be falsified. One could falsify it by coming up with a better explanation of the widespread distribution of conscience which treats conscience as a purely cultural artifact. The likelihood that someone will succeed in doing so, however, is uncertain. (Freud's theory isn't an example since the psychological mechanisms it postulates to explain conscience are, or so Freud thinks, natural and universal.)

Conclusion

How, then, are we to assess Newman's argument? Its first premise is true, or at least highly plausible. Newman has accurately described the phenomenology of at least some consciences. Conscience is often experienced as a "voice" or "magisterial dictate," an intimation of something beyond the self; and the common inference from these intimations to a holy judge or moral ruler is typically spontaneous and natural.

Newman's third premise is also plausible; it is reasonable to trust our natural faculties in the absence of compelling reasons for not doing so. Appealing to this truth blunts the force of critiques like Freud's by placing the burden of proof squarely on their advocates.

---

35   This shouldn't be confused with the claim that the best explanation of the phenomena of conscience (the intimations of a higher sanction, the sense of standing under judgment, and the like) is that God is their cause. I have argued that this is not a premise in Newman's argument (although he may very well have thought that it is true). The claim we are now considering is that the hypothesis that conscience is part of our natural noetic equipment is the best explanation of its distribution across times and cultures.

Newman's most problematic premise is perhaps the second, for one may doubt that conscience, as described by Newman, is as natural or as universal as he thinks. We have seen, though, that it may not be easy to show that Newman is mistaken on this point. Until someone succeeds in doing so, we are justified in concluding that Newman's argument is a qualified success.

Even if the argument is successful, however, it does have an apparent limitation. As Grave points out, "the phenomena of a conscience commanding and prohibiting, and accusing or condemning," may "point to the existence of a God who is holy, all-seeing, retributive," but "what in our experience of the working of conscience points in a similar way to loving-kindness and mercy in God?" Not a *good* conscience, for "all that seems to bring is an untroubled mind." A good conscience is simply the absence of a bad conscience, and hence doesn't point beyond itself.[36]

While Newman thinks that conscience does have its consolations, its intimations of hope and mercy, and the like, he agrees with the main thrust of Grave's remarks. "Now conscience suggests to us many things about that Master whom by means of it we perceive, but its most prominent teaching . . . is that he is our Judge." Given that "our shortcomings are far more frequent and important than our fulfillment of the duties enjoined upon us," the object of conscience typically appears as "One who is angry with us, and threatens evil." (*Grammar* 303–5) The "large and deep foundation" of religion "is [thus] the sense of sin and guilt," without which "there is . . . no genuine religion." (*Grammar* 311)

The limitation to which Grave calls our attention, however, is a limitation not so much of Newman's *argument* as of natural religion. The need and desire for revelation, and the yearning for consolation and forgiveness, are natural effects of conscience. We crave to know more clearly the one who speaks to us in conscience, and guilt cries out for expiation and atonement. In Newman's opinion, the religion of nature (that is, of conscience) cries out for its completion in the Christian revelation of an immeasurable love which redeems us by taking our sins upon itself.

Appendix

Premise 3 reads: It is reasonable to trust our natural faculties in the absence of compelling reasons for doubting them. Newman himself, however, is reluctant to speak of "trust" or "faith" in our faculties. His reasons are these:

1 I can no more doubt that I reason, remember, or experience the phenomena of conscience than I can doubt my own existence, for my awareness of the operations of these faculties is inseparable from my awareness of my own being.

---

36 Grave, *Conscience in Newman's Thought*, pp. 67–8.

2   Nor can I doubt the occurrence of the *contents* of these acts of consciousness. For example, not only can I not doubt that I (seem to) remember, I cannot doubt that I (seem to) remember having toast and marmalade for breakfast this morning.

3   Properly speaking, what we trust in are "particular acts of memory and reasoning." Thus, I implicitly trust my judgment that I spent my summer vacation in Southeast Asia or that the column of figures adds up to 874. "But, in doing so, we imply no recognition of a general power or faculty . . . over and above the particular act. We know indeed that we have a faculty by which we remember, as we know we have a faculty by which we breathe; but we gain this knowledge by abstraction or inference from its particular acts, not by direct experience." (*Grammar* 66)

4   "Nor do we trust in the faculty of memory or reasoning as such, even after we have inferred its existence; for its acts are often inaccurate, nor do we invariably assent to them." (*Grammar* 66)

5   Finally, our faculties are (part of) ourselves. To trust our faculties would be to trust or have faith in ourselves. But this is double nonsense. For in the first place, "we do not confront or bargain with ourselves." Trust presupposes a distinction between the person who trusts and the object of his or her trust. Since our faculties *are* our selves, trust, in the strict sense, is impossible. And in the second, talk of trust implies that we can withhold it. But "we are as little able to accept or reject our mental constitution, as our being. We have not the option . . . " (*Grammar* 66–7)

These reasons aren't compelling. Newman's first two points are irrelevant since what is at issue is not whether we *possess* reason, memory, or conscience, or whether we *think* that a given set of premises supports a conclusion, or *seem* to remember having toast and marmalade for breakfast, or *experience* the pangs of conscience on lying to a friend, but whether the *deliverances* of reason, memory, and conscience are generally reliable.

Newman's third point can be granted: in trusting the verdicts of reason or memory or conscience, we aren't typically thinking of the *faculties* of which these acts are the expression. But it is surely true that we habitually act *as if* these faculties were generally reliable and, in that sense, implicitly presuppose that they are.

Newman's fourth point rests on a false assumption. Trusting in another's memory or powers of reasoning doesn't entail a belief that her memory is *always* accurate or that her ratiocinations are *always* correct—merely that they are *generally* so. Similarly here. Trusting in my own memory, for example, only entails believing that my memory is generally reliable.

Newman's last point is more substantial but it too isn't fully convincing. In the first place, his argument, if sound, would show that a global skepticism is not only unreasonable but impossible. Yet global skeptics exist, and attempts to show that global skepticism is incoherent haven't proved universally compelling. (Some good philosophers remain unconvinced by them.) In the second place, even if I can't coherently distance myself from *all* my epistemic faculties and call all of them into question at once, I *can* distance myself from some of them. I can use reason, for example, to cast doubt on the reliability of sense perception and memory—or, more to the point, use reason, memory, and the like, to cast doubt on the deliverances of conscience.

Finally, there are two positive reasons for thinking that (*pace* Newman) the use of "trust" or "faith" is appropriate here. The first is that Newman himself admits that talk of "faith" or "trust" is in order when speaking of belief in "an external or outward being"—the existence of material objects, for example, or the real occurrence of my breakfasting on toast and marmalade this morning, or the objective reality of God. (Proof 108–9) Yet when we speak of relying on our faculties, the reliability of judgments of this sort is precisely what is at issue. The second is that, as we have seen, Newman provides arguments for the general reliability of our mental faculties. These arguments would be pointless if distrust (and hence *trust*) weren't real possibilities.

CHAPTER 4

The Argument from the Objectivity of Value

This chapter examines the claim that the objectivity of values provides evidence for theism. Two questions must be considered: are values objective? And, if they are, does the existence of objective values provide evidence for religious conclusions? I shall argue that the answer to both questions is "yes."

The Objectivity of Value

What conditions must be met if values are to be objective? First, value claims are either true or false. Second, values are universal. If something is good or right or beautiful, it is good or right or beautiful at all times and places.[1] Third, values aren't products of our desires. The goodness of truthfulness or friendship, for example, can't be reduced to the fact that we desire them or would desire them if we were fully informed.

But while these conditions are necessary, they are not sufficient. To be objective in the intended sense, values must also be part of the "furniture of the universe." Goodness and rightness, for example, must be real properties of the things that have them. The difference between people who believe in the objectivity of values and those who don't is, in this respect, like that between men and women who believe in the real existence of material substance underlying phenomenal qualities of color, shape, and so on, and phenomenalists or Berkeleyan idealists who do not.[2]

J. L. Mackie has persuasively argued that a belief in the objectivity of *moral* values at least is embedded in most mainstream Western moral philosophy, and presupposed in ordinary moral thought and discourse. "The ordinary user of moral language means to say something about" the object that he "characterizes morally," and not about his or anyone elses attitudes toward it, "something that involves a call for action or for the refraining from action . . . that is . . . not contingent upon any

---

1   This shouldn't be misunderstood. Truthfulness is an important value but there can be circumstances in which one's commitment to truthfulness is trumped by more important values. It would be wrong not to lie if a consequence of speaking the truth would be delivering an innocent Jewish child into the hands of the Gestapo. It is nonetheless true that, at all times and places, one has a *prima facie* obligation to speak the truth.
2   Cf. J. L. Mackie, *Ethics: Inventing Right and Wrong*. Harmondsworth, Middlesex: Penguin Books 1977, pp. 20–24.

desire or preference . . . or choice" of "his own or anyone else's."[3] An indication that this belief is deeply ingrained in ordinary moral thought is the fact that a loss of it often leads to profound uneasiness, a sense that moral values may not really matter.

Mackie himself thinks that the belief in objective values is mistaken. For one thing, value qualities, if real, would be "queer" properties, "utterly different from everything else in the universe." (Unlike all other facts, moral facts would have either requiredness or "not-to-be-doneness somehow built into" them, and an objective goodness would have "to-be-pursuedness somehow built into it."[4] Yet how a thing's objective value properties are related to its natural features is a total mystery.) For another, it is unclear how we could *know* these nonnatural properties since they don't stand in causal relations to us. (Values aren't causes.)

Finally, if we can provide an explanation of people's *belief* in the objectivity of values which doesn't appeal to their objectivity, the postulation of objective values seems otiose. And we can. The belief can be explained in terms of the mind's "propensity to spread itself on external objects," by our projecting our attitudes on to their objects, by our tendency to reverse "the direction of dependence" between desires and goodness, "making the desire depend upon the goodness, instead of the goodness on the desire," by our unconsciously suppressing the fact that statements of obligation are implicitly hypothetical (asserting that so-and-so should be done *if* we or others *want* such-and-such), by "the persistence of a belief in something like divine law when the belief in the divine legislator has faded out," and the like.[5]

How might one respond to this? Many theists believe that they can provide an explanation of values which respects the appearance of objectivity and meets Mackie's objections. If their account provides a *better* explanation of the apparent objectivity of values than Mackie's does, then their apparent objectivity provides a good reason for preferring the theist's account of values to Mackie's.[6] Theistic accounts do have two serious rivals, however. Both naturalism and constructivism preserve at least some of the appearances.

Naturalism identifies goodness, say, with a natural (that is, empirical) property such as pleasure or happiness, or with a cluster of natural properties. For example, Richard Boyd identifies goodness with what he calls a "homeostatic property cluster"—"things which satisfy important human needs" together with the

---

3   Ibid., p. 33.
4   Ibid., pp. 38–41.
5   Ibid., pp. 42–6. Mackie also appeals to the diversity of moral and aesthetic opinion. This is less persuasive, however, since it is fairly easy for the moral objectivist to account for it in terms of empirical or logical error, the different concrete circumstances to which general moral principles are applied, and so on.
6   The relevant principle is that if a theory T1 provides a better explanation of a body of evidence, E, than its rivals T2, T3, . . . , Tn, then T is more probable on E than T1, T2, . . . , or Tn.

"homeostatic mechanisms which unify them," that is, tend to produce or maintain the others when enough of them are present.[7]

G. E. Moore's "open question argument" isn't sufficient to dispose of naturalism. Moore's argument was this: suppose that we identify goodness with some natural property, N. Then the question "Is N good?" is equivalent to "Is N N?", and "x is N but x isn't good" is equivalent to "x is N but x isn't N." The question "Is N good?" is *not* otiose, however, and the claim that something is N but not good is *not* a contradiction. For any natural property you please, it makes sense to ask whether it is good, and a person who denies that it is, while perhaps mistaken, is not contradicting herself.

Moore's argument doesn't defeat naturalism, however. The most it shows is that, for any natural property, N, "x is good" doesn't *mean* "x is N." It doesn't show that x's goodness doesn't *consist in* its being N. An analogy helps make this clear. A form of Moore's open question argument can be used to show that "x is water" doesn't *mean* "x is H_2O." My five-year-old grandson knows how to use the word "water" correctly. But if he asks "Is water H_2O?", his question isn't otiose, and if he denies that water is H_2O, he isn't contradicting himself (merely exhibiting his ignorance of chemistry). These facts are perfectly compatible with water's *being* H_2O, however, and whether it is or not is a matter for empirical investigation. Similarly with ethical naturalism. The sophisticated naturalist is not claiming that "good" means happiness, say, but that happiness is what *constitutes* goodness, what goodness *really is*.

Naturalism has several advantages. Perhaps the most important is that it makes values robustly objective. In its view, values are ordinary empirical properties (or sets of properties). They are therefore part of the furniture of the universe, and claims about them are either true or false. They also appear to be universal in the relevant sense. If something is pleasant, for example, it is reasonable to assume that it will be pleasant at other times and places.[8]

Whether naturalism preserves all the appearances, however, is doubtful. Mackie has pointed out that, in the ordinary view, moral facts have "requiredness" or "not-to-be-doneness" built into them, and the property (or set of properties) picked out by "goodness" has "to-be-pursuedness" built into it. Yet it is difficult to see how *purely empirical* properties could have these characteristics built into them.

Suppose, for example, that we identify goodness with the satisfaction of our more important wants and needs. Given that we have these wants and needs, we

---

7 Richard Boyd, "How to be a Moral Realist," in Geoffrey Sayre-McCord, ed., *Essays on Moral Realism*. Ithaca: Cornell University Press, 1988, pp. 181–228.

8 This should not be misunderstood, however. I enjoy apple pie. But eating apple pie isn't pleasant when one has the flu, or is already surfeited. All that follows, though, is that the subject of the sentence, "Eating apple pie is pleasant," hasn't been fully specified. What is pleasant isn't eating apple pie *simpliciter*, but eating apple pie when one is well, moderately hungry, and so on. When fully specified, the claim *is* universal in the intended sense.

will pursue their satisfaction. But the "to-be-pursuedness" of their satisfaction appears to be an artifact of our needs and wants, not an intrinsic feature of the satisfactions themselves. If so, then the third criterion of objectivity isn't met: values don't have the necessary independence from our desires or interests. And if goodness is identified with a natural property or set of properties that are less immediately connected to our wants and interests—health, say, or psychological integration, or social order[9]—it is even less obvious that "to-be-pursuedness" is built into them. The only obvious answers to why we should pursue them is that we simply *want* them or things they lead to—in which case, their goodness is an artifact of our desires; or that they or the things they lead to are *good*, where their goodness is an objective but *non*natural property with to-be-pursuedness built into it—which is inconsistent with naturalism.[10]

The other important rival to theistic accounts of the objectivity of value is constructivism. Constructivists believe that while there are moral facts or truths, these facts or truths are the *products* of rational deliberation and choice. For example, John Rawls argues that adequate principles of justice are those which would be chosen under fair conditions by rational agents concerned to maximize their share of such things as "rights and liberties, opportunities and powers, income and wealth," and "a sense of one's own worth."[11] David Gauthier identifies moral principles with those that would be chosen by rational self-interested agents,[12]

---

9   Less immediately connected with our desires because our desires aren't part of their concept as they are part of the concept of the satisfaction of our desires.

10   Robert Adams has another objection. By identifying goodness with a natural property or set of them, we abandon the "critical stance" which is an essential feature of our use of moral terms. "For any natural, empirically identifiable property or action type," it is "*always* open in principle" to ask whether it "is *really* good or right, or to issue an evaluative or normative challenge by denying that it is *really* good or right." He then suggests that the proper alternative to naturalism "is a realist view of the Good as transcendent" since, "given that our knowledge of the Good is necessarily imperfect and fragmentary, it can never be out of order to question or challenge any human view about the Good." (Robert M. Adams, *Finite and Infinite Goods* [New York: Oxford University Press, 1999], pp. 78, 81. Henceforth Adams) Although I am sympathetic to Adams's remarks, I am not fully persuaded by them. For one thing, I wonder if a critical stance which is prepared to call every value claim into question is a feature of ordinary moral thought and discourse in general, or only of *modern* moral thought and discourse, and of certain strands of western philosophical ethics. For another, Adams's remarks fail to do justice to the important critical role played by the concepts of pleasure and happiness in the hands of social reformers like Jeremy Bentham and J. S. Mill. Natural properties can be, and have been, used as touchstones to critically assess human mental states, acts, institutions, and practices.

11   John Rawls, *A Theory of Justice*. Cambridge: Harvard University Press, 1971, p. 92.

12   David Gauthier, *Morals by Agreement*. Oxford: Clarendon Press, 1986. It should be noted that Gauthier does *not* think that the principle that would be chosen by rational self-interested agents is "Choose actions which have the greatest expected value." Rational self-interested agents would instead select principles whereby choices would be made on a cooperative basis.

while Christine Korsgaard argues that "value is grounded in rational nature—in particular in the structure of reflective consciousness." Moral values are bound up with our "practical identity," descriptions under which we value ourselves, "find [our] life to be worth living and [our] actions to be worth undertaking."[13]

On constructivist views like these, value claims are objective in the sense that they are true or false (or, alternatively, correct or incorrect, reasonable or unreasonable). Whether they meet the other three conditions for objectivity is less clear.

Gauthier's theory is a sophisticated form of ethical egoism: the binding force of moral obligation is ultimately dependent on our desire to further our own interests. So the third condition isn't met. Rawls now admits that his procedures will yield the intuitively "correct" results only when applied by rational agents committed to the values of modern Western liberal democracies.[14] The moral claims supported by the procedures aren't truly universal, then. The fourth condition isn't met either. Korsgaard, I think, speaks for all of them when she says that the value which "is grounded in . . . the structure of rational consciousness . . . is projected on to the world. So the reflection in question is practical and not theoretical: it is a reflection about what to do, *not reflection about what is to be found in the normative part of the world*."[15]

Another problem with constructivism is this: normative objectivity normally requires the possibility of error. (Judgments of taste like "I like vanilla ice cream" aren't objective because they can't be mistaken.) Suppose that the constructivists' methods don't yield convergence on the answers to some moral questions (or that they only yield convergence for those who initially accept a controversial procedural analysis of practical rationality such as Rawls's). Suppose further that moral realism is false; there are no mind-independent moral facts. Then it is totally unclear what moral error could consist in in cases in which two persons correctly employ the recommended procedures and get conflicting results, or in cases in which conflicting results are reached by persons who correctly employ different procedures neither of which is clearly irrational.

One wants to say that at least one of the results in these cases is mistaken. Suppose, for example, that, without either party misapplying the relevant proce-

---

13   Christine M. Korsgaard, *The Sources of Normativity*. Cambridge: Cambridge University Press, 1996, pp. 101, 116.

14   John Rawls, *Political Liberalism*. New York: Columbia University Press, 1993.

15   Korsgaard, *Sources of Normativity*, p. 116, my emphasis. This claim must be qualified, however. For example, that Rawlsian rational agents, choosing under Rawlsian fair conditions, would opt for his principle that social and economic inequalities are justified only if they work for the advantage of the least well off is—if true—as much a part of the furniture of the world as any other hypothetical fact (that water will freeze if the temperature drops below 32 degrees Fahrenheit, for instance). It is also mind-independent in the sense that its truth doesn't depend on any mind embracing it. Nevertheless, it remains the case that there aren't any mind-independent non-hypothetical moral facts. The categorical features of the world can be exhaustively described without referring to values.

dures, one draws the conclusion that a radically equalitarian democracy is the best political system while the other derives its denial. It is difficult to see what "error" (and hence "being right") could mean here. The constructivist should probably bite the bullet at this point, and simply admit that neither person is mistaken. Yet this seems counter-intuitive.

It isn't clear then, that either naturalism or constructivism adequately accommodates the appearance of objectivity built into our ordinary thinking and speaking about values. Can theism do better? To answer this question, we will examine the theories of W. R. Sorley and Robert M. Adams.

W. R. Sorley and the Inference from Objective Values to a Supreme Mind

Sorley's argument can be formulated as follows:

1 Moral values are objective.
2 If moral values are objective, they must exist "somehow and somewhere."
3 They don't exist in "material things" or "in the mind of this or that individual."
4 They must therefore exist in "a Supreme Mind."[16]

Assume that moral values are objective. Why think that Sorley's *other* premises are true? Consider premise (3). The laws of nature and of mathematics "are already embodied in the processes of nature."[17] The laws of logic "too receive verification in reality and in thought in so far as it does not end in confusion." It is different with ethical values, however. They needn't be (and only imperfectly are) "embodied" or "verified" in natural processes or in human thought and behavior.[18] (Sorley 353) Values such as justice, for instance, are only imperfectly understood, and reality doesn't always behave justly.

Yet suppose that we grant (3). Why accept premise (2)? "Why is it assumed that the moral ideal must exist somewhere and somehow?" Isn't the "validity" of our ideals being confused with their "existence"? Sorley's answer is that "the validity of the moral ideal, like all validity, is a *validity for existents*. Without this

---

16 W. R. Sorley, *Moral Values and the Idea of God.* Cambridge: The University Press, 1918, pp. 351–6. Henceforth Sorley.
17 Sorley thinks that the laws of mathematics "are merely an abstract of the natural order, when considered solely in its formal aspect." (Sorley 353) However, this is, at best, true only of those mathematical systems which are *realized* in the physical order.
18 Note that being embodied or verified in human thought is very different from being embodied or verified in human behavior. A moral ideal or value is "embodied" in thought when it is more or less perfectly understood and appreciated. It is "embodied" in behavior when it is *instantiated* in our conduct. Sorley runs these two sorts of "embodiment" or "verification" together. His doing so doesn't clearly vitiate his argument, however.

reference to existents there seems no meaning in asserting validity." (Sorley 355, my emphasis)

But this response isn't helpful. The most natural interpretation of "Moral ideals are valid for existents" is that existents *should* instantiate them. It doesn't follow from this, however, that moral ideals exist somewhere in ontological space, let alone in a "Supreme Mind." So just what is going on here? There are at least two possibilities.

The first is this. Sorley *might* be assuming that truth is a relation of correspondence or adequation or conformity between minds, on the one hand, and reality, on the other. If it is, then absolute truth implies an absolute mind—one fully adequate to, or in perfect correspondence with, reality. If this *is* what Sorley has in mind, however, it won't clearly do.

An absolute mind would presumably be an *omniscient* or *perfect* mind, one fully adequate to reality in its entirety or as a whole. But Sorley's premises, together with this conception of truth, don't demonstrate the reality of a mind like *that*. They at most establish the existence of an intellect in perfect possession of *moral* truth. Admittedly, one can't be in perfect possession of moral truth without understanding many nonmoral truths. There is no reason to think that one must understand all of them, however. An understanding of justice, for example, involves some understanding of rational agents. It does not require an understanding of microphysics or the more arcane aspects of set theory. The inference to a *supreme* mind thus seems unwarranted.

Moreover, it isn't clear that this line of thought even succeeds in establishing the existence of a mind that is in perfect possession of *moral* truth. For *even if* truth should be understood as a relation between minds and reality, why not define the absolute truth about mathematics, say, or morality as those claims about mathematics or morality that *would* be endorsed by a perfect mathematician or ethical reasoner *if* there were one? The reference to *actually existing* minds seems unnecessary.[19]

The other possibility is that Sorley is assuming that truths must be, or be anchored in, *facts*, express or reflect (aspects of) *reality*. If so, then truths about value must be grounded in real, that is, existent, goodness. This, by itself, is insufficient to establish theism since the condition would be met by Platonism. If the form of the Good and the Beautiful is an actual existent, as Plato thought, then goodness is embedded in the structure of reality, and value propositions have an objectively existing referent. Yet Plato's form of the Good is not "a Supreme Mind." It is possible, however, that Sorley's argument is governed not only by this assumption

---

19 But in that case, wouldn't mathematical or moral truth be merely *possible* truth? On the assumption that truth consists in an adequation between mind and reality, doesn't *actual* truth presuppose *actual* minds? Only if actual truth is defined as a relation between real *relata*. But the suggestion here is that it need not be; it can be defined as a relation between a real *relatum* and an ideal one, namely, an ideal mathematician, or chemist, or moralist, or what have you.

but by another, namely, that all *real* existents are *concreta* or aspects of *concreta*, and *concreta* are exhaustively divided into minds and material objects.[20] If we grant this, and there really are objective values, then the values must be rooted in physical objects or minds. Since they don't exist in "material things" or "in the mind of this or that individual," they must exist "in a Supreme Mind."

Whether we *should* grant this assumption, however, is debatable. Platonisms which countenance the real existence of numbers, sets, and other abstract objects are common in the history of philosophy, and it is unclear that opposition to them is rooted in anything stronger than a (contested) intuition that only *concreta* are genuinely real, or in a taste for desert landscapes.

Sorley's argument isn't fully persuasive, then, because its rests on one or more controversial assumptions—that truth is a relation between minds and reality, that truths are part of or reflect the structure of reality, that *concreta* alone are truly real. Nevertheless, Sorley's assumptions are not clearly mistaken, and there are no knock-down-drag-out arguments against them.

W. T. Maclagan has an argument against views like Sorley's, though, which would, if sound, be devastating. Sorley thinks that "moral distinctions are . . . neither . . . the product of [God's] will nor . . . altogether independent of him, but [are] constitutive of his understanding, and" have "'reality' only thus." Yet this is nonsense. "What we know, and our knowing it are . . . never the same thing, and to claim that something is the case includes the affirmation that it is the case apart from our knowledge." So either God does not understand moral distinctions, or they are what they are *independent* of his understanding of them and thus aren't constituted *by* his understanding them.[21]

This isn't convincing. That what we know is distinct from our *understanding* of it does not imply that it is distinct from *us*. My irascibility, for instance, is distinct

---

20   A. C. Ewing, who offers an argument similar to Sorley's, clearly does make this
      assumption. To the objection that moral law (and presumably values) "need only be
      conceived as subsisting and not as existing" as concrete objects do, Ewing responds
      that "the subsistence of the law . . . can be understood only in relation to an existent
      . . . " "Subsistence" has no "clear meaning by itself, but is merely a technical way of
      expressing the point that moral judgments [and presumably other judgments which
      tempt us to posit subsisting facts to which they correspond or in which they are
      anchored] have some kind of objectivity, we know not what without the addition of
      some further explanation . . . given by reference to an existent." (A. C. Ewing, *Value
      and Reality* [London: George Allen and Unwin, 1973], pp. 195–6)
21   Maclagan, *Theological Frontier of Ethics*, p. 70. A. C. Ewing adds that if moral laws
      are true because God thinks them (rather than God thinking them because they are
      true), then their truth is "essentially arbitrary." ("The Autonomy of Ethics," in Ian
      Ramsey, ed., *Prospect for Metaphysics* [London: George Allen and Unwin, 1961], pp.
      41f.) This doesn't follow, however. If God thinks moral truths ("Lying is *prima facie*
      wrong," for instance) *in all possible worlds*, and their truth consists in his thinking
      them, then they are *true* in all possible words and hence necessary. Since they couldn't
      be false, they aren't "arbitrary."

from my cognizance of it but is not distinct *from me.* Similarly, if God is the Good, as many classical theists have believed, then, while *what* God knows (the Good) is distinct from his *cognizance* of it,[22] it is *not* distinct from *him.*

This response, however, shifts the emphasis from God's understanding to his nature. Value is constituted by God's being and characteristic activity, and not (primarily at least) by his understanding of it. We will examine a view of this sort in the next section.

Robert Adams and the Transcendent Good

Sorley thinks that the objectivity of values consists in God's thinking them. Robert Adams's theory, too, involves essential references to divine mentation.[23] Even so, there are few traces of the view that God's mind is the *place* of values.[24] Adams's emphasis is instead upon the idea that *God himself* is value or the Good.

1   Adams's Theory of Value

Excellence is a property of "persons . . . ; physical objects; some kinds of abstraction (such as poems and mathematical proofs); qualities (such as a beautiful shade of blue); deeds; lives—but not in general of states of affairs." It is an object of eros both in "its moments of admiration" and in its moments of pursuit. (The latter is grounded in the former.) Moreover, "to the extent that anything is good, in the sense of 'excellent,' it is *good* for us to love it, admire it, and want to be related to it, whether we do in fact or not." (Adams 17, 19–20)

Now, "the character of our pursuit of excellence, including the character of the things we think are excellent," points in the direction of "a single property or nature" that "would best satisfy the pursuit." "That property or nature," whatever it may be, is excellence. (Adams 22) In Adams's view, the nature or property we refer to by "excellence" is constituted by resemblance to the Good.[25] Since (as Adams will argue) *God* is the Good, excellence is ultimately constituted by resemblance to

---

22   There is at least a "notional" distinction between the Good and God's knowledge of it. If the doctrine of divine simplicity is correct, however, there is no "*real*" distinction between them. While "God," "the Good," and "God's knowledge of the Good" don't have the same *meaning*, they have the same *referent*, namely, God's being or nature.

23   Adams says, for example, that "God's view of things" is "the definitive standard . . . of resemblance" to God, and hence (as we shall see) of the excellence that resemblance constitutes. (Adams 34) Adams also thinks that the fact that x's resemblance to God constitutes an excellence is explained by that resemblance's constituting a *reason* for God's loving x.

24   But see Adams's "Divine Necessity," discussed below.

25   "x is excellent" doesn't *mean* "x resembles the Good," however. Adams's theory of the good isn't a theory of meaning.

God. Adams's responses to objections to this identification of excellence and resemblance to the divinity clarifies his meaning.

On the face of it, resemblance to God is neither a necessary nor sufficient condition of excellence. It isn't necessary since some excellences don't resemble God. Excellence in cooking, for example, is a real excellence, but God is not a great chef. Or consider human excellences that "depend on our finitude" such as temperance or courage. God isn't temperate or brave because he lacks appetites and desires which need to be controlled and he can't be threatened by dangers. Nor is resemblance to God sufficient. Hitler's power resembles God's, and a three-leaf clover resembles the trinity, but neither are thereby excellent. How dispose of counter-examples like these? (Adams 30–31)

God isn't a great cook, and God isn't temperate or brave, but "saying that A resembles B in respect of A's Φ-ing does not entail that Φ-ing is a property that A and B share or that B Φ's too. It is enough if A's Φ-ing manifests resemblance to some aspect of B." "One's cooking," for example, "might manifest a resemblance to the divine creativity," and virtues like courage or temperance "may resemble or image God" with respect to "what we care about, and the strength and effectiveness of our caring." (Adams 30–31)

What the second pair of counter-examples shows is that "not every sharing of a property constitutes a resemblance" in the intended sense. "Judgments of resemblance are more holistic than that." A squirrel and I don't resemble each other simply because we have the same number of hairs on our bodies. Nor would I "become more Godlike by coming to believe I was God." But even holistic resemblance is not enough, for caricatures holistically resemble their originals yet do not share their excellences. To constitute excellence, the holistic image or resemblance must be "faithful" rather than "distorted." (Adams 32–3)

These remarks are helpful. Nevertheless, they do not fully capture Adams's intention. God loves himself and therefore loves what resembles him. That is, x's resembling God "contributes to God's reasons for loving" x. (God may, of course, love x for other reasons as well.) That it does so "helps explain . . . the resemblances' constituting excellence." The most accurate statement of Adams's view, then, is this: the excellence of finite things consists in holistic resemblances to God that can "serve God as a reason for loving that thing." (Adams 36)

Yet why should the Good be identified with God in the first place? For a number of converging reasons. First, the Good must be personal. Since most important excellences "are excellences of persons, or of qualities or actions or works or lives or stories of persons," and since the excellence of finite things "consists in resembling or imaging" the Good, the Good must be "a person or importantly like a person." (Adams 42)

It must also be actual. For suppose that it isn't. "Mere possibilities have no standing in the world except as objects of understanding." Now, "*we* do not understand the Good itself, in all its perfections." Hence, the Good will have no standing in the world unless *God* understands it. If God understands it, however, then God exists and "is there as a real being to fill the role of the Good." Assuming that he has the other characteristics needed to fit something for the role of the Good, it is thus reasonable to identify God with the "objective standard of excellence." (Adams 44–5)

We can reach the same conclusion from a different direction. To be useful, a standard of excellence must be determinate. Mere possibilities, however, aren't sufficiently determinate to "serve as the standard of excellence" because there are "too many" of them and they are too "various." An adequate standard of excellence must therefore be actual. But what actual entity can serve as "an objective standard of excellence"? If God "really exists," he "is surely the salient candidate."[26] (Adams 44–5)

There are still other reasons for identifying the Good with God. Adams has suggested that a finite thing's excellence consists in its resemblance to the Good's being a reason for the Good's loving it. But persons alone love and have reasons. The Good must therefore be personal. It must also be best. "Let X be the Good itself; and suppose that excellence therefore consists in a sort of resemblance to X." Since "no being could be more like X than X itself is . . . , no being could be more excellent than X is." Now God has been traditionally conceived as maximally perfect, "a being than which nothing greater can be conceived." It is therefore reasonable to identify the Good with God. (Adams 45)

Again, it isn't a contingent matter that knowledge or beauty, say, or fidelity are excellences, and that ignorance, ugliness, and treachery are not. Knowledge, for example, would be good in all possible worlds. But if it would, and if excellence consists in a certain sort of resemblance to something, G, playing the role of the Good, then *G* must exist in all possible worlds.[27] Now, the God of classical theism has typically[28] been regarded as a necessary being. So if God has a sufficient

---

26 For the argument from determinateness to be convincing, I think that Adams must not only insist that the members of the relevant set of possibilities are "many" and "various;" he must also insist that the members of the set are themselves indeterminate. For suppose he doesn't. Then each of the relevant possibilities (and hence the set of them) is fully determinate although our grasp of them (in most cases) is not. But of course we don't fully grasp all the excellences of the actually existing (and hence fully determinate) God either. There is the same ontological determinateness in both cases and the same epistemic indeterminateness. So why is God a better candidate for the standard of excellence than the set of these possibilities? Adams might argue, though, that if the members of the set aren't corealizable, we must artibrarily pick one rather than the other, and are thus left without practical guidance. By contrast, it is *not* arbitrary to pick an actual existent for the role of the standard of excellence if it is the most salient of the available candidates.

27 Why can't excellence in all possible worlds consist in faithfully resembling an entity which exists in only *one* of them (and is therefore not necessary)? Perhaps for this reason. Resemblance to an entity E would not be a viable standard in worlds in which E doesn't exist and reveal itself, because persons in those worlds would have no epistemic access to that standard.

28 Although not always.

number of the other characteristics needed to play the role of the Good, it is reasonable to identify the Good with God. And God does. God's essential attributes *do* fit him for that role. Examples are loving or prizing such things as courage and personality, and "hating" or misprizing such things as cruelty or the violation of persons. (What plays the role of the Good must square, in a rough and ready way, with ordinary judgments of excellence. If God prized cruelty, for instance, then imaging or resembling the divine nature couldn't plausibly be identified with excellence.)

Note that, on Adams's account, values meet all four of the conditions that must be satisfied if they are to be considered objective. Since claims that things resemble God in the right way are either true or false, value claims are true or false. Values are also universal. If courage, for example, or human fidelity faithfully images or resembles God, it does so at all times and places. Nor are the facts of resemblance in which excellence consists dependent on our desires. If visual beauty, for instance, faithfully images God, it does so whether we admire and desire it or not.[29] Finally, God, and the facts of resemblance, are part of the "furniture of the universe." That human love resembles God's love, for example, is as objectively real a feature of human love, as a photograph's resemblance to its original or a child's resemblance to its parents. Adams's theory thus saves the appearance of value's objectivity.

A theory like Adams's also dispels Mackie's two main worries. By identifying objective value with resemblance to God, it eliminates, or at least reduces, its ontological "queerness." The existence of objective value is no "queerer" than the existence of God himself. It can also explain our epistemic access to objective value. If theism is true, then it is reasonable to believe that "God causes . . . human beings to regard as excellent approximately those things that are Godlike in the relevant way." (He may do so by fashioning their consciences, by endowing them with appropriate emotions and capacities for practical reasoning, by direct revelation, and the like.) If he does so, however, "there is a causal and explanatory connection between facts of excellence and beliefs that we may regard as justified about excellence." (Adams 70) Our epistemic access to objective value thus isn't mysterious.

Whereas Sorley's argument was deductive, Adams's is best viewed as an inference to the best explanation. The fact to be explained is value realism—that excellence is an objectively real property of things. The *explicans* is that excellence consists in a certain kind to resemblance to a Good which is identical with, that is, constituted by, the Godhead. If Adams's theistic theory of the Good accounts for value's appearance of objectivity more adequately than alternative theories (including debunking theories like Mackie's), then that appearance is *a* reason for theism.[30]

---

29   However, visual beauty's, or knowledge's, excellence does entail that we *should* desire or admire them.

30   That is, it raises the probability of theism. How much it does so depends in part on the theist's success in defusing standard objections to theism. Note that Adams's argument

2   Objections

Adams's theory is exposed to two important objections, however.

First objection   The first objection is this. If we think of God as a *person*, we can only think of him as "fully and perfectly *exemplifying*" "the order of values," "not as *being* . . . it." "He will be, so to say, the Great Exemplar." He won't be Goodness itself.[31] The objection, in short, is that God is a *particular*, and particulars can't be standards.

Furthermore, that God is to be praised and glorified for his goodness is fundamental to theism.[32] But that God is to be praised for his goodness seems to imply that, rather than *being* a standard, God *meets* standards. (We don't praise standards. We praise things for meeting them.)

The distinction between perfect examples and standards is not that sharp, however. Examples are sometimes *prior* to the rules or norms which state that things like the example are good or right, in the sense that the rules or norms are *derived from* the examples. A person, or a pattern of behavior, or a work of art, or a new wine strikes as exemplary even though it fails to meet existing norms in some respects. Under the impact of the example, we construct new rules or reconstruct old ones. In situations like these the example is more than a perfect instance of the new or reconstructed norm. It is, in a real sense, its ground or source.

Nor is the priority of the examples in these cases purely epistemological. It is not as if, under the impact of the examples, we discover standards that can be stated *without reference to them*. For, in the cases in question, the standards can only be stated in the form "Paintings like this (or behavior like this, or scientific work like this, or . . .) are good or right." Reference to the exemplar is (ontologically) *essential* to them. William Alston's distinction between "'Platonic' predicates" and "'particularistic' predicates" is helpful here. The former "can be specified in purely general terms." The latter make "essential reference to one or more individuals." "Triangle" is an example of the first. "Meter" is an example of the second, since what makes something "a meter in length is not its conformity to a Platonic essence but its conformity to a certain existing individual," namely, "the standard meter-stick kept in Paris."[33] It is not clear, then, that there need be anything logically

---

is not, in the first instance, an argument for theism but, rather, for a certain account of value. That account entails theism, however. So any evidence which supports that account supports theism. (If E raises the probability of H, it raises the probability of any relevant proposition, P, entailed by H.)

31   Maclagan, *Theological Frontier of Ethics*, p. 88.
32   Think of the role praise plays in the religious life of devout Muslims, Christians, and Jews, for example.
33   William Alston, "Some Suggestions for Divine Command Theorists," in William P. Alston, *Divine Nature and Human Language: Essays in Philosophical Theology*. Ithaca: Cornell University Press, 1989, p. 269.

idiosyncratic in suggesting that *God* is both Goodness's perfect exemplar *and* its standard.[34]

Note, too, that where the standard *is* a particular, praise or commendation are sometimes in order. Arguably, where particulars function as standards, they do so because they are perfect instances of the class of things being evaluated. Thus, the standard meter bar is (*pace* Wittgenstein) exactly one meter long since it is the same length as itself. If a particular chef's bratwurst sandwiches provide the paradigm for all bratwurst sandwiches, then his sandwiches are perfect bratwurst sandwiches.[35] Moreover, while it would be nonsense to praise the rule which states that the chef's sandwiches provide the paradigm for all bratwurst sandwiches, it is not nonsense to praise the chef's sandwiches themselves. Even if we do praise things for meeting standards rather than for being standards, it isn't clear that we can't praise the exemplary sandwiches for their perfect conformity to the rule which states that they are the paradigmatic instances of their class. Similarly, it isn't clear that God's being the standard of goodness is incompatible with praise. Standard examples cannot, of course, fail to match themselves. Whether this precludes praise, however, is doubtful. Classical theists, at least, have no reason to think so. For while they believe that praising God is always in order, they *also* think that God, being essentially good, cannot fail to meet the appropriate standards.

The first objection to Adams's thesis thus fails.

Second objection   A second objection questions the *need* for theories like Sorley's and Adams's. Suppose that basic value facts are *necessary* facts.[36] Suppose, for instance, that "Lying is *prima facie* wrong," or "Loyalty is an excellence," are *necessarily* true, that is, true in all possible worlds. This view is not implausible.

---

34   Colin Strong argues that a particular can be a standard for something only if there is a rule or "logos" which asserts that it is the standard for that thing. Thus the standard meter bar in Paris functions as a standard only in virtue of a rule which asserts that its length is the length of a meter. Analogously, if God functions as a standard of goodness, he does so only in virtue of a standard which asserts that a thing's goodness is measured by its resemblance to God. Since particulars function as standards solely in virtue of rules of this kind, the *rules* are the standards in the primary sense. (Colin Strong, "Plato and the Third Man," *Proceedings of the Aristotelian Society*, Supplementary vol. 37 [1963], pp. 147–64) I am not sure how much force these points have. Even if particulars aren't standards in the *primary* sense, it doesn't follow that they aren't *standards* (which is the point at issue). Furthermore, since the rules are derived from the exemplars, and make essential reference to them, it is not clear that they really are the standards in the primary sense.

35   This is not to deny the logical uniqueness of the particulars which furnish the standard. Other bratwurst sandwiches are perfect only in so far as they match the chef's sandwiches, and they can fail to do so. By contrast, the paradigmatic sandwiches can't fail to resemble themselves.

36   *Non*-basic value claims can be contingent. "It was wrong of Mary to lie to her mother" entails the existence of both Mary and her mother. Since their existence is contingent, the proposition, if true, is only contingently true.

Are there any conceivable circumstances in which there wouldn't be a moral *presumption* against lying, for instance,[37] or in which loyalty[38] wouldn't be a good-making feature of the attitudes, actions, and patterns of behavior which exhibit it? I, for one, doubt it.

Suppose, then, that basic value facts *are* necessary. If they are, then values meet our four criteria for objectivity. Claims about basic values are either necessarily *true* or necessarily *false*.[39] The values in question are also universal: since propositions expressing value facts are necessarily true, they are true in all possible worlds. Our third criterion is met as well. Necessary facts, such as the facts of logic or mathematics, aren't constituted by our willing or desiring them. They thus have the necessary independence.

Is the fourth criterion met too? It is difficult to see why not. If (some) value claims are necessarily true, then the facts that they express are as much a part of the structure of reality as the facts of logic and mathematics. If the latter are rightly regarded as objective, then so too are the former. Moreover, value properties are *real* properties of the things that have them. If it is necessarily true that lying is *prima facie* wrong and that loyalty is an excellence, then *prima facie* wrongness and excellence are *essential* properties of lying and loyalty, respectively. But surely essential properties of a thing are *real* properties of it.[40]

---

37 Presumptions can, of course, sometimes be overridden.

38 Suitably qualified, of course. Loyalty can be misguided or misdirected. But assuming it isn't, can it fail to be excellent?

39 If true basic value claims are necessarily true, then the *denials* of true basic value claims are necessarily false.

40 There are problems here. For example, G. E. Moore argues that goodness is not an intrinsic property of the things that have it, where P is an intrinsic property of x if and only if (1) P is a descriptive property of x and (2) P depends only on x's nature, so that anything with that nature must have that property. Thus, while pleasurable consciousness is necessarily good (the second condition is met), a description of pleasurable consciousness can be complete which omits all references to its value (the first condition is not met). Hence, goodness is not an intrinsic property of pleasurable consciousness. (G. E. Moore, "The Conception of Intrinsic Value," in G. E. Moore, *Philosophical Studies* [New York: The Humanities Press, 1951], pp. 253–75) So if a thing's real properties are identified with its *intrinsic* properties, then not all of a thing's essential properties are real properties of it. Whether Moore himself would have identified the two is doubtful, but doing so highlights the difficulty of defining "real property." If we identify a thing's real properties with the set of properties that can be truly ascribed to it, then *not having a square root* is a real property of frogs. If a thing's real properties include its *essential* properties, we get the same result since it is necessarily true that frogs don't have square roots. If a thing's real properties are those which would be included in a complete description of it, however, then *not having a square root* probably isn't a real property of frogs. (Would one object to someone's description of frogs, "You've left something out—you forgot to mention that they don't have square roots"?!) Whether goodness could be omitted in a complete description of (e.g.) pleasurable consciousness is less clear. As we have seen, Moore believed that it could. W. D. Ross, on the other hand, thought that Moore was misled by the fact

The objection, therefore, is this. There is some reason to think that basic value claims are necessarily true. If they are, their objectivity is assured, and there is no reason to bring God into the picture. The appeal to theistic metaphysics is otiose.

There are at least two possible responses to this objection. The first is that *all* necessary facts require an explanation. Thus, in the penultimate paragraph of an essay first published in 1980, Adams writes: "Both of the following views seem . . . plausible. (1) Possibilities and necessary truths are discovered, not made, by our thought . . . (2) Possibilities and necessary truths cannot be there except in so far as they, or the ideas involved in them, are thought by some mind." These apparently inconsistent claims "can be held together," however, "if we suppose a nonhuman mind that eternally and necessarily exists and thinks all the possibilities and necessary truths."[41]

Sorley's view (that the place of values is God's mind) can be reinterpreted along the lines of this suggestion. Suppose that

1   Lying is *prima facie* wrong

is a necessary truth. Suppose further that God necessarily exists and is essentially omniscient. Then 1 is logically equivalent to

2   God believes (1),[42] and
3   Necessarily, lying is *prima facie* wrong

is logically equivalent to

4   God exists and it is part of his nature to believe that lying is *prima facie* wrong.[43]

---

that descriptions which omit all reference to value are often complete *for certain purposes* (doing science, say). However, a *truly* complete description of such things as pleasurable consciousness would mention their goodness. (W. D. Ross, *The Right and the Good* [Oxford: Clarendon Press, 1930], pp. 120f.) I am inclined to follow Ross on this point. In my view, any essential property of x which would figure in a truly complete description of x is a real property of it. Since goodness is an essential property of pleasurable consciousness or loyalty, and since (following Ross) their goodness would figure in their complete description, goodness is a real property of them. (But what ought to be included in "a truly complete description"? For a first approximation, any predicate which would be genuinely informative in some context or other.)

41   Robert Adams, "Divine Necessity," in Robert M. Adams, *The Virtue of Faith and Other Essays in Philosophical Theology*. New York: Oxford University Press, 1987, p. 218. I find few traces of this suggestion in *Finite and Infinite Goods*, however.
42   Since in any world in which (1) is true, (2) is true, and vice versa.
43   For (3) is logically equivalent to

If we add that (1) and (3) are grounded in, or explained by, (2) and (4), respectively, we have a position like Sorley's.[44]

But views like these are problematic. While the relation of logical dependence between (1) and (3), on the one hand, and (2) and (4), on the other, runs both ways, "there is a *causal* or ontological dependence running in only one direction, rendering" (2) and (4) "somehow ultimately more revealing than" (1) and (3).[45] Necessary facts, and hence necessary value facts, are the products of God's thinking them in all possible worlds—and this is what accounts for or explains them.

This has a very counter-intuitive consequence, however. For consider the propositions

5 God is omniscient, and
6 Necessarily, God is omniscient.

If God necessarily exists and is essentially omniscient, then (5) and (6) are logically equivalent to

7 God believes that he is omniscient, and
8 God exists and it is part of his nature to believe that he is omniscient,

respectively. Now, on the type of view we are considering, (5) and (6) are *logically* dependent on (7) and (8), respectively, and (7) and (8) are *logically* dependent on (5) and (6).[46] The relation of *ontological* dependence, however, runs only one way—from (5) and (6) to (7) and (8), respectively, but *not* from (7) and (8) to (5) and (6). And this is curious to say the least. For it amounts to saying that God's belief that he is omniscient is the explanatory *ground* of his omniscience, and its being part of his nature to believe in his essential omniscience is the *ontological foundation* of his essential omniscience.

One could avoid these consequences by insisting that only *some* necessary facts (those of logic, mathematics, and ethics, for example, but not the sort of facts

---

(3′) "Lying is *prima facie* wrong" is true in all possible worlds,
(3') is logically equivalent to
(4′) God believes "Lying is *prima facie* wrong" in all possible worlds,
and (4') is logically equivalent to (4).

44 For suggestions along these lines with respect to mathematical and logical propositions, see Alvin Plantinga, *Does God Have a Nature?* (Milwaukee, WI: Marquette University Press, 1980), pp. 142–6.
45 Thomas Morris, "Absolute Creation," in Thomas V. Morris, *Anselmian Explorations*. Notre Dame, IN: University of Notre Dame Press, 1987, p. 165. Note that causal and ontological dependence aren't the same thing. Attributes are ontologically dependent on the substances in which they inhere. They aren't causally dependent on them.
46 Since they mutually entail one another.

expressed by [5] and [6]) are constituted by God's thinking them. Any restriction of this kind seems arbitrary, though. I conclude that this attempt to ground necessary value facts in God's nature and activity is unsuccessful.

There is, however, a second response to the objection that, like facts of logic and mathematics, basic value facts are necessary and hence need no further explanation.

There is an important difference between logical or mathematical facts, on the once hand, and necessary value facts, on the other. The former are logically necessary in the "narrow" sense. Their truth is analytic, a consequence of definitions and logical or syntactic rules.[47] Some necessary truths, however, are not analytic. Typical examples are "Nothing is red and green all over," "Nothing is larger than itself," or (more controversially) "No contingent being exists without some reason for its existence." While propositions like these are true in all possible worlds, their truth can't be deduced from definitions and logical rules. The constraints that truths of this sort impose are *substantive*, and not merely *formal*. Perhaps narrowly necessary truths stand in no need of explanation. But "broadly" necessary truths[48] do. That there is some reason for the existence of contingent beings, for instance, presupposes the world's (partial) intelligibility, and that the world *is* intelligible cries out for explanation. Now necessary value truths aren't analytic either.[49] Hence there is more reason for thinking that these truths stand in need of explanation than for thinking that truths of logic and mathematics do.

The metaphysical "queerness" of necessary value facts can be brought out in another way. On objectivist accounts, the property of beauty supervenes on a splendid sunset or a Mozart string quartet, rightness supervenes on instances of truth telling, and goodness supervenes on pleasurable consciousness and certain character types (those exhibited by Marcus Aurelius, for example, or St Francis). In addition, the connection between the base properties and the supervenient properties is necessary. In any possible world containing a faithful performance of Mozart's sixth Haydn Quartet, for instance, beauty would supervene on it. Yet the connection between the base property and the supervenient property can seem mysterious. For, in the absence of further explanation, the (necessary) connection between these radically different sorts of property (the auditory qualities constituting a faithful performance of the Mozart quartet and the "nonnatural" [that is, non-empirical] property of beauty) is just an inexplicable brute fact.[50]

---

47   Since definitions and rules are consequences of (entail) themselves, they too are analytically true in this sense.

48   Or at least some of them.

49   Or, more accurately, the more interesting ones aren't. "If x is obligatory, x is permissible" appears to be analytic. "Lying is *prima facie* wrong" does not.

50   This is a bit like the problem of *qualia*. Why should phenomenal redness, say, rather than phenomenal greenness, be associated with the physiological states which in fact underlie it? That the connection holds appears to be both true and unexplained. (See Robert Adams, "Flavors, Colors, and God," in *The Virtue of Faith*. See also Richard

Theistic metaphysics can mitigate this problem since "the theist has a suitably 'queer' world-view into which to fit these 'queer' objects."[51] Robert Adams's theistic theory of the Good, for example, explains the connection by appealing to the notion of resemblance. The property of beauty supervenes upon glorious sunsets, for example, because the latter resembles the Good (that is, God) in the right way.[52]

Our conclusion is therefore this. If value facts are necessary facts, their objectivity is assured whether or not God exists. Moreover, it is tempting to regard necessary facts as self-explanatory, standing in no need of further explanation. We have examined reasons for thinking that at least some necessary facts aren't intrinsically intelligible, however. Necessary value facts are examples. Their existence does seem to cry out for explanation—an explanation which at least some forms of theistic metaphysics can provide.

The general point is this: naturalists believe that the space-time world is all there is; the story of the world is ultimately a story of "atoms, and time and space and economics and politics."[53] But "values and obligations cannot be deep in such a world. They have a grip only upon surface phenomena, probably only upon man. What is deep" in a world of this sort "must be such things as matter and energy, or perhaps natural law, chance, or chaos." In a Platonic or theistic world, on the other hand, the Good is "much more fundamental to reality than are the atoms," and those who align themselves with the Good align themselves "with what is deepest and most basic in existence."[54] The existence of objective values, or of necessary connections between natural properties and the value properties which supervene upon them, are surely less surprising in a world of this sort than in one in which what is deepest is matter, energy, natural law, or chance. As a result, religious views like theism or Platonism can illuminate the existence of objective value in a way in which naturalism cannot. That they can provides a reason for embracing views of this sort.

Swinburne, *The Evolution of Soul* [Oxford: Clarendon Press, 1986], especially chapters 3 and 10.)

51 Robert Gay, "Moral Arguments for the Existence of God," *Modern Theology* 3 (1987), p. 123.

52 It is worth noting that Adams's theory isn't open to the objection raised against arguments like Sorley's, for it does not entail that necessary facts are constituted by God's thinking them (although Adams may indeed believe that they are). It should also be noted that Adams's theory is a theory of the *Good*, not of the right or obligatory. Adams explains the connections between certain actions and obligatoriness or rightness by introducing a divine command theory. (See Chapter 6 below.)

53 C. S. Lewis, *Miracles*. New York: Macmillan, 1947, p. 102.

54 George I. Mavrodes, "Religion and the Queerness of Morality," in Robert Audi and William J. Wainwright, eds, *Rationality, Religious Belief, and Moral Commitment*. Ithaca: Cornell University Press, 1986, pp. 224f. Mavrodes's emphasis, however, is rather different from mine. His primary concern is with the "queerness," in a naturalistic world, of objective obligations that would require me to sacrifice my own interests.

Conclusion

Our results in this chapter can be summarized as follows: a belief in the objectivity of value is built into ordinary evaluative thought and discourse. Ethical naturalism and constructivism are not entirely successful in preserving the appearance of objectivity. To see whether theism can do better we examined the theories of W. R. Sorley and Robert Adams. Sorley preserves the objectivity of values by placing them in a "Supreme Mind." On Adams's account, excellence consists in a resemblance to the Good (namely God), so that if God's existence is objective, so too is the existence of value. Sorley's argument has some force if one is willing to grant his assumptions (that values must exist in a place, for example). Adams's account is more richly developed but is subject to two important objections—that concrete existents like God can't be standards, and that necessary facts, *including basic value facts*, don't need explanation. Neither of these objections is decisive.

The conclusion of this chapter is therefore this. Theism can account for the apparent objectivity of value. Moreover, it does this at least as successfully as debunking theories like Mackie's or rival objectivist theories such as naturalism or constructivism. As a result, those of us who are convinced that at least some values are objective have some reason for embracing theism.

Appendix: Moral Commitment and the Objectivity of Values

In "The Sentiment of Rationality," William James contrasts those who think "that the words 'good' and 'bad' have no sense apart from subjective passions and interests which we may, if we please, play fast and loose with at will . . . ," and those who believe that moral facts are embedded in the structure of reality. The moral conduct of either will be indistinguishable in most situations. But in the "lonely emergencies of life," in which our ideals clash with our interests, the former will tend to adjust his ideals to his interests while the latter will not. "Resistance . . . , poverty, martyrdom if need be, tragedy in a word,—such are the solemn feasts of his inward faith."[55]

What James's remarks suggest is that moral *seriousness*—a deep and unswerving commitment to the moral life—implicitly presupposes that moral values are not only objective but part of the deep structure of reality, that the universe is, as James puts it, a "moral universe." There is, in other words, a kind of incoherence in wholeheartedly committing oneself to the moral life while denying that "the law of right and wrong is as much part and parcel of the structure of the universe as the

---

55   William James, "The Sentiment of Rationality," in William James, *The Will to Believe and Other Essays on Popular Philosophy*. New York: Dover Publications, 1956, pp. 103–5.

law of gravitation or the law of conservation of energy."[56] For such a person, "duty and reality are radically split asunder. He cannot be wholly serious about his" duty, for he knows that if he violates it, he will not be "living out of harmony with reality."[57]

Is an implicit commitment to the claim that moral values are part of the deep structure of reality religious? The work of the anthropologist Clifford Geertz suggests the presence of "a minimal common form to all religions," namely, an attempt "to integrate the world-view and the ethos of a society," to express the thought that "the deepest human values and the most fundamental ontological structures cohere."[58] Is the converse true as well? That is, does a conviction of their coherence itself involve an implicit commitment to religion? One can at least say this. Their coherence is less surprising in a theistic or Platonic or Hindu or Buddhist universe, in which a supreme Goodness is the deepest fact about reality, than in the anti-supernaturalist's world in which the deepest facts are facts about "atoms, and time and space and economics and politics."

What sort of argument is this? It is broadly Kantian in the sense that it traces the alleged implications of our moral commitments. But whereas Kant's arguments draw conclusions from our commitments to specific duties (to be perfect, and to seek the highest good), the argument presently under consideration draws conclusions from the fact of moral commitment itself (and thus, potentially, has a broader appeal).

It also differs from arguments which appeal to our alleged need to believe that our duty and happiness aren't in permanent conflict. In the "Concluding Chapter" of his *Methods of Ethics*, Henry Sidgwick asserts that the judgment that the aims of self-interest and morality ultimately coincide "expresses the vital need that our Practical Reason feels of proving or postulating this connexion of virtue and self-interest, if it is to be made consistent with itself. For the negation of the connexion must force us to admit an ultimate and fundamental contradiction in our apparent intuitions of what is Reasonable in conduct," an admission which, in turn, implies "that the apparently intuitive operation of the Practical Reason, manifested in these contradictory judgments is, after all illusory."[59] In short, if it is reasonable to act in one's own interest and also reasonable to act morally, then, if the demands of prudential reason and moral reason ultimately conflict, there is a deep incoherence at the very heart of practical reason. And John Hare makes a related point. If the moral agent thought that her commitment to morality would ultimately *thwart* her happiness—that, in the last analysis, the two were *inconsistent*—it would be difficult for her commitment to morality to remain "wholehearted."[60]

---

56   A. E. Taylor, *Does God Exist?* London: Macmillan, 1948, pp. 96f.
57   J. Brenton Stearns, "A Moral Argument," *Idealistic Studies* 8 (1978), pp. 200–201.
58   Byrne, *Moral Interpretation of Religion*, pp. 90–91.
59   Henry Sidgwick, *The Methods of Ethics*. London: Macmillan, 1913, p. 508.
60   Hare, *Moral Gap*, pp. 72–95.

However, if reality is fundamentally good, as the world's great religions attest, both Sidgwick's and Hare's problems are solved. For it would be reasonable to believe that the demands of self-interest and morality *aren't* ultimately in conflict, and that a commitment to morality *won't* permanently thwart one's happiness.

The argument we are presently considering, however, makes no appeal to the claims of self-interest or to our desire for happiness. Its point, rather, is that if moral demands can't be disregarded—even in "the lonely emergencies of life"— they must be more than a reflection of our own interests and subjective feelings.[61]

The argument we are discussing also differs from those examined in the main body of this chapter. The latter assume, or argue for, the claim that values *are* objective, and proceed to draw out that claim's religious implications. The current argument agrees that the objectivity of moral values has religious implications but, instead of assuming or attempting to establish their objectivity, insists only that a wholehearted commitment to the moral enterprise implicitly presupposes a *belief* in their objectivity. Thus, unlike the other arguments in this chapter, it is a *practical*, not theoretical, argument, its probative force depending on the depth of one's own moral commitment.

61　Even our interests in, and feelings for, other people. For, as James points out, we will be tempted to modify those interests and feelings when they come in conflict with other interests. Even "when a materialist says that it is better for him to suffer great inconvenience than to break a promise," say, "he only means that his social interests have become so knit up with keeping faith that, those interests once being granted, it *is* better for him to keep the promise in spite of everything. But the interests themselves are neither right nor wrong, except possibly with reference to some ulterior order of interests which themselves again are mere subjective data without character, either good or bad . . . The subjectivist in morals, when his moral feelings are at war" with his other interests, is thus "always free to seek harmony by toning down the sensitiveness of the feelings." (James, "The Sentiment of Rationality," pp. 103–4) Note that, as James pictures her, the "absolute moralist" does not do her duty because, in contrast to the subjective moralist, she believes that doing so *won't* thwart her interests; she does it because she regards her duty as an obdurate fact which she can neither evade nor modify but must come to terms with.

PART II
DIVINE COMMAND THEORY
AND ITS CRITICS

CHAPTER 5

The Euthyphro Problem

The *Euthyphro* recounts a conversation between Socrates and Euthryphro. The latter is planning to prosecute his father for an unintentional homicide in order to avoid any religious pollution that might accrue to him as a result of his association with the "murderer." Socrates' immediate reaction is amazement: "Good heavens, Euthyphro! and is your knowledge of religion and of things pious and impious so very exact that, supposing the circumstances to be as you state them, you are not afraid lest you too may be doing an impious thing in bringing an action against your father?" Euthyphro is unperturbed, however, professing "exact knowledge of all such matters." The conversation then turns to a discussion of the nature of piety. After some preliminary fencing, Euthyphro proposes that the pious or holy is what is loved by the gods, and this leads to the central question of the dialogue: "whether the pious or holy is beloved by the gods because it is holy, or holy because it is beloved of the gods?"[1]

While the *Euthyphro* ends inconclusively, Socrates clearly favors the first alternative. Goodness or rightness or holiness is neither explained nor constituted by the gods loving it or approving it or willing it. On the contrary: what is good or right or holy is good or right or holy independently of anyone's attitudes toward it— including those of the gods. The gods love or approve of or will the good or right or holy because they discern its intrinsic excellence—an excellence it possesses independently of their approval or love of it.

Socrates's position has dominated Christian philosophical theology. Some important Christian thinkers have embraced the second alternative, however—what is good or right is good or right only because God wills or commands it. This view is called "divine command theory" or "theological voluntarism." The present chapter examines some historically significant versions of this theory. The remaining chapters in Part II discuss contemporary attempts to defend divine command theory against its critics and to offer positive arguments in support of it.

Some Classical Statements of Divine Command Theory

Pierre d'Ailly (1350–1420), Chancellor of the University of Paris and later bishop and cardinal, states the voluntarist position quite clearly: "nothing is good or evil

---

1   Plato, *Euthyphro*, in Benjamin Jowett, trans., *The Dialogues of Plato*, vol. 1. New York: Random House, 1937, pp. 385–6, 391.

which God necessarily or from the nature of the thing [loved or hated], loves or hates . . . Neither is any quality connected with justice on account of its own nature, but from sheer divine acceptance; nor is God just because He loves justice, but rather, the contrary is the case: something is possessed of justice because God loves it, that is accepts it . . . " "Nor therefore does He command good actions because they are good, or prohibit evil ones because they are evil; but . . . these are therefore good because they are commanded and evil because prohibited."[2]

D'Ailly's position is echoed by his student Jean de Gerson (1363–1429), who succeeded him as Chancellor: "nothing is evil except because prohibited [by God]; and nothing good except because accepted by God; and God does not therefore will and approve our actions because they are good, but they are therefore good because he approves them. Similarly, they are therefore evil because he prohibits and disapproves of them."[3]

Why would anyone endorse a position like this? For at least two closely connected reasons. The first is God's absolute sovereignty. If God is Lord of everything, then God depends on nothing, and nothing escapes his sovereignty. The claim that God's will is guided or shaped by independent standards of good and evil, right and wrong, threatens both assertions. For if God is *subject* to independent standards, he depends on them and so isn't Lord *of* those standards. This point emerges clearly in the following passage from Martin Luther:

> He is God, and for his will there is no cause or reason that can be laid down as a rule or measure for it, since there is nothing equal or superior to it, but it is itself the rule of all things. For if there were any rule or standard for it, either as cause or reason, it could no longer be the will of God. For it is not because he is or was obliged so to will that what he wills is right, but on the contrary, because he himself so wills, therefore what happens [or is commanded] must be right. Cause and reason can be assigned for a creature's will, but not for the will of the Creator, unless you set up over him another creator.[4]

The view that God's will is subject to independent standards of right and wrong, good and evil, also appears to compromise his omnipotence. Thus, Descartes asserts that an "idea of good" did not impel God to create one thing rather than another. For example,

---

2   Pierre d'Ailly, *Questions on the Books of the Sentences*, Book I, Question 9, Article 2, and Book I, Question 14, in Janine Marie Idziak, ed., *Divine Command Morality: Historical and Contemporary Readings*. New York and Toronto: Edwin Mellen Press, 1979, pp. 63–4.

3   Jean de Gerson, *On the Spiritual Life of the Soul*, Reading I, Corollary X, in Idziak, *Divine Command Morality*, p. 66.

4   Martin Luther, *The Bondage of the Will*, in E. Gordon Rupp and Philip S. Watson, eds, *Luther and Erasmus: Free Will and Salvation*. Philadelphia: Westminster Press, 1969, pp. 236–7.

God did not will to create the world in time [that is, with a beginning] because he saw that it would be better thus than if he created it from all eternity; nor did he will the three angles of a triangle to be equal to two right angles because he knew that they could not be otherwise. On the contrary, because he worked to create the world in time it is for that reason better than if he had created it from all eternity; and it is because he willed the three angles of a triangle to be necessarily equal to two right angles that this is true and cannot be otherwise; and so in other cases.

Indeed, "nothing at all can exist which does not depend on him. This is true not only of everything that subsists. but of all order, of every law, and of every reason of truth and goodness. . . . For if any reason for what is good had preceded his preordination, it would have determined him towards that which it was best to bring about." And that would be inconsistent with his omnipotence. "Supreme indifference in God is the supreme proof of his omnipotence." "Eternal truths," such as those of mathematics or morality, "depend on God alone, who, as the supreme legislator, ordained them from all eternity."[5]

These considerations are reinforced by another. Humble submission to God's will is a central strand of theistic piety. Passage after passage of the Hebrew Bible or Christian New Testament suggest that rebellion or disobedience is the essence of sin. And "Islam" simply means submission to God's will. Couple this with the widely held view that God's revealed will[6] is the proper measure or standard of human conduct, and it may seem just obvious that the Lord of heaven and earth's omnipotent will can't be subject to an external standard. Why, then, have so many orthodox theists rejected it? To answer this question, let us turn to one of the most thorough attempts to respond to theological voluntarism—Ralph Cudworth's *A Treatise Concerning True and Immutable Morality* (1731).

Cudworth and Theological Voluntarism

Cudworth (1617–88) begins by calling attention to three apparent—and unpalatable—consequences of the claim "that there is nothing absolutely, intrinsically and

---

5 René Descartes, "Reply to the Sixth Set of Objections," nos 6 and 8, *Objections and Replies*, in Elizabeth S. Haldane and G. R. T. Ross, trans., *The Philosophical Works of Descartes*, vol. 2. New York: Dover Publications, 1955, pp. 248, 250–51. The assumption that God could have made it the case that what is in fact true and necessary (that the angles of a triangle are equal to two right angles, say, or that promise keeping is *prima facie* wrong) is not true or not necessary implies that an axiom of the stronger systems of modal logic, S4 and S5, is false: it is not the case that what is necessary is necessarily necessary. This axiom is intuitively plausible. It is not universally accepted, however, and some coherent systems of modal logic (S3, for instance) dispense with it. So its rejection by theological voluntarists like Descartes isn't a conclusive objection to divine command theory.

6 As revealed in the Bible, for example, or in the *Quran*.

naturally good and evil, just and unjust, antecedently to any positive command or prohibition of God; but that the arbitrary will and pleasure of God ... by its commands and prohibitions, is the first and only rule and measure thereof."[7]

The first is that "nothing can be imagined so grossly wicked ... but if it were supposed to be commanded by this omnipotent deity, must needs ... forthwith become holy, just and righteous." If God were to command us to blaspheme, for example, or to torture an innocent child, doing so would be morally obligatory. The second is that "to love God," or protect the innocent, "is by nature an indifferent [that is, morally neutral] thing." Hatred of God or the persecution of the innocent becomes wrong only when or if God prohibits it. The third unpalatable implication is that it is consistent with God's essential nature "to command blasphemy, perjury, lying, etc." Commanding "the hatred of God," for example, "is not inconsistent with the *nature* of God," but only with what God has in fact commanded. (Cudworth 10–11, my emphasis)

And to these points we may add a fourth: theological voluntarism appears to undercut the very possibility of morality as divine command theorists understand it, namely, as unreserved obedience to what one rightly believes to be God's will. For, as George Rust (d. 1679) points out, if God isn't *essentially* just and truthful, if nothing in his nature prevents him from lying to us or breaking his covenant with us, then we have no basis for trusting him or for believing that what he has *declared* to be his will (in scripture, through the church, and so on) really *is* his will. A commitment to theological voluntarism thus makes the practice of morality impossible.[8]

Cudworth believes that consequences like these are unavoidable if "nothing [is] so essential to the Deity, as uncontrollable power and an arbitrary will, and therefore that God could not be God if there should be anything evil in its own nature which he could not do." (Cudworth 10) Descartes had argued from God's "uncontrollable power" to theological voluntarism. Cudworth, however, thinks that Descartes's argument should be stood on its head: since the consequences of theological voluntarism are unacceptable, we should reject the conception of divine omnipotence from which they follow.

In Cudworth's opinion, such things as triangles or promise breaking or contempt of God have fixed natures or essences. As a result, it is logically impossible to "make a body triangular ... without having three angles equal to two right ones," for instance, or to permit or bring about an act of promising breaking which isn't morally wrong. And "the reason ... is plain, because" things like these "imply a

---

7   Ralph Cudworth, *A Treatise Concerning True and Immutable Morality*. London: J. & J. Knapton, 1731. (Reprint, New York: Garland, 1976.) p. 9. Henceforth Cudworth.

8   George Rust, "A Discourse of Truth." From Joseph Glanville, *Two Choice and Useful Treatises* (London: James Collins and Sam Lowndes, 1682), sections xi, xii. Reprinted in Idziak, *Divine Command Morality*, pp. 192–3. Is Rust's argument acceptable? That God is not *essentially* just and truthful only implies that God *might not have been* just and truthful. That God might not have been just and truthful, however, does not entail that he *isn't* just and truthful, or that we have no reason to believe that he is.

manifest contradiction." That triangles have angles which aren't equal to two right angles, or that acts of promising breaking aren't morally wrong, are necessarily false. (Cudworth 14–15)

In short, moral truths, like truths of mathematics and logic, are *necessarily* true, and their denials are logically impossible. So if God can make it false that promise breaking is wrong, say, or that hatred of God is morally evil, he can make necessary truths false.[9] Or, as Cudworth puts it, God would have the power to alter the essences of things, making it true that the angles of a triangle aren't equivalent to two right angles, for instance, or that human beings aren't animals, or that promise breaking isn't wrong. And this would have two absurd consequences.

First, if the "essences of things [are] dependent upon an arbitrary will in God," then *God's* essence is dependent on an arbitrary will of God. But in that case, God could have willed that "there . . . be no such thing as knowledge in God himself," or "that neither his own power nor knowledge should be infinite." For if God freely determines the constituents of his own essence, he could determine that it not include power or infinite power, or knowledge or infinite knowledge, and thus determine that there be logically possible worlds in which his power or knowledge is limited, and possible worlds in which he has no power or knows nothing at all. (Cudworth 33–4)

Second, the view in question "destroys all knowledge." (Ibid. 32) Why? Presumably because a logically impossible proposition entails all propositions.[10] So in

---

9   Which is, of course, equivalent to making logically impossible propositions true.
10 There are at least two arguments for this. First, a proposition, q, is entailed by another proposition, p, if and only if it is logically impossible for p to be true and q to be false. Now suppose that p is a logically impossible proposition. If it is, then it is impossible for p to be true. But if it is impossible for p to be true, then, for any proposition q, it is impossible for p to be true and q to be false. So p entails q. This argument is question-begging in the present context, however, since it relies on the claim that logically impossible propositions can't be true—which is the point at issue. A second argument is less obviously circular. Cudworth makes the common assumption that logically impossible propositions are or entail contradictions. Suppose that they are or do. Then we can show that a logically impossible proposition entails all propositions. Let p and q be any propositions.

(1) p and not p (Assumption) Therefore,
(2) p (From [1])
(3) p or q (From [2]) Therefore,
(4) not-p (From [1]) Therefore,
(5) q (From 3 and 4)

If this is the sort of argument Cudworth has in mind, however, it may miss Descartes's point, namely, that God can make the impossible *possible* (and hence *not* self-contradictory). If God were to will that the angles of a triangle are not equal to two right angles, for example, or that promising breaking isn't wrong, he would thereby will that these things be possible (because true), and hence not self-contradictory.

making a logically impossible proposition true, God make *all* propositions true. If all propositions are true, however, then, for any proposition p, both p and its denial are true, and the distinction between true and false beliefs collapses. (The belief that God exists and the belief that he doesn't would both be true, for example, and similarly for any other belief.) And this undermines the very notion of knowledge. For "A knows that p" entails that A knows that not-p is false. And "A knows that not-p is false" entails "Not-p *is* false." Yet if all propositions are true, not-p *isn't* false. So knowledge, as Cudworth says, is "destroyed." If there is no such thing as knowledge, though, there is no such thing as knowledge of God's will, and the injunction to obey him becomes pointless.

But suppose we grant that theological voluntarism is problematic. Still, isn't it the *only* position compatible with God's absolute power and sovereignty? Cudworth thinks it is not.

Omnipotence is (roughly) the power to do anything possible. Since moral truths are necessarily true, their denials aren't logically possible. Hence the fact that God can't make it false that promise keeping is morally obligatory, say, or that infidelity is wrong doesn't count against his omnipotence. God's power ranges over contingent states of affairs, not necessary ones. "The will and power of God have an absolute, infinite and unlimited command upon the existences of all created things to make them to be, or not to be at pleasure; yet when things exist, they are what they are . . . by the necessity of their own nature."[11] (Cudworth 16) For example, God is free to either make or not make triangular surfaces, just as he pleases. But he is *not* free to make a triangular surface whose angles aren't equal to two right angles, for doing so isn't possible. Similarly, God is free to create or not create worlds in which promise breaking occurs. But he is *not* free to create a world in which promise breaking occurs and isn't morally wrong since that state of affairs, too, is logically impossible.

Yet in spite of Cudworth's protestations, isn't God's inability to bring about impossible states of affairs a limitation of his power, as Descartes thought? Cudworth believes it isn't. For "a contradiction is a non-entity, and therefore cannot be the object of divine power." (Cudworth 32)

Precisely what is Cudworth claiming? Perhaps he thinks that a contradiction can't be the object or content of an act of will. I can't, for example, will that 'twas

---

11 Cudworth doesn't mean that *each* of a thing's properties is essential to it but, rather, that each property that is *included in its nature or essence* is essential to it. God can't make a triangular surface whose angles aren't equal to two right angles, but he *is* free to make triangular surfaces that are red or not red, "at pleasure," since neither redness nor nonredness are included in the nature of a triangle. Compare Richard Price, *A Review of the Principal Questions in Morals* (Oxford: Clarendon Press, 1974; originally published in London, 1787), chapter I, section III: Moral truths are *necessary* truths, and "omnipotence does not consist in a power to alter the [essential] nature of things, and to destroy necessary truth (for this is contradictory . . .) but in an absolute command over all *particular, external* existences, to create or destroy them, or produce any possible changes among them."

brillig and the slithy toves did gyre and gymble in the wabe since nonsensical strings of words don't pick out states of affairs that could be willed or chosen. So if contradictions are meaningless, as some have claimed, then they too can't be objects of possible acts of will. But the trouble with this is that self-contradictory propositions are *not* meaningless. It is precisely *because* we understand the meaning of "A triangular surface exists whose angles aren't equal to two right angles" that we realize that it cannot be true.

Or perhaps Cudworth is arguing that contradictions are *nothing* (nonentities) because they can't possibly *be* or obtain, whereas power ranges over actual and potential *being*. But if he is, his argument begs the question, for radical theological voluntarists like Descartes maintain that "contradictions" (triangles whose angles don't equal two right angles, for example) *can* be or obtain—if God wills them. Or perhaps Cudworth thinks that his claim is simply self-evident. The problem with this, though, is that it isn't evident to the theological voluntarist.

And *isn't* God's power in fact constrained or limited (and hence imperfect) if his creative decisions are limited by the Good and other essences, as Cudworth and others think? To this George Rust replies: "It is no imperfection for God to be determined to Good; it is no bondage, slavery, or contraction, to be bound up to the eternal laws of right and justice." On the contrary, "it is the greatest weakness and impotency in the world to have a power to evil . . . " Indeed, "the more any being partakes of reason and understanding, the worse is the imputation of acting arbitrariously . . . " Liberty to choose is a perfection only where there is a moral "indifference in the things or actions about which it is conversant."[12] And Cudworth would agree.

But would or should a traditional theological voluntarist be impressed by this argument? Note first that, on her view, everything, including promise breaking or lying or taking an innocent life, *is* intrinsically indifferent. Things become good or bad only when and if God commands or prohibits them. Hence, it is no imperfection in God to be at liberty with respect to them. Nor does God's power to command or do what we believe to be evil (break a promise, say) imply a defect in his understanding, as the passage from Rust implies. For if there *are* no "eternal verities" or moral truths to know (as most traditional voluntarists believe), that God doesn't know them implies no intellectual defect. Finally, on the voluntarist's view, God's power to lie, say, or make lying right, is not a power to *do evil*, since good and evil are *constituted* or *made* by whatever God freely wills or prohibits.

Let us suppose, however, that attempts to show that perfect or unlimited *power* doesn't entail theological voluntarism are successful. Isn't it nonetheless true that voluntarism is a necessary consequence of God's *sovereignty*? Cudworth, and like-minded philosophers and theologians, think that it is not.

---

12 Rust, "A Discourse of Truth," pp. 198–9; reprinted in Idziak, *Divine Command Morality*, pp. 196f.

Note first that not even the voluntarist can reasonably claim that *everything* depends on God's will, "for instance; this will itself; his own existence . . . ," and so on. "To suppose these dependent on his will, is so extravagant, that no one can assert it."[13] Nor can one reasonably assert that the fact that God's will and existence don't depend on his will limits his sovereignty.[14] So the fact that something exists or obtains which doesn't depend on God's will isn't *in principle* objectionable or inconsistent with his sovereignty.

Yet suppose that we grant this. Doesn't the doctrine of God's sovereignty nevertheless entail that everything *other than* God depends on his will? And doesn't that, in turn, imply that necessary truths in general, and moral truths in particular, do so? Cudworth thinks that it does not. That essences and necessary truths do not depend *on God's will* does not imply that they don't depend *on God*. The "essences and verities of things" are included in God's "eternal and immutable wisdom" which is, in turn, an expression of "his essential goodness."[15] (Cudworth 34–7) Eternal truths, including moral truths, aren't independent of God because they are part of his *nature*. Richard Price concurs. "None have reason to be offended when *morality* is represented as eternal and immutable; for it appears that is only saying that God himself is eternal and immutable, and making his nature the high and sacred original of virtue."[16] Whether this response is satisfactory depends on the plausibility of the sorts of view examined in Chapter 4.

Conclusion

Where do we stand at this point? Cudworth, and the theological mainstream, have presented an attractive alternative to theological voluntarism's conceptions of God's power and sovereignty. It is not clear that they have demonstrated its superiority, however. Many of their arguments against the theological voluntarist's conception of divine power beg the question,[17] and their response to the sovereignty objection

---

13 Price, *Review of the Principal Questions in Morals*, chapter 5, p. 86. Cf. the discussion of this point in Chapter 4, pp. 65–6.

14 This can be challenged. Some have suggested that infinite power and total control entail an ability to commit suicide. So God's (continued) existence and willing *do* depend upon his will. The standard response is that since God necessarily exists, it is logically impossible that he (or anything else) bring about his nonexistence. This move won't impress a *radical* voluntarist like Descartes, however, because the radical voluntarist thinks that God's power and control aren't restricted to the possible.

15 Cudworth's conception, I think, is essentially Neoplatonic. The eternal essences are not just objects of the divine intellect. They are also expressions or reflections of the Good. But the Good for Cudworth, as for other Christian Platonists, isn't *distinct* from God; it is his being or nature or character.

16 Price, *Review of the Principal Questions in Morals*, chapter 5, p. 89.

17 Question begging is endemic in responses to radical voluntarism. For two more examples, consider these arguments of Richard Price: (1) that (1a) God is "eternally and

depends on controversial views about God's nature (that he is the Good, for example, or that necessary truths are contained in his intellect and have no being apart from it). The plausibility of their position also depends on the claim that basic moral truths are necessarily true, and that they are can be doubted. Suppose, for example, that moral utterances don't express propositions that are true or false but, instead, express attitudes of approval or disapproval, or commend or condemn certain courses of action. Since moral propositions aren't true (or false), on this view, they aren't necessarily true (or necessarily false), and so can't limit what God can do or command.[18]

We will turn to modern defenses of divine command theory in Chapter 6. But before doing so, it is worth considering one last argument of Cudworth's.

Acts of will create obligations where none previously existed *only* against a background of *already existing* obligations. For example, I have no obligation to lend Margaret my copy of Cudworth's *True Intellectual System of the Universe*. If I promise to do so, however, I *am* obligated to lend it to her, but only because of my *pre-existing obligation* to keep any promises I make. Similarly, if the legislature passes a law requiring everyone to drive on the right-hand side of the road, I am

---

unalterably" (that is, necessarily) righteous and holy implies that (1b) there is an eternal and unalterable (that is, necessary) distinction between right and wrong, holiness and unholiness. (2) (2a) "To conceive of truth as depending on God's will, is to conceive of his intelligence and knowledge as depending on his will." (2b) Yet this is incompatible with the concept of will "which from the nature of it, *requires something* to guide and determine it." (Price, *Review*, chapter 5, p. 86f.) Neither argument either will or should convince the committed radical voluntarist. (1) If righteousness or holiness is a purely "formal" notion, as voluntarists sometimes imply (so that righteous and holy actions are *whatever* actions God wills that we perform), then (1b) can be admitted without abandoning voluntarism. Since there is no time at which God wills *every* action, there is, at each time, a distinction between those actions God wills us to perform and those he doesn't, that is, between those actions that are right and those that aren't. There is thus an "eternal and unalterable" distinction between right actions and actions that aren't right. Of course this rejoinder wouldn't satisfy Price since it leaves open the possibility that the *content* of God's will, and thus of rightness, varies and so isn't "unalterable." But could one *show* that this rejoinder is inadequate without begging the question against voluntarism (by rejecting its "formal" conception of righteousness, for example)? (2) As for the second argument, that the *contents* of God's intelligence, that is, truths, depend on his will doesn't imply that *God's intelligence* does so. So (2a) is false. Nor is it just obvious that the will "from the nature of it, requires something to guide and determine it." The possibility of a purely gratuitous choice has its defenders, and lies at the heart of the voluntarist's conception of a God of unlimited power and sovereignty. So to deny the possibility of gratuitous choice is to deny the coherence of her conception of deity. One can't, then, simply *assume* that gratuitous choice is impossible without begging the question against theological voluntarism.

18 This view seems to me false (see Chapter 4), but the point is that the anti-voluntarist's response rests on a number of controversial assumptions. Many important modern moral philosophers *are* non-cognitivists.

obligated to drive on the right, but only because of my prior obligation to obey "civil powers, that have lawful authority of commanding." (Cudworth 22) So while acts of will or commanding can, in a sense, create obligations where none previously existed, they cannot be the source of *all* obligations.

To say even this, however, is to concede too much since, "if we would speak . . . more accurately and precisely," we should "rather say" that acts of will do not "make anything morally good or evil, just and unjust, which nature had not made such before." For morally indifferent things, "considered materially in themselves," remain indifferent even after they have been promised, say, or legitimately commanded. The moral goodness of my keeping my promise to lend Margaret my copy of Cudworth's *True Intellectual System* lies not in the action of lending her my book, considered "in its own nature," but in the "formality of keeping faith and performing covenants." Similarly, the moral rightness of obeying traffic laws does not lie in the rightness of driving on the right or stopping at red lights as such, but in "the formality of yielding obedience to the commands of lawful authority." The goodness of *promise keeping*, on the other and, or the rightness of *obeying lawful authority* depends not on will or command but on the "eternal verities," that is, on necessary moral truths.[19] (Cudworth 20–26)

Yet why can't *God's* will be the source of our obligation to keep our promises, say, or to obey lawful temporal authority? Perhaps it can. Even so, one pivotal question remains unanswered. For what is the source of our obligation *to conform to God's will*? Could that, too, be grounded in a divine command?

It could not, for willing and commanding as such create no obligations. It is, rather, "natural justice or equity, which gives to one the *right* or *authority* of commanding, and begets in another *duty* and *obligation* to obedience." (My emphases) Willing or commanding creates obligations only where there is a *prior obligation to obey*. Willing or commanding, then, can't be the source of *all* obligation. If all obligation were grounded in God's will, for example, then the obligation to obey God[20] would be grounded in God's will. But it is "ridiculous and absurd" to

---

19   Richard Price makes a similar point. "No will can make anything good and right which was not so antecedently and from eternity; or any action right that is not so in itself." Commands and promises don't alter the moral nature of *what* is commanded or promised, but produce "a change in the circumstances of the agent" so "that, what in consequence of it becomes obligatory, is not the same with what *before* was indifferent." What is obligatory is not lending my book to Margaret, or observing the Sabbath, considered in themselves, but keeping a promise I have made or "*obeying the divine will*, and *just authority*"—and that *these* things are obligatory is necessarily true. "Had there been no reason from the [necessary] natures of things for obeying God's will," for instance, "it is certain [that God's commands] could have induced no obligation . . . So far . . . is it from being possible, that any will or laws should *create* right; that they can have no effect, but in virtue of natural and antecedent right." (Price, *Review of the Principal Questions in Morals*, chapter 1, section iii, pp. 50–52.

20   Without which God's commands would lack authority.

suppose that "any one should make a positive law to require that others should be obliged, or bound to obey him . . . for if they were obliged before, then this law would be in vain, and to no purpose; and if they were not before obliged, then they could not be obliged by any positive law, because they were not previously bound to obey such a person's commands." If I already have an obligation to obey Mary's commands, for instance, it is pointless for her to command me to obey them. If I do not, then the mere fact that Mary tells me to do something puts me under no obligation to do it. It would seem, then, that even if God is the source of each of our other obligations, he cannot be the source of our obligation to obey God. (Cudworth 17–20)

Cudworth's argument is powerful and appears to leave the divine command theorist with only two alternatives. One is to deny that we are morally obligated to obey God's commands. The other is to limit the theory to obligations other than the obligation to obey God. The first seems counter-intuitive, although the divine command theorist may be able to partially dispel the appearance of oddity by providing *non*moral reasons for obedience such as God's power, or benevolence, or goodness.[21] The second alternative involves abandoning the fine generality of the theory, and leaves at least one obligation (namely, our obligation to obey God) unaccounted for. These and other issues will be explored further in the next three chapters.

---

21 These reasons are nonmoral in the sense that they don't (or needn't) appeal to moral *obligations*. Some of them may be moral in a broad sense, however. (As William Alston says, in "Some Suggestions for Divine Command Theorists," moral goodness isn't exhausted by the morally obligatory.) If my reason for obeying God is his goodness, for example, then my reason is moral in this wider sense.

CHAPTER 6

Two Recent Divine Command Theories

Few modern philosophers have taken divine command theories seriously. They have either not discussed them, dismissed them for reasons similar to those of Cudworth and Price, or attacked them as an assault on moral autonomy. The recent resuscitation of divine command ethics thus took many by surprise. Yet, in retrospect, its reemergence could have been anticipated. For the past quarter of century, analytic philosophers of religion have turned their attention from standard topics like the proofs for the existence of God, the coherence of the divine attributes, and the problem of evil to traditional theological doctrines such as the trinity or the atonement. Many of these philosophers concluded that standard objections to traditional religious beliefs and theological doctrines are less compelling than their authors had thought, and offered sympathetic defenses of them. It was thus only a matter of time before similar attention was paid to divine command theory. This chapter examines the two most fully developed and sophisticated attempts to articulate and defend it.

Robert Adams's "Modified Divine Command Theory"

Robert Adams believes that God's commands are the best candidate for the role that is "semantically indicated" by our use of the expression "moral obligation." Among the more salient features of our concept of moral obligation are the following: (1) Moral obligations are "something one should take seriously and care about." (2) As a consequence, it is appropriate for agents to feel guilty when they fail to discharge an obligation, and appropriate for others to blame them. (3) Moral obligations are also "something that one can be motivated to comply with," and (4) "should be such as to ground *reasons* for compliance." Finally, (5) "it is part of the roles of moral obligation and wrongness that fulfillment of obligation and opposition to wrong actions should be publicly inculcated."[1]

Morality is inherently social. The fifth condition explicitly "connect[s] morality with society." Guilt, too, points to obligation's social nature: "In typical cases, guilt

---

1   Adams, *Finite and Infinite Goods*, pp. 235–6. Henceforth Adams 1999. Adams notes that (3) and (4) are connected. They *are* different, however. Motives are what Francis Hutcheson called "*exciting* reasons," considerations which (causally) prompt me to do something. Adams's reasons are what Hutcheson called "*justifying* reasons," considerations which not only *prompt* me to do something but *justify* my doing it. Reasons can sometimes be motives, but the distinction between motives and reasons remains.

involves alienation from *someone else* who required or expected of us what we were obligated to do and have not done, or who has been harmed by what we have done and might reasonably have required us not to do it." "Typically there is someone who is, or might well be, understandably angry with me," a fact that "is connected with such practices as punishing and apologizing."[2] (Adams 1999: 237, 241, 239, my emphasis)

These considerations are reinforced by another. The fact that "obligations constitute reasons [and motives] for doing that which one is obligated to do" is best explained by obligation's social nature.[3] "According to social theories . . . , having an obligation to do something consists in being required (in a certain way, under certain circumstances or conditions), by another person or group of persons, to do it." Motivation is supplied by "fear [of] punishment or retaliation for noncompli-

---

2 But what about the claim that a *morally mature* person is motivated by *principles*, not personal relationships? Adams agrees that it is possible to love principles, but insists that this "has more to do with ideals than with obligations. To love truthfulness is one thing; to feel that one *has* to tell the truth is something else. Similarly, failing to act on a principle one loves seems, as such, more an occasion of shame than of guilt." If I haven't significantly harmed "anyone, or alienated myself from anyone," then apologies aren't called for, and "it is neither natural nor appropriate for me to feel *guilty* in such a situation" even if it *is* appropriate for me and others "to think less of me for the deed." (Adams 1999: 240) I find this less obvious than Adams does. One may doubt whether the distinction between shame and guilt is that clear cut. (See Bernard Williams, *Shame and Necessity*.) There is also something odd about saying, "Even though no one could have been harmed by my behavior [behaving cowardly, say, or exhibiting an egregious lack of self-control], I am deeply ashamed of it. I do not feel guilty, however, nor do I deserve any blame."

3 If being morally obligated could be identified with being required by moral reasons, there would be no compelling reason to accept a *social* account of the nature of obligation. If our sense of obligation can be explained by the pressure of pure practical reason, appeals to *society's* pressures seem otiose. Although Adams rejects the identification, I find his counter-example unpersuasive. The example is this: the balance of moral reasons favors "not walking on the lawn but also favors . . . not worrying very much about it and not feeling guilty if you do it—perhaps because it would be better, on balance, ...if we do not worry much about such things." For similar reasons, it is probably "morally irrational for us to try to make people feel they *must* not walk on the grass." If these considerations are correct, "walking on the lawn does not violate [a moral] obligation." (Adams 1999: 238) But guilt comes in degrees. That we shouldn't worry very much about not meeting a requirement, or be ridden with guilt when we fail to do what we have good moral reasons for doing, or waste a great deal of time in inculcating a requirement, hardly shows that we shouldn't feel *some* guilt when we violate it (as when we tell a "white lie," for example), or make *some* effort to inculcate it. Moral obligations aren't equally weighty. I suspect, however, that Adams's principal reason for rejecting the identification is his view that moral reasons as such are insufficiently motivating. He says, for example, that the mere rightness of an action (not walking on the lawn, say) is "too abstract" to motivate us. (Adams 1999: 242) Even if this is true (and, like Kant, I am not convinced that it is), is it really part of our concept of moral obligation that moral obligations not only should but *do* motivate us?

ance." It is also supplied by the fact that one *values* one's social bonds. One desires not only to "obtain and maintain" social relationships, but also to *express* one's "valuing and respecting the relationship[s]." (Adams 1999: 241–2)

For obligations arising from social bonds to constitute moral obligations, however, several additional conditions must be met: (1) Not only must the social bonds be valued; they must be *"rightly* valued," that is, they must be *"really* good." (2) The "personal characteristics" of those imposing social requirements are also "relevant to the possibility of [social] requirements constituting moral obligation." Other things being equal, we "have more reason to comply with the requests and demands of the knowledgeable, wise, or saintly." (3) "How much reason one has to comply" depends, in addition, on "how good the demand is," where the goodness of the demand is a function of the goodness of what is demanded, on the appropriateness of the sanctions "implied in the demand," on the degree to which "making the demand" affects the relationship "for the better" and not "for the worse," and on the extent to which the demand is the expression of a good "project or social movement." Demands which meet these conditions at least *approximate* moral requirements.[4] (Adams 1999: 244–5, my emphases)

Yet social theories, "as developed thus far," can't adequately account for the *objectivity* of moral obligations, their independence from our beliefs about them and attitudes toward them. For example, if moral obligations were solely a function of what society demands, then "society would be able to eliminate obligations by just not making certain demands." Moreover, "moral reformers have taught us that there have been situations in which none of the existing human communities demanded as much as they should have . . . " (Until quite recently, for instance, most societies tolerated slavery and the subjugation of women.) Then, too, conflicting demands may arise from different social relationships, where "both sets of demands and relationships will manifest some degree of goodness, but a flawed goodness." (The demands of the family may conflict with those of the state, for example.) In cases like these, there is no clear answer to the question "which, if either constitutes a moral obligation?" Adams's conclusion from these considerations is "that actual human social requirements are simply not good enough," or objective enough, "to constitute the basis of moral obligations." (Adams 1999: 247–8)

"An idealized version of the social requirement theory," namely, divine command theory, can remedy these deficiencies. Unlike human commands, divine

---

4   Note, however, that the Chinese demands of *li* (propriety, decorum) arose in a social system that was rightly valued by its participants; that what was demanded was good—if not intrinsically, then because of the end which the system of demands was designed to achieve (harmony with others and, ultimately, with the cosmos); and that those who imposed the demands were comparatively wise and virtuous. Did the requirements of *li* therefore constitute, or even approximate, *moral* requirements? Do conventional rules of politeness do so? The answer isn't clearly "yes" or "no."

commands are independent of our beliefs about them and our attitudes toward them. They therefore have the necessary objectivity. And because God has properties that make him the "ideal" and "salient" candidate "for the semantically indicated role" of the supreme Good (see Chapter 4), there are no worries about whether his commands, or the relationships in which they are incorporated, are good enough.[5]

Divine commands are suited to the role of constituting moral obligation in other ways as well. For example, they provide motives for compliance—not only fear of punishment and hope of reward but also, and more importantly, motives arising from our valuing our social bonds with God, his excellencies, and the goodness of what he commands. Furthermore, divine command theory "facilitates the understanding of moral guilt as involving offense against a person," and can explain how the facts of moral obligation" can "play a part in our coming to recognize actions as right and wrong." Commands must be communicated to be valid. So if moral obligations are divine commands, God must arrange things in such a way that we know them—either through revelation, by designing our faculties (reason, conscience, social inclinations, and the like) so that we are sensitive to what is morally required, through human socialization, or in some other fashion. (Adams 1999: 257)

Adams's theory is original and impressive. Is it satisfactory? We will consider objections to *any* divine command theory in the following chapter. Objections directed specifically against Adams's version of it will be examined in the next four subsections.

Objections to Identity Theories

Mark Murphy argues that Adams is mistaken in thinking that moral obligations can be identified with divine commands. Why? "Everyone agrees" that moral properties supervene on nonmoral properties. The moral wrongness of cruelty supervenes on its effects on the victim and perpetrator, for example, and the moral rightness of truth telling depends on its nature and consequences. So consider, first, strong supervenience: "If an item has a certain moral property due to its having a certain set of nonmoral properties, then any item in *any possible world* that has that set of nonmoral properties in that world will have that moral property in that world." It follows that if being obligatory strongly supervenes on nonmoral properties, and being obligatory and being commanded by God are identical, then being commanded by God, too, strongly supervenes on, and thus is *"wholly fixed by*, a set of [nonmoral] properties that does not include *being commanded by God*." (First emphasis mine) God's commands thus aren't free.[6] Yet this undercuts the "theo-

---

5 Adams is careful to point out that he is *not* offering a divine command account of divine or human *goodness*, but only of moral obligation. So there is no circle here.

6 Mark C. Murphy, *An Essay on Divine Authority*. Ithaca: Cornell University Press, 2002, pp. 86–7.

logical motivation" for divine command theory, namely, to protect God's sovereignty and independence, by insisting that not even the moral constitutes "an independent constraint on God's commanding activity."[7]

Consider, next, weak supervenience: "If an item has a . . . moral property" in a possible world "due to its having a certain set of nonmoral properties" in that world, "then any item *in that possible world* that has that set of nonmoral properties will have that moral property."[8] Weak supervenience seems initially more promising. For if God is a *rational* commander, he is a *consistent* commander, and so can't command A (a particular instance of promise keeping, say) and not command another act identical to it in all relevant respects. On the other hand, weak supervenience does *not* imply that God's commanding activity is "wholly fixed" by nonmoral facts, since it is consistent with God's not commanding acts identical to A in relevant respects in *other* possible worlds. God is therefore *not* "constrained" or "forced" to command as he does.

But weak supervenience won't do either. It is generally agreed that obligations supervene on general properties. Commands, though, do not. It can be quite reasonable to command someone to do something without commanding another to do it even though the *general* features of their situations are identical. (Murphy's example is two equally competent swimmers, each of whom is equally well situated to save a drowning child, but who would get in each other's way if both tried to do so. "So I give a command 'Jane, jump in and save the child! Tom, stay on the bank!'"[9])

Murphy's conclusion is therefore this. The identity theory entails that divine commands either strongly or weakly supervene on nonmoral properties. Since both alternatives have unacceptable consequences, the identity theory should be rejected.

Murphy's critique isn't fully convincing, however, for it depends on a particular interpretation of the claim that the property of being obligatory is identical with the property of being commanded by God, namely, that the two are identical in the way that the evening and morning stars are identical or that Tully is identical to Cicero. The relevant relation, though, is a *constitutive* one. To say that "water" picks out, or refers to, H_2O is to say that H_2O is the stuff that constitutes water,[10] and implies that

---

7   Mark C. Murphy, "A Trilemma for Divine Command Theory," *Faith and Philosophy* 19 (2002), p. 28.

8   Murphy, *Divine Authority*, p. 87.

9   Ibid., pp. 87–90. This objection would, of course, be equally damaging to the view that God's commands *strongly* supervene on nonmoral properties. It is worth noting that Murphy thinks that, even apart from any role it may play in divine command theory, weak supervenience doesn't adequately capture the relation between moral obligation and nonmoral facts. For consider an act, A, that is obligatory in the actual world. Weak supervenience implies that, in another possible world, an act with the same nonmoral features is *not* obligatory. But, in that case, the fact that A is obligatory in *our* world is just a brute fact about it. Whether this would be so hard for a divine command theorist to swallow, however, seems to me doubtful.

10   By contrast, Tully, say, doesn't *constitute* Cicero, nor does Cicero *constitute* Tully.

the possession of the phenomenal properties of water, such as odorlessness, taste-lessness, and liquidity at room temperature, (weakly) supervene on—*but are not strictly identical with*—being H_2O.[11] Similarly here. On Adams's view, being ob-ligatory is constituted by being commanded by God, and this implies that the functional properties defining the concept of moral obligation[12] (strongly or weakly) supervene on being commanded by God. This view no more implies that being commanded by God supervenes on *something else*, however, than the claim that water is constituted by H_2O implies that being H_2O does.[13]

But while this reply may be satisfactory as far as it goes, it does not get to the heart of Murphy's objection. Adams maintains "that the formal and substantive features of God's commanding activity seem to coincide neatly with the formal and substantive features of [moral] obligation."[14] Yet if moral obligation (strongly or weakly) supervenes on nonmoral properties and God's commanding activity does not, then Adams is mistaken. Being commanded by God lacks an important—indeed central—formal feature of being obligatory.

The wisest course for Adams to take at this point may be to simply admit this dissimilarity between the formal features of moral obligation and of God's com-manding activity, but insist that enough similarities remain to make it reasonable to identify God's commanding activity with what underlies or constitutes moral obli-gation.

Is the Appeal to Divine Commands Superfluous?

John Chandler thinks it is. If Adams is right, moral obligations are the commands of a loving God. A loving God, however, would presumably command all and only loving acts. That is,

1   "*a* is a loving act if and only if God commands *a*."[15]

---

11   Water's phenomenal properties and being H_2O aren't strictly identical because (for example) the former are directly observable and the latter is not.

12   Moral obligations are something one takes seriously and cares about, non-compliance is an appropriate object of blame and guilt, and so on. See the discussion on p. 84.

13   If some statements of moral obligation are necessary, though, and if moral obligations are constituted by divine commands, and God necessarily exists and commands or prohibits actions because of their nonmoral qualities, then *some* of God's commands *will* strongly supervene on nonmoral properties. If "Torturing innocents is wrong," for example, is necessarily true, then being prohibited by God strongly supervenes on torturing innocents. (If God's prohibiting torture is due to its having certain undesir-able nonmoral qualities, then any action that has those properties in any possible world will be prohibited by God in that world.)

14   Murphy, "A Trilemma," p. 28.

15   Adams does not in fact think that God commands *all* loving acts because he does not think that God commands us to do everything he would prefer that we do. But let this pass.

And because theories like Adams's identify being morally right with being commanded by God, it is also true that

2   "God commands *a* if and only if *a* is right (obligatory)."

It thus follows that

3   "*a* is a loving act if and only if *a* is right (obligatory)."

So "if an action's being loving is a good . . . reason for a loving God to command it [as (1) implies], it must be an equally good reason for us to perform it [as (3) implies] . . . That loving actions are commanded by God may be an additional reason for believers to perform them; but there is already sufficient (justificatory) reason . . . The content of the moral code can in principle be read off from the knowledge of which acts are loving without reference to God." God's commands are consequently superfluous, and Adams's divine command theory is otiose.[16]

There are problems with Chandler's objection. In the first place, (1) and (3) are merely biconditionals. *Pace* Chandler, they do not tell us that the propositions on the left side of the equations provide *reasons* or *justifications* for the propositions on their right. Of course, if we know that a biconditional is true, and know that one side of the biconditional obtains, we know that the other obtains. It doesn't follow, though, that the former is a reason or justification for the latter. I know, for example, that $2 + 2 = 4$ if and only if basketballs are material objects. Yet it would be odd indeed to offer the first as a reason or justification for the second.

A more important problem, however, is this. Even if *a*'s being a loving action can't be a good reason for God to command it without it also being a good reason for us to perform it, it doesn't follow that *a*'s being a loving action is a good reason for our regarding *a* as *morally obligatory*. Adams can therefore argue that what makes loving actions not only good but obligatory is the fact that God has commanded them.[17]

Finally Adams explicitly denies that we must *know* that God has commanded *a* before we can know that *a* is morally obligatory. Many, if not most, of our obligations can be discovered by reason, by consulting our consciences or social affections, and the like. Adams's theory is not a theory of moral epistemology.[18] Nor is it primarily a theory of divine motivation.[19] It is, rather, a *metaphysical* theory, or *constitutive explanation*, of moral obligation.

---

16   John Chandler, "Divine Command Theories and the Appeal to Love," *American Philosophical Quarterly* 22 (1985), p. 236.

17   Adams makes a similar point in Adams 1999, p. 250 fn.

18   Although his theory has consequences for moral epistemology. It can explain why our moral faculties (reason, conscience, social feelings, and the like) are generally reliable.

19   Although Adams thinks that God's nature helps explain why God issues the commands that he does.

Constitutive explanations, like "Ice is water because ice is composed of H_2O molecules," differ from motivational explanations like "Jane slapped Tom because she was angry with him," and from etiological causal explanations like "The brats were charred because John kept them on the grill too long." Constitutive explanations don't tell us *why* an agent did what she did, or explain an event by citing its antecedent causes; instead, they explicate or lay out the factors that constitute a thing or make it up. The core of Adams's theory is that an "Action A is right only *constitutively*-because God commands it," that is, A's "being right *consists* exclusively in God's commanding it." Adams may also wish to assert that "God commands A *motivationally*-because he has some reason for doing so." That A is loving, for example, may be his agent reason for commanding us to care for our neighbors. But while "given the transitivity of 'because,' it does indeed follow that . . . A is right because A is loving[20] . . . it does *not* follow that . . . A is right *constitutively*-because A is loving (i.e., [that] its being right *consists* in its being loving)." So (*pace* Chandler) Adams's claim that the moral rightness of an action consists exclusively in God's commanding it—which is the heart of his divine command theory—is entirely consistent with his citing motivational explanations for God's commanding what he does.[21]

Doesn't this response to Chandler suggest another way of formulating the problem, however? Robert Westmoreland thinks it does. Adams allows that if God doesn't exist, something other than his commands might constitute rightness and wrongness. Call this X. (X might be compliance or noncompliance with Kant's categorical imperative,[22] for example, or furthering or hindering human happiness *à la* Richard Boyd.) But "if wrongness," say, "is identical to something like contrariety to [the] categorical imperative in case there is no loving God, how could it be that [that] imperative has no independent obligation-generating force in case there *is* a loving God?" Yet if it does, our obligations are overdetermined and, in that case, lying, refusing to help the needy, and the like would be wrong even if God didn't prohibit them. So God's commands are superfluous after all.[23]

This objection misfires, however. In the first place, Adams's claim is that in a world in which God prohibits such things as lying, his commands are the *best* candidate for the role semantically indicated by our use of "morally wrong." The fact that in worlds in which a loving God *doesn't* prohibit them, something else, such as contrariety to the categorical imperative, would be the best candidate for

20 If A is right because God commands A, and if God commands A because A is loving, then A is right because A is loving.

21 Stephen J. Sullivan, "Arbitrariness, Divine Commands, and Morality," *International Journal for Philosophy of Religion* 33 (1993), pp. 37–8.

22 Act so that you can will that the maxim of your action (the principle on which you act) could be a universal law of nature.

23 Robert Westmoreland, "Two Recent Metaphysical Divine Command Theories of Ethics," *International Journal for Philosophy of Religion* 39 (1996), pp. 29–30.

that role is irrelevant; it has no tendency to show that God's commands aren't the best candidate in *this* world.

In the second place, if "obligation-generating force" means no more than "provides a ground or reason for regarding something as obligatory," then Adams needn't balk at Westmoreland's contention that truth telling's compliance with the categorical imperative, say, has obligation-generating force—*even if* a loving God in fact commands it. Many things can be *reasons* for regarding something as obligatory even if only *one* thing *constitutes* its obligatoriness.

Can Obligations be Constituted by Divine Commands?

Suppose that a loving God commands us to tell the truth, care for the needy, and so on. Is Adams justified in identifying these commands with moral obligations? Stephen J. Sullivan directs our attention to something which suggests that he isn't.

Adams's theory is a modified version of Hilary Putnam's approach to natural kinds. According to Putnam, "the word 'water' does not *mean* H_2O." Nevertheless, "it is the nature of water to be H_2O . . . ; and the property of water is, necessarily, identical with the property of being H_2O." (Adams 1999: 15) H_2O is the substance that underlies and accounts for the phenomenal features of water that are part of the ordinary meaning of the term "water." It is also the (a?) terminus of the causal chain accounting for our use of "water."

An attribute like wrongness, on Adams's view, should be treated similarly. It is whatever property can "account for the wrongness of a major portion of the types of action we have believed to be wrong,"[24] and can help "explain causally our coming to hold those beliefs." Adams believes that this property is being prohibited by a loving God.[25] It belongs to all and only wrong actions, and their being prohibited by a loving God helps to causally explain our classifying them as wrong "in so far as [he] has created our moral faculties to reflect his" prohibitions.[26]

The problem, however, is this: if love, justice, faithfulness, and the like motivate God's commands and prohibitions, then the relevant causal chain terminates *in these qualities* and not in his commands and prohibitions. It should therefore follow that conformity or nonconformity to the dictates of love,[27] and not to God's commands and prohibitions, are the properties that "moral rightness" and "moral wrongness" refer to.[28]

---

24 Adams, "Divine Command Metaethics Modified Again," in Adams, *Virtue of Faith*, p. 137.

25 Where God's love is suitably tempered by his justice, faithfulness, love of all excellence, and the like.

26 Stephen J. Sullivan, "Why Adams Needs to Modify his Divine Command Theory One More Time," *Faith and Philosophy* 11 (1994), p. 76.

27 Suitably tempered by justice, faithfulness, and so on.

28 Note that this objection is distinct from Westmoreland's. Sullivan's point is not that God's love, and so on, provide *reasons* for what he commands and prohibits (though

There are problems with Sullivan's argument. For example, it won't clearly work unless we suppose that God's love (suitably tempered) is *sufficient* to determine his commands and prohibitions. If it isn't, God's commanding and prohibiting is *a* terminus of the causal chain eventuating in our use of "right" and "wrong," and it is open to Adams to identify rightness and wrongness with them. Note, too, that if we were to identify moral rightness and wrongness with conformity and non-conformity to the divine love, respectively, our theory would still be a *theistic* one since the love in question is *God's* love, not love in general or in the abstract. (Love in general or in the abstract isn't a *cause* of anything.) That being said, Sullivan's objection remains powerful.

He notes, though, that Putnam himself provides a way out. As Putnam points out, his causal theory of reference does not imply that "'the members of the extension of a natural-kind word necessarily have a common hidden structure'[29] or even a small number of such structures ... [I]n the case of certain disease terms," for example, "the paradigmatic examples 'have ... *so many* that "hidden structure" becomes irrelevant, and superficial characteristics become the decisive ones'."[30] Sullivan suggests that Adams could modify his theory in the light of Putnam's remarks: the relevant causal chain does indeed stretch back to God's reasons or motives for issuing the commands he does.

> But God has so *many* ... reasons or motives[31] that the first *semantically important* link in the chain is His commands themselves. These provide a *better* causal/historical explanation of our use of moral terms than do His multifarious motives, just as the superficial features of a given natural kind may provide a better explanation of our use of the relevant natural kind term than do the overabundant hidden structures of the kind.[32]

Yet while Adams *could* modify his theory in this way, Sullivan thinks that to postulate "an overabundance of divine motives" is "quite *ad hoc* ... "[33] The real problem seems to me to lie deeper, however. Putnam does not think that diseases are *constituted* by their superficial features whereas Adams wants to say that moral obligations *are* constituted by God's commands. Sullivan's suggested modification would preclude him from saying that, since the multifarious divine motives, and not God's commands, would be the only "micro structures" underlying moral obligation.

---

they do) but, rather, that his love, and so on, are *causes* of his commands and prohibitions.

29   "Jade," for example, does not since it "applies to two minerals" with "two quite different micro structures." (Sullivan, "Why Adams Needs to Modify," p. 77.)

30   Ibid. The internal quotations are from Putnam.

31   Although love may be the most central or pervasive motive.

32   Sullivan, "Why Adams Needs to Modify," p. 77.

33   Ibid.

Adams's Theory and Necessary Moral Truths

We are morally obligated to avoid harming innocents, to speak the truth, to help those in need, and many other things. If these obligations consist in God's commanding them, then, if God doesn't exist or command us to do them, we are under no obligation to do them.[34] And this seems counter-intuitive.

How does Adams handle this difficulty? We can approach the issue obliquely by considering his response to a similar objection to his theory of the Good. Adams thinks that God is Goodness itself, and that the excellence of other things consists in their resemblance to God. (See Chapter 4.) So if God doesn't exist, or is relevantly different from what we believe him to be (cruel, perhaps), then Adams's "theory [of value] is false," although "there may be some other salient, suitable candidate" for the role of supreme Good, "or some other theory of the nature of the good may be true." (Adams 1999: 46)

Suppose, however, that God *does* exist and *is* a suitable candidate for the role of the supreme Good. What should we say about excellence in possible worlds in which such a God *doesn't* exist? There are four possibilities. (1) We might say that nothing is excellent in those worlds although "beings like us might have a concept subjectively indistinguishable from our concept of excellence [that is, a concept playing the same semantic role] and there might be an objective property . . . signified by it . . . " (2) We might say that excellence is a disjunctive property, where the disjuncts are what best fulfills the semantically indicated role of the Good in each of the various possible worlds. (3) Or we might say "that excellence in any possible world is measured by conformity to the standard of excellence as it is in the actual world—so that . . . what God is like in the actual world will determine the nature of excellence in all possible worlds." (4) Or we might say that it is necessarily true that such a God exists; God could not "have failed to exist or to be a good candidate for the role of the Good." (Adams 1999: 46f.)

Adams concedes that (2) and (3) aren't very satisfactory; (2), for example, seems "too artificial" and too "relative in too many dimensions."[35] He expresses a preference for (4), because "excellence is so closely tied to what things are like that it should not be a contingent matter what it would be excellent to be like."[36] But having no proof of the necessary existence of a God of the required sort (loving, supremely beautiful, and the like), Adams wishes to leave (1) open. (Adams 1999: p. 46f.)

---

34 Although it may be *good* to do them.
35 Too relative because the best candidates for the semantically indicated role of the supreme Good in the various worlds may be quite diverse. Adams doesn't explain why (3) is unsatisfactory. One may conjecture, however, that it is unsatisfactory because, if (3) is true, the standard in a possible world in which God doesn't exist (namely, God) will be a mere possibility or ideal in that world, and (as Adams has insisted) a suitable standard in a world should be actual in that world.
36 As it would be if the most suitable candidate for the role of the supreme Good varied significantly from possible world to possible world.

But *should* we leave (1) open? Why assume that in every possible world in which such a God doesn't exist, there will *be* a suitable candidate for the role of the supreme Good? Should we even assume that there will be a suitable candidate in every possible world in which, intuitively, some things are better than others (more beautiful, say)? It is not clear that we should. Yet if there isn't (and Adams's account of the semantics of "good" is more or less correct), then the term "good" doesn't pick out a real property in those worlds; the concept of good will be as empty in those worlds as the concept of phlogiston is in ours. Whether this consequence is acceptable, however, seems doubtful.

Similar questions arise with respect to Adams's theory of moral obligation, and similar responses are available. Adams admits that "if there were no loving God, then . . . no acts . . . would have the property" that the theory identifies with moral wrongness, say, and, hence, no actions would *be* wrong. Nevertheless, "some other property (which . . . *is not* moral wrongness, but only similar to it) might be a good enough candidate, and the best available, for the semantically indicated role of moral wrongness." (Adams 1999: 281f.) And, of course, the same might also be true in possible but non-actual worlds in which a loving God doesn't exist or issue commands and in which, as a consequence, moral wrongness can't be identified with non-compliance with God's commands. (This corresponds to Adams's first response to a similar worry about the Good.)

As in the case of the Good, though, why assume that there *is* or *would be* such a property? Indeed, the question about obligation seems even more worrisome. Adams advocates a social theory of moral obligation because, among other things, it helps explain how the recognition that something is morally right can be a *reason* or *motive* for doing it. (Compliance with reasonable demands expresses our positive evaluation of the relevant social bonds, for example.) But Adams *also* thinks that divine command theory is superior to other social theories of obligation because it explains how moral reformers can be right in thinking that we are morally obligated to do things which aren't demanded by the human communities to which we belong. As Adams says, "there have been situations in which none of the existing [comparatively good] human communities [have] demanded as much as they should have." The only social theory that can adequately accommodate this fact is divine command theory. (Adams 1999: 248) But in that case, if God doesn't exist in a possible world, or his commands aren't a salient candidate for the semantically indicated role of obligation in those worlds,[37] then actions which transcend the demands of the various human communities in those worlds aren't obligatory. No one would have an obligation to work for the abolition of slavery, for example, or to oppose the exploitation of women, if none of the human communities to which people belong demands it. Many of us will find this hard to swallow.

---

37   Because he isn't good, for example, or doesn't command or prohibit anything.

As in the case of the Good, however, other responses are possible. We might identify moral obligation with a disjunctive property, for example, or, assuming that a loving God exists and issues the right sort of commands, moral obligation in possible worlds in which God doesn't exist or issue commands could be identified with what God *actually* commands in the *actual* world. Yet neither response is particularly plausible. Like disjunctive accounts of the Good, disjunctive accounts of moral obligation would be "too artificial" and too "relative in too many dimensions." The third response is a non-starter since, as Adams argues at length, commands must be *promulgated* to create obligations, and divine commands aren't promulgated in possible worlds in which he fails to exist or issue commands.[38]

Perhaps a fourth response is again best: God necessarily exists and is such that in any possible world in which creatures like us exist, he commands them not to lie, to protect the innocent, and so.[39] Adams clearly doesn't want to take this line with respect to all moral obligations. (He says, for instance, that he does "not believe that there is a unique set of commands that would be issued by any supremely good God." [Adams 1999: 255]) But one might agree with Adams on this score and yet consistently claim that there are *some* commands that any "supremely good God" would *necessarily* issue to beings sufficiently like us. The second table of the Decalogue is a possible example. The *motivation* behind the claim that some statements of moral obligation are necessarily true is that it seems impossible that there be a world in which the innocent are tortured, say, or friends are betrayed, and yet those acts wouldn't be *prima facie* wrong—that there wouldn't be a moral presumption against them. If moral obligations are best understood as divine commands, then these necessary moral truths must be construed as commands God necessarily issues in the appropriate circumstances.

But even though this line of thought is attractive, Adams can't adopt it. Adams thinks that grounding goodness and moral obligation in God somehow explains them. This *may* be true of goodness. If God exists and is what we believe him to be,

---

38 Mark Murphy's and Philip Quinn's identification of moral obligations with God's antecedent intentions, rather than with his commands, isn't subject to this objection. Adams, however, explicitly rejects Murphy's and Quinn's identification. See his "Response to my Critics," *Philosophy and Phenomenological Research* 64 (2002), pp. 474–90. Henceforth Adams 2002.

39 "Failing to protect the innocent is wrong" isn't a necessary truth on this view since some possible worlds don't contain creatures like us (either because there are no created beings in those worlds; or because the created beings that exist in those worlds aren't appropriate recipients of commands [they aren't rational beings, for instance]; or because they aren't appropriate recipients of *this* command [because, in those worlds, innocents can't be harmed, for example]). Since they don't contain creatures relevantly like us, God doesn't command anyone to protect the innocent in those worlds. And if he doesn't, and obligations are constituted by divine commands, there is no obligation to protect the innocent in those worlds. What *is* necessarily true in the worlds in question, however, is that if there *were* beings like us, God would command them to protect the innocent, and so they *would* have an obligation to do so.

Adams's account of moral and other forms of goodness is plausible. (See Chapter 4.) And if he *necessarily* exists and is *necessarily* what we believe him to be, then some judgments of excellence are necessarily true. But moral *obligation*, in Adams's view, is grounded in divine commands and hence in God's *will*. And this creates a problem with respect to necessary moral truths. For if all moral obligations are grounded in God's will, and some moral obligations are necessary, then God necessarily wills that we not torture the innocent, say, or commit acts of betrayal, and one may doubt that necessity is compatible with willing.

Not everyone does. Aquinas, for example, thought that we necessarily will our own happiness, and Jonathan Edwards's theological premises commit him to the claim that God necessarily wills to create some world or other.[40] Adams, however, has explicitly said that willing implies real alternatives. "For the will seems to be an efficient cause," and efficient causes presuppose alternatives, the cause explaining why one alternative is realized rather than another. If this is true, then God's willings appear to "presuppose alternatives in some sense possible."[41] It would thus seem that Adams is faced with three choices. He can deny that there are any necessary moral obligations. He can admit that some moral obligations (namely, necessary ones) aren't grounded in God's will, and hence aren't constituted by his commands. Or he can abandon the view that willing necessarily implies real alternatives. Since the first option is strongly counter-intuitive, and the second considerably narrows the scope of his divine command theory, Adams would be well advised to embrace the third.

Philip Quinn's Causal Divine Command Theory

In an essay that appeared in 1979, Philip Quinn proposed a causal theory of divine commands. p is a causally sufficient condition of q = def. "it is causally . . . but not logically necessary that if p then q." And p is a causally necessary condition of q = def. "it is causally . . . but not logically necessary that if q then p." With these definitions in hand, the "relation between divine commands and moral duty" can be characterized as follows: where God's commanding p is logically possible and p is contingent, God's commanding p is a causally sufficient and necessary condition of p's being morally obligatory.[42]

---

40   For Edwards, see my "Jonathan Edwards, William Rowe, and the Necessity of Creation," in Jeff Jordan and Daniel Howard-Snyder, eds, *Faith, Freedom and Rationality*. Lanham, MD: Rowman and Littlefield, 1996, pp. 119–33.

41   Robert M. Adams, *Leibniz: Determinist, Theist, Idealist*. New York: Oxford University Press, 1994, pp. 184–5.

42   Philip L. Quinn, "Divine Command Ethics: A Causal Theory," in Idziak, *Divine Command Morality*, pp. 310–12. Henceforth Quinn 1979. Analogous accounts can be given of p's being morally forbidden or morally permitted.

The theory as it stands is subject to an important objection, however. Some statements of moral requiredness appear to be necessarily true. For example, it seems necessarily true "that everyone refrains from gratuitous torture of innocents is obligatory." But if it is, then God's commanding that everyone refrain from the gratuitous torture of innocents is not a *causally* sufficient condition of its being obligatory. (If "It is obligatory that everyone refrains from torturing innocents" is necessarily true, then it is necessarily true that if God commands everyone to refrain from torturing innocents, refraining from torturing innocents is obligatory.[43] God's command is thus a *logically* sufficient condition of the obligation obtaining. Given our definitions, it therefore follows that God's command is not a *causally* sufficient condition of the actions's moral requiredness.)

Furthermore, it seems, intuitively, that necessary states of affairs aren't caused. Hence, if everyone's refraining from torturing innocents being obligatory is a necessary state of affairs, then nothing—not even God' commands—*causes* it to obtain.

Quinn's response to this objection was twofold. (1) He alluded to Ockham's view that the moral status of actions is contingent. If it is, then *no* statement of the form "x is obligatory" is necessarily true, and the problem evaporates. (2) Or perhaps some statements of moral obligation *are* necessarily true.[44] If they are, then the theory doesn't apply to them. *Other* obligations are plausibly contingent, however, and our causal theory provides the best account of *them*.[45] (Quinn 1979: 322–3) Neither response seems adequate.

The first falls foul of deeply seated intuitions. It seems clear to many of us, for example, that there are *no* possible worlds in which torturing innocents would be permissible.

The second response empties divine command theory of much of its interest by severely limiting its scope. For consider true statements of *prima facie* obligation like "There is a *prima facie* obligation to keep one's promises" or "There is a *prima facie* obligation to refrain from torturing innocents." To say that one has a *prima facie* obligation to keep one's promises, or to refrain from torturing innocents, is roughly equivalent to saying that, other things being equal, one has a moral obligation to keep one's promises or to refrain from torturing innocents, that there is a moral presumption for or against doing these things. *Prima facie* obligations are distinguished from actual obligations. Actual obligations are what one is obligated to do all things considered. For example, although I have a *prima facie* obligation

---

43   Conditionals with necessary consequents are necessarily true. Since it is impossible for their consequents to be false, it is impossible that their antecedents be true and their consequents false. It is thus impossible that the conditionals be false, that is, they are necessarily true.

44   Although Quinn professes to be "not at all sure whether there are any necessary truths about obligations and prohibitions." (Quinn 1979: 322)

45   The Jews' obligation to observe the Sabbath might be an example.

to keep my promises, I also have a *prima facie* obligation not to abet murder, and the second typically outweighs the first. If I can keep my promise only by abetting murder, I will not normally have an obligation to keep my promise.

Now, arguably, true statements of *prima facie* obligation are necessarily true. There is no possible world in which there wouldn't be a moral *presumption* against promise breaking, torturing innocents, and the like. If they are necessarily true, however, and God is not a causally sufficient condition of necessary states of affairs, then God isn't a causally sufficient condition of *prima facie* moral obligations.

Moreover, God is a causally sufficient condition of most actual moral obligations only in the sense that he is the causally sufficient condition of the states of affairs that transform *prima facie* obligations into actual ones. For example, God is the cause of my actual obligation to keep my promise to have lunch with my daughter on Sunday only in so far as he is the causally sufficient condition of the fact that no morally relevant circumstances will arise between now and Sunday which will outweigh my *prima facie* obligation to have lunch with her as I promised. That I have an actual obligation to keep my promise isn't wholly explained by God's causal activity because the relevant true statements of *prima facie* obligation must also be included in any satisfactory explanation and these, being necessary, are not *made* true by God. God can, of course, make things which are morally "indifferent,"[46] obligatory or forbidden by commanding that we do or not do them. But even here their being obligatory or forbidden seems to depend on its being necessary that we are obligated to obey God's commands—a state of affairs which, like all necessary states of affairs, is not commanded by God.

The upshot of these considerations is therefore this: if God is not a cause of necessary states of affairs, his causal role in bringing about moral obligations is severely limited.

By 1990 Quinn had shifted his position, admitting that he had since come to think that some "deontological states of affairs obtain in every possible world" and are thus necessary. He believes, however, that the existence of necessary deontological states of affairs is compatible with theological voluntarism after all, since "the divine will too" may be "in some respects necessary and immutable."[47] How should this be understood?

---

46 In the sense that there is no *prima facie* obligation to either do or not do them.
47 Philip L. Quinn, "An Argument for Divine Command Ethics," in Michael D. Beaty, ed., *Christian Theism and the Problems of Philosophy*. Notre Dame, IN: University of Notre Dame Press 1990, p. 301. Henceforth Quinn 1990a. In an article published the same year, Quinn does note a possible problem with this position since there will be "possible worlds in which God does not create beings capable of freely obeying moral injunctions" and, in those worlds, "it may be that . . . there are no divine commands, because they would be pointless, and so no moral requirements or prohibitions." ("The Recent Revival of Divine Command Ethics," *Philosophy and Phenomenological Research* 50 [1990], p. 364. Henceforth Quinn 1990b) Notice, however, that even in those worlds, related counterfactuals would obtain. (See note 39) For example, it will be

Quinn invites us to consider Michael Loux's formulation of the view that necessary facts are grounded in God: "Facts are necessarily as they are because God has the relevant strong beliefs," where "a person S strongly believes that p if and only if S believes that p and does not entertain that not-p." (Entertaining not-p involves believing that not-p is possible.) On this view, even if some moral facts necessarily obtain, they depend upon God since God strongly believes that they obtain. (Quinn 1990b: 360–61)

But do they depend on God's *will*, as divine command theories imply? They do (1) if God's believing p is identical with his willing p, as strong doctrines of God's simplicity imply since, in that case, "divine strong beliefs will be identical with divine commands that are invariant across all possible worlds," or (2) if, while not identical, divine believings and willings are so "tightly integrated in God" that they "are perfectly correlated." (Quinn 1990b: 362)

Strong doctrines of divine simplicity are dubious. The second alternative is more promising, however, and can be developed in three ways: (1) Moral facts are "causally overdetermined, and . . . perfectly correlated divine commands and divine beliefs operate independently to bring it about that moral propositions are true." (2) "Divine volitions . . . bring about divine beliefs which . . . , in turn, bring about the truth of moral propositions." (3) Divine beliefs bring about divine volitions which, in turn, bring about the truth of moral propositions. Quinn thinks that the third approach has "a slight edge over the other two in terms of intuitive naturalness or plausibility" (since volitions are typically grounded in beliefs), but that each of them can accommodate both the intuition that at least some moral facts are necessary *and* the claim that God causes all moral facts. (Quinn 1990b: 362–3)

Quinn's 1990 proposal is promising. It isn't entirely satisfactory, however, since each of his three ways of developing the claim that divine believings and willings are perfectly coordinated is problematic. If divine volitions and divine beliefs operate independently and each is a causally *sufficient* condition of the relevant moral facts (as the first approach implies), then divine volitions aren't causally

---

counterfactually true that if God *were* to create beings capable of freely obeying moral injunctions, he would necessarily command them to refrain from torturing any innocents there might be. So if theological voluntarism is true, it will also be true, in those worlds, that if God were to create beings capable of freely obeying moral injunctions, they would be morally obligated to refrain from torturing innocents. Given that God necessarily exists, that it is necessarily true that rational beings are capable of freely obeying moral injunctions, that God necessarily commands any rational beings there may be to refrain from torturing innocents (if there are any), and that theological voluntarism is necessarily true (as it presumably must be if it is true at all), then it follows that it is necessarily true that if there are rational beings they are morally obligated to refrain from torturing any innocents there might be. But surely this is all that was ever meant by the claim that it is necessarily true that there is a moral obligation to refrain from torturing innocents.

necessary conditions of those facts.[48] And this is inconsistent with divine command theory.[49] The second is problematic for the reasons Quinn gives. But the third, too, is problematic since the idea that God's will is the *ultimate* cause of moral facts seems essential to any robust divine command theory.

It is perhaps for these reasons among others that Quinn's most recent formulation of divine command theory takes a somewhat different tack. As he now sees it, "it is at the deepest level God's will, and not divine commands, which merely express or reveal God's will, that determines the deontological status of human actions."[50] He therefore proposes to follow Mark Murphy in identifying the ground of moral obligation with God's "antecedent intentions," that is, with "what God intends the agent to do antecedent to choice."[51] These antecedent intentions are the total, exclusive, active, immediate, and *necessitating* causes of moral obligations. For example, God's antecedently intending that John keep his promise to Mary is the total "and sole cause" of his obligation to do so, is an "exercise" of God's "active power," brings about the obligation "immediately rather than by means of secondary causes or instruments," and "necessitates" it.[52] (Quinn 2000: 55)

---

48 Since divine beliefs are causally sufficient to produce them, the facts in question would obtain *even if* God didn't will them.

49 It is also inconsistent with Quinn's 1979 claim that God's commands are causally sufficient *and* causally necessary conditions of moral facts, and his 2000 claim (see below) that God's will is the "total" and "sole" cause of the moral facts he brings about.

50 Philip L. Quinn, "Divine Command Theory," in Hugh La Follette, ed., *The Blackwell Guide to Ethical Theory*. Malden, MA: Blackwell, 2000, p. 55. Henceforth, Quinn 2000.

51 Philip L. Quinn, "Obligation, Divine Commands, and Abraham's Dilemma," *Philosophy and Phenomenological Research* 64 (2002), p. 460. Henceforth, Quinn 2002.

52 God's antecedent intentions are distinguished from his consequent intentions. Since nothing occurs that is contrary to what God intends to occur all things considered, everything that occurs is an expression of God's consequent intentions. If I break a promise for my own advantage, for instance, my doing so is not contrary to what God intends to occur all things considered. He intends that I make "free, effective choices," and permits or accepts my misuse of my freedom since his doing so is a necessary condition of that freedom. But God surely *prefers* that I keep it. So we can say that, abstracting from my free choice and the conditions needed to sustain it, God *antecedently* intends that I keep it. One's *actual* obligations—"those moral obligations by which we are bound, all things considered"—depend "on God's antecedent intentions concerning one's actions which take into account *all* circumstances of action apart from what one actually chooses to do. One's merely *prima facie* obligations . . . depend on those of God's antecedent intentions concerning one's actions that abstract even more completely from the particular circumstances in which one must choose what do." For example, suppose that I have promised to have lunch with my daughter but on my way to her house encounter an accident. The injured driver needs help and I alone am in a position to assist him. I can do so, however, only by breaking my promise. Suppose further that these are the only relevant circumstances. Taking *everything* into account, God antecedently intends that I help him even though doing so involves breaking my promise. I

Michael Loux's account of God's relation to necessary truths can be modified to accommodate the new approach. *Necessary* moral facts are brought about by God's *strong* antecedent intentions. What precisely is a strong intention? As we have seen, "S strongly believes that p if and only if S believes that p and does not entertain that not-p." Presumably, then, strongly intending that x do A is intending that x do A and not entertaining not intending that x do A.[53] (Quinn 2000: 64) And note that[54] Quinn's latest account neatly sidesteps the problems raised by his earlier view that necessary moral obligations are grounded in divine beliefs that are perfectly coordinated with divine willings. For, on the new account, necessary moral obligations are immediately grounded in God's *intentions*, that is, in God's *will*.

Adams, Quinn, and Traditional Divine Command Theory

What critics of traditional divine command theories find most objectionable is their implication that God could command us to torture innocents, say, or betray our friends, and that, if he were to do so, torturing innocents or betraying our friends would be morally obligatory. We will consider this objection further in Chapter 7. Notice, though, that neither Adams's theory nor Quinn's has this implication. For Adams, morally obligatory acts are those commanded by a *loving* God. Since a loving God *couldn't* command us to torture innocents, torturing innocents could not be obligatory. And since Quinn thinks that some true statements of moral obligation are *necessarily* true, some actions could not have been obligatory. If "Refraining from torturing innocents is morally obligatory" is necessarily true, God *necessarily* wills that we refrain from torturing them. If he does,[55] God could not have willed that we

---

therefore have an actual obligation to help the injured driver. But, abstracting from the special circumstances of the case (the accident), God antecedently intends that I keep my promise, and so I have a *prima facie*, though not an actual, obligation to keep it. (Mark C. Murphy, "Divine Command, Divine Will, and Moral Obligation," *Faith and Philosophy* 15 [1998], pp. 19–20) Robert Adams has objected, however, that it is unclear how antecedent intentions differ from mere preferences, and that God simply *prefers* (even strongly prefers) that we do something doesn't make it obligatory. "We do sometimes speak of an agent (A) intending another agent or thing (X) to do something, but ... that normally implies an intention on A's part to do something to see to it, or at least make it significantly more likely, that X will do what was intended." If A doesn't, "it would surely be more accurate to say" only that A "hoped" or wanted or preferred that X do it. Since God's antecedent intention that I break my promise to help the injured driver doesn't bring it about or make it significantly more likely that I will do so, it is best construed as a mere preference, not as a volition. (Adams 2002: 484)

53 Not "intending that x do A and not entertaining x's not doing A"—as a strict analogy with strong beliefs would suggest. For when God antecedently intends that x do A, he *knows* that x may *not* do A, and hence entertains x's not doing it.
54 Although Quinn doesn't mention it.
55 And God can't will inconsistent things.

torture innocents and so torturing innocents could not have been obligatory. Are views like these consistent with traditional divine command theory, however?

In commenting on Adams's view that moral obligations should be identified with the commands of a *loving* God, John Chandler remarks: "The stress on love or similar attributes of God [such as his goodness or fairness] introduces" an element into divine command theory "which coheres poorly with the deontological emphasis in the theory on commands and obedience for its own sake ... [T]he divine command theory has traditionally been associated with a particular conception of God's nature, one which emphasizes his absolute power and freedom, and consequently the unknowability of his will by human reason." Divine command theories "which emphasize God's love [or goodness or fairness] on the other hand suppose a greater grasp of his nature by analogy with human nature, and a lesser gulf between world and God."[56] Similar points can be made about Quinn. On the most recent versions of his theory, God is not free to make things like the torture of innocents or the betrayal of one's spouse morally obligatory.

There is more than a little truth in Chandler's remarks. But—for a Christian theist at least—the obvious response is that the Bible not only depicts a God who is absolutely sovereign, whose ways are inscrutable, and whose commands create and abrogate obligations; it also depicts a God who is loving and faithful, and who writes his laws on the human heart. For a Christian theist, then, the best theory of moral obligation is one that accommodates both of these strands of the Christian tradition. Arguably, both Adams's theory and Quinn's[57] successfully do so.

Appendix: Are there Substantive Necessary Moral Truths?

In "The Recent Revival of Divine Command Ethics," Quinn points out that not all necessary moral truths are made true by God. For *some* necessarily true moral propositions are *analytically* true—true simply in virtue of the concepts they contain. Because "murder," for example, just *means* "the wrongful killing of a human being," "Murder is wrong" is trivially true, and so isn't plausibly regarded as having been *made* true by God. If God forbids that Able kill Baker and also forbids that Able murder Baker, God's prohibition may bring it about that it is wrong that Able kill Baker but does not bring it about that it is wrong that Able murder Baker (though it is). And this seems correct. It points to a potential problem, however.

T. J. Mawson has recently argued that all "necessary moral truths" are "truths about moral concepts. They are logically or analytically necessary," and "as such ... tell us no more about how the world ought to be than necessary truths about other concepts tell us about how the world is." "We are obligated to pay our debts,"

---

56   Chandler, "Divine Command Theories," p. 238.
57   Or at least its later versions.

for example, reduces to the (trivial) "We are obligated to pay whatever monies we are obligated to pay people." "One is obligated to care for one's children" is *necessarily* true only if "one's children" is *defined* as "one's biological children who are such that one has a duty to care for them." "One ought not to punish the innocent" reduces to "One ought not to punish those whom one ought not to punish." Again, "One ought not to tell lies (subject to the appropriate qualifications)" may be necessarily true, but only because "if one makes whatever qualifications are needed to make [it] logically necessary, then [it] will be logically necessary." Moral properties trivially entail (that is, analytically imply) moral properties. Purely descriptive properties, however, do not.[58]

If Mawson is right, then necessary moral truths impose no substantive restrictions upon what God or anyone else is entitled to do or command.[59] God doesn't *make* necessary moral truths true. But because these truths aren't *substantive*, tell us nothing "about how the world ought to be," God's inability to make them true is like his inability to make it true that bachelors are unmarried or that triangles aren't plane figures; it is not a genuine limitation.

It isn't clear that this will do. For one thing, there appear to be necessary but non-analytic *non*moral truths which tell us something about the world. Examples of necessary synthetic nonmoral truths are "Nothing can be green and red all over," "Nothing is taller than itself," or (more controversially) "Every event has at least necessary causal conditions."[60] More to the point, Mawson's claim implies that all the purely descriptive properties of an instance of gratuitous cruelty, say, could be instantiated without the action that instantiates them being wrong.[61] And that seems counter-intuitive.

Mawson has a reply to moves of this sort. Richard Swinburne has claimed "that two [possible] worlds exactly alike in all non-moral respects could not differ in moral ones" (which entails that the non-moral properties in question *entail* moral ones). But "the sense of 'could not' in which two worlds identical in all non-moral properties could not differ in moral ones" either is or is not "an analytic/logical one."[62]

---

58   T. J. Mawson, "God's Creation of Morality," *Religious Studies* 38 (2002), pp. 3–4.

59   And hence, because God is able to do anything he is entitled to do, necessary moral truths impose no restrictions on what he can do.

60   These sentences can't be reduced to contradictions by substituting definitions for the terms they contain, and therefore aren't analytic in the strict sense. Nor is it sufficient to protest that the propositions in question *must* be analytic because one can't fully understand them without grasping their truth. For those who think that some necessary truths are synthetic say precisely the same thing of a number of *those* necessary truths: they, too, can't be rejected by someone who fully understands them.

61   Let P, Q, R . . . be the relevant descriptive properties. If Mawson is right, "If action A exhibits P, Q, R . . . , it is wrong" isn't *analytically* true (true by virtue of the concepts it contains). And since (in Mawson's view) all necessary truths are analytic, it isn't necessarily true either. It is therefore possible for an action to exhibit P, Q, R . . . and not be wrong.

62   Mawson, "God's Creation of Morality," p. 5.

If it is, "this could only be because we are not specifying the worlds in entirely non-moral properties . . . ; otherwise," there is no entailment. Nonmoral properties do not entail moral ones. Any appearance to the contrary is due to the fact that allegedly nonmoral properties which *seem* to entail moral properties aren't really nonmoral. Consider "extreme pain," for instance. "The 'qualia-tative' [*sic*] feel of experiences can sometimes analytically/logically entail moral facts. It is analytically/logically necessary that severe pain is bad for people and thus that the infliction of it is something one has *prima facie* reason to avoid. To think otherwise requires one to hold either that meaning can be separated from use or that the meanings of a term such as 'severe pain' can be given by its use in genuinely non-moral contexts," and "neither of these positions is tenable."[63]

Suppose, on the other hand, that the "could not" in Swinburne's claim is not an analytic/logical "could not." If it isn't, then "the truth that two worlds identical in all non-moral properties could not differ in moral properties . . . would not be an analytically/logically necessary" truth but, rather, some sort of metaphysically necessary one.[64]

But precisely what, one may ask, is objectionable about *that*? Certainly not that if its necessity is only metaphysical, the relevant nonmoral properties can't *entail* moral properties, for metaphysical necessity (as usually understood) is a *form* of logical necessity. That is, metaphysically necessary conditionals, like analytically necessary ones, are true *in all possible worlds*; it is impossible for their antecedents to be true and their consequents false. Furthermore, to *deny* Swinburne's claim is to deny the supervenience thesis (see pp. 87–9)—a thesis that appears to be implied by the very logic of moral concepts.[65] I conclude, then, that Mawson's attack on substantive necessary moral truths is unsuccessful.

---

63 Ibid., p. 6. Mawson admits that this is controversial but claims that "to attribute to you a mind requires me to see you as sharing the values, aims and strategies which characterize people. One [of these] is the value associated with avoiding unnecessary suffering . . . " (Ibid., p. 24fn.) The concept of pain is inherently value laden. But how convincing is this? For the sake of argument suppose we grant that attributing pain to someone involves attributing to them the *purely descriptive* properties of trying to avoid it and of *thinking* that they have reason to avoid it. It doesn't follow that our use of language commits us to saying that they *have* a (good) reason to avoid the pain or that *we* have a (good) reason to care about it. Ascribing purposeful behavior and reasons to a person doesn't *conceptually* commit us to endorsing them. (Not even when the person in question is *me*. For I can refuse to endorse both my behavior and my first-order reasons for engaging in it.) It isn't clear, then, that the ascription of pain to myself or others *analytically* implies any judgment about its value or disvalue. That is, it isn't clear that the badness of severe pain is part of its *concept* or, what comes to the same thing, that a failure to endorse "Severe pain is bad" involves a failure to grasp "severe pain"'s conceptual *meaning*.

64 Mawson, "God's Creation of Morality," p. 5.

65 As R. M. Hare was among the first to point out.

CHAPTER 7

Objections to Divine Command Theory

That nontheists reject divine command theory is neither surprising nor particularly interesting. What *is* interesting is that nontheists offer reasons why believers should reject it, and many theists accept them. This chapter examines these reasons.

Semantic, Epistemic, and Logical Objections to Divine Command Theory

Semantic Objections

"x is a bachelor" means "x is an unmarried adult male." As a consequence, "x is a bachelor but x isn't an unmarried adult male" is false on its face; and "If x is a bachelor, x is an unmarried adult male" and "If x is an unmarried adult male, x is a bachelor" are tautologies. By contrast, "x is obligatory but God did not command x" is not false on its face; and "If x is obligatory, God commands x" and "If God commands x, x is obligatory" are not bare tautologies. Hence, "x is obligatory" does not *mean* "God commands x."

Arguments of this sort are sufficient to dispose of the claim that "being obligatory" and "being commanded by God" have the same meaning, and divine command theorists who have maintained that they do are mistaken. But they are not sufficient to show that the property of being obligatory and the property of being commanded by God aren't the same property. As we have seen in Chapter 4, "x is water but x isn't H_2O" isn't false on its face; and "If x is water, x is H_2O" and "If x is H_2O, x is water" aren't empty tautologies. So "water" doesn't *mean* "H_2O." It doesn't follow, however, that water isn't *identical with*, or *constituted by*, H_2O. Similarly, the fact that "being obligatory" doesn't mean "being commanded by God" doesn't show that being obligatory isn't identical with, or constituted by, being commanded by God, and hence doesn't show that Robert Adams's divine command theory is mistaken. Nor does it show that Philip Quinn is mistaken in claiming that God's commands cause or bring about moral obligations. The moral of the semantic objection, then, is not that divine command theories are false but only that their central contentions should not be formulated as claims about the meaning of expressions such as "morally obligatory" and "morally prohibited."

Epistemic Objections

Divine command theories appear to imply "that only those people who have religious knowledge [who know that God commands truth telling, for instance, or forbids cruelty] can have moral knowledge." (Quinn 1979: 314) But this, as Edward Wierenga points out, is absurd. Any plausible version of divine command theory will allow that one can discern an action's rightness or wrongness without recognizing that God commands or prohibits it. To deny that one can is to deny that atheists and agnostics have moral knowledge when they patently do. If moral knowledge doesn't depend on religious knowledge, however, divine command theory seems devoid of practical interest.[1]

There are two responses to this objection. The first is that recent versions of divine command theory, at least, are metaphysical, not epistemological, doctrines. Even if "the sole epistemic access we have to God's will and what he has commanded is through moral inquiry of the usual sort,"[2] it may still be true that moral obligations are caused by God's commands (Quinn) or constituted by them (Adams). For, as Quinn puts it,

> the causal order and the order of learning need not be the same. Even if effects are sometimes known through their causes, causes are sometimes known through their effects. So it is consistent with our [causal] theory to maintain that we can come to know what is obligatory and forbidden without prior causal knowledge of why these things have the moral status they do. (Quinn 1979: 314)

And similar claims can be made for Adams's theory. That one can know that x is water without knowing that x is H_2O is no objection to the claim that water is identical with, or constituted by, H_2O. Similarly, that one can know that x is obligatory without knowing that God has commanded x is no objection to the claim that being obligatory is identical with, or constituted by, being commanded by God. The first response, then, is that the objection is irrelevant because recent versions of divine command theory, at least, are not making epistemic claims.

The second response is that even if one can possess (some) moral knowledge without possessing religious knowledge, divine commands can still have an important bearing on our knowledge of what we morally should and should not do. For, as Wierenga points out, "at least in some cases, it [may be] easier to discern God's commands" (through consulting scripture, for example) than to independently determine whether an action has the property of moral rightness or moral wrongness.[3] William Paley offers the following analogy. Even though an ambassador who is acquainted with his sovereign's disposition and designs "may take his measures in many cases with safety; and presume, with great probability, how his master would have him act on most occasions that arise: . . . [yet] if he has his commission and instructions in his pocket, it would be strange not to look into

---

1   Edward R. Wierenga, *The Nature of God: An Inquiry into Divine Attributes*. Ithaca, NY: Cornell University Press, 1989, pp. 226–7.
2   Philip L. Quinn, *Divine Commands and Moral Requirements*. Oxford: Clarendon Press, 1978, p. 44. Henceforth Quinn 1978.
3   Wierenga, *Nature of God*, p. 226f.

them."[4] Similarly, even if the theist assumes that God has created us in such a way that the proper use of our reason and the guidance of our moral sentiments are normally sufficient to determine our moral obligations, it would be strange for her not to consult God's revealed will if she believes that she has access to it (through scripture or in some other way).

To this we may add that just as theory may be used to correct common sense judgments about the external world, so God's revealed will may be employed to correct our fallible moral intuitions. The discovery that a liquid which looks and tastes like water isn't H_2O might lead us to conclude that it *isn't* water. In the same way, the discovery that God commands or forbids what common sense regards as morally indifferent might provide us with a conclusive reason for correcting our common-sense moral judgements. For example, the discovery that God commands us to love our enemies and do good to those who hate us may lead us to revise our opinion that we have no moral obligations to do so.[5]

"Is" Doesn't Imply "Ought"

That ought-statements can't be validly deduced from is-statements has been a philosophical commonplace since David Hume. Hume expresses his surprise at finding that the typical moral philosopher

> proceeds for some time in the ordinary way of reasoning, and establishes the being of a God, or makes observations concerning human affairs; when of a sudden . . . instead of the usual copulations of propositions, *is*, and *is not*, I meet with no proposition that is not connected with an *ought*, or an *ought not*. This change is imperceptible; but is, however, of the last consequence. For as *ought*, or *ought not*, expresses some new relation or affirmation, 'tis necessary that it should be . . . explained; and . . . a reason . . . given, for what seems altogether inconceivable, how this new relation can be a deduction from others, which are entirely different from it.[6]

If an *ought* can't be validly deduced from an *is*, however, then "God commands x" does *not* entail "x is obligatory," and divine command theories are false.

Philip Quinn's initial response to the difficulty was this: the divine command theorist needn't deny Hume's claim. For she does not (for example) deduce "Truth

---

4   William Paley, *Principles of Moral and Political Philosophy*, 4th American ed. Boston: John West, 1819, pp. 61–2. Quoted in Wierenga, *Nature of God*, p. 227.

5   Divine commands would have no bearing on moral knowledge if the only way of discovering that God has commanded x is by *first* discovering that x is morally obligatory. There is little or no reason to believe that this is true, however. Note, too, that the fact (if it is fact—see Chapter 10) that we should discount a claim that God has commanded x if we are strongly convinced that x is morally abhorrent doesn't entail that we can't sometimes discover God's will for us in a particular situation without prior knowledge of what our moral obligations are in that situation.

6   David Hume, *A Treatise of Human Nature*. Oxford: Clarendon Press, 1955, p. 469.

telling is obligatory" from "God commands x" *alone*, since she employs a principle of her theory "as an *additional* premise in [her] argument." For instance, she may invoke the principle that whatever God commands is obligatory which, in conjunction with "God commands truth telling," clearly does entail that truth telling is obligatory. (Quinn 1978: 45–6, my emphasis)

But this seems inadequate. For, on Quinn's view, the principles in question are *necessarily* true. (The postulates of the divine command theories formulated in *Divine Commands and Moral Requirements* were intended to express metaphysically necessary connections between God's commands on the one hand, and what is morally required, permitted, or forbidden on the other.[7]) Yet anyone who objects to the inference from "God commands x" to "x is obligatory" will also object to the claim that it is necessarily true that if God commands x, x is obligatory. ("The inference from 'God commands x' to 'x is obligatory' is valid" is logically equivalent to "The antecedent of 'if God commands x, x is obligatory' entails its consequent." The inference's validity and the necessary truth of the conditional stand or fall together.) On the other hand, if the additional principle *is* necessarily true, then "God commands x" *does* entail "x is obligatory," and no fallacy has been committed.[8] The wisest course for divine command theorists who believe that the connections between divine commands and moral obligations are metaphysically necessary, then, may be simply to deny Hume's thesis: an *ought* sometimes *can* be deduced from an *is*.

But this way of dismissing the problem is probably too quick. To see this consider a related objection which Quinn examines a few pages later: since moral

---

7 Shortly after completing this work, Quinn shifted his attention from divine command theories "based on logical relations such as strict equivalence" to causal theories. (Quinn 1979: 310) The principle in question would still appear to be necessary, however. If God's commanding x is the only thing that does or can make x obligatory, then it is presumably impossible for God to command x and x not be obligatory. It is true that causal sufficiency and necessity are, in general, distinct from logical sufficiency and necessity. For example, the temperature dropping below 32 degrees Fahrenheit is causally but not logically sufficient for water to freeze under standard conditions. But this sort of causal sufficiency and necessity is determined by the causal laws that contingently obtain. In other possible worlds, with different causal laws, water might not freeze at that temperature. *God's* causal activity is *not* governed by causal laws, however, since he is their *author*. If it isn't, then the distinction between causal and broadly logical necessity collapses in his case, and there is no possible world in which God commands x and x isn't obligatory. The principle in question is therefore necessarily true. Notice that the same result follows from Robert Adams's claim that being obligatory is identical with, or constituted by, being commanded by God. For if x is *identical* with y, "y is x" is a *de re* necessary truth. If water is identical with H_2O, for example, then it is necessarily true that whatever is H_2O is water. Similarly, if being obligatory is identical with being commanded by God, then it is necessarily true that whatever God commands is obligatory.

8 If "p implies q" is necessarily true, then "p implies q" is true in every possible world. And if "p implies q" is true in every possible world, then there is no possible world in which p is true and q is false, that is, p *entails* q.

statements have prescriptive force and factual statements do not, statements about what God commands *cannot* be logically equivalent to statements about what is morally required, permitted, or forbidden. Although Quinn treats this as a separate objection, I believe it captures the *real* force or thrust of the is–ought objection. How does Quinn respond to it?

Quinn's first reply seems inadequate.[9]

> Even if statements about God's commands were not by themselves used with prescriptive force, this would not establish the falsity of any of the theoretical principles of a divine command theory. Each such principle as a whole has prescriptive force ... by virtue of the ethical terms contained in it, but this does not imply that each sentential part of every such principle must have this feature ... If a hedonist asserts that something is good if and only if it produces a balance of pleasure over pain, he is commending something, and it is pleasure that he commends [even though "it produces a balance of pleasure over pain," by itself, lacks prescriptive force]. Similarly, a divine command theorist [who asserts that something is obligatory if and only if God commands it] is prescribing something, and it is obedience to God that he prescribes [even if "God commands it," by itself, has no prescriptive force]. (Quinn 1978: 53)

But does this really meet the difficulty? For the objection is *not* that the divine command theorist isn't prescribing, and hence isn't making moral claims. It is, rather, that, because statements about God's commands and prohibitions *lack* prescriptive force whereas statements about what we morally ought and ought not to do *have* prescriptive force, the divine command theorist's biconditional doesn't express a *logical* equivalence. "God commands x" neither entails nor is entailed by "x is morally obligatory."

Quinn's second response is more persuasive, however. "Within the context of religious ethical discourse, statements about divine commands" are normally used "to guide or direct action," and hence *do* have prescriptive force; they are not merely fact stating. (Quinn 1978: 52f.)

Moral Objections

Divine command theories appear to imply that if God doesn't exist, or commands nothing, then nothing is obligatory and nothing is forbidden (that is, everything is permitted). Quinn's initial response to this difficulty was to admit that this hypothetical *is* a consequence of divine command theories, concede that the hypothetical's consequent ("everything is permitted") *is* unacceptable, but insist that the hypothetical isn't known to be false. (The hypothetical would be known to be false only if its antecedent were known to be true and its consequent false. The falsity of the

---

9   I am inverting the order of Quinn's responses.

consequent has been granted. The hypothetical's antecedent, however, is *not* known to be true.) (Quinn 1979: 316–18)

This response seems a bit lame, however. What bothers us, I think, is the theory's apparent implication that in worlds in which God fails to exist or commands nothing, such things as promise keeping or fidelity wouldn't be obligatory, and gratuitous cruelty, treachery, and the like wouldn't be forbidden. For it seems to many of us, at least, that promise keeping or fidelity would be obligatory in all possible circumstances,[10] and that gratuitous cruelty and treachery would be forbidden.

To make matters worse, divine command theories seem to imply that not only might things like gratuitous cruelty be permitted; they might even be obligatory. For if divine command theories are true, then if God *were* to command gratuitous cruelty, gratuitous cruelty would be morally obligatory. Yet one of our most deeply entrenched moral intuitions is that there is *no* possible world in which it would be obligatory to gratuitously inflict pain on others.

Quinn's initial response to this objection was this: if attention is restricted to the actual world, then the divine command theorist will agree with "the intuition that gratuitous cruelty is morally forbidden," since he believes that God has in fact prohibited it. Disagreement arises only when we consider "various hypothetical and counterfactual" cases. For the divine command theorist thinks that "if God had commanded what we call 'gratuitous cruelty' . . . , what we call 'gratuitous cruelty' would have been morally required . . . ," whereas the critic's moral intuitions lead him to believe that even if God *had* commanded it, "what we call 'gratuitous cruelty' would still have been morally forbidden . . . " What isn't clear, though, is that the critic's intuitions should be trusted. (Quinn 1978: 58–9)

The unreliability or insufficiency of at least some of our moral intuitions is shown by their failure "to produce agreement about controversial issues" such as abortion or euthanasia or capital punishment. We have even less reason to trust them when we "go beyond actual moral problems into the realm of the merely possible." Counterfactuals are true when their antecedents and consequents are both true in possible worlds with "the greatest over-all similarity to the actual world." Where the closest possible worlds in which the antecedent of the relevant counterfactual is true "differ very little from the actual world," our intuitions can often be trusted. But where the differences are great, they cannot be. In particular, "possible worlds . . . in which God commands what we call 'gratuitous cruelty'" would be "so dissimilar" to the actual world that our intuitions are an unreliable guide to what is required and forbidden there. It might be, for example, that "in such worlds what we call 'gratuitous cruelty' provides cathartic release for its perpetrators without causing pain to is victims . . . Indeed, since the divine command theorist holds that the difference between God's commands [in] the actual world and [in] such possible worlds is just what *makes* a difference in the moral

---

10   With the usual qualifications, of course.

order between worlds, he will have some reason to think that his critic's intuitions about the moral order in such possible worlds are faulty." (Quinn 1978: 58–60, my emphasis)

The first thing to be said is that Quinn's *example* isn't convincing since, if the acts in question cause no pain to their victims, they aren't appropriately described as acts of *cruelty*. In other words, the antecedents of the relevant counterfactuals don't hold in the world Quinn has described because the acts which God commands in that world (acts providing catharsis to their perpetrators without pain to their 'victims') are *not* instances of "what we call 'gratuitous cruelty.'" Nevertheless, Quinn's *general* point about the unreliability of intuitions in controversial and hypothetical cases may be sound.

Thomas Talbott begs to differ. "Moral judgments about possible cases are often less dubious and far easier to agree upon than those about actual cases." For in actual cases the facts are frequently unclear. An example is the controversy over capital punishment. (Does or doesn't it deter crime, for instance.) "Moreover, whereas possible cases can often be simplified" for purposes of clarification, actual cases "are apt to involve . . . knotty conceptual problems that cannot be eliminated by the mere expedient of more precise stipulations." (An example might be the problem of determining just when the foetus becomes a human person.) In any case, that our moral intuitions may be unreliable guides in controversial cases like capital punishment or abortion provides "no grounds for skepticism concerning non-controversial matters, such as the [necessary] immorality of inflicting pain upon others simply for one's own pleasure." The important distinction is not between actual and merely possible cases, but between noncontroversial cases and controversial ones. Intuitions *are* sometimes unreliable or insufficient in the latter. That "cruelty for its own sake" could have been obligatory, however, is *not* controversial because it is so "obviously," indeed "outrageously," false.[11]

This isn't compelling. In the first place, it isn't obvious that all of the relevant facts *are* clear in hypothetical cases in which God commands gratuitous cruelty. Quinn's own example may be (and I think is) unpersuasive, but he is right about one thing. We have only the sketchiest idea of what possible worlds in which God commands gratuitous cruelty would be like. We thus aren't in a position to be sure that we are in possession of all the relevant facts. In other words, the reason Talbott offers for distrusting our intuitions in a number of *actual* cases (that some of the relevant facts are, or at least may be, unknown) *also* applies to these hypothetical cases. And to insist that we *do* know everything relevant about these cases, namely that God has commanded gratuitous cruelty and gratuitous cruelty is always wrong is, as Quinn says, the sheerest "moral dogmatism"—or, at the least, begs the question.

---

11   Thomas Talbott, "Quinn on Divine Commands and Moral Requirements," *International Journal for Philosophy of Religion* 13 (1982), pp. 203–5.

In the second place, the very fact that many divine command theorists don't *share* Talbott's intuition strongly suggests that it isn't noncontroversial. As Quinn points out, just as the moral intuitions of divine command theory's critics have been formed by a secular education or by membership in one of the more liberal theistic traditions, so the divine command theorists' moral intuitions have been shaped by the theory itself as set forth in scripture, sermons, prayer, and the like. The fact is that moral intuitions concerning these hypothetical cases differ. That they do is a good reason for regarding them as controversial.

There is more to be said, however, for the critic's intuitions *may* reflect her conviction that true statements of (basic) moral requirement and prohibition are *necessary,* so that if, say, "Gratuitous cruelty is wrong" is true at all, it is *necessarily* true.[12] Indeed, what most troubles divine command theory's critics may be the suggestion that basic moral requirements and prohibitions are merely contingent for—in some cases at least—this seems very hard to swallow. The prohibition of gratuitous cruelty is a clear example.

Quinn returns to the problem in "Divine Command Theory." Divine command theory implies that

1   If God were to command (or antecedently will) that "someone at some time bring about the torture to death of an innocent child," then doing so would be morally obligatory.

Furthermore, if God's commandings and willings are free, it seems that

2   There is a possible world in which God commands (or antecedently wills) that "someone at some time bring about the torture to death of an innocent child."

Yet strong intuitions suggest that

3   There is no possible world in which bringing about the torture to death of an innocent child would be obligatory.[13]

But (1) through (3) constitute an inconsistent triad.[14] At least one of them must therefore be abandoned, and Quinn suggests that the divine command theorist's best move is to deny (2). Because God is "essentially just," he *couldn't* command or will that "someone at some time bring about the torture to death of an innocent

---

12   Note that the claim that basic moral truths are necessarily true is compatible with divine command theory *if* God necessarily commands truth telling, say, or necessarily forbids gratuitous cruelty. (See Chapter 6.)

13   I am inverting the order of Quinn's second and third propositions.

14   (3) entails the falsity of (1)'s consequent and (2) entails the truth of (1)'s antecedent. So the truth of (2) and (3) entails the falsity of (1).

child."[15] Since conditionals with logically impossible antecedents are trivially true, however, (1) *is* true, as divine command theory implies.[16] (Quinn 2000: 70–71)

Quinn's solution[17] depends upon the claim that counterfactuals with logically impossible antecedents are necessarily true. And this is plausible. If there is no possible world in which a conditional's antecedent is true, there is no possible world in which its antecedent is true and its consequent false. If there is no possible world in which its antecedent is true and its consequent false, however, then there is no possible world in which the conditional is false. The conditional is thus *necessarily* true.

But note that if this is the *only* reason for assenting to (1), then we may be in trouble. For consider

4   If God were to command (or antecedently will) that "someone at some time bring about the torture to death of an innocent child," then doing so would *not* be morally obligatory.

Since (4)'s antecedent is logically impossible, (4), too, is necessarily true. Should the divine command theorist who accepts (3) be satisfied to save (1) at the expense of regarding it as *trivially* true and, indeed, *no more* true than (4)?

There is an alternative. Call counterfactuals with logically impossible antecedents "counterpossibles." Some metaphysically significant counterpossibles seem true while others seem false. Linda Zagzebski invites us to consider the following propositions:

---

15   Note that this solution does not entail that *God's* justice consists in obedience to his own commands or fulfilment of his own intentions—things "which provide no constraints on the [commands or] antecedent intentions that God can [issue or] form . . . While in the human case justice is both good and made obligatory by God, in the divine case justice is good but not obligatory. God's essential perfect goodness entails God's essential justice . . . It is the divine nature itself, and not divine commands or intentions, that constrains the [commands and] antecedent intentions God can [issue or] form." (Quinn 2000: 71) Note that the same result can be obtained by stressing other aspects of God's character. That God is "essentially loving," for example, "precludes his commanding [acts of gratuitous cruelty] in any possible world . . . " (Edward R. Wierenga, "A Defensible Divine Command Theory," *Nous* 17 [1983], p. 395. Cf. Wierenga, *Nature of God*, pp. 219–21, and the discussion in Adams 1999, chapter 6)

16   One could also solve the problem by accepting (2) and denying (3). Doing so would preserve (1)'s truth, since (1)'s antecedent and consequent would both be true "at the appropriate possible world or worlds," namely, a world or worlds in which God commands or antecedently wills that "someone brings about the torture to death of an innocent child." Quinn's earlier writings on divine command theory were clearly sympathetic to this solution. He now regards it as less plausible than its alternative, however—except possibly in a few exceptional cases such as God's commanding that Abraham sacrifice Isaac. (Quinn 2000: 70–71)

17   And a similar solution of Wierenga's. See "A Defensible Divine Command Theory" and *The Nature of God*.

5   If God weren't good, there would be more evil in the world than there is.
6   If God weren't good, there would be less evil in the world than there is.
7   If God had wanted to do evil, he would have been able to.
8   If God had wanted to do evil, he would not have been able to.

If God is essentially good, all four propositions have impossible antecedents. Nevertheless, Zagzebski thinks that (5) and (7) are true and that (6) and (8) are false. But *why* are (5) and (7) true, and (6) and (8) false?

She suggests the following: if metaphysically necessary truths explain other truths, then "it is reasonable to say that if they were false, these other propositions might be false."[18] (5) is true because God's essential goodness (together with his essential omniscience and omnipotence) entails his providence, and the latter explains why there isn't more evil in the world than there is. (7)'s truth and (8)'s falsity are needed "to capture the difference between impossibility due to lack of power and impossibility due to lack of willing." God's inability to do evil is explained by the firmness of his will, not by a lack of power.[19] Following Zagzebski's lead, then, one might suggest that (1) is (nontrivially) true because God's commands or antecedent intentions explain the existence of moral obligations.[20]

Theological Objections

If divine command theory is correct, it would seem that God's goodness can only consist in his doing whatever he wills to do. A "goodness" of *that* sort, however, is no goodness at all. As Leibniz says, divine command theorists seem to "deprive God of the designation *good*: for what cause could one have to praise him

---

18   Linda Zagzebski, *The Dilemma of Freedom and Foreknowledge*. New York: Oxford University Press, 1991, p. 160.
19   Linda Zagzebski, "What if the Impossible had been Actual?," in Beaty, *Christian Theism*, pp. 180.
20   Zagzebski's claims can be doubted, however. For consider the proposition that

>   (9) John's striking a match (under standard conditions) explains its ignition.

>   (9) implies that

>   (10) If John hadn't struck the match, it wouldn't have ignited, and that
>   (11) If John hadn't struck the match, it would have ignited anyway,

>   is false. Indeed, (10), and (11)'s denial, appear to be part of what is *meant* in asserting (9). But if this result can be generalized, then the claim that God's goodness explains why there isn't more evil in the world than there is *includes* the assertion of (5) and the denial of (6). So if we are puzzled by the (alleged) fact that (5) is true and (6) is false, it seems that we should be equally puzzled by the explanation introduced to ground it.

for what he does, if in doing something quite different he would have done equally well?"[21] More precisely, if an action's moral requiredness consists in its being commanded by God, then God can't coherently be said to be required or obligated to do anything, and so can't be praised for doing what he is morally obligated to do. If divine command theory is correct, then God's doing what he is obligated to do would be equivalent to his doing what he has commanded himself to do. The notion of commanding oneself to do something,[22] however, is incoherent. Nor can divine command theorists ascribe *moral virtues* to God since they construe moral virtues as dispositions to do things because God has commanded one to do them. If God can't command himself to do anything, then he can't coherently be said to possess dispositions to do things because he has commanded himself to do them, and so can't coherently be said to possess moral virtues. (Quinn 1978: 135)

It doesn't follow, however, that the critics are right in thinking that divine command theorists can't make sense of God's moral goodness. For "God may very well have character traits which are very much like some of the human moral virtues." For example, he may be disposed to love his creatures, or to treat them fairly or equitably, even though he is not *obligated* to do so, and even though his disposition to do so isn't grounded in a disposition to obey God. (Quinn 1978: 135) Moreover, if these dispositions are essential to his nature, God possesses them in every possible world in which he exists. If he does, then, while "it is true that whatever God were to do would be good, . . . the range of 'whatever God were to do' includes no actions for which God would not be praiseworthy."[23]

William Alston embraces this solution but also deepens it. "The moral goodness of an action must be distinguished from its moral obligatoriness." A necessary condition of my having an obligation to do something is that there are "practical rules" or "principles" requiring me to do it. But "practical principles are in force, in a nondegenerate way, with respect to a given population of agents only if there is at least a possibility of their playing a governing or regulative function; and this is possible only where there is a possibility of agents in that population violating them."[24] Because God is essentially good, there is no possibility of his deviating from the standards of moral goodness reflected in practical principles.[25] Consequently, the concept of obligation or requiredness doesn't apply to him. Since

---

21   G. W. Leibniz, *Theodicy*. London: Routledge and Kegan Paul, 1951, p. 236.
22   As distinguished from forming an intention to do it or judging that it would be good to do it.
23   Wierenga, *Nature of God*, p. 222.
24   Alston, *Divine Nature and Human Language*, pp. 261–2. Rules have a governing or regulative function where "behavior can be guided, monitored, controlled, corrected, criticized, praised, blamed, punished, or rewarded" on their basis.
25   For example, the moral goodness of truth telling is reflected in the principle "One ought to speak the truth," and the moral goodness of charity or benevolence is reflected in "One ought to help others."

divine command theory is a theory of *moral obligation*, that it doesn't apply to God is precisely what one would expect.

It doesn't follow, however, that God and his actions aren't *morally good*. "The morally good things that we are obligated to do can perfectly well have the status for God of morally good things to do ... Some of God's moral goodness [his benevolence and justice, for instance] can be supervenient on the same behavior or tendencies on which, in us, satisfaction of moral obligations as well as moral goodness is supervenient."[26]

The distinction between moral goodness and moral obligatoriness can also explain why divine command theory needn't imply that morality is arbitrary in the sense that "God could have no ... *moral* reason for issuing the commands he does issue."[27] It is true that the moral obligatoriness of truth telling, for instance, could not have been God's reason for commanding us to speak the truth. Since, prior to his commanding it, truth telling wasn't morally obligatory, its obligatoriness wasn't a reason God *could* have had for commanding it. It doesn't follow that he does not have moral reasons for commanding us to speak the truth, help others, and the like. For the fact that such things as truth telling and helping others are *morally good* is a sufficient reason for God's commanding them, and thus making them morally obligatory as well as morally good.

The Autonomy Objection

Kant famously argued that autonomy is essential to morality. The principles one employs to select the maxims that will guide one's conduct should be grounded in pure practical reason alone. (See Chapter 2.) "If the will seeks the law which is to determine it any where else than in the fitness of its maxims to its own universal legislation, and if it goes outside itself ... heteronomy always results." Grounding our principles in our desire for happiness, for instance, "supports morality with incentives which undermine it ... , for it puts the motives to virtue and those to vice [namely, our own happiness] in the same class, teaching us only to make a better calculation [of what will lead to happiness] while obliterating the specific difference between them."[28] More generally, submission to anything external to reason yields only hypothetical imperatives of the form "Do so and so *if* you want to achieve such and such." Hypothetical imperatives can't serve as moral principles, however. For moral principles are binding on *all* rational beings, whereas hypothetical imperatives only bind those who endorse the end to which the hypothetical imperative prescribes the means.

---

26   Alston, *Divine Nature and Human Language*, p. 266.
27   Ibid., p. 267. My emphasis.
28   Immanuel Kant, *Foundations of the Metaphysics of Morals*, trans. Lewis White Beck. Indianapolis: Bobbs-Merrill, 1959, pp. 59, 61.

Divine command morality, according to Kant, is either circular or heteronomous. For God's will is conceived of as morally perfect or else "the concept of the divine will is made up of the attributes of desire for glory and dominion combined with the awful conceptions of might and vengeance." If the former, then any derivation of morality from the divine will is circular: although morality is derived from the divine will, the divine will itself is morally authoritative because and only because it expresses the principles of pure practical reason. If the latter, then "any system of ethics based on [it] would be directly opposed to morality." It would be grounded in incentives of fear and prudence, and would thus consist solely in hypothetical imperatives such as "Submit to God's demand for truthfulness if you want to avoid punishment."[29]

In one form or another, Kant's insistence on the necessity of moral autonomy has become a philosophical commonplace. For example, R. M. Hare says that "to become morally adult" is to learn how "to make decisions of principle," that is, how to freely determine the basic standards which shall govern one's conduct. As Kant points out, "judgments which are *properly* moral must rest upon 'the property the will has of being a law to itself.'" To unreflectively assimilate the principles of others without making our own decisions is to behave like "ants" or "automata," not moral agents. An autonomy which includes the reflective choice of first principles is *essential* to morality in the "proper" sense, and is a *necessary* feature of moral "maturity."[30]

R. T. Nuyen has recently argued that Kant's own views on divine command ethics are much more nuanced than the views of those like Hare who consider themselves his heirs.[31]

A fair amount of textual evidence supports the claim that Kant himself was a kind of divine command theorist. For example: "Moral religion" consists "in the heart's disposition to fulfil all human duties as divine commands." "As soon as anything is recognized as a duty obedience to it is also a divine command." "When [human beings] fulfil their duties to men . . . they are, by these very acts, performing God's commands." "Religion is (subjectively regarded) the recognition of all duties as divine commands." The idea of God includes the idea of God "as holy legislator;" God is "the legislator of all duties." Indeed, "agreement with the bare idea of a moral lawgiver for all men is . . . *identical* [my emphasis] with the general moral concept of duty." Just as earthly commonwealths depend for their existence on a legislator so, too, "an ethical commonwealth" cannot exist without "a public lawgiver," namely, God conceived as the moral ruler of the world. (*Religion* 6, 79, 90–91, 94, 131, 142, 148)

---

29   Ibid., pp. 61–2.
30   R. M. Hare, *The Language of Morals*. Oxford: Clarendon Press, 1952, pp. 74–8, 196. My emphases.
31   R. T. Nuyen, "Is Kant a Divine Command Theorist?," *History of Philosophy Quarterly* 15 (1998), pp. 441–53.

On the other hand, a number of passages appear to unambiguously *repudiate* divine command ethics: we should "not look upon actions as obligatory because they are commands of God" but, on the contrary, "regard them as divine commands because we have an inward obligation to them."[32] In the *Religion*, Kant says that the Bible, or any other purported divine revelation, should be interpreted according to our moral principles, not vice versa. (*Religion* 100–101, and elsewhere) And again, "even though something is represented as commanded by God, through a direct manifestation of Him, yet if it flatly contradicts morality, it cannot, despite all appearances, be of God (for example, were a father ordered to kill his son who is, so far as he knows, perfectly innocent.)" (*Religion* 81–2)

How can these conflicting texts be reconciled? Nuyen suggests that we look at a paper entitled "A New Exposition of the First principles of Metaphysics" in which Kant distinguishes a thing's *ratio essendi* from its *ratio cognoscendi*.[33] A is the *ratio cognoscendi* of B if B is known through A. A is the *ratio essendi* of B if, when "the first is not supplied, the determined thing is not intelligible."[34] As Nuyen puts it, A is B's *ratio essendi* if it "determines the logical grounds for B, or the logical connections between B as a subject and its predicates, thus enabling us to understand why [B] is what it is." Thus, Kant thinks, "freedom is the *ratio essendi* of the moral law"—it is what makes morality or the moral law possible. Morality or the moral law, however, "is the *ratio cognoscendi* of freedom, "that through which we become aware of it."[35]

Similarly, Nuyen suggests, Kant thinks that while the moral law is the *ratio cognoscendi* of God, God is the *ratio essendi* of the moral law. "The holiness, the universal authority, the binding force of moral laws derives from God's nature itself as a holy, universally authoritative Being capable of commanding obedience." But if God really is the ground of the moral law, how can Kant be so sure that no divine command can contradict what we perceive to be the demands of morality? Because, on Kant's view, God is only *known* through the moral law. There is thus no possible world in which God commands what we discern to be evil because "no such possible world is conceivable by practical reason."[36]

How does all this bear on the autonomy objection? Autonomy can be understood in various ways. If it means that, in making ethical decisions, we must ultimately rely on our *own* moral insights or the dictates of our *own* practical reason, then Kant's insistence on moral autonomy is as unqualified as anyone's. What allows

---

32   Kant, *Critique of Pure Reason*, p. 644.
33   Kant's paper appears as an appendix in F. E. England, *Kant's Conception of God* (London: Allen and Unwin, 1929).
34   Ibid., p. 220.
35   Nuyen, "Is Kant a Divine Command Theorist?," p. 448.
36   Ibid., pp. 449, 451. What strictly follows, however, is not that there is no possible world in which God commands what we discern to be evil but, rather, that there is no possible world in which *we would have reason to believe* that God commands what we discern to be evil.

Kant to preserve the autonomy thesis while endorsing a brand of divine command ethics is the fact that, for him, our sole access to God is through moral reason.

But autonomy, for Kant, *also* includes self-legislation. How can *this* be compatible with a divine command theory? Presumably because "the set of moral laws is identical with the set of divine commands."[37] Considered in relation to us, moral laws are dictates of pure practical reason—laws which, as rational beings, we freely impose upon ourselves. Considered in relation to God, however, they are divine commands. Moral laws are thus *both* self-imposed *and* divinely commanded.

It is doubtful that this solves the problem. For it is essential to Kant's position that laws and principles lack moral authority if they aren't self-legislated. Divine command theorists, on the other hand, think that God's commands *alone* are sufficient to create moral obligations. If they are right, then self-legislation isn't also needed, and Kant is mistaken in thinking that self-legislation is a necessary condition of a law's possessing moral authority. Kant's insistence that a moral autonomy which includes self-legislation *is* essential to morality is therefore incompatible with divine command theory.

So is divine command theory compatible with moral autonomy or not? Robert Adams agrees that divine command theory is incompatible with the claim that mature moral agents are self-legislative, imposing the moral law on themselves. It is also incompatible with the claim that mature moral agents should rely only on their "own reasoning and/or feelings in adopting moral principles, values, and priorities"—never being "swayed ... by the moral stance of others whom one respects, and by the pressure of their demands as a *moral* pressure by which one's own conception of one's moral obligations *may* need to be corrected." (Adams 1999: 271)

On the other hand, Adams insists that a divine command theory *is* compatible with moral responsibility. It is compatible with responsibility for heeding or not heeding God's commands, for example. It is also compatible with responsibility for attempting to understand them correctly, and for applying them accurately to the circumstances in which one finds oneself. It is thus consistent with responsibility for one's "moral competence," the ability to make "moral judgments about particular cases, based on [one's] own principles, perceptions and feelings." In addition, *Adams's* divine command theory at least is compatible with a self-critical attitude toward "all claims and beliefs about *what* God has commanded." (My emphasis) Since God transcends human beliefs about him, claims to speak for God, or to have grasped God's will, must be viewed with caution. In evaluating a purported divine command we must perforce rely on our independent judgments of excellence in deciding whether it really does have a divine origin—our judgments of the excellence "of God's character," for example, and "especially" of the excellence of the

---

37   Ibid., p. 452.

command's content. Indeed, on Adams's view, our very accession to God's commands is based on our *independent* valuation of him as the Supreme Good. (Adams 1999: 272–6)

But even if they do preserve a role for human moral autonomy, don't views like Adams's face another problem? James Rachels,[38] for example, has argued that "a theist who uses his own moral judgments as a basis for deciding whether or not to obey commands cannot be yielding the appropriate sort of unqualified obedience which is owed to a being that is worthy of worship." (Quinn 1978: 9)

Quinn thinks that this is mistaken. Rachels confuses

1   "If God commands P to do A, then P ought to do A only if conditions C are satisfied,"

and

2   "P ought to assent to the claim that God commands P to do A only if conditions C′ are satisfied."

The theist can consistently endorse (2) while rejecting (1). Endorsing (1) is incompatible with the unconditional obedience the theist owes God. God is to be obeyed—period, not just when certain conditions are met. But this does not preclude accepting (2). That one's deeply held and reflectively endorsed moral judgments can provide good reasons for withholding one's assent to the claim that God commands one to do A is fully compatible with a commitment to unconditionally do A if one ascertains that God has in fact commanded that one do it. Unconditional submission to God's commands and reliance on one's own ethical judgments aren't inconsistent. The relevance of the latter is most immediately epistemic: one relies on one's own ethical judgments[39] in determining *what* God has commanded. But one does not rely on them to determine what one should do *once one has settled the epistemic question*, and ascertained that God has indeed commanded one to do such and such. (Quinn 1978: 9–10)

There is a larger problem, however, as Quinn points out. For one may have good inductive reasons for thinking that God commands one to do something that conflicts with one's settled moral judgments. And it is at least possible that one's reasons for thinking that God has commanded one to do it are sufficiently strong, and one's settled moral convictions sufficiently doubtful,[40] to put one in a morally ambiguous situation. The story of Abraham and Isaac may provide an example. If God has in fact commanded Abraham to kill Isaac, then Abraham ought to kill Isaac. His submission to God commits him to it, and his not doing it would be

---

38   James Rachels, "God and Human Attitudes," *Religious Studies* 7 (1971), pp. 325–37.
39   Among other things.
40   For one's moral judgments are, after all, fallible.

morally wrong. If, on the other hand, his deeply held conviction that killing his son would be morally wrong is correct (as it seems to him to be), then he ought *not* to kill Isaac, and doing so would be morally wrong. His reasons pull him in two directions, and it is unclear what he should do.

Even more strongly, it is in principle possible for Abraham's reasons for thinking that God has commanded him to kill Isaac are sufficiently strong to *outweigh* his settled moral conviction that he ought not to kill Isaac. Suppose that they do. If moral autonomy implies that one's independent moral reflections should always determine one's conduct, then, if Abraham should function autonomously, he ought not to obey what he has sufficient reasons to believe are God's commands. Moral autonomy in *this* sense is indeed incompatible with an unconditional submission to God's commands.[41]

The larger question, of course, is whether moral autonomy of this sort is genuinely admirable. Adams thinks it is not. "A person who is autonomous in this . . . sense will rely exclusively on her own reasoning and/or feelings in adopting moral principles, values and priorities." But "the morality that any one of us could have invented from scratch would have been a pretty inferior product . . . We learn morality from others, and [never] wholly outgrow the need to do so . . . Refusal ever to be swayed . . . by the moral stance of others whom one respects, and by the pressure of their demands, as a *moral* pressure by which one's own moral obligations *may* need to be corrected" is "an unattractive rather than an admirable independence." (Adams 1999: 271) Moreover, when the other in question is *God*, a being to whom one unconditionally submits because one recognizes him as the *Good*, insistence on one's own independence seems not only unattractive but childish (or, perhaps more accurately, adolescent). It is not (*pace* Hare) a sign of "moral maturity."

A Final Word

At the conclusion of his discussion of objections to divine command theory in *Divine Commands and Moral Requirements*, Quinn observes that successfully refuting objections has no tendency "to show that any divine command theory is plausible or worthy of acceptance." (Quinn 1978: 64) This seems wrong, though, or at least misleading. Refuting objections to divine command theory increases its credibility by removing obstacles to belief in it. The reason why most moderns dismiss divine command theory as a nonstarter is that they regard one or more of the objections considered in this chapter as decisive. If (as these critics believe) the soundness of these objections lowers the probability of divine command theory to the point that belief in it becomes irrational, their refutation can only raise the

---

41   For more on Abraham's "dilemma" see Chapter 10.

theory's probability. It may not raise it to the point that belief in divine command theory becomes more reasonable than not, however. For that we need strong positive arguments in support of the theory. We will examine the most important of these in the next chapter.

CHAPTER 8

The Case for Divine Command Theory

Can a positive case be made for divine command theory? This chapter examines a number of the more important reasons which have been offered in support of it. As we shall see, these vary in strength. We will begin with some comparatively weak arguments for divine command theory, and proceed to more compelling ones.

The Arguments from Impeccability, Omnipotence, and Analogy

An Argument from God's Impeccability

Some have thought that divine command theory follows from God's inability to sin. Thus the Puritan theologian, John Preston (1587–1628) insisted that God's will must be the "rule of justice and equity" since, if it were not, it would be possible that "the *Lord* could erre, though he did never erre: that which goes by a rule, though it doth not swarve, yet it may; but if it be the rule itselfe, it is impossible to erre."[1]

It is true that a rule or standard can't depart from itself. The standard meter, for example, can't be more or less than a meter long. But *is* it necessarily true that things measured by a rule can fail to meet it? Other versions of theological ethics such as Ralph Cudworth's (see Chapter 5) deny it; God's will isn't the rule but (since God is essentially good) necessarily conforms to it. Preston's argument thus begs the question against anti-voluntarist theories like these.

There may also be *non*-theological counter-examples to the alleged necessary truth that things measured by a rule can fail to meet it. Consider the rules of logic, for a example, and a valid proof such as "All humans are mortal; Socrates is human; therefore Socrates is mortal." Since the latter *necessarily* conforms to the logical rules which measure it, it can't fail to meet them.

---

1   John Preston, *Life Eternall or, A Treatise of the Knowledge of the Divine Essence and Attributes*, 4th edn, Part I, Sermon VIII, Second Attribute of God. London: E. Purslowe, 1634. Quoted in Janine Marie Idziak, "In Search of 'Good Positive Reasons' for an Ethics of Divine Commands: A Catalogue of Arguments," *Faith and Philosophy* 6 (1989), p. 51.

An Argument from Omnipotence

Others appeal to God's omnipotence. Janine Idziak puts it this way: "Let us suppose . . . that there is something, x, which is evil in its own nature entirely apart from a divine prohibition. If this is so, then God, being good, cannot do x. But then, if God cannot do x, God is not omnipotent—which is impossible . . . An ethics of divine commands, on the other hand, respects God's omnipotence, for if God can make anything right which he wants to, then there is nothing which he is morally prevented from doing."[2]

This argument won't work, though, if some moral truths are *necessarily* true and God's power is "confined" to the logically possible. As a first approximation, God's omnipotence can be defined as his ability to do anything that it is logically possible for him to do. God's power includes the ability to create life, for example, or part the Red Sea, but not the ability to bring it about that two apples and two more apples don't equal four apples or to create beings not created by God. If God is essentially good, however, and it is necessarily true that no good being breaks his word, say, or inflicts gratuitous pain on another, then it is logically impossible that God does these things. So if God's perfect power is "restricted" to the logically possible, the fact that God can't break his word or inflict gratuitous pain is not inconsistent with his omnipotence.

An Argument from Analogy

This argument hinges on an analogy between "God as 'first being'" and "God as 'first good.'" Thus, Andrew of Neufchateau (flourished around 1360) maintained that just as "the 'first being' is the contingent and free cause of all other beings, and that on account of which each being is such a being," so "the 'first good,' that is, God, is the contingent and free cause of all other goods, and that on account of which each good is such a good."[3] Similarly, Pierre d'Ailly argued that "just as there is not an infinite regress in efficient causes, . . . so there is not an infinite regress in obligatory laws . . . No created law is absolutely first," for "as no created thing has of itself the power of creating, so no created law has of itself the power of binding." There must, then, be an "absolutely first" law, and this is the divine will. For "just as it is ascribed to the divine will to be the first efficient cause, so it must be ascribed to the same thing to be the first obligatory law; for just as the former belongs to perfection, so [too] does the latter."[4]

---

2   Idziak, "Search," p. 52.
3   Andrew of Neufchateau, *Primum Scriptum Sententiarum*, d. 48, q. 1. Paris: John Granjon, 1514. Quoted in Idziak, "Search," p. 56.
4   Pierre d'Ailly, *Quaestiones super libros sententiarum cum quibusdam in fine adjunctis,* Principium in Primum Sententiarum, D. Strassburg, 1490. Quoted in Idziak, "Search," pp. 57–8.

This argument is suggestive but begs an essential question, namely, *does* being "the first obligatory law" belong to divine perfection or, more generally, *is* divine command theory entailed by God's perfection? We will take up this issue later in the chapter.

The Argument from God's Sovereignty and Independence

Important strands of the Christian tradition stress God's absolute sovereignty. This emphasis is particularly clear in Augustine, Martin Luther, and John Calvin. It is also an important theme in Islam and in Dvaita Vedānta. If God's sovereignty is indeed unlimited and unqualified, as these traditions attest, then there is nothing distinct from God on which he is dependent and nothing distinct from him which is not dependent on him. It seems to follow that moral truths aren't independent of God. If God is truly sovereign, his will must somehow make them true or constitute the moral facts which they express.

For suppose it doesn't, and that God's will is wholly or partly determined by independent standards of value. If it is, then God's activity is not wholly *self-determined*; he is subject to causes that exist independently of him. John Preston put the point this way: "If the *Lord* be without all cause, . . . he doth not will any thing, because it is just, or desire it, because it is good, or love any thing, because it is pleasant; for there is no cause without him. . . . The creatures indeed desire things, because they are good, and love them, because they are pleasant; because they seek for perfection out of themselves, because they are caused by that which is out of themselves: but this is not so in *God*, who is first cause, because of the first cause there is no cause."[5] Or as Idziak says, "if God were to choose something because he perceived it to possess goodness or justice" or pleasantness, "then God would be causally affected by something external to himself, which is impossible."[6]

Yet "causally affected" *in what sense*? Suppose that God chooses A because he perceives that A is good. God's perception of A's goodness may be a cause of his electing it, but his *perception* isn't external to him. A's goodness *is* external to him, but it doesn't clearly follow that it is a cause of God's electing it. "God perceives that A is good" does entail "A is good." But that, and the fact that God's perception of A's goodness is a cause of his electing A, entails that A's goodness is a cause of God's electing A only if "x is a cause of y" entails that whatever x entails is a cause of y, and it doesn't. John's striking a match, for example, entails that $2 + 2 = 4$, and that John, the match, physical objects, and contingent beings exist. Even so, 2 and 2 equaling 4, the existence of contingent beings, and the like aren't *causes* of the match's ignition since they don't *bring the match's ignition about*.[7]

---

5   Preston, *Life Eternall.* Quoted in Idziak, "Search," pp. 50–51.
6   Idziak, "Search," p. 51.
7   One might argue that, like the presence of oxygen, John's existence and the existence

Moreover, if A's goodness is essential to it, then, necessarily, anything with A's qualities is good; and necessary facts aren't (efficient) causes. (My perception that $2 + 3 = 5$ isn't *brought about* by 2 plus 3 equaling 5.) So even if God's perception of A's goodness (and consequent election of A) are *dependent* on A's goodness in the sense that if A hadn't been independently good, God would not have perceived that A was good and elected it, God's perception and election of A aren't caused by A's goodness. Contrary to Preston, then, God's *causal* independence is compatible with the existence of independent value facts.

If, on the other hand, God's sovereignty rules out *any* kind of dependence on states of affairs that are external to God, and are not constituted or made to obtain by him, then an inference like Preston's goes through; God's sovereignty precludes his choosing things because he perceives that they are independently good or just or pleasant.

Furthermore, questions of divine dependence aside, the *very existence* of independent moral and value facts compromises God's sovereignty. For if essences, eternal truths (including moral truths), values, and the like aren't "part" of God or created by him, then God's sovereignty does not extend over all being. So by making moral facts dependent on God's will divine command theory effectively protects his sovereignty—and this is an important consideration in its favor.

Philip Quinn attempts to formulate the sovereignty intuition more precisely. He begins with the following definitions:

1   "The state of affairs p involves the state of affairs q = Df. p is necessarily such that whoever conceives it, conceives q . . . "
2   "The state of affairs p entails the state of affairs q = Df. p is necessarily such that (i) if it obtains, then q obtains and (ii) whoever accepts it accepts q."
3   "The state of affairs p is identical with the state of affairs q = Df. p both involves and entails q, and q both involves and entails p."
4   "The state of affairs p is wholly distinct from the state of affairs q = Df. p neither involves nor entails q, and q neither involves nor entails p."[8]
5   "The state of affairs p is metaphysically dependent on the state of affairs q = Df. q contributes to bringing about p, and it is not the case that p contributes to bringing about q."

Employing these definitions we can formulate the following (strong) principle of divine sovereignty:

---

of the match are part of a larger causal story explaining the match's ignition. But is the existence of contingent being or the fact that $2 + 2 = 4$ part of that story? Not clearly.
8   Given these definitions, "such states of affairs as $7 = 5$ being equal to 12, . . . theft being wrong, and the number 2 existing are wholly distinct from God existing. . . . God being omniscient . . . [or] God existing or roses being red," on the other hand, are not. (Quinn 1990a: 295)

6   "Necessarily, for all states of affairs p, if p obtains and p is wholly distinct from the state of affairs of God existing, then p is metaphysically dependent on being willed by God."

If we add that

7   "Truth telling being obligatory obtains," and
8   "Truth telling being obligatory is wholly distinct from the state of affairs of God existing,"

we can conclude that

9   "Truth telling being obligatory is metaphysically dependent on being willed by God."

Similar arguments can be constructed for other "deontological states of affairs" such as "promise keeping being obligatory" or "torturing children being forbidden." (Quinn 1990a: 294–8)

But Quinn notes that arguments of this kind *won't* show that the state of affairs consisting in obedience to God being obligatory is metaphysically dependent on God's will, because *that* state of affairs is *not* wholly distinct from the state of affairs of God existing. (Obedience to God being obligatory "both involves and entails God existing" since if obedience to God is obligatory God exists, and I can't conceive of the first without conceiving the second or affirm the first without affirming the second.) And yet the sovereignty intuition surely implies that *all* deontological states of affairs are dependent on God's will. (Quinn 1990a: 298)

There are three ways one might handle this anomaly. The first is by strengthening the principle of divine sovereignty. For example, we might replace (6) with

10   "Necessarily, for all states of affairs p, if p obtains and p is not identical with the state of affairs of God existing, then p is metaphysically dependent on being willed by God."

Since God's existing "neither involves nor entails obedience to God being obligatory, the latter ... is not identical with the former,"[9] and so (10) implies that obeying God being obligatory is metaphysically dependent on God's willing it. (Quinn 1990a: 299)

---

9   As Mark Murphy points out in *Divine Authority*, even if God's existing involves or entails obeying God being prudent or good, it doesn't, in any obvious way, involve or entail obeying God being *morally obligatory*.

Quinn thinks that this solution has a counter-intuitive consequence. Since one can conceive and affirm God's existence without conceiving his omniscience and omnipotence, God's existence, and his omniscience and omnipotence, aren't identical. (10) therefore implies that God's omniscience and omnipotence are metaphysically dependent on his willing them—which is surely unacceptable.[10]

A second response to the anomaly would be to bite the bullet and simply *deny* that the state of affairs of obeying God being obligatory is metaphysically dependent on God willing it. But because this would be unacceptable to "a thoroughgoing theological voluntarist," Quinn thinks that a better response is to persist in one's insistence that the state of affairs consisting in obedience to God being obligatory *is* metaphysically dependent on God willing it, "but concede that this is not" established by considerations of divine sovereignty. (Quinn 1990a: 299) This third response seems unsatisfactory, however, for if the claim that obeying God being obligatory is dependent on God's will *isn't* established by considerations of divine sovereignty, it is not clear why one should insist on it.

Does the anomaly really follow from Quinn's argument, though? It may not. On Quinn's view, states of affairs are dependent on God's will only if they neither involve nor entail God's existence. Since the state of affairs of obeying God being obligatory involves and entails God's existence, he concludes that it is not dependent on God's will. But as Mark Murphy points out, it isn't really obvious that the state of affairs of obeying God being obligatory is *not* wholly distinct from God's existence. Just as promise keeping can be obligatory even if there are no promises, so obeying God can be obligatory even if God doesn't exist. One can conceive "Promise keeping is morally obligatory" although no one has made a promise, and one can affirm "Promise keeping is morally obligatory" without affirming "There are promises to accept." Similarly, one can conceive "It is morally obligatory to obey God"[11] while at the same time conceiving "God does not exist," and one can

---

10 Is this line of reasoning correct, though? One can undoubtedly conceive and affirm a *divine being*'s existing without conceiving and affirming its omniscience and omnipotence. Whether one can conceive and affirm *God*'s existence without conceiving and affirming his omniscience and omnipotence is another matter. If to conceive and affirm God's existing is to conceive and affirm a maximally perfect being's existing, then it is doubtful that one can. And that aside, that one can conceive and affirm p without conceiving or affirming q is not an adequate criterion of p's and q's nonidentity. One can conceive and affirm the existence of water, for instance, without conceiving or affirming the existence of H_2O, and yet water and H_2O are identical. So *even if* one can conceive and affirm God's existence without conceiving and affirming his omniscience and omnipotence, it doesn't follow that being God and being omniscient and omnipotent aren't identical. (Particularly if, as some think, omniscience and omnipotence entail moral impeccability. [For arguments that they do see Richard Swinburne, *The Existence of God* (Oxford: Oxford University Press, 1979), pp. 97f., and James Ross, *Philosophical Theology* (Indianapolis: Bobbs-Merrill, 1969), pp. 228–34.]) The flaw in the argument may thus lie in (3) rather than in (10).

11 That is, it is morally obligatory to obey God if he exists.

affirm "Obeying God is morally obligatory" without affirming "God exists."[12] Since one can also conceive and affirm God's existence without conceiving and affirming obeying God being obligatory,[13] (4) implies that obeying God being obligatory *is* wholly distinct from God's existence after all. If it is, then (6) implies that it is metaphysically dependent on God's willing it, and the anomaly disappears.

Even if Murphy's remarks are unconvincing, a *fourth* resolution of the anomaly is available which seems more satisfactory than either the second or the third, namely, that the state of affairs of obeying God being obligatory *is* metaphysically dependent on God, but *not* metaphysically dependent on his *willing* it. It might be metaphysically dependent on his thinking it, for example. Or it might be metaphysically dependent on God's being the Supreme Good (standard of value), so that the standard contributes to the existence of the obligation but the existence of the obligation doesn't contribute to the existence of the standard.

Quinn assumes that the notion of metaphysical dependence "is at bottom causal" (Quinn 1990a: 296), but this may be doubted. A substance's contingent properties aren't caused by the substance in which they inhere.[14] They are nevertheless metaphysically dependent on it. Again, Anna Karenina is metaphysically dependent on the creative activity of Leo Tolstoy. But Tolstoy's authorial activity isn't precisely the *cause* of Anna Karenina's being because that cause is the procreational activity of her parents. And these possible counter-examples aside, why can't the relation between the Supreme Good or standard of value, and moral obligations such as the obligation to obey God, be quasi-causal? The Platonic tradition, at least, has supposed that it could. A Platonic form like Beauty itself is not only the measure of the beauty of bodies or fair thoughts and practices, it is also their source.

The fourth resolution does have an important implication for divine command theory, however. If it is a live option, then theological voluntarism isn't the only way of preserving the sovereignty intuition. If it isn't, one can't argue that divine command theory is needed to protect it.

The "Immoralities" of the Patriarchs

Consider the following three cases: Abraham's willingness to kill his beloved son, Isaac, at God's command (Genesis 22: 1–19); the Israelite's plunder of the Egyp-

---

12   Mark C. Murphy, "Divine Command, Divine Will, and Moral Obligation," *Faith and Philosophy* 15 (1998), p. 13.
13   As distinguished, perhaps, from its being a good or wise thing to do.
14   Even though they are "wholly distinct" from it. I can conceive and affirm my daughter's existence, for instance, without conceiving and affirming that she has brown hair and is married to a Frenchman, and I can conceive and affirm that those properties exist and are instantiated (by something or other) without conceiving and affirming her existence.

tians because God commands them to do so (Exodus 12: 35–36); Hosea's illicit sexual relations with a harlot at God's order (Hosea 1: 2–3). Not only would these actions ordinarily be regarded as immoral; they are explicitly forbidden in the Decalogue. Yet the Bible clearly implies that Abraham, the Israelites, and Hosea committed no wrong. How can this be?

A suggestion offered by Augustine and Bernard is that God's general directives (for example, the Decalogue) admit of exceptions, since God can release "individuals or groups" from the general obligations he imposes on them by commanding them to do things "which would have been wrong in the absence of those commands." (Quinn 1990b: 356)

A more interesting take on these cases is Aquinas's. In his view, the divine precepts that are formulated in the Decalogue "admit of no dispensation whatsoever." But the actions of the patriarchs *do not violate them*. God is the "lord of life and death" who justly "inflicts the punishment of death on all men . . . on account of the sin of our first parent." Having justly condemned everyone to death for the sin of Adam, God can commission whomever he pleases to carry out the sentence. Since murder is *wrongful* killing, and God *commands* Abraham to kill Isaac, as he has every right to do, Abraham's willingness to kill Isaac does not violate the injunction against murder.[15]

Moreover, since God is the owner of everything, what rightfully belongs to a person is what God has directly allotted to her. Because God allotted the silver ornaments and gold of the Egyptians to the Israelites, the silver and gold rightfully belonged to them. Hence they did not commit theft in taking them. Finally, God is the "*author* of the institution of marriage;" one's lawful spouse is the person whom God has allotted to one (normally—but not always—through the divinely ordained institution of marriage). Since licit sexual relations are those God ordains, and God commands Hosea to cohabitate with a prostitute, his sexual relations with her didn't violate the divine injunction against illicit sexual relations.[16]

We needn't decide between Augustine's and Bernard's interpretation, and Aquinas's. The important point is that, on either view, "divine commands addressed to particular individuals or groups make a difference in the moral statuses of actions they perform out of obedience." And even if one doubts the historicity of these stories, the Christian or Jewish theist (and perhaps other theists as well) would be prepared to admit that *were* God to command things like these in situations like the ones described in the Old Testament, "the divine commands would make a moral difference of the sort" Augustine, Bernard, and Aquinas "were convinced they did in fact make" (Quinn 1990b: 356, 359)

Nevertheless, while a consideration of these cases provides *some* support for divine command theory, the extent of that support should not be exaggerated; for "a

---

15   Thomas Aquinas, *The Summa Theologica*. New York: Benziger Bros, 1947, I–II, Q. 100, a. 8.

16   Ibid., my emphasis.

few particular cases in which moral statuses do or would depend upon divine commands might be exceptional. . . . They do not show that God is the sole source of moral obligation." (Quinn 1990b: 359) I would only add that not only are these cases by themselves insufficient to show that *all* moral obligations depend upon God's will, they are not (if one doubts their historicity) sufficient to show that *any* *actual* obligation derives its moral status from God's commanding it. The most these stories establish is that (almost?) any act (taking the life of one's beloved child, for example) *could* be made obligatory by God's command, and that (almost?) any act (such as sparing her life) *could* be made non-obligatory by a divine command not to do it. While this conclusion isn't trivial, the support it provides for divine command theory seems fairly weak.

The Love Commandment and Christian Practice

The Love Commandment

Philip Quinn believes that another argument for divine command morality can be derived from Jesus' injunction to love our neighbor as ourselves. His argument is essentially this. Not only is the love commandment's *content* (loving others as we love ourselves) central to Christian ethics, it is imperative that that content be expressed in the *form of a command*.

Quinn's first point can be easily granted. Yet why insist on the second? "To a first approximation," because "the love of neighbor of which Jesus speaks is unnatural for humans in their present condition. . . . It must therefore be an obligatory love with the feel of something that represents a curb or check on our natural desires and predilections." A comparison with Kant may be helpful. Kant thought that, because of the drag imposed on the will by our desire for happiness and our other natural inclinations, the moral law necessarily appears to us as a command or imperative—something we ought to follow but are strongly tempted not to. Christian ethics presents a particularly salient instance of Kant's point. For the tension between our inclinations and the love requirement is even more acute than that between our natural inclinations and the moral law's demand for truthfulness, say, or benevolence.[17] Why is it so acute? Quinn answers this question by appealing to Søren Kierkegaard, who "has seen with greater clarity" than any other Christian thinker "just how radical the demands of love of neighbor are."[18]

---

17   But *is* it more acute than the tension between our desire for happiness and the moral law's demand for *moral purity*, that is, for the will's perfect conformity to the moral law? This is at least doubtful.

18   Philip L. Quinn, "The Primacy of God's Will in Christian Ethics," *Philosophical Perspectives* 6 (1992), p. 504. Henceforth Quinn 1992.

In the first place, because "the command tells us that the neighbor is to be loved as we love ourselves, everyone . . . ought to be regarded as just as near to us as we are to ourselves. . . . [E]very human, including one's beloved, one's friend and one's very self is" (that is, should be) "at the same distance from one as one's worst enemy or millions of people with whom one has had no contact." Since Christian love is completely "impartial" or indiscriminate, it can't be based on preference or liking, or on objectively valuable properties which one person has and another lacks. As a result, neighbor love has no basis in our natural inclinations or affections and, indeed, runs counter to them. Quinn then argues as follows: since our natural affections are limited in scope,[19] "only a dutiful love"—a love that is "a matter of duty or obligation"—"can be sufficiently extensive in scope to embrace everyone without distinction." (Quinn 1992: 505–7)

In the second place, erotic love and friendship are "vulnerable to changes in their objects." For example, Aristotle argues that in the best sort of friendship each friend loves the other for his virtue. As a result, friendship dies if one's friend loses his virtue or if one outstrips him in virtue. Again, an erotic love based on the beloved's beauty and sweetness of deposition won't survive their loss. "[O]nly a dutiful love can be invulnerable" to changes like these. (Quinn 1992: 506–7)

How forceful is Quinn's argument? One might wonder whether the requirements of the love commandment are as "unnatural" as he thinks. Mark Murphy, for example, concedes that "natural practical" rationality[20] can't show that we are morally obligated to meet the love requirement, but nonetheless insists that living "as that precept dictates is, in itself, a reasonable commitment: the reasons to live this way are simply the goods to be promoted in all of the persons capable of enjoying those goods."[21]

But this isn't convincing. In the first place, even if there are reasons for living this way, they may not be sufficiently strong to trump those for not living as the precept dictates—our desire for our own happiness, or the fact that some people have few or no objectively valuable properties, our liking for some people and not others, and the like. In the second, Murphy's remarks aren't sufficient to show that commitment to love as the requirement dictates is reasonable for men and women who live in a *fallen* world, a world where most people will *not* adhere to it. (Cf. Hume's argument that a commitment to justice is unreasonable in a world in which,

---

19   Writers such as Jean-Jacques Rousseau and Francis Hutcheson have argued that not only are other regarding impulses such as pity natural; we can pity those we neither esteem nor are attracted to. But, as Aristotle points out, pity is *not* unrestricted in scope. We only pity those whose sufferings we regard as undeserved or disproportionate to any fault they have committed. Unlike neighbor love, it is not totally indiscriminate.

20   That is, rationality unassisted by revelation.

21   Murphy, *Divine Authority*, p. 186.

because of extreme scarcity or extreme selfishness, or both, most people will not act justly.)[22] Murphy's objection thus fails.

Another objection is more telling, however. While Quinn's argument may show that neighbor love should be regarded as *obligatory* or a matter of *duty*, it doesn't clearly show that it should be regarded as (literally) *commanded*. To convince us of *that* we must already be persuaded that moral obligations are best construed as divine commands; that is, we must already be persuaded that divine command theory is correct. The argument is thus circular.

Nor is it sufficient to argue that, because neighbor love is unnatural, God would command us to love our neighbor if he wished us to do so. That there may be good reasons for God's commanding neighbor love doesn't entail that there are good reasons for thinking that God's commanding neighbor love *constitutes* or *brings it about* that neighbor love is obligatory; that is, it does not entail that there are good reasons for divine command theory.

Christian Practice

Quinn also appeals to a consideration adduced by Janine Idziak. "Christian [devotional] practice emphasizes the theme of conformity to the divine will." (Quinn 2000: 59) For example, Thomas à Kempis's *Imitation of Christ* "depicts Christ counseling a disciple 'to learn perfect self surrender, and to accept My will without argument or complaint.' ... The colonial American saint Elizabeth Seton enjoins that 'the first purpose of our daily work is to do the will of God; secondly, to do it in the manner he wills; and thirdly, to do it because it is his will.'" The Presbyterian manual of *Daily Prayer* contains examples like these: "'Eternal God, send your Holy Spirit into our hearts, to direct and rule us according to your will.' ... 'May we live according to your holy will revealed in Jesus Christ.' ... 'Purify our desires that we may seek your will.'" And so on. Idziak concludes that divine command theory "can be defended as a formalization of an important theme of Christian spiritual life, namely, conformity to the divine will."[23] Or as Quinn puts it, "theological voluntarism in ethics expresses this theme at the level of moral theory. ... the fact that conformity to the will of God is an important theme in Christian devotional and liturgical practices is a good reason for Christians to adopt a moral theory in which the will of God is a source of obligations." And non-Christian

---

22   Murphy expresses surprise that Quinn doesn't discuss the fact that secular moral theories like utilitarianism are equally demanding, and in the same way. But, in the first place, they are *not* equally demanding if only altruistic *actions*, and not altruistic *attitudes*, are required or morally obligatory. And, in the second, it is precisely *because* the demands made by utilitarianism are so extraordinary or "unnatural" that so many find utilitarianism unreasonable.

23   Janine Marie Idziak, "Divine Command Ethics," in Philip Quinn and Charles Taliaferro, eds, *A Companion to the Philosophy of Religion*. Cambridge, MA and Oxford: Blackwell, 1997, pp. 45–7.

theists could undoubtedly find similar reasons for embracing divine command theory in their own practices. (Quinn 2000: 60)

As in the previous argument, the facts adduced for explanation are undeniable.[24] What is less clear is the conclusion that should be drawn from them. Christian devotional and liturgical practice meshes neatly with an ethics of divine command. The question is, however, whether there aren't *other* theological views which fit the facts as easily. That theists have good reasons for conforming their will to God's will, or (more strongly) that they are *morally obligated* to do so, doesn't entail that God's will *makes* what we do to conform to God's will obligatory. Perhaps we should conform our will to God's, not because he commands it, but because his will is the *paradigm* of a morally good will (Kant), or because he is the *exemplar* of moral goodness. (We will examine a version of the second suggestion at the end of this chapter.) The point is this: while theological voluntarism may explain or illuminate the Christian emphasis on conformity to God's will, it isn't obvious that other theological views can't do an equally good job of accounting for it. If they can, we are not entitled to infer that divine command theory offers the best explanation of the facts in question.

A Cumulative Case for Divine Command Theory?

None of the arguments examined so far is coercive. Even when they are valid, their premises can be questioned, some are susceptible to charges of circularity, and alternative explanations can be provided of the phenomena which furnish the arguments' data. These criticisms may miss the point, however. In "Divine Command Theory," Quinn confesses that he is "now inclined to doubt that constructing deductive arguments is the most promising way of supporting theological voluntarism. ... [A] more fruitful approach is to support it by a cumulative case argument" that appeals to a number of the points adduced in the arguments discussed up to now in this chapter. (Quinn 2000: 57)

Cumulative case arguments attempt to justify their conclusion by introducing a variety of diverse considerations in support of it. When taken singly, none of them is sufficient to establish the conclusion. Yet taken together, they make an impressive case for it.

Cumulative case arguments are inferences to the best explanation. A hypothesis is accepted because it makes more sense of a range of data than its alternatives do. In the case that concerns us, the data include such things as God's independence and sovereignty, the "immoralities of the patriarchs," the love commandment, and theistic worship and spiritual practice; and the claim is that theological voluntarism

---

24 The "impossibly high" demands of the love requirement in the first case, a spiritual and liturgical practice which emphasizes conformity to the divine will in the second.

provides a more illuminating or satisfying account of these facts as a whole than alternative explanations do.

Inferences to the best explanation can be attacked by impugning the data. (Cumulative case arguments lose their force if the facts they purport to explain turn out to have been misdescribed or illusory.) But normally, the most effective way of defusing an inference to the best explanation is by showing that other hypotheses explain the relevant data as well or better. The question, then, is this: are there competing accounts of the relevant theological and ethical data which are at least as illuminating as divine command theory? If there are, then the cumulative case argument for theological voluntarism isn't compelling.

We will address this question in the last section of the chapter. But before doing so, it may be useful to examine a consideration which (to the best of my knowledge) has not been offered in support of divine command theory but can, I think, contribute to a cumulative case for it, namely, that the mere fact that God tells us to do something is a decisive reason for doing it.[25]

An Appeal to Divine Authority

Theological anti-voluntarists typically talk as if God's commands can't themselves be sufficient reasons for obedience. That God commands us to do A *is* a reason for doing it—but only because doing A is independently (of God's will) obligatory, and, being omniscient, God knows that it is; or because God will punish us if we don't do A and/or reward us if we do; or because we are independently (of God's will) obligated to obey God. This presupposes that, abstracting from other considerations, God's commanding something isn't *itself* a decisive reason for doing it. In other words, God lacks what Mark Murphy calls "practical authority." Showing that God *does* possess practical authority would therefore contribute to the case for theological voluntarism.

Murphy thinks this can't be done. Neither God's omniscience, omnipotence, nor perfect moral goodness entail that God possesses practical authority over rational beings. God's omniscience, for example, entails that he knows what we have decisive reasons for doing, and God's perfect moral goodness entails that he wouldn't tell us to do something when we lacked a decisive reason for doing it. But his omniscience and perfect moral goodness do not entail that his merely *telling* us to do something would *itself* constitute a decisive reason for doing it, and so doesn't entail that God enjoys practical authority.

---

25 Quinn and others have noted that the Old and New Testaments (and, I venture to say, the *Quran*) depict a God whose commands are themselves decisive reasons for doing what they prescribe. The datum that I will be discussing, however, is a bit different, namely, that the very concept of a maximally perfect being entails his having this kind of authority.

An appeal to omnipotence seems initially more promising. For if God can't provide us with a decisive reason for doing something by simply telling us to do it, then he lacks a power he apparently could have had,[26] and hence is not genuinely omnipotent. But while this argument has some force, it isn't decisive because it can be countered by another.

If practical authority is entailed by omnipotence, then, since omnipotence is an essential divine property, so too is practical authority. Yet if practical authority over rational beings *is* an essential divine property, then God can't create rational beings who are *not* under his authority. That is, God can't create rational beings for whom his commands are not themselves decisive reasons for obedience. He can't, for example, create rational beings who are under divine authority only if they freely consent to submit to him. But this too seems to be a limitation of God's power.

The rather obvious response to these arguments is that, whether or not it follows from omniscience, omnipotence, or perfect moral goodness, practical authority is *itself* a divine perfection—an excellence a maximally perfect being would necessarily have. Murphy marshals two proofs to show that this is a mistake, however. I shall argue that neither is compelling.

First Argument

Murphy's first argument is this:

1   Divine perfections must have an intrinsic maximum (upper limit).
2   Practical authority does not have an intrinsic maximum. Therefore,
3   Practical authority can't be a divine perfection.

Premise (1) is supported by two considerations. First, all non-controversial divine perfections (power, for instance, knowledge, and moral goodness) have an upper limit. Second (and more important), if a divine perfection *doesn't* have an upper limit, then it is possible for God to be more perfect than he is—and, in that case, he is not *maximally* perfect.

The second premise is also true. "The extent to which one is practically authoritative seems to depend on two factors: . . . the scope of the actions with respect to which one's dictates" are authoritative, and the number of beings over whom one exercises authority. The first may have an intrinsic maximum, namely, "the range of all actions open to a rational agent in any given situation." But the second does not since, for any number, n, of rational beings, there could always be more.[27]

In spite of Murphy's contentions, however, both premises are suspect. As for the first, some non-controversial divine perfections seem to lack intrinsic maxima.

---

26   And which others do have—drill sergeants, for example.
27   Mark C. Murphy, "Divine Authority and Divine Perfection," *International Journal for Philosophy of Religion* 49 (2001), p. 168.

Love appears to be an example. Murphy thinks it isn't: if "God's being loving involves God's just valuing each thing at least as much as it merits, then *being loving* possesses an intrinsic maximum [namely, valuing each thing at least as much as it deserves]. But if it involves God's loving things more than they merit, then I doubt that we should call this a divine perfection: for if this love is freely and gratuitously given, then it must be possible that God not love those beings in this way." If it is, then God would not have this "perfection" in some possible worlds. If he wouldn't, loving beings in this way isn't an excellence a perfect being *necessarily* has, and thus isn't an *essential* feature of our concept of a perfect being; that is, maximal perfection does not entail it.[28]

Yet even if Murphy is right about this, other alleged divine perfections without intrinsic maxima can't be so easily disposed of. Joy or bliss is an example. So too is the dissemination or diffusion of God's goodness *ad extra*.[29] Perfect moral goodness may also provide a counter-example to Murphy's claim. Murphy thinks that perfect moral goodness *does* have an upper limit, namely, "perfectly acting in accordance with true moral principles."[30] But if perfect moral goodness includes acting according to virtues such as generosity, it is *not* clear that it has an intrinsic maximum. No matter how generous God is, for example, he could always be more generous.

Furthermore, at least one plausible interpretation of maximal excellence is consistent with the rejection of Murphy's first premise. God, we might say, is unsurpassable in the sense that (1) for each perfection which has an intrinsic maximum, God exhibits it to the utmost degree, and (2) for each perfection that lacks an intrinsic maximum, God exhibits it to a superlative degree and is such that no *other* possible being[31] exhibits it to a greater degree. On this construal of maximal perfection, it is simply false that all divine excellences must have upper limits.

The second premise is equally suspect. For example, one might argue that "the extent of practical authority is not an additive notion but a *completeness* notion." Since "in every world, God has authority over every rational being in that world, . . . God has an equal maximal amount of practical authority in every world." Alternatively, one could "relativize the notion of maximum authority to each possible world:" in each possible world, one "has maximum authority possible in that world," namely, "authority over all created rational beings in that world . . . with

---

28　Ibid., p. 169.
29　The latter is controversial, however, since (*pace* Jonathan Edwards [see my "Edwards, William Rowe, and the Necessity of Creation"] and Norman Kretzmann [see his "A General Problem of Creation: Why would God Create Anything at All?," in Scott MacDonald, ed., *Being and Goodness* (Ithaca: Cornell University Press, 1991)]) it is controversial that God necessarily diffuses his goodness *ad extra*. But if he does, there appears to be no upper limit to the self-diffusion of his internal goodness.
30　Murphy, "Divine Authority and Divine Perfection," p. 169.
31　That is, no possible being other than God.

respect to all actions." The intrinsic maximum of practical authority would thus be "having [the] maximal authority possible in a world in *every* world."[32]

Murphy thinks neither approach is satisfactory. The first implies "that [1] a person who is practically authoritative over two out of two people has" more "practical authority than one who has practical authority over 4.99999 billion out of 5 billion people" (since the former's practical authority is complete and the latter's is not); and that (2) A, who has authority "over no one at all" in a world, because there are no other rational beings in that world, has as much authority as B, who has authority over 5 billion out of "5 billion people in a world."[33] The "completeness criterion" also implies that (3) a being who has practical authority over all created rational beings in a world can lose complete authority "simply by the emergence of rational life on the other side of the universe," or that a being who lacks complete practical authority can gain it "by killing those not under [its] authority."[34]

The second alternative fares no better. God's possession of the relativized property of maximal perfection "requires only that *if* a created rational being should come into existence, *then* God will have complete rational authority over" it. This has two "unhappy" implications. First, since God might not choose to create rational beings, God could "have the perfection of practical authority without actually having any authority." And second, "for any finite amount of practical authority that God possesses in a possible world, it seems that if that world were actual, we could say truly that God could have had a hundred times as much authority as God actually has [since he could have created a hundred times as many rational beings as he has], while asserting in the same breath that . . . God fully possesses the perfection of practical authority."[35]

I do not find these consequences as absurd as Murphy does. Some divine perfections admit of a distinction between their possession and their exercise. Others do not. No meaningful distinction can be drawn between the possession of immutability or simplicity, for example, and their exercise. But we *can* distinguish between God's creative power and its exercise, or between his goodness and its products or manifestations. In these cases, the exercises or products or manifestations are not the proper measure of the perfection in question. That God creates 5 billion rational beings in possible world w1 and 150 billion rational beings in possible world w2 doesn't entail that God has more creative power in w2 than in w1 since, while God has created 5 billion rational beings in w1, he could have created more. Again, God

---

32   Murphy, "Divine Authority and Divine Perfection," pp. 171–2.

33   A being's practical authority in a world is complete if, for any other rational being in that world, it has practical authority over it. Since one's authority over an *empty* set of created rational beings would be complete and hence maximal (for there would be *no* rational being in that set over whom one *wouldn't* be practically authoritative), A's and B's practical authority are both maximal.

34   Murphy, "Divine Authority and Divine Perfection," p. 171.

35   Ibid., pp. 172–3.

may exercise or manifest more power in some worlds that in others (by performing more miracles, for example, or gratuitously redeeming more people). Or the products and tokens of his goodness may be better or more striking in some worlds than in others. It doesn't follow that God is more powerful or more good in the former worlds than he is in the latter.[36]

Now practical authority, too, seems to admit of a distinction between possession and exercise.[37] If it does, then the fact that (because there are fewer rational beings in possible world w1 than in possible world w2) God *exercises* less practical authority in w1 than in w2 doesn't show that he *possesses* less practical authority (that his practical authority is less perfect) in w1 than in w2.

Since its second premise is as dubious as its first, Murphy's first proof that practical authority is not itself a divine perfection is unsuccessful. He has a second argument, however.

Second Argument

"Practical authority is had in relation to contingent objects. . . . If there had been no created rational beings, God would have lacked practical authority. Since God might have lacked practical authority" then, since he possess his perfections essentially, practical authority "cannot be a divine perfection . . . " Nor will it help to argue that since perfect goodness is necessarily self-diffusive, God necessarily creates some rational beings or other. "For [on this view] God's possessing practical authority over created rational beings is logically posterior to there being created rational beings" and this, in turn, "is logically posterior, given the self-diffusiveness argument for God's necessary creativity, to God's being absolutely perfect. God's possessing practical authority, then, is *logically posterior* to God's perfection," and so cannot be included "*among* the divine perfections."[38]

I do not think that these considerations are sound. In the first place, "has practical authority," in Murphy's argument, must be taken in the sense of "exercises practical authority," and the fact (if it is one) that the *exercise* of practical authority is not an essential property of God does not entail that its *possession* isn't. Moreover, similar arguments would show that God's love and the communication of his goodness to others aren't divine perfections since they, too, require the existence of contingent beings.[39] And this is surely counter-intuitive.

---

36   If for any world God creates, he could have created a better (as Aquinas and others have claimed), then the fact that he could have produced more good than he has does not entail that his goodness is less than perfect. (See my "Jonathan Edwards, William Rowe, and the Necessity of Creation.")

37   It clearly does if we relativize it to possible worlds.

38   Murphy, "Divine Authority and Divine Perfection," p. 170. My emphases.

39   This argument is complicated by Trinitarian considerations, however. If God is triune, then the Father, for example, loves, and communicates his goodness to, the Son; and the need for contingent objects of God's love and desire to communicate himself

In the second place, it isn't clear that the self-diffusiveness argument *does* imply that God's practical authority is logically posterior to his perfection (and so can't be a part of it). It is true that God's having practical authority over created rational beings entails (and thus logically presupposes) that there are created rational beings; and that the latter entails (and thus logically presupposes) that God has diffused himself *ad extra*. And since God's necessary diffusion of himself *ad extra* is an *aspect* of his perfection (according to the self-diffusion argument), God's practical authority over created rational beings entails (and thus logically presupposes) the divine perfection.[40]

But on the self-diffusion view, the entailments *also* run the other way. God's necessary self-diffusion entails the existence of created rational beings; and, *pace* Murphy, advocates of the self-diffusion argument think that the existence of created rational beings entails that God has practical authority over them.[41] If they are right, then God's perfections entail his practical authority. Yet surely any excellence entailed by a divine perfection is *itself* a divine perfection, and hence an aspect or part of it.[42] It therefore is *not* logically posterior to it.

I conclude, then, that Murphy has not succeeded in showing that practical authority isn't a divine perfection. If it is, however, then the fact that our concept of God implicitly includes practical authority can contribute to the cumulative case argument for theological voluntarism. Since anti-voluntarist theistic theories typically assume that God does *not* have practical authority, reasons for thinking that he does buttress the case for theological voluntarism.

Is Divine Command Theory the Best Account of the Relevant Data?

The cumulative case for theological voluntarism is compelling only if theological voluntarism is more illuminating than other accounts of the relevant theological and ethical data. Is it? To bring out some of the issues that are at stake, we will conclude this chapter by briefly considering a recent proposal of Linda Zagzebski's.

---

becomes less obvious. It should be noted, though, that Jonathan Edwards thought that the Son, too, must communicate his goodness, and can do so only by creating contingent rational beings.

40 In a footnote which was dropped when "Divine Authority and Divine Perfection" was incorporated into chapter 3 of *Divine Authority*, Murphy identified God's perfection with the "totality" of his perfections. ("Divine Authority and Divine Perfection," p. 177, fn 19) If God's perfection and the totality of his perfections are identical, and God's self-diffusion is a divine perfection, then his self-diffusion is clearly a *part* of his perfection.

41 This is clearly the view of Jonathan Edwards, who developed one of the more sophisticated versions of the self-diffusion argument.

42 If God's self-diffusion *is* a divine perfection, as advocates of the self-diffusion argument maintain, then it is obviously included in the *totality* of divine perfections. See note 40.

Zagzebski calls her view "divine motivation theory." "Divine motivation theory makes the ground of what is morally good and morally right God's motives rather than God's will." Divine motivational states "such as love and compassion . . . are components of God's virtues," and "constitute the metaphysical basis for moral value."[43]

Divine motivation theory is "a virtue theory because the moral properties of persons [namely, virtues and vices] are more basic than the moral properties of acts and outcomes." "A virtue is an enduring trait consisting of a good" motive "and reliable success in bringing about the aim, if any, of the good motive." A vice is an enduring human trait consisting in a bad motive and reliable success in bringing about the aim, if any, of the bad motive. "Outcomes [and acts] get their moral value by their relation to good and bad motivations." Good acts, for example, are the sort of acts which express the good emotional dispositions that are constituents of the virtues.[44]

Divine motivation theory is not only a virtue theory, however. It is also "exemplarist because the moral properties of persons, acts, and outcomes are defined via an indexical reference to an exemplar of a good person." "The paradigmatically good person is God. . . . God's motives are perfectly good and human motives are good in so far as they are like the divine motives as those motives would be expressed in finite and embodied beings." Human virtues are good personal traits that "imitate God's virtues" in the sense that they are the way those virtues "would be expressed by human beings in human circumstances."[45]

Zagzebski believes that divine motivation theory has several advantages over divine command theory. For example, in divine command theory, "God's own goodness and the rightness of God's own acts . . . are not connected to divine commands because God does not give commands to himself." Divine motivation theory, on the other hand, "has the theoretical advantage of providing a unitary theory of all [moral] evaluative properties, divine as well as human:" "Both divine and human goodness are explained in terms of good motives, and the goodness of human motives is derived from the goodness of the divine motives." And "for those who prefer virtue ethics to deontological ethics the theory" has the added "advantage of being a form of virtue theory."[46]

Whether divine motivation theory adequately accounts for the data canvased in this chapter is another matter. It does seem to do an equally good job of protecting God's sovereignty and independence. If God's motivational states are the meta-

---

43   Linda Zagzebski, "Religion and Morality," in William J. Wainwright, ed., *The Oxford Handbook for Philosophy of Religion*. New York: Oxford University Press, 2004, p. 357. See also her "Perfect Goodness and Divine Motivation Theory," *Midwest Studies in Philosophy* 21 (1997), pp. 296–309 and *Divine Motivation Theory*. Cambridge: Cambridge University Press, 2004.

44   "Religion and Morality," p. 358.

45   Ibid.

46   Ibid., pp. 360f.

physical basis of the goodness or badness of persons and the rightness or wrong-ness of their actions, then the fact that certain human motivational states are good and others are bad, and some human actions are morally right while others are morally wrong, is not metaphysically independent of God.

Divine motivational theory also illuminates the centrality of love in Christian ethics. If self-giving love is God's most salient motivational state, and if human virtue consists in imaging forth God's virtue, then the Christian emphasis on neighbor love is precisely what one would expect if divine motivation theory were true. Whether it can provide an illuminating account of the fact that neighbor love is *commanded*, however, is more doubtful.

It is also unclear that divine motivation theory has the resources for making sense of the "immoralities" of the patriarchs or for illuminating the fact that practical authority is a divine perfection. Both seem to cohere better with divine command theory.

In addition, the emphasis placed on obedience to God seems more at home in divine command theory than in divine motivation theory considered simply as such. A specifically *Christian* divine motivation theory may be able to do so[47] since Christians believe that God was made man in Jesus of Nazareth and hence *does* exhibit the virtue of obedience. In mirroring Jesus' obedience, the Christian's obedience therefore mirrors God's own obedience. A move of this sort is not available to *non*-Christian theists, however.

Finally, the plausibility of divine motivation theory depends on the plausibility of *virtue* theory. Whether virtue theory can adequately account for our sense of moral *obligation*, however, is controversial.[48]

What conclusion should be drawn from these considerations? Divine motivation theory does have some advantages over divine command theory. (For example, it provides a unitary account of divine and human virtue whereas divine command theory does not.) But there are also disadvantages. The "immoralities" of the patriarchs, the fact that neighbor love is commanded, God's practical authority, and the emphasis placed on obedience to God's will in both Christian and *non*-Christian theism seem to comport better with divine command theory than with divine motivation theory. On the other hand, divine motivation theory hasn't yet been worked out with the same thoroughness as divine command theory.[49] When it has, the apparent advantages of the latter may turn out to be illusory.

---

47   As Zagzebski points out.

48   Zagzebski attempts to show that it can in chapter 4 of her *Divine Motivation Theory*. Whether one regards her attempt as successful or not will partly depend on one's attitude towards Kant's accounts of moral duty and moral obligation, however, since the latter don't comport well with virtue theory.

49   Divine command theory has been subjected to centuries of intense critical scrutiny and, as a consequence, has become increasingly refined. Divine motivation theory is a bold new hypothesis which hasn't yet been subjected to the same kind of extensive scrutiny.

Furthermore, there are *other* theistic ethical theories to consider. Natural law theory is an example though, in my view, it is less promising than either divine command theory or divine motivation theory. Natural law theory attempts to derive "moral precepts from true statements about human nature," truths about what human beings desire or aim at. But as John Hare points out, human nature is fallen. As a result, our desires are misdirected and we don't aim at the good. Aristotle's ethical theory provides an example. Aristotle thought that we naturally (and legitimately) desire power and prestige. We may agree with Aristotle that we *do* desire them. *Pace* Aristotle, however, they are not part of the human good. For one thing, they are "competitive goods" that "can be possessed by some only if they are not possessed, or are possessed less, by others," and are thus "objectionable to a supporter of altruism or even impartial justice."[50] For another, they are incompatible with Christian neighbor love, and the theist's emphasis on humility and submission to God's will.[51]

The upshot of these reflections is this. At this point in time, it is not unreasonable to prefer theological voluntarism to other forms of theistic ethical theory. Because the issues are complicated, however, and more work needs to be done, the case for divine command theory is far from closed.

---

50   John Hare, *God's Call: Moral Realism, God's Commands, and Human Autonomy.* Grand Rapids, MI: William B. Eerdmans, 2001, pp. 54–5, 30.

51   It is worth noting that a pursuit of these goods is also incompatible with Buddhist selflessness and *karunā* (compassion). The tension between natural law theory and Buddhist ethics is at least as great as that between natural law theory and the demands of Christianity.

PART III
HUMAN MORALITY AND
RELIGIOUS REQUIREMENTS

CHAPTER 9

Religious Ethics and Rational Morality

In arguing for "continued public support of religion," Timothy Dwight, President of Yale and leader of the Second Great Awakening, declared: "Morality, as every sober man who knows anything of the subject discerns with a glance, is merely a branch of Religion; and where there is no religion, there is no morality . . . [W]here God is not worshiped . . . justice, kindness, and truth, the great hinges on which free Society hangs, will be unpracticed, because there are no motives to the practice, or sufficient forces to resist the passions of men."[1] Dwight's opinion was widely held in the eighteenth and nineteenth centuries, and continues to be expressed by significant portions of the American public. The view has not lacked dissenters, however. Responding to Cleanthes's claim that, because it "is so strong and necessary a security to morals," "religion, however corrupted, is . . . better than no religion at all," Philo replies that if religion were "so salutary to society," then history would not abound "so much with accounts of its pernicious consequences on public affairs. Factions, civil wars, persecutions, . . . oppression . . . ; these are the dismal consequences which always attend its prevalency over the minds of men. If the religious spirit be ever mentioned in any historical narration, we are sure to meet afterwards with a detail of the miseries which attend it."[2]

So does religion support or, on the contrary, undermine morality? The third and final part of this book explores these issues by examining three topics. The present chapter discusses tensions between certain religious assessments and requirements and the assessments and requirements of any purely natural or rational morality.[3] Its first section examines the conflict between Buddhist and Christian pacifism and rational morality. Its second section defends the claim that, from a theistic (or at least Christian) perspective, virtues that aren't rooted in the love of God are no more than "splendid vices." Chapter 10 examines the possibility that God might

---

1 *Travels; in New-England and New York*, vol. 4. New Haven, 1822, p. 403. Quoted in Robert T. Handy, *A Christian America: Protestant Hopes and Historical Realities*, 2nd edn, New York: Oxford University Press, 1984, p. 21.

2 David Hume, *Dialogues Concerning Natural Religion*, ed. with intro. by Norman Kemp Smith. Indianapolis: Bobbs-Merrill, *c.* 1947, pp. 219–20. It is usually assumed that Philo speaks here for Hume.

3 By a purely natural or rational morality, I mean any system of morality based exclusively on human reason, natural feelings, desires, and sentiments, and facts that can be acknowledged by both naturalists and supernaturalists. In what follows I shall use "rational morality" as shorthand for the phrase "purely natural or rational morality." Natural law, moral sense, Kantian, and utilitarian moral theories are all rational moralities in this sense.

command actions which seem clearly *im*moral, and Chapter 11 explores the ambiguous relations between religious mysticism, on the one hand, and morality, on the other. What will emerge from Part III is that the connections between religion and morality are not as straightforward as either Dwight or Hume supposed.

Buddhist and Christian Pacifism and the Demands of Rational Morality

Theravāda Buddhism and War[4]

Sallie B. King begins a recent paper by stating that "Buddhism has a problem with respect to war."[5] The five precepts are "the foundation of Theravāda Buddhist morality." The first is abstention "from the taking of life." (King 1) One important reason for doing so is that killing has negative karmic consequences for the person who kills. So killing is "not only . . . morally wrong;" it is "bad for oneself." It "is also inefficacious." As the *Dhammapada* says, "not by enmity are enmities quelled . . . By the absence of enmity are they quelled. This is an ancient truth." Moreover, Buddhist practice, if engaged in "seriously and over time," tends to "make one less and less capable of intentionally causing any harm to any sentient being." By weakening "feelings of fear, anger, enmity, and separation or alienation" from others, and by strengthening "feelings of universal benevolence . . . and compassion," one becomes less and less capable of violence. (King 1–2)

Even so, "Buddhist countries have always had armies and Buddhists have in large numbers always served in those armies and killed other human beings." Furthermore, Asoka is generally regarded as the closest historical approximation to the *cakravartin* or "ideal Buddhist monarch who rules by Dharma" (that is, "by Buddhist principles"). It is therefore significant that while Asoka renounces aggressive warfare upon converting to Buddhism, "he publicly announces to the [peoples in the remote sections of the conquered territory] that . . . despite his repentance" for the suffering caused by the aggressive wars he had undertaken before his conversion, he will exercise his "power to punish . . . in order to induce them to desist from their crimes and escape execution." Again, in the *Cakkavatti Sihananda Sutta* of the *Digha Nikaya*, the Buddha advises "an aspiring cakravartin [to] . . . 'establish guard, ward, and protection according to Dhamma for your own household, your troops, your nobles and vassals, for Brahmins and householders, . . . for beasts and birds.'" (King 2–4)

---

4   Theravāda Buddhism is the only surviving school of Hīnayāna Buddhism. It is the dominant form of Buddhism in Southeast Asia.

5   Sallie B. King, "Buddhism and War," delivered at the Annual Meeting of the American Academy of Religion, Toronto, 2002, p. 1. All quotations in this section are from this paper. A version of it will appear in King's forthcoming *For the Sake of All Beings: The Social Ethics of Engaged Buddhism* (Honolulu: University Press of Hawaii).

Does Buddhist participation in war and the *cakravartin* ideal imply, then, that Buddhists are justified in exercising violence to repel unjust aggression and punish evil doers? While it may seem to, "it is significant that no Buddhist thinker has ever produced" a just war theory (King 4). And, in fact, "the Buddha states in the *Samyutta Nikaya* that a soldier fighting with the intention of killing others who is himself killed in the course of battle will be born in the 'Battle-Slain Hell'" (King 5).

There are, nonetheless, "two examples . . . of Buddhist attempts to" at least "address the karma problem as part of an effort to justify war." The first is found in the Sri Lanka chronicle *Mahavamsa*. A Buddhist king is deeply distressed by the large number of casualties caused by his war against a Hindu Tamil king. Enlightened *arhats*[6] tell him not to worry, however, since his "deed presents no obstacle on [his] path to heaven." Only two Buddhists were slain. "'The rest were wicked men of wrong view who died like (or: considered as) beasts' . . . In other words," because the Hindu dead were not really human, no more bad karma is generated by killing them than would have been generated by killing animals. Furthermore, even the negative karma caused by killing the two Buddhists is counterbalanced by the fact that the king's war strengthened Buddhism in Sri Lanka. What is significant is that while some contemporary Sinhalese Buddhists have used this text to justify the government's war against the Tamil separatists, other Sinhalese Buddhists have opposed their stance, and "outside Sri Lanka, the *Mahavamsa* has no authority." The second example is that of the Thai Buddhist monk Kittividdho, who "stated in 1976 [that] 'killing Communists is not demeritorious [because] such killing is not the killing of persons . . . [but the killing of the] Devil.'" It is important to note, however, that "the Supreme Patriarch of Thai Buddhism denounced Kittividdho's statements and there were attempts to have him disciplined." (King 5–7)

The fact is that Theravāda Buddhists have not developed a just war theory and, given the importance of the first precept, it is difficult to see just how they could do so. There are some paths contemporary Buddhists might pursue, however.

One would be to develop a just war theory "drawing upon the" importance "of intention in determining karmic outcomes," and the notion of "degrees of violence." As one modern Buddhist points out, "even if we take pride in being vegetarian . . . we have to acknowledge that the water in which we boil our vegetables contains many tiny microorganisms. We can not be completely nonviolent, but by being vegetarian, we are going in the direction of nonviolence. If we want to head north we can use the North Star to guide us, but it is impossible to arrive at the North Star. Our effort is only to proceed in that direction. Any one can practice some nonviolence, even army generals"—by avoiding killing innocent people, for example.[7] By using concepts like these, Buddhists might be able to construct a just war

---

6   An arhat is a follower of the Buddha who has succeeded in putting the Buddha's teachings into practice and achieved enlightenment.

7   Thich Nhat Hanh, *For a Future to be Possible: Commentaries on the Five Wonderful Precepts*. Berkeley, CA: Parallax Press, 1993, pp. 16–17. Quoted in King 10.

theory—perhaps limiting the military's role to defense against unjust aggression and international peacekeeping. Alternatively, Buddhists can "hold fast to principled nonviolence and give up the idea that Buddhism is compatible with national rule." Or they could try "to pioneer ways to have national rule without a military. The Dalai Lama, for example, has proposed making of Tibet a Zone of Peace free of any militarization whatsoever." (King 14–15)

Realization of the third possibility, however, depends on the forbearance of other nations, or on the willingness of other national states to use force to preserve its nonmilitarized status. The first seems unrealistic and the second indirectly involves the demilitarized nation in violence. By relying on the armies of other nations for protection, it is complicit in their implicit threat of force.

The first alternative is also problematic from a Buddhist perspective. One's intention is still to kill, and even defensive wars and peacekeeping missions can result in large numbers of casualties. Implicitly comparing the deaths caused by NATO's intervention in Kosovo, for example, to the destruction of the microorganisms incurred by boiling water to cook one's vegetables trivializes them. Moreover, on the Buddhist view, *any* killing remains harmful, and generates bad consequences for the killer.

The second alternative seems most consistent with Buddhist principles but, unfortunately, fails to come to grips with the fact that the refusal to intervene militarily can sometimes result in even greater suffering. The recent genocide in Rwanda is an example. Christian pacifists, on the other hand, *have* been forced to address these issues since the Christian tradition, as a whole, has sanctioned the occasional use of violence, and a number of its ablest thinkers have developed principled reasons for Christians sometimes engaging in it. As a consequence of this controversy, both Christian pacifism and theological critiques of it have been developed with considerable sophistication. We will discuss this debate in the next section.

Christian Pacifism and its Critics

The Early Church   It has often been said that, up to the time of Constantine, the Christian Church was largely pacifist. Ronald H. Baintain is typical of those who believe that, on the whole, this is true. "Until the decade A. D. 170–80" there is little explicit evidence of Christian military service. "From then on the references to Christian soldiers increase." Their "numbers cannot be computed," although "the most extensive Christian participation in warfare" appears to have been along the empire's eastern frontier. Not surprisingly, "the period in which we have no evidence of Christians in the ranks is also the period in which there is no specific prohibition of such service." After 180 there are "a number of more or less explicit condemnations of military service" in both East and West, although "the greatest objection to military service appears to have been in the Hellenistic East," where some Christians were actively participating in warfare. "The Christians in North

Africa," on the other hand, "were divided" on the issue, and it may be significant that "the Roman Church in the late second and third centuries did not forbid epitaphs recording the military profession."[8] What is *clearly* significant is that "Celsus, the pagan critic of Christianity," assumes that Christians won't serve in the military, and condemns them for not doing so (Baintain 68). Celsus's assumption is borne out by the witness of a number of the early church fathers.

Tertullian, for example, condemns voluntary enlistment, and affirms "that many upon conversion withdrew from military service." He also argued that even though "Christians were sufficiently numerous to offer successful resistance to persecuting emperors," they counted "it better to be slain than to slay." (Baintain 70, 73) Again, "Lactantius, writing [in] A. D. 304–5 asserted: 'God in prohibiting killing discountenances not only brigandage, which is contrary to human laws, but also that which men regard as legal. Participation in warfare therefore will not be legitimate to a just man'" (Baintain 73). And Minucius Felix exclaims: "'It is not right for us either to see or hear a man being killed' ... Arnobius thought it better to pour out one's own blood than to stain one's hands ... with the blood of another." And the Canons of Hippolytus state "that 'a soldier of civil authority must be taught not to kill men and to refuse to do so if he is commanded.'" (Baintain 78)

Perhaps the clearest witness to early Christian pacifism is Origen's. "The Jews ... were allowed to take up arms in defense of their possessions and to kill their enemies" but "the Christian Lawgiver ... made homicide absolutely forbidden." He "taught that his disciples were never justified in taking such action against a man even if he were the greatest wrongdoer. [Jesus] considered it contrary to his divinely inspired legislation to approve any kind of homicide whatsoever." (*Against Celsus* 3:8). Again, "to those who ask about our origin and our founder we reply that we have come in response to Jesus' commands to beat into ploughshares the rational swords of conflict and arrogance and to change into pruning hooks those spears that we used to fight with. For we no longer take up the sword against any nation, nor do we learn the art of war any more" (*Against Celsus* 5:33).[9]

What was the basis of the church fathers' condemnation of warfare? Some scholars have suggested that the antimilitarism of the early church was fueled by the eschatological expectation of the Lord's immanent return, and a consequent indifference to the social and political consequences of refusing to fight. But as Baintain points out, the trouble with this view is that these millenarist expectations were no longer common in the period in question (AD 100 to 300). Other scholars insist that the principal reason for the church's opposition to military service was its horror of idolatry. And indeed, "the cult of the deified emperor was particularly

---

8   Roland H. Baintain, *Christian Attitudes Toward War and Peace*. London: Hodder and Stoughton, 1961, pp. 71–2. Henceforth Baintain.

9   Quoted in John Helgeland, Robert J. Daly, and J. Partout Burns, *Christians and the Military: The Early Experience*. Philadelphia: Fortress Press, 1985, p. 39. Henceforth Helgeland.

prevalent in the camps . . . On the other hand, Tertullian indicated that the problem was not so acute" for the common "soldier, who was not called on to actually perform a sacrifice." Nor would the church "have permitted its members—as it did—to remain in the service even in peace time . . . if idolatry had been unavoidable." (Baintain 73–4)

On the whole, according to Baintain, the position of the early church was this: in peacetime, the Roman army more or less functioned as a police force and the early church did not, by and large, repudiate the state or the state's exercise of its police powers.[10] Moreover, the first few centuries of the Christian era were largely peaceful except on the empire's frontiers. It was therefore quite possible to pass one's life in the *army* without ever being called upon to participate in *battle*. Christians could therefore be permitted to serve in the military. They should, however, refuse to engage in battle. Thus, after his conversion, Martin of Tours "remained in the army for two years, until an actual battle was imminent, and only then declined longer to serve." (Baintain 81)

Views like Baintain's have been widely endorsed. In *Christians and the Military*, however, John Helgeland, Robert J. Daly, and J. Partout Burns contend that the case for the early church's pacifism has been vastly overstated. They argue, for example, that (contrary to Baintain) the early church's *primary* objection to military service was idolatry, and that there was no systematic or concerted attempt to argue for pacifism.

Consider Tertullian, who is often cited as a major early pacifist. In his *Apology*, Tertullian claims that "without ceasing" Christians pray "for all our emperors . . . We pray . . . for security to the empire, for *brave armies*, a faithful senate, a virtuous people, the world at rest." (Quoted in Helgeland 21, my emphasis) Moreover, it is significant that one of Tertullian's most important discussions of military service occurs in his *Treatise on Idolatry*. Helgeland, Daly, and Burns convincingly argue that Tertullian's discussion in the *Treatise* reveals that his principal objection to military service was *not* that it involved killing but that it involved the soldier in idolatry. Even if common soldiers were not called upon to participate in the frequent sacrifices but only to witness them, *all* aspects of Roman military life were infused with Roman religion. The standards of a legion, for example, and the oaths required of soldiers had tremendous religious significance.[11] As Tertullian clearly saw, it was impossible to serve in the Roman army without being directly or indirectly implicated in the Roman religion, and careful examination of the "ac-

---

10   Although note that the church's acquiescence in Christian participation in the state's exercise of its police powers is incompatible with a policy of strict *non*resistance, and hence with the most straightforward interpretation of Jesus' injunctions against violence. (More on this later.)

11   The standards, together with "the insignia on the uniforms of the soldiers," were believed by the Romans to be "the chief radiators of religious power to the legions." (Helgeland 25)

counts of the military martyrs" reveal that, in practice, "soldiers got in trouble with the army because of religious policy, never on the basis of a refusal to kill or to serve in combat" (Helgeland 66). More generally, Tertullian's scattered remarks about violence and the military are "nowhere . . . developed into an argument of any kind." Nor "is there any statement that a soldier should not enlist because killing in combat is wrong." "Statements such as 'Christians would rather be killed than kill' [*Apology* 37.5] . . . were not uttered in any context dealing with the military . . . ; to use them to build or support a theory of Christian pacifism is totally irresponsible to the text." (Helgeland 29)

Baintain's (and others') treatment of other texts is equally irresponsible. For example, while Hippolytus does indeed say that a soldier "must be told not to execute men; if he should be ordered to do it, he shall not do it" (quoted in Helgeland 37), "it seems clear that the train of thought before and after rules out the taking of life in combat as its meaning." (Helgeland 36)

Helgeland, Daly, and Burns acknowledge that Origen's position was broadly pacifist. Even so, Origen says that "as the priests and ministers of God," Christians, while "keeping their hands pure," should wrestle "in prayers to God on behalf of those who are fighting in a righteous cause, and for the king who reigns right-eously, that whatever is opposed to those who act righteously may be destroyed. And as we by our prayers vanquish all demons who stir up war, . . . and disturb the peace, we in this way are much more helpful to the kings than those who go into the field to fight for them." (*Against Celsus* 8:73, quoted in Helgeland 41) Origen's position, in their view, was that Christians are obligated "to support 'those who are fighting in a righteous cause.' But because all Christians are 'priests,' it is not proper for them (no more than it is for pagan priests [who were never enlisted in the army]) to fight with anything but spiritual arms." As for Celsus's "dilemma . . . (if all became Christians, no one would be left to protect the emperor)," it "would never materialize" because, as more and more became Christians, war and conflict would eventually disappear. (Helgeland 41) Finally, Origen's position is obviously an idealization. He "accepts the fact of Celsus's complaint that Christians do not serve in the army." Yet he must have known that this was in fact false. One can only conclude that Origen chose "to defend, for the purposes of his polemic, only what he perceived to be the ideal Christian stance rather than what he knew to be the actual situation." (Helgeland 42)

In sum, the authors conclude that "there is . . . little significant evidence" for "any general theory of pacifism in the church" of this period "as a whole." Expres-sions of abhorrence of war, and "general prohibitions against killing," are no evidence to the contrary since both are compatible with (for example) just war theory. (Helgeland 69)

Helgeland's and his coauthors' case against Baintain and like-minded writers is impressive but seems to downplay the rather frequent allusions to the tension between the committed Christian life, on the one hand, and participation in warfare or violence on the other. (The historical church's uneasiness on this score is reflected in its eventual endorsement of Christian "vocationalism," the view that some are called to more perfectly imitate Christ by observing his "counsels of perfection"—which include, among other things, the renunciation of violence.)

Their extended treatment of Tertullian is a case in point. A number of Tertullian's remarks in his discussion of the military strongly suggest that he saw at least a *tension* between killing and a Christian profession. For example, in *On Idolatry* 19, Tertullian states that not only idolatry but also participation in capital punishment (which was sometimes a soldier's duty) is proscribed for Christians and, in the same passage, asks "How will a Christian man go to war? Indeed how will he serve even in peacetime without a sword which the Lord has taken away? . . . The Lord in . . . disarming Peter, disarmed every soldier." (Quoted in Helgeland 23) Or again, "Shall it be held lawful to make an occupation of the sword, when the Lord proclaims that he who uses the sword shall perish by the sword? And shall the son of peace take part in the battle when it does not become him even to sue at law?" (*Treatise on the Crown*, chapter 11, quoted in Helgeland 26–7) Granted that idolatry, and not killing, is Tertullian's primary objection to military service, and that pacifism was not one of his major concerns, it seems disingenuous to simply discount these statements.

As for the *Canons of Hippolytus*, it can be admitted that the context of the injunction against participating in executions is a discussion of occupations that are impermissible for Christians, and that Hippolytus's major concern is (as the authors argue) idolatry and personal immorality. Nevertheless, it is difficult to see how one can allow participation in battle if one proscribes participation in executions. (Note that, from the standpoint of worldly wisdom, *both* are sometimes needed to establish justice and protect the innocent.)

Nor is it plausible to dismiss Origen's position as a mere idealization. Granted that he must have known that many Christians did serve in the military. All the same, both Celsus's complaint and Origen's defense would have been pointless unless significant numbers of Christians *had* refused to do so. Nevertheless the authors do rightly point out that Origen concedes that *some* wars *are* fought in just causes. His claim is only that *Christians* are called to a more rigorous standard, and therefore can't participate in them. Origen thus anticipates later Christian vocationalism—especially in the form it was to assume in the historic peace churches.

The historic peace churches   "The Anabaptists," for instance, "made a sharp distinction between . . . the kingdom of the world and the kingdom of Christ." (Baintain 153) For example, the Schleitheim Confession of 1527 states: "The sword is an ordering of God outside the perfection of Christ. It punishes and kills the wicked, and guards and protects the good. In the [Hebrew] law the sword is established for punishment and for death, and the secular rulers are established to wield the same. But within the perfection of Christ only the ban [excommunication] is used for the admonition and exclusion of the one who has sinned, without the death of the flesh."[12] The state has been ordained by God to restrain human wickedness—by force if necessary. Christians, however, are to abstain from all violence. "Our fortress is Christ, our defense is patience, our sword is the Word of God, and our victory is ... faith in Jesus Christ. Spears and swords of iron we leave to those who, alas, consider human blood and swine's blood well-nigh of equal value." (Menno Simons, quoted in Baintain 153.)

The injunction against violence applies not only to individuals but to the church, which must be restored to its primitive purity. Its renunciation of the ways of the world, including the state's exercise of its police powers and right of defense, will inevitably lead to persecution. Yet this is only to be expected as long as the world remains the world and the church is the church. To the objection that if Christians refused to serve as magistrates, or to exercise the sword, "justice would suffer, they answered that there would never be any lack of persons ready to assume the office of the magistrate." As Baintain observes, "this rejoinder savors very much of vocationalism," the notion common after Constantine that only some have a special vocation to follow the New Testament's more radical teachings. (Baintain 156) There is this important difference, however. The church, after Constantine, has by and large maintained that only some Christians are called to observe the counsels of perfection. The Anabaptists, like Origen, argue that *all* Christians are called to do so.

In a pair of recent articles, Caleb Miller offers an interesting reconstruction and defense of the Anabaptist position.[13] Most Christians would agree that the human good consists in fulfilling one's telos as a human being by living "only in ways consistent with the love of God and the love of other human beings." (Miller 1999: 368) This good is absolute, the same for everyone. The *virtues*, however, are relative. The virtues for a particular human being or community are "those character traits which contribute to [its] redemption" by being "best suited to overcome the impediments of sin to the fulfillment of our *telos*." (Ibid.: 369) These vary from one person to another, and from community to community.

Miller explicates his position by offering the following definitions:

1   "A person, P, aspires to fulfil an action-guiding principle, R, if and only if: (i) P believes that she is morally obligated to fulfill R, and (ii) P seeks to fulfill R, in order to fulfill her moral obligation."
2   "A person, P, constructively aspires to fulfill an action-guiding principle, R, if and only if: (i) P aspires to fulfill R, and (ii) P's aspiring to fulfill R, tends to improve her conformity to the love of God and others."
3   "An action-guiding principle, R, is redemptive for a person, P, if and only if: (i) P can constructively aspire to fulfill R, and (ii) there is no action-guiding

---

12   Quoted in Caleb Miller, "Character and Independent Duty: An Anabaptist Approach," *Faith and Philosophy* 17 (2000), pp. 293–4. Henceforth Miller 2000.
13   Caleb Miller, "Creation, Redemption, and Virtue," *Faith and Philosophy* 16 (1999), pp. 368–77, henceforth Miller 1999; and Miller 2000, pp. 291–305.

principle, N, incompatible with R, such that P's aspiring to fulfill N would tend to improve P's conformity to the love of God and others as strongly as would P's aspiring to fulfill R."

Obligatory principles (the principles God *requires* of us) are those which are redemptive for us.[14] (Miller 2000: 297–9)

An example may make the implication of these definitions clearer. For those prone to impose disproportionate penalties for injuries, the appropriate standard may be the *lex talionis*, and the appropriate virtues dispositions to act in accordance with it. For others, the appropriate standards may be those of the Sermon on the Mount, and the appropriate dispositions include those leading to nonresistance and the return of good for evil. For the ancient Israelites, for instance, the *lex talionis* and its corresponding virtues may have been the highest standard "to which they could constructively aspire . . . If they had regarded unconditional love as a standard to which they were subject when it was utterly beyond their moral capacities to meet it, it would only have discouraged them from the project of improving their lives morally, and habituated them to the violation of their moral standards." For them, therefore, "the disposition . . . to treat others as one has been treated by them," and the corresponding standard, were "redemptive." (Miller 1999: 371)

"Our character is" not only "subject . . . to such causal factors as habituation and social influence," however. It is also subject "to God's enabling grace." Because God has revealed his will for us in the New Testament, and because he empowers those who "close with Christ," Christians can[15] constructively aspire to the perfection of Christ. Moreover, since they can, and since no incompatible action-guiding principle would be more redemptive for them, they are *obligated* to fulfill Christ's "law" of perfection. (Miller 2000: 301) For them, therefore, "unconditional love is a virtue," and a disposition to take an eye for an eye, or a tooth for a tooth "is a vice." (Miller 1999: 371)

Miller claims that this "reconstruction of traditional Anabaptist ethics . . . explains why Anabaptists have traditionally denied that pacifism is" obligatory for non-Christians. (Miller 2000: 302) It would not be redemptive for them or their communities. They would quickly find themselves unable to fulfill standards enjoining nonresistance and the return of good for evil, and, in the absence of other relevant principles to which they *could* constructively aspire,[16] would tend to wage war without moral restraint. It can also account for the sharp moral divergences between the morality of the Old and New Testaments without denying that the

---

14   Miller notes that if two principles are *tied* with respect to their redemptive tendencies but "they beat out" the "competition, then their *disjunction* is redemptive," and what is obligatory is that one fulfill one or the other. (Miller 2000: 305)

15   Both individually and collectively.

16   Just war principles, for example, such as fighting only in a just cause, sparing noncombatants, and proportioning the means to the end.

moral requirements of the Old Testament were divinely inspired, and explain why the actions of saints like Mother Teresa are regarded as supererogatory by most while the saints themselves think they are only doing their duty. The New Testament's law of perfection would not have been redemptive for the ancient Israelites, and the burdens assumed by figures like Mother Teresa are indeed obligatory for the "saints" (the redeemed) but not for non-Christians for whom they *are* supererogatory.[17]

Finally, Miller thinks that his reconstructed Anabaptist moral theory can defuse one of the more common objections to pacifism—"that there can never be a successful pacifist nation-state, since, without the recourse to deadly force, there is no effective way to restrain the evil of its worst citizens and adversaries . . . For those reasons, among others, the prescription by God of pacifism for nation-states would not be redemptive." (Miller 2000: 302) (The idea, I take it, is that depriving states of the tool of violence would almost invariably lead to tyranny[18] or Hobbesian anarchy, and an ethos of lies, treachery, and violence—to situations, in short, in which the moral climate would make it more difficult for most people to constructively aspire to any but the lowest standards.)

Niebuhr and Christian Pacifism

Reinhold Niebuhr's assessment of Christian pacifism is both nuanced and trenchant. According to Niebuhr, the New Testament's success "in gauging the full dimension of human life" is a result of two things—"its love perfectionism, on the one hand, and its moral realism, on the other."[19] The Christian must affirm both. She should neither "deny that the [love] ethic of Jesus is an absolute and uncompromising ethic," nor that attempts to fully implement it come into immediate collision with the depth of human sin.[20]

Love and justice By rejecting any form of self-love, the love commandment not only "sets itself uncompromisingly . . . against the natural self-regarding impulses, but against the necessary prudent defenses of the self, required because of the

---

17 Miller thinks his reconstructed Anabaptist moral theory can also help us "understand cultural diversity in moral attitudes," without simply dismissing those that differ from our own as false or misguided. For, in its view, "there can be enormous diversity in the *objective* obligations of different cultures owing to differences in what is redemptive from culture to culture." (Miller 2000: 304, my emphasis)

18 Since the state would have no effective way of resisting usurpation or conquest by evil men and women who would take advantage of its weakness.

19 Reinhold Niebuhr, *An Interpretation of Christian Ethics*. New York and London: Harper, 1935, p. 65. Henceforth Niebuhr 1935.

20 Reinhold Niebuhr, "Why the Christian Church is not Pacifist," chapter 1 of Niebuhr's *Christianity and Power Politics*. New York: Charles Scribner's Sons, 1940, p. 8. Henceforth Niebuhr 1940.

egoism of others." (Niebuhr 1935: 39) "The very basis of self-love is the natural will to survive . . . Therefore, in the ethic of Jesus, concern for physical existence is prohibited: 'Take no thought for your life, what ye shall eat, or what ye shall drink.'" (Ibid.: 41) Since "the most natural expansion of the self is . . . through possessions . . . , the love of possessions" is condemned, and the rich young man "is advised" to sell all that he has "and give to the poor." (Ibid.: 42) Again, "self-assertion when the self is in peril or the victim of injustice expresses itself as a natural impulse" to resist, yet Jesus urges his disciples to neither insist on their rights nor retaliate. "Both resistance and resentment are forbidden. The self is not to assert its interests against those who encroach upon it, and not to resent the injustice done to it . . . Nowhere is the ethic of Jesus in more obvious conflict with both the impulses and the necessities of ordinary men in typical social situations." (Ibid.: 45–6)

Moreover, Jesus does not promise his disciples "any concrete or obvious reward:" they can expect only "sacrifice, abnegation, and loss." (Ibid.: 52) The way of Jesus is the way of the Cross.[21] The justification for so acting does not lie in its consequences but in God's nature. We are to forgive because God forgives, love our enemies because God loves both the just and the unjust, take up our cross because God himself has done so.

Niebuhr is convinced that the "uncompromising" ethic of Jesus provides the proper critical standard for assessing every relative value and achievement. He also believes that no "social ethic which deals with present realities . . . can be directly derived from" it. (Ibid.: 51)[22] Why not?

Largely because of how people behave in social groups. While individuals may sometimes act altruistically, groups and classes do not. Whatever their pretensions

---

21 Niebuhr notes that the way of the Cross *does* lead "to a higher form of self-realization," but one which is an "unintended" (!?) though "inevitable consequence of unselfish action." (Niebuhr 1935: 53)

22 Unlikz,ʺaul Ramsey who, in effect, reduces the Christian love ethic to a kind of utilitarianism—although with one important modification, namely, that one is not to include oneself in one's utilitarian calculations. Thus Ramsey praises Augustine and early just war theorists for getting it right: when acting as a magistrate (or as an impartial third party), the Christian may, and indeed should, employ the sword when doing so is necessary to restrain evil and repel aggression. *Self*-defense, on the other hand, is impermissible (except in cases where defending oneself is necessary to meet the needs of third parties). Christian love excludes egoism or self-regard, not the use of force. (See Paul Ramsey, *Basic Christian Ethics*. New York: Charles Scribner's Sons, 1950) If what Christian love demands is simply the maximization of the well-being of others, however, then (*pace* Niebuhr), its standard *can* be directly applied to social, economic, and political realities. The trouble is that Christian love as sketched by Ramsey doesn't look much like the love of the New Testament. For one thing, it comes perilously close to making *humanity* (minus one) the object of one's love rather than one's neighbor, the concrete individual I happen to meet. For another, the only obvious difference between Ramsey's vision of Christian ethics and a purely secular utilitarian-ism isapts refusal to include one's own interests in its calculations.

and professions,[23] groups and classes act in their own interests. As John Stuart Mill pointed out in *Representative Government*, the interests of other groups or classes are either overlooked; or when not overlooked, not fully appreciated; or, if appreciated, assigned less weight than one assigns one's own.[24]

Human egoism is insidious and pervasive. "If it is defeated on a lower or more obvious level, it will express itself in more subtle forms. If it is defeated by social impulse, it insinuates itself into the social impulse, so that a man's devotion to his community always means the expression of a transferred egoism as well as of altruism." (Niebuhr 1932: 40). "Patriotism," for example, "is a high form of altruism, when compared with lesser and more parochial loyalties; but from an absolute perspective it is simply another form of selfishness." (Ibid.: 48) "Group relations can never be as ethical as those which [sometimes] characterize individual relations." (Ibid.: 83)

A consequence of individual and group egoism is that violence is not only inevitable but necessary. For "the sentiments of benevolence and social good will will never be so pure or powerful, and the rational capacity to consider the rights and needs of others in fair competition with our own will never be so fully developed," as to make it possible to dispense with "a measure of coercion" in any but "the most intimate social group[s]." (Ibid.: 3) "Tolstoian pacifists and other advocates of nonresistance" discern "the evils which force introduces into society" more clearly that most. But they are deluded in thinking that it can or should be "completely eliminated." (Ibid.: 20) The continued existence of the organized communities that human social life and well-being require depends upon the threat, and occasional exercise, of violence. State violence, for example, can be limited or restrained. Eliminating it entirely, however, would result in even more evil than is caused by its occasional exercise.

The upshot of these considerations is that while "the dream of perpetual peace and brotherhood" is "prompted by the conscience and insight of individual man," it is "incapable of fulfillment by collective man. It is like all true religious visions, possible of [very imperfect] approximation but not of realization in actual history." (Ibid.: 21–2) Christ "on the cross turned defeat into victory and prophesied the day when love would be triumphant in the world. But the triumph" would only "come

---

23 However sincere they may be. Classes and groups may consciously believe they are acting in the interests of the whole, but those beliefs are always, at least in part, an expression of false consciousness, a blindness to the real nature of their actions. "Perhaps the best that can be expected of nations," for example, "is that they should justify their hypocrisies [their claim to be acting in the cause of impartial justice or for the greater human good] by a slight measure of real international achievement, and learn how to do justice to wider interests than their own, while they pursue their own." (Reinhold Niebuhr, *Moral Man and Immoral Society*. New York: Charles Scribner's Sons, 1932. Reprinted 1960, p. 108. Henceforth Niebuhr 1932)

24 John Stuart Mill, *Considerations on Representative Government*. New York: Liberal Arts Press, 1958.

through the intervention of God," not through human effort—not even efforts to follow the love ethic of Jesus. (Ibid.: 82) Pure non-resistance, for instance, "has nothing to do with the problem of social justice ... Jesus did not counsel his disciples to forgive seventy times seven in order that they might convert their enemies or make them more favorably disposed.[25] He counseled it as an effort to approximate complete moral perfection, the perfection of God." (Ibid.: 263)[26]

But even if Christian perfectionism has nothing to say directly about problems of social justice, the love commandment and standards of justice aren't unrelated. Just what is the connection between them?

The aim of "a *rational* ethic" is justice. (Ibid.: 57, my emphasis.) But David Hume and John Rawls have convincingly argued that institutions of justice are called for only under conditions of moderate scarcity and limited altruism, that is, when (1) goods are limited (so that not everyone can have everything they want) and yet not so scarce as to make good lives impossible for most, and (2) people are neither wholly altruistic nor wholly selfish. Under these conditions, principles of justice are needed to adjudicate competing claims to the limited stock of goods. "It is [thus] impossible to construct a social ethic out of the ideal of love in its pure form, because the ideal presupposes the resolution [or, more accurately, abolition] of the conflict of" interest with interest "which it is the concern of law [that is, justice] to mitigate and restrain." (Niebuhr 1935: 149f.) Justice "seeks to bring the needs of others into equal consideration with those of the self." An ethics of love, on the other hand, demands "that the needs of the neighbor shall be met without a careful computation of relative needs" and, in doing so, goes beyond justice. (Niebuhr 1932: 57) And, in fact, "anything *less* than perfect love in human life [including every form of human justice] is destructive of life ... Egoism," an insistence on one's own needs and interests, "is always destructive." (Niebuhr 1935: 60, my emphasis.)

Yet "perfect love," too, can be "destructive" when one tries to apply the standard of love directly to situations of social conflict. For suppose that some, but not all, obey the love commandment under conditions of moderate scarcity and limited altruism. Evil is not resisted (or at least not effectively) and, as a consequence, goods and evil aren't distributed in accordance with justice. Niebuhr says that love *transcends* justice, and this is true when the love in question is *mutual*. As Aristotle says, friendship (which is a form of mutual love) is "the truest form of justice" and,

---

25   Though Paul seems to suggest something of the sort in Romans 12: 21.

26   Niebuhr admits that refusing to assert one's own claims, loving one's enemies, and forgiveness may sometimes "have redemptive social consequences ... within the area of individual and personal relationships." (Niebuhr 1932, 264) The enemy's heart may sometimes be softened and the wrong-doer may sometimes repent. There is absolutely no guarantee, however, that consequences like these will occur and, in any case, the justification of nonresistance, love, and forgiveness does not depend on the probability of their occurring.

where it exists, makes ordinary justice unnecessary.[27] Where love is not mutual, however, its effect can be to subvert justice by allowing injustice to flourish with impunity.

The demands of love and justice aren't simply opposed, however. Why not? In the first place, "the law of love is . . . the source of norms of justice" (Niebuhr 1935: 140), for mutual self-giving love is the only perfect expression of the unity and harmony to which seekers after justice aspire. Second, "the law of love" provides "an ultimate perspective" from which the "limitations" of "all approximations of justice" are starkly revealed. (Ibid.) Third, the law of love "suggests possibilities" of reform and improvement "which immediately transcend any achievements of justice by which society has" so far managed to mitigate the conflicts setting one person or social group against another. (Ibid.: 144) Religion's "millennial hope," its vision of a Kingdom in which "nation shall not lift up sword against nation" and "the wolf shall lie down with the lamb" (Isaiah 2: 4, 11: 6) is also a source of the strength and courage needed to struggle for a better society, "for the task of building a just society seems always to be a hopeless one when only present realities and immediate possibilities are envisaged." (Niebuhr 1932: 61) Finally, "the principles of equal justice are . . . *approximations* of the law of love in the kind of imperfect world which we know,"[28] even though they mustn't be *confused* with it since they presuppose the existence of competing egoisms. (Niebuhr 1935: 149, my emphasis)

Love, then, is an "impossible possibility." Because God is the world's creator and redeemer, "actions which flow" from God's command to love are "in harmony and not in conflict with reality." (Ibid.: 55) Furthermore, "the kingdom of God is always at hand in the sense that [apparent] impossibilities" (such as ending segregation or destroying apartheid) "are really possible and lead to new actualities in given moments of history . . . [On the other hand,] every actuality of history reveals itself, after the event, as only an approximation of the ideal; and the Kingdom of God is therefore [always] not here." (Ibid.: 58) It will never be realized in mundane history and, in that sense, is impossible. Love is an impossible possibility in our own lives as well. "The grace of God which is revealed in Christ is, . . . on the one hand, an actual 'power of righteousness' which heals the contradiction within our hearts" between "the law in our minds" (the law of love) and the "law in our members" (our egoism). In this sense love is a real possibility for us. "On the other hand," God's "grace is conceived as 'justification,' as pardon rather than power, as the forgiveness of God, which is vouchsafed to man despite the fact that he never achieves the full measure of Christ. In that sense Christ is the '*impossible* possibility.' Loyalty to him means realization *in intention,* but does not actually mean the full realization of the measure of Christ" in fact. (Niebuhr 1940: 3, my emphases)

---

27   Aristotle, *Nichomachean Ethics*, 1155a 27.
28   And, by extension, the (limited) achievements of justice are approximations to the Kingdom of love in "the kind of imperfect world which we know."

Niebuhr's critique of pacifism   Niebuhr points out that modern Christian pacifism tends to differ from that of the traditional peace churches. It also differs from the "pacifism" of Christian perfectionists who regarded a strict adherence to Christ's counsels of perfection (including nonresistance) as a special vocation which was not incumbent on all Christians. Like Gandhi (who often serves as their model), modern Christian pacifists confuse the "spirituality" of "pure nonresistance" ("truth force" and "soul force") with nonviolent *resistance*. The latter, by entering "the field of social," political, and economic "relations, places" external "restraints upon the desires and activities of others," and is thus "a form of physical coercion." Pure nonresistance, on the other hand, appeals "to the reason and good will of an opponent in a social struggle," but "places no external constraints" on his or her behavior. (Niebuhr 1932: 242, 244)

Modern Christian pacifism is flawed on two counts. In the first place, it is impossible to "draw any absolute line of demarcation between violent and nonviolent coercion." (Ibid.: 172) The only difference is that in the former case "the destruction of life or property" is directly intended and in the latter case it is not. Even so "that destruction is [often] the inevitable consequence of nonviolent coercion." Boycotts such as Gandhi's boycott of British cotton, for instance, "may rob a whole community of its livelihood and, if maintained long enough, . . . will certainly destroy life." Nor does non-violent resistance when directed against groups isolate "the guilty from the innocent more successfully than violent coercion." The children of the British cotton workers suffered although they were innocent of any wrong-doing. (Ibid., 240–41)

Since there is no absolute distinction between violent and nonviolent coercion, the decisions of a Christian entering the social and political arena should be made on pragmatic grounds. Nonviolent resistance is often preferable to violent resistance "because social violence is a great evil and ought to be avoided if at all possible." (Ibid.: 189) But because the choice of nonviolent over violent methods of resisting injustice is pragmatic, it is justified only when nonviolent resistance will be at least as effective as violence. Modern pacifism's failure to recognize this is a consequence of its blindness to the fact that there is no absolute distinction between these two forms of resistance.

It is also a consequence of an overestimation of the power of nonviolent resistance which is based on its obliviousness to the corrosive effects of human sin. (And this is its second flaw.) Modern liberal "Christian pacifists, rationalists like Bertrand Russell, and mystics like Aldous Huxley believe essentially the same thing." Liberal Christian pacifists "make Christ into the symbol of their faith in man. But their faith is really identical with that of Russell or Huxley." All three believe in humanity's essential goodness. They believe, in other words, that if you only cultivate the reason and altruistic feelings which all humans share, or "some mystic–universal element in the deeper levels of man's consciousness, you will be able to eliminate human selfishness and the consequent conflict of life with life." (Niebuhr 1940: 7) However, because this belief is not simply delusive but incorporates a willful blindness to the reality of human sin, most modern pacifism is a form of false consciousness.

Some pacifist responses   Many thoughtful pacifists have endorsed a number of Niebuhr's more important observations. Culbert G. Rutenbar is an example. He agrees that the state is an ordinance of God for restraining wickedness and promoting the public good even though, as a *natural* ordinance, part of the order of creation and not of grace, the most the state can achieve is relative justice. (Like Niebuhr, Rutenbar insists that the standard by which the state's attempts at relative justice must be judged is the law of love.)[29] Rutenbar also agrees that the state may legitimately exercise its police powers in the course of fulfilling its functions.

It doesn't follow that the Christian can countenance war, however. For "the Christian is a minister of reconciliation" whereas "the professed and deliberate purpose of war . . . is to kill, i.e., to put the other man wholly beyond the reach of any conceivable appeal or concern of love." Moreover, "modern war is so impersonal and indiscriminate that any kind of personal relationship in which love might be expressed between Christian and enemy is rarely possible." Finally, "war is accompanied by things like lying, subterfuge, and treachery"—to which we might add the unintended[30] killing and maiming of the enemy soldier's children, friends, and relatives[31]—"which poison personal relations at their roots." (Rutenbar 63) The point is not just that war doesn't *aim* at reconciliation for neither does police action (at least not directly). It is, rather, that war makes reconciliation impossible.

Nevertheless, Rutenbar and a number of other Christian pacifists also agree with Niebuhr on two further points, First, many modern pacifists have been more or less willfully blind to the depth of human sin. Modern pacifism has too often been "built upon a view of human nature that seems scarcely realistic, let alone Christian." Its faith is ultimately in "man," in the potentialities of human nature, not in God. The consequence is a simple-minded "optimism about history that makes them think that if they try hard enough, they'll secure a warless world." (Rutenbar 29–30) The trouble with this is that "sin is not something peripheral" but "has penetrated" to humanity's "very core," and "tainted [its] very best, even [its] virtue." Humanity's "radical evil" cannot be cured by human effort but "only by the even more radical grace of God in Jesus Christ." (Rutenbar 34)

The second point on which these pacifists agree with Niebuhr is that Christian pacifists should not try to justify their behavior by appealing to consequences. We *are* to meet evil with good in the faith that good will prevail. But prevail in what sense? Some Christian pacifists think that "overcoming evil" means "that the evil will of the enemy will be changed and redeemed so that the enemy-relation will

---

29   Culbert G. Rutenbar, *The Dagger and the Cross: An Examination of Christian Pacifism*. Nyack, New York: Fellowship Publications, 1957, pp. 83–6. Henceforth Rutenbar.
30   Or at least not directly intended.
31   So-called "collateral damage."

vanish." But while this *may* happen, it does not always, or perhaps even often, happen. "The emphasis of the New Testament, in its appeals for returning good for evil, is not upon possible consequences. Niebuhr is certainly right when he points out that nothing is said in the Sermon on the Mount about transmuting enmity into friendship by the practice of forgiveness." (Rutenbar 65) "The Christian knows too much of the reality of sin to be optimistic" about the mundane success of his attempts to obey Jesus' "hard" precepts. (Rutenbar 125) The New Testament, after all, "does not teach that a warless world is a historical possibility." On the contrary, its last days are envisaged "as times of unprecedented world tumult," not "of perfect peace." (Rutenbar 137) Indeed, "the cross of Christ suggests the strong probability that Niebuhr is right when he reminds pacifists that there is reason for believing that love may be suffering rather than triumphant in this world." (Rutenbar 136–7)

Why, then, should the Christian renounce violence? Because God himself does so. As Stanley Hauerwas says,

> pacifism is . . . first of all . . . an affirmation that God wills to rule his creation not through violence and coercion but by love . . . Though it counts individual passages of scripture such as *Matthew* 5: 38–48 as important, [Christian] pacifism does not derive its sole justification from them. Rather pacifism follows from our understanding of God which we believe has been most decisively revealed in the cross of Jesus Christ. Just as God refused to use violence to ensure the success of his cause, so must we.[32]

The Christian pacifist cannot honestly rest her case on the beneficial consequences of her nonviolent efforts after peace, justice, and reconciliation. Rather, "at its most Christian point, pacifism is Christian witness . . . to the reality of the love and will of God in Jesus Christ." (Rutenbar 138)[33] (Notice that on this point, too, Rutenbar, Hauerwas, and a number of other recent Christian pacifists turn out to agree with Niebuhr. Christian pacifism is not a *strategy*—effective or otherwise—for dealing with social problems, but a witness or testimony to a more than human possibility.)

Still, while Christian pacifists should be realistic about their chances for mundane success, their "relative pessimism" is wrapped in "an ultimate optimism," although "that ultimate optimism is centered in God and not in man, not even redeemed man." (Rutenbar 125) It is precisely on this point that John H. Yoder thinks that Niebuhr's theological inadequacies become most apparent.

In the first place, "although the New Testament understands the cross only in the light of the resurrection, Niebuhr speaks of the cross repeatedly, of the resurrection

---

32   Stanley Hauerwas, "Pacifism: Some Philosophical Considerations," *Faith and Philosophy* 2 (1985), p. 99. Notice, however, that the God of the New Testament is *also* the God of its apocalyptic strands which (at least *symbolically*) depict him as coercively intervening to defeat the powers of darkness (the war in heaven, Armageddon, and so on).

33   And, I would add, that to be effective the witness must be costly, self-sacrificial.

of Christ not at all." Second, the New Testament regards the church, Christ's body, as "the bearer of meaning in history." Yet "the concept of the church is quite absent from [Niebuhr's] thought." Third, the New Testament "teaches that there is a significant difference between the saint and the unbeliever by virtue of a change of motives so basic as to be called a new birth." Niebuhr, on the other hand, "has no place for the doctrine of regeneration since the saint for him is still a sinner." Finally, the New Testament regards "the resurrection, the church, and regeneration" as the work of the Holy Spirit, but "the Holy Spirit is likewise neglected in Niebuhr's ethics."[34]

Yoder thinks that these emphases and omissions have serious consequences for the topic at hand. Grace for Niebuhr is primarily forgiveness, which gives us peace, and enables us to act in spite of the "contradiction in our own souls" between our recognition that we should love our neighbors as ourselves and our inability to do so. The New Testament, on the other hand, "speaks of our 'resurrection with Christ' as opening new ethical possibilities," and of the Holy Spirit as a *power* which enables the Christian to lead a new life under new principles. Moreover, the church or body of Christ, to which every redeemed Christian belongs, "differs from other social bodies in that it is" *more* rather than "less moral than its individual members." The Christian is a redeemed person, and the society to which he or she belongs (the church or body of Christ) is a *society* of redeemed persons. Because Niebuhr neglects the doctrine of regeneration, he fails to see that "ethics for Christians and ethics for unregenerate society are two distinct disciplines," and that what may be an impossible possibility for the unregenerate is not impossible for Christians. "The triumph of love over sin is not reserved for some Platonic realm (such as Niebuhr's 'super history') where the eschatological judgment takes place" (and which Niebuhr understands mythically or symbolically). Rather, "sin is vanquished every time a Christian, in the power of God, chooses the better instead of the good, . . . love instead of compromise . . . That this triumph over sin is incomplete changes in no way the fact that it is possible."[35]

Yoder's remarks aren't entirely fair to Niebuhr, for the latter's point is that Christians are *simultaneously* sinners *and* redeemed. Even so, Yoder is correct when he points out that Niebuhr's emphasis is on the first, and that his understanding of redemption tends to be restricted to forgiveness.[36] On the other hand, Yoder can be accused of overemphasizing the second. The body of Christ, for instance, may be a supernatural entity which is more moral that the individuals who constitute it. The *church*, however—including the historic peace churches—is also a

---

34 John H. Yoder, *Reinhold Niebuhr and Christian Pacifism*, A Concern Reprint, n.d., pp. 17–18. This pamphlet originally appeared as an article in the *Mennonite Quarterly Review* 29 (1955), pp. 101ff.
35 Ibid., pp. 17–18.
36 Or, more accurately, that forgiveness is emphasized so heavily that regeneration tends to be neglected.

human institution that stands under God's judgment, and is not always more moral than its individual members. (Think, for example, of the crusades, the wars of religion, the church's support of slavery, the identification of Christianity with the American way of life, and so on.) Nevertheless, Yoder's principal point is well taken. As a member of Christ's body, empowered by the Holy Spirit, and living in the light of the resurrection, the Christian is, however imperfectly, able to follow Christ's love commandment.

But, of course, Niebuhr doesn't deny that *some* Christians are able to do so. There have always been Christians who have, however imperfectly, implemented the counsels of perfection in their own lives. What Niebuhr does deny is that *all* Christians are called to do so, and that the consequences would be anything less than tragic if they *were* to do so. Given the grim realities of history, injustice and evil must sometimes be met with force. Violence is indeed evil, but the failure to use it (as in the case of the Western nations' inaction in Rwanda) can result in even worse evil.

Rutenbar, Yoder, et al. are surely right in insisting that the New Testament does not discriminate between Christians who are called to rigorously enact the law of love in their lives and those who are permitted (or even called) to compromise the love principle because of the exigencies of history. Even so, on at least one important point, the position of the peace churches, in any case, is not as far removed from Niebuhr's as one might think. On the one hand, Niebuhr believes that it is good that some (however imperfectly) follow Jesus' path of nonresistance, for in doing so they serve as witnesses, "symbol[s] of the final ideal of love, under the tension of which all men stand." (Niebuhr 1935: 187)[37] The historic peace churches, on the other hand, have tended to think that *true* Christians (those who genuinely answer God's call) will always be few. So, in practice, the consequences of Christian perfectionism will not be tragic. Most men and women of good will—including most of those who think of themselves as Christian—will resort to the sword when doing so appears necessary to restrain evil. Caleb Miller even goes so far as to suggest that they may be *justified* in doing so. (See pages 155–7) In effect, then, both Niebuhr and the historic peace churches distinguish between those who choose to witness to God's love by following the path of nonresistance and professing Christians who believe themselves justified in resorting to the sword to secure or maintain justice. The difference between them is only that the historic peace churches deny that the latter are truly Christian while Niebuhr does not.

Four alternatives   So what should a Christian's attitude toward violence be? Traditional pacifists like the Mennonites say: "Obey Christ's injunctions in all their rigor and purity and, as a consequence, practice nonresistance and return good for evil." It is difficult to deny that this is in fact the teaching of the New Testament.

---

37   The tension in question is "between the Christian ideal and the realities and compromises in which we are all involved." (Niebuhr 1935: 187)

Indeed, Niebuhr himself insists that while it is foolish to deny that the love commandment "is not immediately applicable to the task of securing justice in a sinful world," it is just as "foolish to deny that the ethic of Jesus [which includes nonresistance] is an absolute and uncompromising ethic." (Niebuhr 1940: 8–9) And Richard J. Mouw admits that a number of New Testament passages, especially those recording "the teachings and example of Jesus," are "awkward" for Christian just war theorists like himself. (Mouw argues, however, that these passages must be understood in a way "which fits into . . . the over all sense of the scriptures," and "it is a clear fact of Old Testament history that God did endorse the use of violence . . . That lethal violence is on occasion morally justified seems to square with our moral intuitions" as well.[38] These considerations aren't decisive, though. It is a question of just how much weight Christians should place on the Old Testament when it seems to conflict with the teachings of the New. Without denying [as Marcion did] that God is revealed in the Old Testament, it is arguable that Christians should say that the New Testament trumps the Old in cases of apparent conflict.[39] Again, while our moral intuitions undeniably support the claim that the use of lethal force is sometimes morally justified, it is unclear how much weight this has. Given that our epistemic capacities have been marred by sin [as traditional Christians believe] our moral intuitions may not be entirely reliable.)

The second alternative is Niebuhr's, and the one historically taken by most Christians: while the path of nonresistance is legitimate for some, most should get their hands dirty when doing so is necessary to preserve or secure justice. The religious person "is tempted either to leave the world of political and economic relations to take the course which natural impulse prompts [as traditional pacifists too often do], or [like many Christian disciples of Tolstoy and Gandhi] to assume that his principles are influencing political life more profoundly than they really are. He is tempted, in other words, either to [withdrawal and] defeatism or to sentimentality." (Niebuhr 1932: 75f.) What the Christian *should* normally do, however, is enter the social and political arena, and "use the forces of nature to defeat nature, . . . use force in order to establish justice." This strategy can lead to "corruption" and is therefore perilous as the "religious spirit" well knows. But "if that fear can be overcome religious ideals may yet achieve social and political significance." (Ibid.: 81)[40]

---

38   Richard J. Mouw, "Christianity and Pacifism," *Faith and Philosophy* 2 (1985), p. 106.

39   For a Mennonite attempt to reconcile the two see the discussion of Caleb Miller on p. 156f.

40   Yoder criticizes Niebuhr's contention that the exigencies imposed by sin require us to set the love commandment aside in the political and social arena: "There is no necessity of abandoning love as an ethical absolute unless something more important than love stands to be lost." And this is the case "only if there is a moral absolute higher than love"—which no Christian (including Niebuhr) can admit. (Yoder, *Reinhold Niebuhr*, p. 15) But this misrepresents Niebuhr. *Love itself* requires us to set "love" aside when the only way to counter injustice is through violence. Moreover, Niebuhr

The first two alternatives are irreconcilable. There is, however, a third alternative. Traditional pacifism repudiates *all* resistance. In its view, "Gandhi's method, unlike that of Christ, is a method of [economic, social, and psychological] compulsion, whose function is to *force* the opposition to change in the desired direction." (Rutenbar 25, my emphasis) But Stanley Hauerwas denies that Christianity implies that one should not *resist* evil.[41] And, indeed, nonviolent *resistance* to injustice and oppression has seemed an attractive alternative to many modern Christian pacifists because it appears to take "them off a very embarrassing hook: the appearance of indifference to the monstrous evils of our time." (Rutenbar 22f.) As we have seen, Niebuhr rather plausibly argues that the New Testament teaches *non*resistance rather than nonviolent (or violent) resistance. Yet even if Jesus does enjoin nonresistance, "nonviolent resistance is so much *nearer* the New Testament ideal of love than bloodshed, war and violence" that it "is at least the *minimum* position the Christian ought to take where large social groups are involved." (Rutenbar 26–7) As even Niebuhr admits, nonviolent and self-sacrificial resistance that is infused with a spirit of love free from any "personal resentments" and "selfish ambition" "is usually the better method of expressing goodwill." By "enduring more suffering than it causes . . . , it mitigates resentment, which" the suffering of the object of one's resistance "usually creates, by enduring more pain than it inflicts." (Niebuhr 1932: 246–7)

The question, of course, is whether Christian pacifists like Rutenbar and Hauerwas can maintain any sort of principled distinction between nonviolent and violent resistance. If the distinction is made on purely pragmatic grounds, then Niebuhr is

---

doesn't really set the love commandment aside. It continues to be the standard by which all relative moral and social achievements are to be judged, and the source of an ideal aspiration which should motivate any attempt to improve the social, economic, and political environment. Nevertheless, a problem for Niebuhr does lurk in the neighborhood. Niebuhr claims that because Christ's way of life is "the 'impossible possibility,' loyalty to him means realization in intention," but not "the full realization of the measure of Christ" in fact. (Niebuhr 1940: 3) Notice, though, that a Christian who adopts Niebuhr's views would *not* realize the law of love in intention. For she would not intend to *follow* it but merely use it as a yardstick for exposing the sinfulness of all human solutions to the problems of history and making relative distinctions between closer and more distant approximations to the ideal of love, and as a source of aspiration. Her actual intention in engaging in history is to achieve closer approximations to justice. In short, *justice*, not love, becomes the standard that guides her in practice. Of course, Niebuhr might object that justice is an *image* or *simulacrum* of love in a world of conflicting egoisms so that, in aiming at a more perfect justice, we are, in effect, aiming at a more perfect image of love. The problem with this, however, is that the "image" badly distorts what it images or shadows forth since (as Niebuhr recognizes) justice presupposes conflicting interests, and hence conflicting egos. *All* achievable justice is (as Niebuhr says) tainted by selfishness.

41 Whether this is true or not depends on what one *means* by "resistance" (violent resistance, nonviolent resistance, or merely speaking the truth fearlessly to perpetrators and abettors of injustice).

surely right in thinking they cannot. Whether the practical consequences of nonviolent resistance are preferable to those of violent resistance depends upon the circumstances. Gandhi's methods were effective in India and the American South, but would not have succeeded in Nazi Germany or Stalin's Russia. Pragmatic considerations may not be decisive, of course. But even if they aren't, it remains unclear just how these pacifists can draw a principled distinction between the state's participation in a just war and its use of lethal force in carrying out internal policing functions.

Rutenbar, for example, argues that police activity has four characteristics which war lacks: (1) It "is aimed only at the aggressor or the wrong doer," not at his family, or acquaintances, or friends. (2) Its aim is not to kill the offender "if this can be done without endangering the lives of innocent victims." (3) "Police activity summons the offender to an impartial court, and punishment is inflicted by disinterested people." (4) "Police activity is capable of successfully achieving its objects."[42] (Rutenbar 40)

The line between the state's police actions and its engagement in just wars is not that clear-cut, however. (1) In a just war, the death of innocents, while foreseen, is not directly *intended* or "aimed at." (2) The proximate aim of a just war is the *capitulation* of the enemy, not their deaths.[43] (3) Where the society is unjust or (as is frequently the case) governmental machinery is in the hands of an economic or social class (or race, or religious or ethnic group) with its own special interests, the tribunals of the state are never completely impartial. (4) *Limited* wars, such as those in Kosovo, sometimes achieve their objectives. The upshot of these considerations is that the difference between legitimate police action and just wars is at best a difference of degree (though these do, of course, matter). So it is difficult to see how these pacifists can countenance police action without, at least in principle, countenancing some wars.

The only fully coherent or stable path for the Christian pacifist appears, then, to be that of nonresistance. The consequences of her absolute repudiation of violence may well be tragic, but this is equally true of the modern pacifists' refusal to use violence when nonviolent resistance would be futile.[44] The fact is that all Christians—pacifists and nonpacifists alike—must be clear-eyed about the probable consequences of their acts and take full responsibility for those that prove unfortu-

---

42 Rutenbar is quoting Leslie Dixon Weatherhead, *Thinking Aloud in War-Time*. New York: Abingdon, 1940, p. 38.

43 The ultimate aim of a just war is the prevention or elimination of a great evil which could not be forestalled or removed in any other way.

44 Though it is important to remember that, as Stanley Hauerwas points out, it is difficult to "see how those who support the use of violence provide any less tragic 'solution.'" (Hauerwas, "Pacifism," p. 100) For example, just war theorists argue that, under certain conditions (the cause is just, the means are proportionate to the end, and so on), one may be justified in acting in such a way that innocent lives are lost provided only that their deaths are foreseen and not directly intended.

nate. In a fallen world, *everyone's* hands can't help but be dirty.[45] Indeed, Charles Williams goes so far as to suggest that even God's hands are unavoidably "dirty." "Certainly our sins and faults destroy the good. But our efforts after the good also destroy it . . . It is necessary to behave well here? We do. What is the result? The destruction of some equal good. There is no more significant or more terrible tale in the New Testament than that which surrounded the young Incarnancy with the dying Innocents [who "suffered unknowingly in direct substitution for Christ"]: the chastisement of His peace was upon them."[46]

A fourth take on the issue of violence is Jacques Ellul's. In Ellul's view, violence and hatred are inseparable. The notion (expressed by some Christians) that one can exercise "necessary" violence without hatred is a delusion. "Far too often intellectuals," including Christian intellectuals, "imagine that there is a sort of pure, bloodless violence, an abstract violence like that of Robespierre who dispassionately ordered executions." Leaders may more or less sincerely avow their lack of hatred (although their professions of *love* or universal *benevolence* ring more hollow). Their "intermediaries," however, (those who do the actual killing) can't help but hate, or at least dehumanize, those they are injuring.[47]

Ellul agrees with Niebuhr that "violence is natural and normal to man and society," an inextricable feature of a fallen world. But it is "precisely *because*, apart from Christ, violence[48] is the form human relations normally and necessarily take" that the Christian must "struggle against" it. (Ellul 127) "For the role of the Christian in society . . . is to shatter fatalities and necessities. And he cannot fulfill this role by using violent means, simply because violence is of the order of necessity." (Ibid. 129) To insist that violence is necessary is to implicitly deny that the coming of the Kingdom is in *God's* hands, and to more or less consciously "decide that" we must, instead, "build the Kingdom on earth with [our] own hands." (Ibid. 150)

What must the Christian do, then? Not withdraw from the world but mediate "between the powerful and the oppressed" by "representing" the latter before the former, speaking truth to those who would try to evade it. (Ibid. 151–2) This can be difficult, time-consuming, and costly. (One can hardly speak the truth to a consum-

---

45   This does not mean that everyone should necessarily be *blamed*. It may sometimes be one's duty to act in a way that one knows will harm innocents. It does mean that one should experience anguish for having done so and, where possible, make costly amends for the harm one has caused.

46   Charles Williams, "The Cross." Quoted in Mary McDermott Shideler, *The Theology of Romantic Love: A Study of the Writings of Charles Williams*. Grand Rapids, MI: Eerdmans, 1962, p. 169. The quote in brackets is from Charles Williams, *Witchcraft*. New York: Meridian Books, 1959, p. 118.

47   Jacques Ellul, *Violence: Reflections from a Christian Perspective*. New York: Seabury Press, 1969, pp. 104–5. Henceforth Ellul. First-person accounts by combat veterans tend to bear out the essential accuracy of Ellul's remarks.

48   Whether physical, psychological, social, or economic.

erist culture, for example, if one's way of life shows that one shares its values, or effectively protest militarism if one's own actions[49] indirectly abet it.) The Christian should be under no illusions about the effectiveness of her efforts to witness to the truth. (John the Baptist, after all, did not change Herod's mind.) What she must *not* do, though, is resort to violence.

But what if the Christian should decide that she has no recourse *but* violence? In answering this question, Ellul stakes out a position which differs significantly from both traditional Christian pacifism *and* views like Niebuhr's. The Christian who, after full reflection, *does* participate in violence (Ellul was a member of the French Resistance) cannot do so *as a Christian* but in the knowledge that "he is doing wrong, is sinning against the God of Love," is "no longer a witness to the truth." (Ellul 137) Yet even though he cannot participate in violence *as* a Christian, he can still bear witness to Christian truth—most importantly perhaps by refusing "to accept whatever justifications of violence are advanced."[50] For the *"justification* of violence" is even more "unacceptable to Christian faith" than the violence itself. (Ibid. 140, my emphasis) "Even as he acts with the others," he must proclaim "the injustice and the unacceptability of what he and they are doing;" he must be "the mirror of truth in which his comrades perceive the horror of their action, . . . and the one who, in behalf of his unbelieving comrades, repents, bears humiliation, and prays to the Lord." (Ibid. 141–2)[51] In short, Ellul agrees with traditional Christian pacifists that Christianity wholly precludes any use of violence. But, like Niebuhr, he recognizes that Christian men and women may honestly decide that in some circumstances they have no other recourse. Unlike Niebuhr, however, Ellul insists that their participation in violence is incompatible with Christianity, and rejects all attempts to justify it.[52]

Is Religious Pacifism Rational?

There are a number of reasons for thinking that the absolute pacifism espoused by some Buddhists and Christians is irrational. I will focus on three—its unrealistic assessment of the requirements of social justice, a failure to fully appreciate the moral significance of consequences, and universalizability problems. For the sake of simplicity I will restrict my comments to Christian pacifism but similar difficulties beset Theravāda Buddhism's commitment to absolute nonviolence.

---

49 Paying taxes, for instance.
50 Including, presumably, the very considerations which led him to his decision.
51 There is something paradoxical about Ellul's appeal to repentance. As usually construed, true repentance involves a sincere intention not to repeat the offense. But the Christian resistance fighter, for example, presumably does not eschew his or her continued participation in violence.
52 Or, perhaps more accurately (?), any attempt to show that some justification for violence can be religiously sanctioned.

The requirements of justice   As Hume and Rawls clearly saw, the problem of social justice is a problem of fairly balancing competing claims to society's material and cultural resources. Because there is a limited supply of these goods and humanity's altruistic impulses are severely limited, the threat or exercise of violence will sometimes be needed to achieve or maintain a relatively just social order. (The state's internal policing activity and humanitarian interventions in situations like Rwanda are cases in point.) Niebuhr is surely right in thinking that, given humanity's selfishness and propensity to violence, religious pacifists are unable to provide realistic nonviolent solutions to many of the problems of social justice.[53]

The problem of consequences   Even nonconsequentialist (or deontological) moral systems,[54] like Kant's or W. D. Ross's, typically incorporate rules enjoining us to promote the happiness of others. The effect of our actions upon the well-being of others isn't the only thing that morally matters. Nevertheless, when the consequences of obeying a moral rule are overwhelmingly harmful, most reasonable deontological moral systems instruct us to set the rule aside because the harmful consequences of obeying the rule in the particular case trump other morally relevant considerations. If I have made a death-bed promise to my father, for example, a deontologist like Ross thinks that I should normally keep it even though the consequences of breaking it might be better. If the consequences of keeping my promise to my father would result in severe harm to others, however, I should break it because, in a case like that, the maxim of beneficence overrides the maxim of promise keeping. Now, arguably, the consequences of refusing to employ the tools of violence are sometimes so horrendous that they outweigh any considerations to the contrary. If they are, then absolute pacifism is as unreasonable as an insistence that one should keep one's promises or speak the truth regardless of the probable consequences of doing so.[55]

The universalizability problem   Traditional Christian pacifists believe that the counsels of perfection, *including* those prohibiting any form of retaliation, are obligatory

---

53   Except, of course, in carefully delimited cases. Gandhi was successful in British India and Martin Luther King was successful in the American South, but Gandhi would not have succeeded in "the Russia of 1925 or the Germany of 1933." (Ellul 15)

54   Consequentialists maintain that the moral rightness or wrongness of our actions is solely determined by their direct or indirect consequences. (Classical act utilitarians, for example, argue that an act of promise keeping is right if and only if keeping it produces more happiness than breaking it. Rule utilitarians think that an act of promise keeping is right if it conforms to a rule [namely "Always keep your promises"] general obedience to which produces more good than general obedience to alternative rules governing promise keeping or a situation in which no rule governs it.)

55   Insisting that one should tell the truth in all circumstances, for example, has the morally absurd consequence that if the Gestapo were to ask me if I am hiding Jews, and I am, I should truthfully say "Yes," and allow them to be captured.

on all Christians. In response to the objection that the state would be left defenseless, Origen replied that as long as Christians were in the minority, the empire would not lack for defenders, and if all were to become Christian the problem would disappear. Caleb Miller makes a related point. *True* Christians (those who take Christ's hard demands seriously and attempt to practice them) will always be comparatively few.[56] Hence, in practice, the consequences of Christians' rejection of violence will not be tragic. Most men and women of good will—including most who think of themselves as Christian—will resort to the sword when doing so appears necessary to restrain evil.

But this seems to introduce a generality problem. For the Christian is endorsing a way of life which he knows would have disastrous consequences if too many people followed it. One must be careful to state the problem correctly, however. The consequences would not be disastrous if *everyone* were to follow it. Quite the contrary. Even so, positions like Miller's have the curious consequence that, in a world rife with evil, the Christian should thank God that not all are Christians!

The prohibition against violence can be usefully compared with the maxim "Be a doctor." One can't rationally endorse the universalization of the latter since, if everyone were a doctor, no one would be a farmer or a plumber or a baker, and we would be deprived of goods and services needed for commodious living. Nevertheless, one *can* universalize a maxim like "Be a doctor if you want to be a doctor, have the requisite ability, and there is a need for doctors." The present case seems similar. In a world in which actions and institutions are tainted by what Kant called "radical evil," and "violence is natural and normal to man and society," one can't consistently universalize "Let no one violently resist evil."[57] One can, however, consistently universalize "Follow Christ's path of nonresistance if a sufficient number of men and women of good will will fail to do so," since the consequences in that case will not be disastrous. But even though the universalization of the qualified maxim is consistent, it is not clear that the *Christian* pacifist can rationally will it.

For one thing, it appears to involve a curious perversion, or at least truncation, of the implications of Christ's call to convert all nations. For adopting the qualified (rather than the unqualified) maxim seems to imply that a commitment to Christ's hard precepts is *reasonable* only if many men and women of good will will remain unconverted and therefore resort to the sword when doing so appears necessary to secure or maintain justice. The call to convert all nations is, in effect, transformed into a call to *either* convert *all* nations *or* convert *some* but not too many.

---

56 Note that, in contradistinction to Origen, Miller does not anticipate the immanent conversion of the world in historical time. Given the history of the world since the third century, this is surely more realistic.

57 While the universalized maxim isn't *formally* inconsistent, it does involve what Kant calls a contradiction in the will since what one wills in willing the universalized maxim conflicts with something else one necessarily wills as a rational being, namely, an effective response to aggression and injustice.

For another, traditional Christian pacifists are faced with a rather obvious free-rider problem. For, in many cases at least, the continued flourishing of their way of life depends on the protection of a state whose continued existence ultimately depends upon a willingness to employ the tools of violence they reject.[58] In benefiting from social institutions and practices which they refuse to support, the Christians in question are uncomfortably like those who make exceptions to rules in their own case on the grounds that, because most others won't follow their example, their doing so will not adversely affect the public good by depriving themselves and others of the benefits that follow from general obedience.

Conclusion

A strong case can be made for the claim that Theravāda Buddhists are committed to nonviolence. An equally good case can be made for the claim that Jesus taught his disciples to totally eschew force: violence should be met by nonresistance and evil by good. At the same time, Mouw is surely right in claiming that absolute pacifism conflicts with ordinary moral intuitions—even when those intuitions have been duly pruned and qualified by reflection. It cannot be defended on purely rational grounds.

Only two conclusions seem possible. The first is that, in spite of appearances, neither the Buddha nor Jesus rejected all use of force. This seems disingenuous. As we have seen, Theravāda Buddhists have few resources for defending military action and other forms of violence. And Niebuhr seems right in insisting that it is foolish to "deny that the ethic of Jesus is an absolute and uncompromising ethic." (Niebuhr 1940: 8) There are two ways of restraining the "egoistic impulse"—the way of the Cross and the exercise of coercion, and "there is . . . no possibility of harmonizing" them. (Niebuhr 1932: 270–71)

The only other conclusion possible is that Theravāda Buddhism's and Jesus' teachings on violence fly in the face of what any purely rational ethics would require. It does not follow that the Buddhist's or Christian's commitment to the path of nonresistance is irrational, for he or she may have good reasons for embracing the religious *system* which includes the prohibition of violence as an essential part. It does follow that we have uncovered a real clash between certain religious requirements and the requirements of rational morality.

Are Ordinary Virtues Real Virtues When Divorced from True Religion?

Some Christians have claimed they are not. Augustine, for example, argued that the "virtues" of the Romans were no more than "splendid vices" since even their most admirable actions were motivated by a desire for "glory, honor, and power." But

---

58   And this remains true even if they refuse to resort to the law to protect their interests, or to invoke police protection.

"the love of praise is a vice," for men and women should seek honor from God alone, and not neglect "things which are generally discredited if they are good . . . [or] right."[59]

Perhaps the Romans were motivated by an excessive love of praise. It is not so easy to see how this criticism applies to the rest of us, however. Far from being motivated by an excessive desire for praise, countless acts of quiet virtue are performed every day without thought being given to the praise or blame of others. Yet Jonathan Edwards has argued that most of what ordinarily counts as virtue is not truly virtuous.

True virtue aims at the good of being in general and therefore also esteems the disposition that promotes it. A truly virtuous person thus loves two things—being and benevolence. A virtuous person not only values benevolence because it promotes the general good, however; he or she "relishes" or delights in it for its own sake as well. Hence, while virtue "most essentially consists in benevolence to being," there is a wider sense in which it includes not only benevolence but also "complacence" (delight) in benevolence's intrinsic excellence or beauty.[60]

God, however, "is infinitely the greatest being," and "infinitely the most beautiful and excellent." True virtue thus principally consists "in a supreme love to God, both of benevolence and complacence." (Edwards 550–51) It follows that "a determination of mind to union and benevolence to a *particular person* or *private system* [whether one's self, one's family, one's nation, or even humanity], which is but a small part of the universal system of being . . . is not of the nature of true virtue" unless it is dependent upon, or "subordinate to benevolence to *Being in general.*" (Edwards 554)

One of the main concerns of such eighteenth-century moral philosophers as the Earl of Shaftesbury and Francis Hutcheson was to refute the popular contention that all action is motivated by self-love. Edwards's attitude toward these attempts is ambivalent. On the one hand, he denies that the *truly* benevolent are motivated by self-love. On the other hand, Edwards argues that (*pace* Hutcheson, for instance) most conscientious and other-regarding behavior is indeed a subtle form of self-love. (As we shall see, acts motivated by pity are the only clear exception.) He also argues that acts motivated by rational self-love, conscience, or natural other-regarding instincts such as parental affection or pity aren't genuinely virtuous.

Edwards begins by distinguishing two senses of "self-love." The first is a love of one's own *happiness*, the second a love of one's "private interest."

Everyone is motivated by self-love in the first sense. This "concession" to psychological egoism is trivial, however. For one's happiness is simply what pleases

---

59   Augustine, *The City of God*, trans. Marcus Dods, vol. 1. New York: Hafner, 1948, book v, sections 12–14.

60   Jonathan Edwards, *The Nature of True Virtue*, in Paul Ramsey, ed., *Ethical Writings* (The Works of Jonathan Edwards, vol. 8). New Haven: Yale University Press, p. 540. Henceforth Edwards.

one or what one seeks, whether this be one's own private interest, the well-being of others, or the glory of God. Saying that people are motivated by self-love in the *first* sense, then, is to say no more than that people are pleased with what pleases them or seek what they seek. It is thus necessarily (and trivially) true that any being with a will (and hence any being with desires[61]) desires or seeks or is pleased with its own happiness.

Thomas Hobbes, Bernard Mandeville, and other advocates of the "selfish theory" claim that everyone is motivated by a desire for their own private interest, however, that is, by self-love in its second (and ordinary) sense. Edwards believes this is false.

If everyone is motivated by self-love in the first sense, then so too are the truly benevolent. It doesn't follow that the truly benevolent are motivated by love of their own private interest. Nor does it follow that their love of their own happiness is the *ground* of their love of God and their neighbor. To suppose that it is is to suppose one of two things:

1   That our love of others is grounded in our *capacity* for desiring this or that thing, that is, in our *having* a will or desires.[62]
2   Our love of others is grounded in our love of our own happiness *construed as consisting in their good.*

But the *capacity* for willing or desiring is common to those who place their happiness in the good of others and those who place it in their own private interest. Since it is common to both, its presence can't explain why some are benevolent and others are not. The second alternative is equally unhelpful since it gets things backwards. We don't love others because our happiness consists in their good; our happiness consists in their good because we love them. Just as the miser's happiness consists in wealth because he loves wealth, and the egoist's happiness consists in his own private good because he loves himself rather than others, so the happiness of the truly benevolent consists in the well-being of others because they love others and selflessly desire their happiness.

But while *true* virtue isn't tainted by self-love in Hobbes's or Mandeville's sense, most of what passes for virtue is. Conscience, for example, is a product of a power of placing ourselves in the situation of others (which is necessary for any sort of mutual understanding), a sense of the natural fitness of certain responses (injury and punishment or disapproval, on the one hand, and benefit and reward or approval, on the other), and self-love. Placing ourselves in the situation of those we have injured, we recognize that being treated in that way would not merely anger us

---

61   Edwards identifies will with preponderate desire.
62   Note that while "having a will or desires" doesn't *mean* "desiring or seeking one's own happiness," the two are logically equivalent. If Edwards is right, it is necessarily true that any being with a will (desires) desires happiness, and vice versa.

but seem unfitting or undeserved, and that disapproval and punishment would seem to us to be fitting responses to the injury. We perceive that we are therefore inconsistent in approving of treating others in ways in which we would not wish to be treated ourselves.[63] The resulting sense of "inconsistence" or "self-opposition" makes us "uneasy" since "self-love implies an inclination to feel and act as one with ourselves." (Edwards 589)

What, though, about instinctual other-regarding impulses such as parental affection, "mutual attraction between the sexes" (as distinct from simple sexual attraction), and pity? Edwards is inclined to think that all except pity are forms of self-love[64] although, for the sake of argument, he is prepared to concede that they aren't. The important point is that even if actions motivated by these impulses *can't* be reduced to self-love, they aren't truly virtuous. To see why, consider pity.[65]

If the only truly virtuous actions are those motivated by benevolence toward being in general, then actions motivated by other-regarding impulses that are ultimately directed to "some particular persons or private system" aren't truly virtuous. (Edwards 601) Pity, for example, is directed to those in extreme distress whose suffering appears to us to be undeserved or excessive. Its object is therefore confined to only part of being in general. (Pity's restricted scope is also evidenced by the fact that we sometimes pity those whose "positive pleasure" we are "indifferent" to, or even those to whom we wish ill when the latter's "calamity goes beyond [our] hatred." [Ibid. 606–7]) Moreover, since instinctual affections aren't "dependent" on "general benevolence,"[66] they potentially conflict with it. Everyone admits that this is true of one's affection for oneself (self-love). Yet the situation is no different when the object of one's affection is any other system that falls "infinitely short of universal existence." (Ibid. 602) Pity, for instance, may motivate a judge to act unjustly, and one can be so wrapped up in one's family that one neglects one's duties toward the larger community to which one belongs.

We can't conclude that natural affection, pity, or even rational self-love are *bad*, however. On the contrary, since they tend toward "the preservation of mankind and

---

63   The inconsistency isn't between propositions like "I approve of injuring Mary (since injuring her is in my interest, or because I am angry with her, or the like)" and "I would disapprove of it if I were in her shoes;" or between my *feeling* of approval and the *judgment* that my action deserves recrimination or punishment; but between my conflicting *feelings* of approval and disapproval. It is not a *formal* inconsistency, in other words, but an inconsistency of attitude.

64   Self-love, for example, is the source of our affection toward those who "are near to us by the ties of nature"—our children, for example, and others in whom we have a proprietary interest. (Edwards 584) This is plausible where the child isn't loved for her own sake but because she reflects well on her parents, carries on the family line, and the like, that is, where one's love for one's child is like one's love for one's possessions and accouterments. It is much less plausible in other cases.

65   It is worth noting that Rousseau sometimes makes pity the natural basis, or biological underpinning, of virtue.

66   When, that is, their "operation" is "detached and unsubordinate."

their comfortably subsisting in the world," things would be much worse without them. (Ibid. 600) A world without pity for example, or without mutual affection between the sexes, would be a much more miserable place. Edwards's point is merely that their goodness isn't a truly *moral* goodness. (Compare Kant's claim that actions exclusively motivated by natural inclinations such as sympathy have worth but not *moral* worth.)

The fact remains that natural virtues are either tainted by self-love or fail to extend to being in general. They are thus mere counterfeits or simulacra of true virtue.[67] While they prompt us to promote the good of others, and to condemn those dispositions and actions with impair it, they fall infinitely "short of the extent of true virtuous benevolence, both in . . . nature and object." (Edwards 609)[68] Edwards concludes that true virtue is not a natural endowment nor a natural achievement, but a supernatural gift.

---

67   Why, though, are actions motivated by conscience, rational self-love, and natural other-regarding impulses so often *mistaken* for truly virtuous actions? For several reasons, including the following: (1) They have many of the same consequences. Actions motivated by pity, natural affection, rational self-interest, and so on tend, on the whole, to benefit humankind, and thus promote the good of being in general. (Although, as Edwards notes, so too do actions motivated by our desire for self-preservation, our desire for affection, and the like; yet no one thinks that *"these* have the nature of true virtue." [Edwards 616, my emphasis]) (2) Our other-regarding desires are *forms* of love (of others) and thus *resemble* true benevolence. (3) A love of private systems, and acts motivated by it, "are beautiful *within their own private sphere*." (Edwards 610, my emphasis) That is, *if* the objects to which these loves are directed were the *whole* of being, the loves would be truly virtuous (and thus truly beautiful). One reason why a love of humanity, or even of one's nation or party, is so often confused with true virtue is that people restrict their attention to these private systems and, in effect, identify them with the whole of (conscious) being. This also explains why even a *rational* self-love is less commonly identified with true virtue; it is more difficult to regard the *self* as the whole of being.

68   Are they therefore *sinful*, as Edwards thinks? Jonathan Kvanvig denies that they are. Saving a child from a fall because of one's compassion for her is virtuous even if one's act isn't motivated by true benevolence. The character of those whose lives aren't motivated by a love of being in general may be flawed but "flaws of character . . . do not infect every action a person performs." (Jonathan L. Kvanvig, *The Problem of Hell*. New York: Oxford University Press, 1993, p. 35) This isn't convincing. If Edwards is right, then every action should be (primarily) motivated by true benevolence. (Edwards notes that this does not imply that whenever one is motivated by true benevolence one is explicitly *thinking* of being in general.) If an action isn't rooted in the motive that *should* have prompted it, however, then the *action* (and not merely the agent's charac-ter) is defective. Kvanvig's distinction between flawless characters and flawless actions is, in this case at least, spurious.

Conclusion

This chapter has argued that the ethical teachings of some mainstream religious traditions have implications that can't help but appear counter-intuitive from the standpoint of nonreligious moral systems.[69] Pacifism is firmly embedded in the Buddhist and Christian traditions, for example, yet it is very difficult to see how absolute pacifism[70] could be defended on nonreligious grounds. The notion that most of what ordinarily passes as virtue is really a "splendid vice" seems equally outrageous. Yet Edwards's identification of true virtue with love toward being in general fits well with a "contemporary agapeistic ethics" which "centers Christian ethics on the gospel imperative to love God with all one's heart, soul and mind and to love one's neighbor as oneself."[71] If this identification is correct, Edwards's "outrageous" conclusion seems to follow.

These tensions between nonreligious and (some) religious moralities should not be exaggerated, however. Absolute pacifists may be dismissed as misguided or irrational but few think of them as immoral. And while Edwards believes that most of what passes for virtue isn't properly motivated, and hence isn't truly virtuous, he admits that the *content* of non-Christian and Christian ethics[72] is pretty much the same.

The tension would be much greater if a tradition were to command actions which almost all of us would regard as clearly *im*moral. We will examine a possibility of this sort in the next chapter.

---

69 Nonreligious does not necessarily mean anti-religious. Natural law ethics, Kantian theories, and classical utilitarianism can be, and have been, adopted by Christian thinkers. How well these systems comport with Christianity is a moot question, however.

70 As distinguished from "nuclear pacifism," say, or a pragmatic pacifism which argues that nonviolence can be an effective tactic in some situations.

71 Philip L. Quinn, "The Master Argument of *The Nature of True Virtue*," in Paul Helm and Oliver D. Crisp, eds, *Jonathan Edwards: Philosophical Theologian*. Aldershot, UK: Ashgate, 2003, p. 96.

72 That is, the *actions* condemned or commended.

CHAPTER 10

Abraham and the Binding of Isaac

Abraham and Sarah are childless but God tells Abraham that he will bless Sarah, and give Abraham a son by her, with whom he will establish a perpetual covenant "to be his God and the God of his descendants after him." (Genesis 17: 19) In spite of the fact that both are long past the age of childbearing, Abraham believes the promise. And, indeed, they have a son and name him Isaac.

But then, after the child is born, God "tests" Abraham, saying "Take your only child Isaac, whom you love, and go to the land of Moriah," and "offer him as a burnt offering on a mountain I will point out to you." So Abraham, accompanied by two servants and his son Isaac, travels three days until the party comes to the place God has indicated. Leaving his servants behind, Abraham loads the wood for the burnt offering on his son Isaac, takes the fire and the knife for the sacrifice, and sets off with Isaac for the mountain. On their journey, Isaac says to his father, "Look . . . here are the fire and the wood, but where is the lamb for the burnt offering?", and Abraham replies "My son, God himself will provide the lamb for the burnt offering." When they arrive Abraham builds an altar, binds Isaac, places "him on the altar on top of the wood," and takes up the knife to sacrifice his son. (Genesis 22: 2–10)

At that point, however, the "angel of Yahweh" calls to Abraham from heaven, saying, "Do not raise your hand against the boy . . . for now I know you fear God" since "you have not refused me your son, your only son." Abraham then sees a ram caught in a thicket by its horns and offers it in place of Isaac. Whereupon the angel speaks to Abraham a second time: "I swear by my own self—it is Yahweh who speaks—because you have done this, because you have not refused me your son, your only son, I will shower blessings on you, I will make your descendants as many as the stars of heaven and the grains of sand on the seashore," and "all the nations of the earth shall bless themselves by your descendants, as a reward for your obedience." (Genesis 22: 11–19)

What are we to make of this? Perhaps the dominant interpretation among mainstream Old Testament scholars is that while the story may have originally "circulated as an independent legend" justifying "the commutation of child sacrifice,"[1] its primary emphasis is on Abraham's obedience.[2]

The fact remains that even though Yahweh tells Abraham to stay his hand, and provides a substitutory offering, he *first* commands him to sacrifice his son, and

---

1   Bernhard W. Anderson, *Understanding the Old Testament*, 4th edn. Upper Saddle River, NJ: Prentice-Hall, 1998, p. 158.
2   See, for example, Helmer Ringgren, *Israelite Religion*. Philadelphia: Fortress Press, 1966, pp. 174–5.

Abraham is prepared to obey him. Nor does the story suggest that there is anything improper or untoward about either God's command or Abraham's willingness to obey it.

This is troubling, and not just if we assume that the account is historical. Even if it is not, it remains true that the God in whom Jews, Christians, and Muslims believe is represented in the story as commanding something that seems clearly immoral. Even if God did not in fact command Abraham to kill an innocent child, the Bible presents us with the picture of a God who would have been within his rights to do so, and extolls sincere compliance with such a command as a model of faithful obedience. How should we understand this troubling story?

Augustine thought that the clue is provided by the fact that "the divine authority" can make "exceptions . . . to its own law that men may not be put to death." It can do this in two ways. God can grant a *general* exemption to those in positions of authority, for the purpose of protecting the citizens of the commonwealth from violent criminals and external aggressors. Or God can make an exception "by a special commission granted for a time to some individual." In either case, where an exception has been made, one person may put another "to death without incurring the guilt of murder."[3]

Thus Abraham "was not merely deemed guiltless of cruelty, but was even applauded for his piety, because he was ready to slay his son in obedience to God, not to his own passion." Because God had made an exception to the commandment "You shall not kill" when he ordered Abraham to sacrifice Isaac, Abraham did not violate God's commands and, *eo ipso*, did not violate God's commandment not to kill.[4] Augustine's "solution" proved influential and was adopted by later medieval theologians such as Bernard of Clairvaux.

Aquinas's interpretation is more carefully nuanced. According to Aquinas, "The intention of every lawgiver is directed first and chiefly to the common good [that is, to the good of the commonwealth]; secondly, to the order of justice and virtue, whereby the common good is preserved and attained."[5] Precepts incorporating and/ or directly expressing these intentions, such as "Do justice," are inviolable. But other precepts admit of dispensation when violating them would serve rather than impair the order of justice or the common good. For example, it is possible that in some cases social justice would be better served by affirmative action than by tying college admissions solely to an applicant's academic merits.

What is true of legislators in general is true of the divine lawgiver. God's legislative intentions are directly expressed in the Decalogue. Each of us is a member of a commonwealth of which God is the ruler and chief magistrate, and the "common and final good" of this commonwealth—that toward which everything in

---

3   Augustine, *The City of God*, trans. Marcus Dods. New York: Hafner, 1948. Book I, chapter 21.

4   Ibid.

5   Thomas Aquinas, *Summa Theologica*, I–II, Q. 100, A. 8.

it is directed—is God himself. "You shall have no other gods before me," and other precepts of the first table, direct us to this common and final good. Precepts of the second table, such as "You shall not bear false witness" and "You shall not unjustly kill another," incorporate and express "the order of justice to be observed among men, that nothing undue be done to anyone, and that each one be given his due." Now God's intention that everything be directed toward himself as the final good of all, and that the "order of justice" be observed, is inviolable. But particular divine precepts, such as those regulating temple worship, can be set aside when doing so best serves God's primary and inviolable intentions.[6]

Against this background we can see that Abraham would not have violated divine law if he had killed Isaac at God's behest. For while Isaac is innocent of any personal offense, and it is a precept of justice that the lives of those innocent of personal offenses should not be taken, God has justly inflicted "the punishment of death on *all* men . . . on account of the sin of our first parent." It follows that "if a man be the executer of that sentence *by Divine authority*, he will be no murderer any more than God would be." Since in killing Isaac "nothing undue" would have been done to Isaac, the precept of the Decalogue prohibiting the taking of human life would not have been violated, "*as to the essence of justice which*" it contains.[7] If Aquinas is right, then, there is no *real* violation of the ethical because Abraham's willingness to sacrifice Isaac preserves the order of justice and subserves the common good. Neither Abraham's willingness to sacrifice Isaac nor the deed itself fails to give Isaac his due since, as a consequence of Adam's sin, Isaac owes God his life, and God has commissioned Abraham to take it. Moreover, Abraham's faithful obedience is directed towards the common and final good of all, namely God.

In spite of their differences, Augustine and Aquinas agree both that Abraham would have acted ethically if he had offered Isaac as a burnt offering at God's behest, and that there was nothing ethically improper or infelicitous in God's commanding Abraham to kill his son. There *appears* to be a conflict between Abraham's religious duty to obey God and his ethical duty to his son Isaac, but the conflict is only apparent.

The most influential modern interpretation of the story, on the other hand, argues that the tension between the religious and the ethical which it evinces is real and not merely apparent.

Kierkegaard and Abraham

Søren Kierkegaard's *Fear and Trembling* is an extended meditation on the faith of Abraham.

---

6   Ibid.
7   Ibid., my emphases.

In an early section its pseudonymous author, Johannes de Silentio, uses a story to draw a distinction between the "Knight of Resignation" and the "Knight of Faith." A young man is deeply in love with a princess. He loves her so intensely that "the whole content of his life" and "the whole significance of reality" is concentrated in the "single wish" to win her. Yet he then discovers that it is impossible that his wish be realized.[8] At this point he makes the "movement of infinite resignation." He does not relinquish his *love*—it remains as young and as fresh "as it was in its first moment." But he *does* relinquish his beloved. He "no longer takes a finite interest in what the princess is doing." He no longer needs to hear news of her, and whether or not the princess marries can no longer "disturb him." (55) For in performing the movement of resignation, the young man's "love for that princess became the expression of an eternal love, assumed a religious character, was transfigured into a love for the Eternal Being." (54)

How should this be understood? Robert Adams suggests that Kierkegaard (or Johannes) is implying that "total devotion to God" requires a perfect detachment from everything finite. Yet, unlike Buddhist detachment, Kierkegaard does not think that this involves the systematic "extinction of desire." Rather, one must focus all one's desire on a single point, and *only then* offer one's love to God by relinquishing love's object *while retaining one's love*.[9] There are two reasons for this. First, our desires for, and our interests in, the finite are normally too many and too various to be successfully combated *in toto*. When we succeed in detaching ourselves from one of our finite interests, another immediately presents itself. If we manage to also detach ourselves from that, we find ourselves faced with a third finite interest. And so on. "It may therefore be advantageous to religion if desire for the finite presents itself in one head that can be severed by a single stroke of resignation." Second, Kierkegaard seems to think that the Knight of Resignation's love of God "draw[s] some of its substance—presumably its concentration—from his love for the princess." Given the immeasurable gulf between the infinite and the finite, "no positive content of a human life" is "inherently suited to express the divine. A negative expression" alone is possible, namely, a renunciation of the finite interest in which one has concentrated the "whole content of [one's] life" and "the whole significance of reality."[10]

---

8   Søren Kierkegaard, *Fear and Trembling*, trans. Walter Lowrie. Garden City, NY: Doubleday Anchor Books, 1954, pp. 52–3. All references in this section are to this work unless otherwise noted.

9   The latter is crucial. If one doesn't *continue* to find the whole meaning and significance of the finite bound up in the object of one's passion, if one's interest in the princess becomes just one more interest among others, then relinquishing the object of one's passion ceases to be a total renunciation of the finite.

10   Robert M. Adams, "The Knight of Faith," *Faith and Philosophy* 7 (1990), pp. 387–90. Adams himself finds this religious strategy defective. In the first place, "the finite objects most apt to engage our love are persons, and . . . sacrificing a person is apt to be harmful to the person sacrificed." In the second, "the knight's passion for his

The movement of resignation is difficult and few of us have the strength of character to make it, but it is not the object of Johannes's wonder. That is reserved for the movement of faith. To make that movement, the young man would have had to relinquish the princess while *at the same time* believing, "Nevertheless . . . I shall get her, in virtue, that is, of the absurd, in virtue of the fact that with God all things are possible." (57) That is, while continuing to resign the princess whom he loves with all his heart, and sincerely believing that it is impossible that the princess be his, he at the same time firmly believes that he will get her since, for God, nothing is impossible. And this, says Johannes, is not merely difficult but "absurd."[11]

Abraham, too, makes the movement of infinite resignation. The "whole content" of Abraham's life is concentrated in Isaac, whom he loves with all his heart, and through whom he believes God's promise will be fulfilled. Yet God commands Abraham to offer Isaac as a burnt offering. And, while Abraham realizes that if he obeys God he will lose the most precious thing he has, and God's promise can't be fulfilled,[12] he performs the movement of resignation: without relinquishing his *love* for Isaac,[13] he relinquishes his son.

But then Abraham performs *another* movement, the movement of faith, and wholeheartedly believes that—in virtue of the absurd—he will nevertheless *not* lose Isaac. And that, says Johannes, is why Abraham is great. "For it is great to give up one's wish, but it is greater to hold it fast after having given it up, it is great to grasp the eternal, but it is greater to hold fast to the temporal after having given it up." (33) Yet Johannes professes to be unable to understand Abraham. He *can* understand how Abraham, or even he, might make the movement of infinite resignation, giving up what he most loves in this world. For "this is a . . . movement which I dare say I am able to make if it is required, and which I can train myself to make. . . . " But I can't make the movement of faith "by my own strength, . . . for I am constantly using my strength to renounce everything." (59–60) Nor can Johannes understand how Abraham can be "joyful again with Isaac" after God stays his hand,

---

'princess'" continues to "define . . . the meaning of his life, and specifically its religious character as devotion to God"—yet this seems idolatrous. Freely adapting a comment of Martin Buber (in *Between Man and Man* [Boston: Beacon Press, 1955], p. 57): "God as the princess's successful rival? Is that still God?" Adams's first point is well taken but his second is unpersuasive. For when all is said and done, the meaning of the Knight of Resignation's life is *not* defined by his passion for the princess but, instead, by the sacrifice of the one thing that (apart from God) he holds dearest. How is this idolatrous?

11   That is, paradoxical, "incomprehensible," although not literally self-contradictory.
12   That is, if attention is restricted to the temporal order, there is no possibility that "something will turn up." From the point of view of the finite, the catastrophe is irreparable.
13   Abraham loves Isaac as few fathers have loved their sons and, indeed, if he does not "then every thought of offering Isaac would be not a trial but a base temptation." (42)

how Abraham can receive Isaac back with joy as though nothing terrible had happened. (46)

But there is yet another, and perhaps even greater, "absurdity"—the "teleological suspension of the ethical." God commands Abraham to sacrifice his son—and Abraham has an "absolute duty" toward God. And yet if Abraham does obey God and kills Isaac, "he sins, even though *realiter* [in reality] his deed were that which it was his absolute duty to do." (80) For while "the religious expression" "for what Abraham did . . . is that he would sacrifice Isaac," "the ethical expression . . . is that he would murder Isaac:" and "precisely in this contradiction consists the dread which can well make a man sleepless." (41)

How should we understand these remarks? "The ethical as such is the universal," that is, incumbent on each of us without exception. Furthermore, each person, in her "particularity," with her own individual outlook, hopes, fears, and desires, has her "telos [aim, end] in the universal." Our "ethical task," therefore, is "to abolish [our] particularity in order to become the universal." Thus Kant, for instance, says that our actions should ultimately be expressions of our basic commitment to a moral law that is incumbent on all rational beings, not of the contingent and varied desires and inclinations we have as finite and limited beings necessarily interested in our own happiness. From the moral point of view, then, an individual sins "as soon as [he] would assert himself in his particularity over against the [ethical] universal." And if he "feels an impulse to assert himself as the particular, he is in temptation." (64–5)

For a Knight of Faith, on the other hand, "the particular is *higher* [my emphasis] than the universal" in virtue of its standing in "an absolute relationship to the absolute"—in virtue, that is, of standing under a special command of a God with whom one has a direct or unmediated personal relationship. (65–6) For such an individual, the *ethical universal* can be the temptation. For while "what ordinarily tempts a man is that which would keep him from doing his [ethical] duty," in a case like Abraham's, "the temptation is itself the ethical . . . which would keep him from doing God's will." For in this case, his real "duty is precisely the expression for God's will." (70) Someone like Abraham is therefore lost unless there is such a thing as a "teleological suspension of the ethical" (67)—unless that is, the ethical can be suspended in the name of "a higher telos" (69), unless, in other words, an ethical duty can be contravened by a higher duty.

Now, as Kierkegaard recognizes, in one sense the idea that an ethical duty can be contravened by a higher duty isn't controversial. A calm prevents the Greek forces from sailing to Troy. The gods inform their commander, Agamemnon, that fair winds will not blow until he sacrifices his beloved daughter, Iphigenia. And, in pain and suffering, he does so. Again, Brutus, one of the first consuls of republican Rome, executes his own sons when they attempt to restore the tyranny of the Tarquins. Both Agamemnon and Brutus violate their duty toward their children for the good of the nation, their duty toward the latter taking precedence over their duty toward the former. But in their cases, their justification is clear—to allow the Greek fleet to sail, and to preserve the Roman republic. Agamemnon and Brutus, as Johannes says, sacrifice the ethical to the ethical. By contrast, what stands against Abraham's ethical duty to his son is not a more stringent ethical universal (such as "Preserve the nation") but a divine command that, in this particular case, Abraham simply suspend the ethical and kill Isaac.

Yet isn't the general duty to obey God's commands *itself* an ethical obligation, perhaps even the highest one? It is tempting to think that it is. But *if* it is, then the ethical is *not* suspended, and Abraham's case seems to be more like Agamemnon's and Brutus's than Johannes thinks. The dread, if not eliminated entirely, is of an altogether different sort. For like Agamemnon and Brutus, Abraham can take comfort in the thought that, no matter how difficult and painful it may be, his willingness to kill Isaac is ethically justified.

This interpretation unduly sanitizes Johannes's understanding of Abraham, however. The ethical is the universal and, as such, is transparent to reason. Kant and Hegel are representative of modern ethical thought in believing that true moral claims can, in principle, be justified by reasons which other rational beings will find compelling. They are also representative of much modern ethical and religious thought in believing that a rational religion relates itself to God only *through* the ethical. Kant, for instance, says that "moral religion" consists "in the heart's disposition to fulfil all *human* duties as divine commands."[14] Johannes's criticism of this view is threefold.

First, in saying that human beings can relate to God only through the ethical, *God* tends to vanish altogether. On this view, "if I say . . . that it is my duty to love God, I am really uttering only a tautology, in as much as 'God' is in this instance used in an entirely abstract sense as the divine, i.e. the universal, i.e. duty. . . . God becomes an invisible vanishing point, a powerless thought, his power being only in the ethical which," on this view, becomes, in effect, the whole "content of human existence." (78) The ethical, in other words, becomes a *substitute* for God. The object of our ultimate concern, what is 'God' for us, is, for all practical purposes, identified with the ethical. And this is idolatrous.

Second, there is no *direct* relationship to God, on this view, since any relation to God that one has is mediated *through* the ethical. Duty may be "referred to God, but in duty itself I do not come into relation to God. Thus it is a duty to love one's neighbor, but in performing this duty I do not come into relation with God but with the neighbor whom I love." (78) In *faith*, on the other hand, "the individual . . . determines his relation to the universal [the ethical] by his relation to the absolute [God], not his relation to the absolute by his relation to the universal." (80) One stands directly before the God who is "fire"[15]—the God of Abraham, Isaac, and Jacob, not of the philosophers— and submits to him in love, fear, and trembling.

---

14   Kant, *Religion*, p. 79. My emphasis.
15   The reference is to a paper found among Pascal's effects after his death in 1662.

Finally, while it may be true that one has an absolute duty to God, it isn't clear that this duty is an essentially moral one, or that it is fully transparent to reason.[16] In the first place, although there may be a sense in which it is "reasonable" to submit unconditionally to God's direct commands, the *ground* of our obligation to do so is presumably his goodness, and God's goodness may not be a wholly *moral* goodness. (More on this later.) Moreover, unlike our purely human duties (to respect others as ends in themselves, to aid the unfortunate, and the like), we may not be able to see the reasonableness of the *content* of the obligations imposed on us by divine commands (to kill Isaac, say). That is, we may be unable to justify what we are commanded to do by appealing to ethical values endorsed by reason. For if the duty to God "is absolute, the ethical is reduced to a position of relativity," that is, can no longer be taken as absolute or indefeasible. It "does not follow that the ethical is to be abolished, but it acquires an entirely different expression . . . —that, for example, love to God may cause the Knight of Faith to give his love to his neighbor the *opposite expression to that which, ethically speaking, is required by duty*." (80, my emphasis) It may cause Abraham, for instance, *to kill Isaac*.

But not only is this "incomprehensible," as Johannes claims, it seems morally repugnant. The next section will therefore examine three recent interpretations of *Fear and Trembling* that attempt to reduce or eliminate the moral repugnancy by domesticating the book's message.

Three Recent Interpretations of Kierkegaard's Abraham

Gellman and the "Existential Trial"

Jerome Gellman and a number of other recent interpreters think that Kierkegaard's Johannes identifies the ethical with Hegel's *Sittlichkeit*—a set of institutionally defined roles (parent, citizen, physician, and so on) each with its own built-in duties, obligations, rights, and privileges. For Hegel, *Sittlichkeit* corrects Kantian personal morality or *Moralität*. By grounding morality in pure reason, the latter tends to be unduly subjective and, in practice, often serves as no more than an excuse for furthering "one's non-moral or even immoral interests in the name of lofty moral principles."[17] For one who exists at what Kierkegaard calls the "ethical stage of life," the ethical is absolute. Indeed, her very identity as a person, the way she defines and understands herself, is largely determined by the socially sanc-

---

16 And, as noted earlier, on the standard view, *moral* demands *are* fully transparent to reason.

17 Jerome I. Gellman, *Abraham! Abraham!: Kierkegaard and the Hasidim on the Binding of Isaac*. Aldershot: Ashgate, 2003, p. 32. All references in this subsection are to this book unless otherwise noted.

tioned roles assigned to her. As a consequence, for such an individual, to reject the ethical is to reject her self.

Now, for Abraham, the most encompassing social entity is not the nation (as it was for Agamemnon and Brutus) but the family. His highest obligation, therefore, is to Isaac. In this context, then, God's demand that he sacrifice Isaac is a demand that he dissociate himself from his social roles, and from his identification of himself as a father and head of a family and, instead, exist as a "single one" in "an absolute relation to the absolute."

Gellman's interpretation takes its clue from Edward F. Mooney.[18] According to Mooney, Abraham faces a genuine dilemma. For there are no objectively valid procedures for deciding between following a universally valid ethical principle and following "a non-moral religious demand." Abraham must therefore decide from what Mooney calls his "deep subjectivity," his "most personal truth." "The right decision . . . would [thus] have been *whatever* Abraham would have decided, as long as Abraham's choice reflected in the deepest way his personal integrity, coming from his deep subjectivity." (30)

Gellman's view is similar. God's call to Abraham is a call to exist as a single one "in unfettered individuality before God." (38) God calls Abraham, as he calls each of us, "to stand alone before the face of God." To stand alone before God's face, however, "is to be measured by total possibility, by freedom to choose oneself, independently of and outside of the imposition of any embodiment of morality." (37) As a result, one's duty to God is, ultimately, "a duty to oneself" (38), "a duty to choose oneself in total freedom." (37) Since this is the *real* content of God's demand, Abraham's *willingness* to sacrifice Isaac is sufficient to meet it; the sacrifice itself is not necessary. And, indeed, Abraham would have responded appropriately to God's command even if he had *refused* to sacrifice Isaac, *provided* that his choice was made in "total freedom."

Gellman's interpretation of Kierkegaard is intriguing but problematic. For one thing, as a number of Kierkegaard scholars have suggested, Johannes's interpretation of the ethical is at least as Kantian as it is Hegelian.[19] If it is, then dissociating oneself from the ethical not only involves dissociating oneself from the roles defined by the institutionally embodied morality which happens to be current at one's time and place; it also involves dissociating oneself from duties that appear to be incumbent on *any* rational being no matter how he or she is culturally situated— duties such as treating others as ends and not as means only, for example, or not killing innocent children. And that would be deeply troubling.

---

18   Edward F. Mooney, "Abraham and Dilemma: Kierkegaard's Teleological Suspension Revisited," *International Journal for Philosophy of Religion* 19 (1986), pp. 23–41.

19   See, for example, Seung-Goo Lee, "The Antithesis Between the Religious View of Ethics and the Rationalist View of Ethics in *Fear and Trembling*," in Robert L. Perkins, ed., *Fear and Trembling and Repetition* (International Kierkegaard Commentary). Macon, GA: Mercer University Press, 1993, pp. 101–26.

For another, it is not clear that Mooney (and, by extension, Gellman) grasps the depths of Abraham's dilemma. For Mooney's Abraham is forced back on himself, and compelled to choose in freedom, because there is no objectively valid procedure for deciding whether to follow a universally valid ethical requirement or a competing nonmoral demand. But notice that precisely the same *sort* of dilemma arises from conflicts between irreconcilable *moral* requirements, for in these cases, too, there are no objectively valid procedures for making a decision. Here, too, we are thrown back on our freedom, and must decide from our "deep subjectivity," our "most personal truth." Yet in *these* cases, we are choosing between conflicting *ethical* demands and so, no matter what we choose, *we remain within the ethical*. Abraham's situation is radically different. The essence of *his* dilemma[20] is that God demands that he *set aside the ethical altogether*.

Finally, for Johannes (and Kierkegaard), one isn't just to choose oneself in freedom; one is to choose oneself as a "single one" *before God*,"[21] that is, *choose God*. Gellman's interpretation has the paradoxical consequence that Abraham could obey God by disobeying him. Yet this surely makes nonsense of the story as Johannes understands it. For Johannes, Abraham is to accede to God's "non-moral religious demand" by choosing to *obey* God and sacrifice Isaac.

Outka and the Teleological Suspension of Conventional Morality

Gene Outka, too, thinks that Johannes's understanding of the ethical is Hegelian. Yet Outka recognizes that the decision confronting Abraham is not just a decision to accept or refuse his authentic self. It is a decision to obey or not obey God's explicit command that he sacrifice Isaac.[22]

Toward the latter part of his essay, Outka raises two questions about choices of this sort: "May the agent employ his own antecedent moral criteria of judgment to evaluate whether a given command really has a divine origin? . . . And should he bring his own [moral] criteria to bear to decide whether to follow a command, even supposing he knows it to be God's?" (235)

Kant thinks that the answer to both questions is "yes." Kierkegaard, however, believes that: "1) God is 'incommensurable with the whole of reality.' 2) He retains the initiative in disclosures to men." And "3) His governance exceeds human understanding of it." (240; the internal quote is from *Fear and Trembling*. [45]) (4) Our "practical reason" suffers not only from finitude, moreover, but from sin. As a consequence, while "human beings may properly challenge each other on the basis

---

20 As described by Johannes.

21 It is important to remember that Kierkegaard (and presumably his pseudonym Johannes) has a theocentric conception of the self.

22 Gene Outka, "Religious and Moral Duty: Notes on *Fear and Trembling*," in Gene Outka and John P. Reeder, eds, *Religion and Morality*. Garden City, NY: Anchor/ Doubleday, 1973, pp. 204–54. References in this subsection are to this article.

of prior criteria of moral evaluation . . . , the 'infinite qualitative difference' be-tween" God's infinity, wisdom, and holiness, on the one hand, and human finiteness, ignorance, and sinfulness, on the other, "prevents any straightforward transfer of this procedure" to God.[23] (241) How, then, should Abraham decide?

As Johannes portrays him, Abraham is rightly convinced that God has com-manded him to sacrifice Isaac. (Neither Johannes nor Kierkegaard doubts that God can make his will clear to someone if he wishes to do so.[24]) So Abraham's trial is not that he must decide whether the demand does or doesn't come from God. It is to decide whether or not to *obey* God, and whether, if he chooses to obey him, he can retain his joyful confidence in God's promises.

Now Outka thinks that Kierkegaard (and Abraham) believes that God is ulti-mately loving, and therefore cannot command anything that "involves turning men finally from himself," from the life of loving communion with God which is their inmost highest possibility. So, given what God is and seeks (namely, loving com-munion with human beings), Abraham "cannot do anything to Isaac which is 'finally' unloving if [he] obeys God." Indeed, "Abraham is confident that *unless* he obeys God, he cannot 'love' Isaac. For God will not, *eo ipso*, command what is unloving." (245, my emphasis)

"To be a knight of faith," therefore, "is to remain confident that the command is loving" in spite of the fact that not only can't one see *how* it is loving, one's antecedent moral criteria would have led one to judge that it was *unloving*. (244) Kierkegaard can thus conclude, "God you are to love in unconditional obedience, even if what he demands of you may seem to you to be to your own harm—*yes, harmful to his cause*. For the wisdom of God is not to be compared with yours, and God's governance is not in duty bound, answerable to your prudence" (*or*, it seems, to your antecedent moral convictions). "All you have to do is to obey in love" trusting that God will not undermine his own loving purposes.[25]

Does Outka's interpretation do justice to Abraham's dilemma as Johannes under-stands it? If Outka is correct, then what is "teleologically suspended" is *not* the ethical *as such* but (1) conventional judgments as to what ethics requires and (2) one's own best judgment as to what would be the most ethical course— *in so far as that judgment has been formed in abstraction from a consideration of what God commands*. Moreover, while, on Outka's view, Abraham's highest obligation is indeed to stand in "an absolute relation to the absolute," this relation isn't just an

---

23 The danger, here, of course, is that if one brackets or suspends one's antecedent moral understanding, one may lose one's grip on the meaning and/or reality of God's good-ness.

24 So is Kierkegaard's answer to Outka's first question "Yes"? Not clearly, since Abraham's certainty that God is addressing him may be based on an "inward inspiration" (Aquinas) directly rooted in God's causal activity or on Abraham's previous experience of God, and not on Abraham's "antecedent moral criteria of judgment."

25 Søren Kierkegaard, *Works of Love*, trans. Howard and Edna Hong. New York: Harper, 1962, p. 36, my emphasis.

obedience relation, not even an obedience relation to a God whom one loves with all one's heart; it is a *loving* communion with a loving God of which obedience is merely the expression or consequence. The result is that while Outka preserves the tension between the religious demand and our (and Abraham's) *understanding* of the ethical, Abraham does not ultimately step *outside* the ethical. Like Agamemnon and Brutus, he only sacrifices the ethical to the ethical—choosing to set aside his obligations to his innocent son in the name of a higher moral obligation, namely, his obligation to obey the commands of a loving God. And indeed, on Outka's view, it is not clear that he even does that. For not only is his killing of Isaac not unloving; it can't frustrate God's loving purposes for Isaac. How then, do the ethical claims Isaac has on him prohibit it? Yet if they don't, the ethical isn't sacrificed *at all*. The upshot is that the tension between the religious and the ethical—which lies at the heart of the story as Johannes understands it—ultimately evaporates.

Evans on the Unconditional Character of the Ethical

In "Faith as the Telos of Morality," C. Stephen Evans argues that "the message of *Fear and Trembling*" is *not* that "the person of faith may be required to act in a way that is contrary to moral duty." If it were, it would be inconsistent with the rest of Kierkegaard's writings.[26] For example, the pseudonymous author of the *Concluding Unscientific Postscript* says that the ethical is "preserved" in the religious. And the *Christian Discourses* (which are written in Kierkegaard's own person) ask, "What, then, is the eternal?" To which his response is "It is the difference between right and wrong. All else is transitory . . . all other differences are evanescent. . . . But the difference between right and wrong remains eternally."[27]

What, then, is *Fear and Trembling*'s target? Evans now thinks that while Johannes's *language* is often Kantian, his *understanding* of the ethical is essentially Hegelian: he identifies the ethical with socially instituted and sanctioned roles and values. Since these always stand under God's judgment, however, our duty can't be straightforwardly identified with the obligations they impose. Even though prebellum southern society sanctioned slavery, for instance, a Christian's duty was to oppose it.

Thus far Evans's interpretation resembles Gellman's and Outka's. But Evans thinks that Johannes's critique of Hegelian ethics goes deeper. The ethical, as Hegel and Johannes conceive it, is "in some sense absolute or final." (Evans 1993: 17) "It . . . has nothing outside itself which is its *telos* but is itself *telos* of everything outside it." (*Fear and Trembling* 64) In Hegel's and Johannes's view, one becomes an ethical self by willing the good—by identifying oneself with the good and

---

26   C. Stephen Evans, "Faith as the Telos of Morality: A Reading of *Fear and Trembling*," in *Fear and Trembling and Repetition*, p. 11. Henceforth Evans 1993.

27   Søren Kierkegaard, *Christian Discourses: The Crisis and a Crisis in the Life of an Actress*. Princeton, NJ: Princeton University Press, 1997, pp. 207–8.

embodying it in one's actions, thoughts, and character or, as Johannes says, by abolishing one's "particularity . . . in the universal." (Ibid.: 64f.) But, contrary to Hegel, Johannes thinks that one cannot become an ethical "self by willing the good" since "actual existence is 'incommensurable' with the demands of ethics." Because one can't in fact *meet* the demands of the universal one is in sin, and a person who by sin "has gone outside the universal . . . can return to it only by virtue of having come as an individual into an absolute relation with the absolute." (Ibid.: 108) "'Ethics' is [therefore] not the final word . . . for if ethics is the final word, then [our] lives are hopeless." Only if God supplies the condition that makes ethical obedience possible can we hope to become ethical selves. (Evans 1993: 19–20)

The religious therefore transcends the ethical, and "the main target" of *Fear and Trembling* is any "view of the religious life that interprets faith as reducible to a life of moral striving." (Ibid.: 15) The ethical is indeed "preserved" in the religious, but one can't *rely* on the ethical for validation in the eyes of eternity since one's very ability to live ethically is a gift of grace. In the last analysis, "a direct and personal relationship with God" alone makes ethical authenticity possible. (Ibid.: 23)

The upshot is that what both the Knight of Resignation and the Knight of Faith sacrifice, when they sacrifice the ethical to the eternal, is the ethical in *this* sense, and doing so is neither irrational nor "absurd." For what they relinquish is (1) the notion of "the ethical as a total self-sufficient view of life and mode of existence," and (2) the identification of the contents of ethics with the values that happen to be socially sanctioned at a particular time and place. (Evans 1993: 23) What is "teleologically suspended," then, is not ethics as such, but ethics' absolutist pretensions, and the tendency to identify the eternal distinction between right and wrong with the values endorsed by one's own society. Neither sacrifice is irrational, however, if one can't become an authentic ethical self by just willing the good, that is, by moral striving, and if society's values are contingent, historically conditioned, and hence frequently false or perverse.

While Evans's views are admirably sane, one can't help but wonder whether they can be identified with Johannes's. For Abraham must decide whether or not to obey God's demand that *he sacrifice Isaac*. And Abraham's obligation not to kill an innocent child is neither false nor perverse, nor reflective of contingent, historically conditioned values. Nor (although this is less certain) is it clear that if Johannes's Abraham *had* chosen not to sacrifice Isaac, that choice would have reflected a belief that ethical conduct is sufficient for authenticity, for validation in the eyes of eternity. One wonders, in short, whether Evans's interpretation, like Gellman's and Outka's, unduly bowdlerizes Kierkegaard's *Fear and Trembling*. One's doubts are reinforced by Evans's most recent treatment of the problem.

In chapter 13 of his recent *Kierkegaard's Ethic of Love: Divine Commands and Moral Obligations*, Evans argues that[28] though it is true that if God were to com-

---

28   Given the truth of divine command theory.

mand us to sacrifice our child, we would be obligated to do so, no Christian or Jew "in a contemporary cultural context . . . could reasonably believe that God has today issued such a command."[29] Kant was thus partly right. For a contemporary Jew or Christian, that God has commanded her to sacrifice her child is always less certain than that she has an overriding obligation not to kill her innocent son or daughter. For our situation is unlike Abraham's. The latter "lived in a culture in which child sacrifice was common and regarded as morally acceptable."[30] Furthermore, "God had not yet . . . given the ten commandments, and the prohibitions of child sacrifice given by various prophets had not yet been given." (Evans 2004: 310) *Our* situation is very different, however. We *know* that God would not demand that we sacrifice our children for, through general and special revelation,[31] we know that God has commanded us not to murder or kill the innocent, and "any alleged divine command must be tested for its consistency with what a person already takes to be the commands of God." (Ibid.: 308)

Yet if God is truly transcendent, how do we know that he might not *revoke* these commands, or override them in special cases? Evans's answer is essentially this: the God in whom the Christian believes is a loving God who merits our obedience

---

29   C. Stephen Evans, *Kierkegaard's Ethic of Love: Divine Commands and Moral Obliga-tions*. New York and London: Oxford University Press, 2004, p. 306. Henceforth Evans 2004.

30   Whether the ancient Israelites condoned child sacrifice in some circumstances is controversial. The standard view among Jewish and Christian biblical scholars appears to be that the only *clear* biblical references to human sacrifice by Israelites "all refer to a specific cultic practice borrowed from the Canaanites" which first appears in the reign of Ahab, and that the passages in which these references occur unanimously view it as "an alien element." (Ringgren, *Israelite Religion*, pp. 175) It should be remembered, however, that the biblical material as we have it reflects the views of the later prophets who explicitly condemned the practice. For a well-reasoned contrary view, see chapter 1 of Jon D. Levenson's *The Death and Resurrection of the Beloved Son* (New Haven: Yale University Press, 1993). And as Robert Adams points out, the fact that, in the earlier biblical period, children were regarded as their parents' property would have made it easier to conceive of child sacrifice "as a maximally precious gift from the *parents* to the deity," and to ignore the independent claims of the child. (*Infinite and Infinite Goods*, p. 288) Adams thinks it significant that the emergence of explicit prophetic critiques of child sacrifice (for example, Jeremiah 19: 1–9, 32: 35; Ezekiel 20: 25–6) more or less coincide with the appearance of the idea that children are only responsible for their *own* good and bad deeds, and not for those of their parents. (Cf. Jeremiah 31: 29–30; Ezekiel 18: 2–4.) A new sense of the "moral distance" between parents and child made the wrongness of child sacrifice much more apparent. Evans's point doesn't stand or fall on the outcome of this controversy, however, for child sacrifice *was* practiced and condoned in the Canaanite culture in which Abraham was operating.

31   General revelation refers to what can be gleaned about God and our duties toward him from the "light of nature" (reason, conscience, our natural sentiments, and the like). Special revelation refers to God's extraordinary revelation through the prophets, the apostles, and so on.

and trust. "A God who revoked commands that were given as universal and absolute," however, would be "so inconsistent and unpredictable in character that it is
questionable whether or not such a God would merit our obedience;" and "a God
who gave *contradictory* commands"[32] would be so erratic that he could not "be
counted on to fulfil his promises." (Evans 2004: 309, my emphasis) Since the God
whom the Christian is obligated to obey is a loving God who commands us not to
take innocent lives, and who merits our obedience and trust, we know that a
command to kill an innocent child cannot come from God.

But *is* this so clear? I may know "that God could not command any act that is
truly evil in the sense of being fundamentally bad." But, as Evans himself admits,
"given that our understanding of good and evil is fallible, this is compatible with
the possibility that God might command an action that *appeared* to be evil, at least
initially." (Evans 2004: 315, my emphasis) But if so, then how can I be sure that
what appears to be a divine command that I sacrifice my innocent son or daughter
isn't *in fact* a divine command to do so? Would a *single* and, for all I know, *unique*
command of this sort be sufficient to show that the source of the command wasn't
the God in whom I had rightly trusted, or that what it commands is inconsistent
with God's transcendent nature?

Evans's response appears to be that while it may be *abstractly* possible that God
would issue a command of this sort, I will never find myself in a situation that
warrants my believing that such a command was from God. For the injunctions
against child sacrifice, or taking innocent lives for no apparent purpose, are so
deeply and centrally entrenched in our prior moral understanding—an understanding be it noted which has itself been shaped by God's general and special revelation,
and our responses to it—that it can never be reasonable for me to believe that God
has commanded me to kill my own child. For my reasons for thinking that he hasn't
swamp whatever reasons (an inner voice, a sudden conviction, or anything else of
the sort) for thinking that he has.

And yet surely "an omnipotent God *could* reveal to a human being that the
human being was commanded to carry out an act of child sacrifice in such a way
that the *human being would be rational to believe it.*" Evans's response to this
objection is that while God could do this, we can be assured that he *won't*. For if
God takes "control of the person's beliefs in such a way that the person cannot help
but believe he has been commanded to perform the act, . . . it is questionable
whether the person would really be morally responsible for the belief and any acts
stemming from it," and God wants our *free* obedience. (Evans 2004: 309–10, my
emphases)

But this won't do. In the first place, it isn't clear that the only way God can bring
it about that it is rational for someone to believe that God has commanded him to
commit the act is by bringing it about that "no other belief is possible for that

---

32   Such as "Kill your innocent son or daughter" and "You shall not kill."

person." (Ibid.: 310) Evans's idea, I take it, is that if I can't help believing p, it is rational for me to believe p. And this is true on a deontological account of epistemic justification, according to which my beliefs are rationally held if I can't be faulted or blamed for holding them.[33] But even on a deontological account, it isn't clear that (one's prior moral understanding to the contrary) God can't provide external or internal evidence (miracles, internal markers, and the like) which, together with one's past experience of God, would make it more reasonable than not to believe that the command to sacrifice one's child comes from God, *without* that evidence being sufficiently strong to *compel* belief.[34]

The more important point, however, is this. Evans's argument rests on a false assumption since, in many normal cases, the moral and factual beliefs on which my *free* actions are based aren't within my control. (Many of my perceptual and inferential beliefs provide examples.) That my *beliefs* aren't freely held doesn't entail that my *actions* aren't free. So, my prior moral and religious understanding to the contrary, God could make it impossible for me not to believe that he has commanded me to kill my child without destroying my freedom.

The upshot of the points made in the last two paragraphs is that Evans hasn't shown that the possibility that God would issue a command that flaunts our moral understanding isn't a real one.

Conclusion

The three accounts of Johannes's Abraham that we have discussed in this section agree that apparent conflicts between the demands of religion and those of ethics are *only* apparent. I have argued, though, that each of these accounts unduly sanitizes Johannes's message. The next section examines a defense of the claim that conflicts of this kind can sometimes be real.

Quinn on Abraham's Dilemma

In "Moral Obligation, Religious Demand, and Practical Conflict," Philip Quinn invites us to consider the following four propositions:

> k (i) God's commanding that Abraham perform a particular act of killing Isaac indefeasibly requires that Abraham perform that act of killing Isaac.

---

33   Although on other accounts of epistemic justification some beliefs I can't help having aren't held rationally. (Suppose, for example, that because of some neurophysiological disorder I can't help but believe that all strangers are out to kill me.)

34   And if the evidence at one's disposal makes believing p more rational than not, then (other things being equal) one's believing p is faultless, and therefore justified in the deontological sense (as well as in other senses).

(ii) Isaac's being an innocent child requires that Abraham refrain from performing that act of killing Isaac.

(iii) The requirement that Abraham refrain from performing that act of killing Isaac . . . is overridden by no state of affairs.

(iv) Abraham and that act of killing Isaac are such that it is physically impossible that he both perform and refrain from performing it.[35]

k(i–iv) is a "situation of Kierkegaardian conflict." Quinn argues that it is possible that k(i–iv), and also possible that Abraham *knows* that k(i–iv); that is, knows that he is in a situation of Kierkegaardian conflict.

k(ii–iv) are clearly compossible. The question, then, is whether k(i) is compossible with k(ii–iv). It would appear that it isn't. For, surely, if Abraham is indefeasibly required to kill Isaac, the requirement that he refrain from killing Isaac is overridden. If it is, then, if k(i) is true, k(iii) is false. The appearance of incompatibility is deceptive, however.

Although God's overwhelming goodness explains why his commands are indefeasible, it is possible that his goodness isn't an "exclusively moral goodness." It may, for example, be partly "metaphysical." Thus Leibniz thought that in choosing to create the best of all possible worlds God chose to create "the world that ranks highest on a scale combining considerations of simplicity of natural laws and variety of creaturely denizens," and "it is not at all obvious that a world that is best in this sense is also best in the sense of maximally realizing the values of the moral realm." Or "perhaps divine goodness has a dimension that is more akin to aesthetic goodness than to any other realm of goodness with which we humans are familiar." Then, too, God's goodness may have dimensions that are and always will be "inscrutable to us." If these are real possibilities, then it is also "possible that some of the values God cares about having his human creatures pursue—enough that by command he imposes on them indefeasible requirements for certain actions—should be non-moral values." (204–6)

But suppose they are. If the values underwriting an indefeasible religious requirement can't be wholly identified with moral values, then that requirement may not be a "moral requirement at all." If the requirement that Abraham kill Isaac isn't a *moral* requirement, however, it isn't an especially *stringent* moral requirement, and hence can't override "the supremely urgent [moral] requirement that Abraham refrain from killing Isaac imposed by the fact that Isaac is an innocent child." Thus, contrary to appearances, k(i) does not entail k(iii)'s falsity. (204–5)

Yet suppose we grant that the moral requirement not to kill an innocent child isn't overridden by any other *moral* requirement. Still, why doesn't the indefeasible *religious* requirement that Abraham kill Isaac override the moral requirement?

35   Philip L. Quinn, "Moral Obligation, Religious Demand, and Practical Conflict," in Robert Audi and William J. Wainwright, eds, *Rationality, Religious Belief, and Moral Commitment*. Ithaca, NY: Cornell University Press, 1986, pp. 202–3. All references in this section are to this essay unless otherwise noted.

Quinn's answer is this: *neither* requirement is overridden. Denying the indefeasibility of the religious requirement "seems . . . to involve . . . a failure to acknowledge the ultimacy of certain religious values and our commitments to them." Similarly, "to suppose that the moral requirement is overridden in this case seems . . . to involve a failure to acknowledge the ultimacy of certain *moral* values and our commitments to *them*." (207, my emphases) Neither requirement is overridden by the other. So Abraham is required to kill Isaac and also required to refrain from killing him, although he cannot do both. His dilemma, therefore, is inescapable.[36]

To suppose that one requirement overrides the other is to suppose that the requirements are commensurable, and it is not clear that they are. In situations of Kierkegaardian conflict there may *be* no "common scale of value" or "more inclusive and more ultimate realm of value," in reference to which, or within which, the pursuit of religious values must be judged better than the pursuit of moral values, or vice versa. If there isn't, then there are no grounds for claiming that "one or the other of the two conflicting requirements is overridden." (208)

It is possible, then, that k(i–iv) is true. It is also possible that someone knows that it is. Abraham, for example, could surely know k(ii), k(iii), and k(iv). He could know that the requirement not to kill Isaac is imposed by the state of affairs consisting in Isaac's being an innocent child. He could also know "that no state of affairs bearing on the promotion of the values internal to the moral realm overrides the requirement" not to kill Isaac and that, because of the incommensurability of the religious and moral realms, "no state of affairs internal to the religious realm, including the state of affairs" consisting in God's command that he kill Isaac, overrides the moral requirement that he not kill Isaac. (210) And Abraham, of course, knows that it is physically impossible that he both kill and not kill Isaac.

But could he know k(i)? As we have seen, k(i) could be true. Furthermore, Abraham could know that "God, if he exists, is essentially perfectly good," and "this would justify for him the belief that" if God commanded him to kill Isaac, he would be indefeasibly required to kill Isaac. Abraham could also know that God has commanded him to kill Isaac. For it is possible both that God has done so and that Abraham has a properly basic belief that he has.[37] Moreover, "the past history

---

36 This presupposes the falsity of "'p is required' entails 'It is not the case that not-p is required.'" The principle may seem obvious but, as Quinn points out, (1) Joel Feinberg and some other "contemporary philosophers" have rejected it, (2) "there are perfectly respectable systems of deontic logic which do not include" it, and (3) there are apparent counter-examples. "Antigone's conflict of obligations" in Sophocles' play of the same name is an example. (Quinn 1979: 320)

37 A properly basic belief is a justified belief which isn't inferred from other beliefs. Possible examples are our beliefs in simple necessary truths and many of our ordinary perceptual and memory beliefs. Alvin Plantinga and others have argued that some religious beliefs about God are properly basic. For a further defense of the claim that Abraham could know that God has commanded him to kill Isaac, see my discussion of Evans in the preceding section.

of his interactions with God" might "serve as independent inductive backing for his belief" that God has commanded him to kill Isaac. (209–10)

Finally, on the basis of the argument given earlier for the compossibility of k(i), k(ii), k(iii), and k(iv), Abraham could come to justifiably believe that k(i) through k(iv) are compossible.

So since Abraham could come to justifiably believe "each of k(i) through k(iv)," and that k(i) through k(iv) are compossible, he could come to justifiably believe that the conjunction of k(i) through k(iv) is true. But if it is possible that the conjunction is true and possible that Abraham justifiably believes the conjunction, it is possible that Abraham *knows* that the conjunction of k(i) through k(iv) is true.[38] It is thus not only possible that k(i–iv) *is* true; it is also possible that someone knows that it is. *Pace* Gellman, Outka, Evans, and others, situations of Kierkegaardian conflict are possible, and it is possible for someone to know that she is in one.[39]

How plausible is this? One *might* argue that "the ultimacy of moral values and our commitments to them" imply that moral requirements trump *all* nonmoral requirements. Or to put it slightly differently, that part of the *meaning* of "s is *morally* required," where s is a state of affairs consisting in an agent doing something at a particular time, is that the requirement overrides any conflicting *non*moral requirements. If this is true, then any nonmoral requirement that conflicts with a moral requirement—such as the requirement imposed by God's commanding Abraham to kill Isaac—is not only defeasible but *defeated*. Quinn thinks that moves of this sort "trivialize" the issue by simply defining "moral requirement" in such a way that situations of Kierkegaardian conflict cannot arise. (204 fn) And this

---

38   Unless, of course, the *truth* of the conjunction is incompatible with Abraham's *justifiably believing* the conjunction. But that possibility appears to be a nonstarter.

39   Quinn notes, though, that this view of Abraham's situation "brings with it a theological difficulty." For "consider the following argument: (1) Suppose God commands Abraham to kill Isaac; (2) If God commands Abraham to kill Isaac, then God commands Abraham to do something wrong; (3) If God commands Abraham to do something wrong, then God himself does wrong; (4) If God himself does wrong, then God is not morally perfect; and so (5) God is not morally perfect." Quinn's response to the difficulty is to "reverse the argument. Since God *is* morally perfect, . . . God does not command Abraham to kill Isaac. The story of Abraham illustrates a *possibility* for tragic conflict, but fortunately it is *only* a possibility . . . " The cost of this "way out of the difficulty," of course, "is denying the scriptural literalist's claim that the narrative of Genesis 22 is in all details sober historical truth." (Philip L. Quinn, "Agamemnon and Abraham: The Tragic Dilemma of Kierkegaard's Knight of Faith," *Journal of Literature and Theology* 4 [1990], pp. 191–2, my emphases) There is another solution to the difficulty, however. For one might argue that, in God's case, moral perfection is "sublated" (*aufheben*) in an even greater perfection that includes much if not most of what we ordinarily mean by moral perfection—*including love*, but cannot be identified with it. This way out accepts the conclusion but questions its force. One could argue, for example, that even though God's command conflicts with a moral requirement, it is not unloving since he intends a great good for both Abraham and Isaac.

seems right. The fact remains that a number of important moral philosophers[40] have thought that this *is* part of our concept of moral obligation, and their claim reflects common intuitions about the supreme importance of moral values. Whether these intuitions are trustworthy is another matter. Bernard Williams and others have called attention to cases in which it is *prima facie* plausible that nonmoral values aren't overridden by moral ones.[41] And Quinn, of course, argues that, on the face of it, cases like Abraham's are cases of this kind.

Another potential difficulty is this. Couldn't we have a *moral* obligation to obey God's commands? If we can, then the conflict between Abraham's obligation to obey God by killing Isaac and his moral obligation not to kill Isaac is (in part at least) *internal* to the moral realm. If it is, the obligations aren't wholly incommensurable.

What are the implications of this suggestion? Abraham's *moral* obligation to obey God—as distinct from any religious obligation he might have to do so—is either absolute or it isn't. If it is, one would think that Abraham's moral obligation to obey God is not only indefeasible but overrides any conflicting obligations. But in that case there is no real dilemma (since when two moral obligations conflict, and one overrides the other, one should discharge the overriding obligation), and there is no "teleological suspension of the ethical" (since, in killing Isaac, Abraham would be discharging a *moral* obligation).

Whether a purely moral obligation to obey God can be absolute in this sense seems doubtful, however. A moral obligation to obey God would presumably be grounded in God's *moral* character (including his loving purposes for human kind), in our promise to obey him (see, for example, Exodus 19: 8), in human gratitude for God's loving kindness, and the like. Such an obligation would be one of the most important moral obligations we have. Even so, it would be no more than one moral obligation among others, many of which seem equally compelling. If the moral obligation to obey God is only one moral obligation among others, however, then it seems at least possible that in certain circumstances (such as God's commanding us to kill an innocent child) the moral obligation to obey God would be overridden by another moral obligation (such as our obligation not to kill an innocent child). But, in that case, the moral obligation to obey God is not absolute since it not only can but would be overridden.

The upshot of these considerations is that if requirements imposed by God's commands *are* indefeasible, as most theists believe, then the requirements imposed by God's commands cannot just be moral requirements but must (as Quinn suggests) be at least partly grounded in nonmoral dimensions of God's goodness. But does this imply that Quinn is also right in thinking that the requirements imposed by God's commands are at least partly *incommensurable* with moral requirements?

---

40   Kant and R. M. Hare, for example.
41   See, for example, Williams's "Moral Luck," in his collection of the same name (Cambridge: Cambridge University Press, 1981).

It is not clear to me that he is. Quinn ties commensurability to the existence of a common scale of value, or "a more inclusive and more ultimate realm of value," in relation to which, or within which, conflicting values can be compared and weighed. Is this justified?

It is, of course, trivially true that if we claim that (some) religious requirements override (some) moral requirements, we are *comparing* religious requirements and moral requirements, and judging one more important than the other. Does this, though, entail a more inclusive and ultimate realm of value, or a common scale of value, within which, or in relation to which, the two sets of values (religious and moral) are compared and weighed? This seems doubtful. Consider the realm of moral values and the realm of aesthetic values, and suppose that there are no religious values.[42] Most of us would think that moral values (usually? always?) trump aesthetic values in cases of conflict. It isn't obvious that there is a common scale of value on which moral and aesthetic values can be compared and weighed, however, or a more inclusive and ultimate realm of value which contains both. But if moral and *aesthetic* values can be compared and weighed in the absence of a common scale, why think that *religious* and moral values can't be compared and weighed in the absence of a common scale? Yet if they *can* be, we can't rule out the possibility that a requirement indefeasibly imposed by a divine command overrides any conflicting moral requirement, in which case k(i) and k(iii) *would* be inconsistent after all.

But, of course, while this *may* be true, it also may not be. That is, it might be the case that, while the requirement imposed by God's command to sacrifice Isaac *can't* be overridden (and is hence indefeasible), the requirement not to kill Isaac imposed by Isaac's being an innocent child is not *in fact* overridden. The upshot is that it is both epistemically possible that,[43] because the conflicting requirements *are* commensurable, k(i) is inconsistent with k(iii), in which case k(i–iv) aren't compossible, *and* epistemically possible that they are compossible. This is a weaker conclusion than Quinn wants,[44] but it is far from trivial. Before concluding, however, we must examine an argument which, if successful, would show that one couldn't know that the conjunction of k(i) through k(iv) is true.

---

42   That is, that religious values are specious. This would be true, for example, if all religious world-views were false.

43   For the reasons given above.

44   I think that Quinn believes that he has *established* the compossibility of k(i) through k(iv), in which case not only is the compossibility of k(i–iv) epistemically possible; the denial of their compossibility is not.

Adams on Abraham's Dilemma

Adams's Abraham (who is not precisely "the biblical Abraham" nor "Kierkegaard's Abraham either") finds himself overwhelmingly inclined to believe each of the following three, mutually inconsistent, propositions:

"1 If God commands me to do something, it is not morally wrong for me to do it.
 2 God commands me to kill my son.
 3 It is morally wrong for me to kill my son." (Adams 1999: 280)

How should he respond?

Adams admits that if his divine command theory is true, then, if God *were* to command something evil or cruel, what God commands would not have the property of moral wrongness, and would not be "(unqualifiedly) bad."[45] The important point, however, is this. "A deity that was what we intuitively call *cruel* would not be a good candidate for the role of supreme Good, and the cruel commands of such a being would not be a good candidate for the standard of moral right and wrong. . . . That being so, [we] should probably identify moral wrongness, not simply with the property of being contrary to the commands of God, but rather with the property of being contrary to the commands . . . of a *loving* God." (Adams 1999: 281) And note (although Adams himself does not) that if we were to replace (1) with

1′ If a loving God commands me to do something, it is not morally wrong for me
     to do it,

then, while (1′) entails

4   If a loving God commands me to do something cruel, it is not morally wrong
     for me to do it,

(4) has an impossible antecedent and is therefore trivially true.[46] (Note, too, that (1) has similar consequences if [as Adams thinks but doesn't pretend to have proved] loving kindness is entailed by God's nature.)

(1) *would* be false if God were to issue contradictory commands—commanding me to kill my son, for example, yet also (via the Decalogue or in some other way)

---

45 Although "it does not follow . . . that . . . it would be wrong or bad to *dis*obey" the command. For Adams's divine command theory, see Chapter 5. Notice, however, that the wrongness or badness of disobeying God's command *would* follow from (1a): If God commands me to do something, it is morally wrong for me not to do it. And won't (most?) divine command theorists who endorse (1) *also* wish to endorse (1a)?

46 Conditionals with impossible antecedents can't have true antecedents and false consequents, and hence (on the standard view) can't be false.

commanding me not to kill an innocent child. For, in that case, since "wrongness is the property of being contrary to God's commands," killing my son *is* morally wrong even though God commands me to do it. (Adams 1999: 282)

Adams thinks that this line of argument is a nonstarter, though, since "requirements cannot plausibly be taken as constituting moral obligations unless they are reasonable, and it cannot be reasonable to require something contradictory or impossible."[47] (IBid.: 283) But (as Quinn points out) since *neither* command is contradictory or impossible when taken by itself, Adams must be presupposing that if doing A is obligatory and doing B is obligatory, then doing A and B is obligatory.

"Agglomeration" principles of this sort may be doubted, however.[48] For example, it would seem "that I have a moral reason not to do what would prevent one from doing what I have a moral reason to do." So if I make conflicting promises, I have "a moral reason not to keep the first" since doing so would prevent me from keeping the second and I have " a moral reason not to keep the second" since doing so would prevent me from keeping the first. But I do *not* have "any moral reason to keep neither promise . . . , or to break both" since doing so "would accomplish nothing." Again, while the consequences of doing A may provide me with a moral reason for doing A, and the consequences of doing B may provide me with a moral reason for doing B, I may not have a moral reason for doing both A and B since "the consequences of doing each of [the] two acts separately can be different from the consequences of doing both acts together."[49]

In responding to Quinn, Adams agrees that he should probably abandon the agglomeration principle but continues to insist that "it cannot be reasonable to impose on someone, at the same time, requirements that contradict each other." (Adams 2002: 485)

Yet this seems doubtful, for it implies that it can never be reasonable to knowingly bring about a situation which confronts someone with a moral dilemma. Suppose, though, that one has good reasons for bringing about s and also has good

---

47   Furthermore, if God were to command Abraham to sacrifice Isaac, the command would seem "to imply a suspension of any contrary commands from the same source" since commands "carry permission to do what is commanded." Denying this principle implies a God too inconsistent and unreasonable to be fit "for the exalted role of defining obligation." (Adams 1999: 284) It should be noted, however, that the principle itself won't yield a contradiction. If God commands Abraham to kill Isaac and also commands him not to do so, then, given the principle, it is permissible for Abraham to kill Isaac and it is permissible for him not to kill Isaac. But propositions of the form "It is permissible for x to do A" and "It is permissible for x not to do A" aren't mutually inconsistent. (Although, of course, it *is* true that the conjunction in question entails that Abraham's killing Isaac is morally indifferent, and that *is* inconsistent with either Abraham's killing Isaac or Abraham's not killing Isaac being morally required.)

48   Philip L. Quinn, "Obligation, Divine Commands, and Abraham's Dilemma," *Philosophy and Phenomenological Research* 64 (2002), pp. 459–66. Henceforth Quinn 2002.

49   Walter Sinnott-Armstrong, *Moral Dilemmas*. Oxford: Basil Blackwell, 1988, chapter 4, pp. 133 and 130.

reasons for bringing about s′ where s (a divine command to kill Isaac, say) makes doing x (killing Isaac in this instance) morally obligatory, and s′ (a created order in which Isaac's innocence is a morally compelling reason for not killing him) makes not doing x morally obligatory. Bringing s about and bringing s′ about may be backed by incommensurable values (metaphysical and religious goods in the first case, perhaps, and moral values in the second). There needn't be anything irrational about embracing or pursuing incommensurable values, however. Even if aesthetic and moral values are incommensurable, for instance, it can be rational to embrace and pursue both.

Adams himself thinks that the best response to Abraham's dilemma is to reject (2) ("God commands me to kill my son"). It is true that we should not be too quick to reject propositions *like* (2). Given God's transcendence and our own fallibility, we should be constantly open to the possibility that what God actually requires of us in a situation is very different from what we *think* it is. For, as the transcendent Good, God's requirements may conflict with our present understanding of moral rightness and moral wrongness. For example, God may legitimately require someone to accept martyrdom rather than betray her principles even though doing so harms not only herself but many others. Nevertheless, in deciding whether a purported revelation really is from God, we must rely (among other things) on the conceptions of the good and the right that we bring to that situation. For, ultimately, we have nothing else to fall back on.

And so it is here. Adams thinks that, in the present case at least, we should side with Kant and reject (2) since the very content of the command is good evidence that God did *not* issue it. Our "vision of the Good, and of God as the Good" (Adams 1999: 284) rules out the possibility that God could command someone to kill his innocent child.

Quinn, however, claims to have described a case in which God causes "a sign that we could not credibly fail to interpret as a genuine command from God to offer otherwise unnecessary human sacrifices." Adams doubts that God could do this.[50] Yet suppose he could. There are two alternatives. One is to obey God, "trusting that God will see to it that obedience works out for the best." The other is to "change deities," to decide that the deity in which one has placed one's trust isn't worthy of one's worship and devotion. (Adams 1999: 290) Which is preferable?

If "we could see the author of the command as the supreme Good . . . , then *perhaps* trusting obedience might seem the right course." (Ibid.: 290, my emphasis) Nevertheless, that God would command me to kill my son is so "unimaginable" that "it is at best a waste of spiritual energy to try to decide [in advance] what one should do in that case." Nor does it "honor God to prepare oneself mentally for

---

50 Adams doesn't explain why. Perhaps because he thinks that the evidence against the claim that God has commanded a person to sacrifice his or her child provided by the fact that doing so is a moral horror is sufficiently strong to outweigh any possible evidence to the contrary.

receiving such a command." For "consider an analogy: It would hardly be an expression of confidence in your spouse to ponder in any but the most abstractly theoretical way what you should do if your spouse demanded your cooperation in a serious crime." (Ibid.: 290–91) Adams's response, in short, is this: because it is "unimaginable" that God would issue such a command, it is either idle or spiritually pernicious to consider what one should do if God *were* to do so—"idle" if one's consideration is "abstract" and "theoretical," pernicious if one engages the question existentially. Adams elaborates this point in responding to Quinn.

"To decide in advance . . . that such and such evidence would justify" the conclusion that, while the commandment may come from a supernatural being, it could not come from a *"loving* God" (and should therefore be disobeyed), "seems religiously presumptuous, and perhaps a proleptic abandonment of faith in one's deity, about whom, we are assuming, one does not actually have that disturbing evidence." It would be equally "presumptuous, 'tempting God,' to decide in advance that such and such evidence would force us to draw a conclusion [that a loving God has commanded me to kill my son] that (if false) would be highly insulting to God." The "wisest" policy, therefore, is probably "not to try to decide" in advance whether one should or shouldn't obey if one were confronted with what appears to be a loving God's command that one kill one's son. (Adams 2002: 487)

This conclusion is reinforced by three further considerations. First, "if we ever actually found ourselves in [that] horrendous situation, we would surely be right to distrust any conditional decision we had made before we experienced it." Second, "it is hardly honoring God to think of this as an issue that demands our attention." And, third, "some biblical precedents (*Genesis* 18: 17–33; *Exodus* 37: 7–14) suggest that if we ever concluded" that God had issued such a command, our "first step" should not be to obey or disobey him, but "to argue with God, in the hope that the apparent command would not be God's final decision in the matter; and it seems, again, presumptuous to set a limit to how persistent we should be in such remonstrance." (Adams 2002: 487) I do not find this convincing.

Just *why* is it religiously presumptuous to decide in advance that such and such evidence would force us to conclude that a God who commanded me to kill my son would not be a *loving* God, and just *why* might such a decision be a "proleptic abandonment of faith"? Because it involves entertaining the possibility that the God in whom one (now) believes might not *be* loving? But merely *entertaining* the possibility does not imply that one (now) has *real* doubts. If it doesn't, then it is difficult to see how merely entertaining the possibility involves a proleptic abandonment of one's faith. The possibility that the God in whom one believes might not be loving would indeed be "abstract" and "theoretical." A consideration of abstract and theoretical possibilities is often relevant in *philosophy*, however, if not always in the hurly-burly of real life.

Neither would it be clearly presumptuous, or "tempting God," to decide in advance that such and such evidence world force me to draw a conclusion that (if false) would be highly insulting to God. For if the evidence is so strong that it would *force* me to conclude that a loving God commands me to kill my son, then the possibility that I might be mistaken, *given that evidence*, wouldn't be live for me. Yet, if it wouldn't, then the possibility that I might be insulting God by *falsely* attributing the command to him wouldn't be live for me either. Why, then, would my decision be presumptuous?

Nor are Adams's final three considerations compelling. Adams claims that if we ever were actually faced with Abraham's horrid choice, we should "distrust any conditional decision" we might have made in advance of experiencing it. But this, if true at all, is presumably true of *any* horrendous moral dilemma in which we have equally compelling moral reasons for performing and not performing a certain action. And why should we think that, in situations of this sort, our decisions will be just as good or better if we *don't* try to anticipate them? The answer isn't obvious.

Adams also thinks that it doesn't honor God "to think of this as an issue which demands our attention," and this may be true. It does not follow, however, that considering the issue *dis*honors him.

Adams's final suggestion is that if we ever were to find ourselves in the situation in question, we should "remonstrate" with God rather than decide to obey or disobey him. But notice that this suggestion, too, expresses a *present* decision to act in such a way should the "unimaginable" situation ever arise. Why should this decision be any more reliable than a present decision to obey or disobey in the envisaged circumstances? Moreover (and in spite of the biblical precedents), isn't it at least equally "presumptuous" to decide in advance to implore the God "in whom there is no shadow of turning" (James 1: 17) to change his mind?

I conclude, then, that Adams's case for the claim that we should refuse to decide what we should do if we ever were in Abraham's shoes isn't fully convincing. Even so, Quinn may be right in saying that this is the best move Adams can make within his "ethical framework." "To preclude the possibility of a credible divine command" to kill one's son "would be to attempt to domesticate the transcendent, which is at odds with its fearful and dangerous character," and Adams is reluctant to do this. Yet "to insist on a decision" to either obey or disobey such a command "would be to demand allying oneself either with the moral horror of human sacrifice or with rebellion against the Good itself . . . " In Adams's view, however, this "is not a forced choice" as long as the envisaged situation "remains a mere possibility," and his refusal to make it does not impugn his ethical framework unless an adequate ethical framework must determine "a decision for every *possible* [and not just every actual] morally significant situation of choice to which it applies." (Quinn 2002: 465, my emphasis)

Nevertheless, Quinn doubts that Adams's solution is superior "to a solution that rejects (1) [If God commands me to do something, it is not morally wrong for me to do to it] on the grounds that the divine command . . . puts Abraham in a moral dilemma," or "to a Kierkegaardian solution that rejects (3) ["It is morally wrong for me to kill my son] because the divine command to sacrifice Isaac brings with it a teleological suspension of the ethical." (Ibid.) (If there are genuine moral dilemmas, then it can be true that, if God were to command Abraham to sacrifice Isaac, he *morally ought* to sacrifice Isaac, and yet it would be *morally wrong* for Abraham to sacrifice Isaac. On the other hand, if God's command "teleologically suspends" the ethical, then it is false that it is morally wrong for Abraham to sacrifice Isaac.)

If my reasons for thinking that Adams's case for suspending judgment is less than compelling are sound, then Quinn's doubts that Adams's solution to Abraham's dilemma is superior to its competitors is even more persuasive.

Conclusion

In his response to Quinn, Adams says that he does not think his view is "contrary to belief in a transcendent, in large measure incomprehensible God who 'screams with the hawk and laughs with the hyenas'." (Adams 2002: 486) But when all is said and done, it seems to me that it is, and that differing judgments as to the weight one should assign to this aspect of the Godhead may largely account for the disagreement between those who, like Quinn, think that religious values may be incommensurable with moral values at significant junctures and those who, like Outka, Evans, and Adams, doubt that our duties to God can ultimately come into conflict with our moral obligations.

Rudolf Otto has effectively argued that important strands of theistic experience resist easy moralization. Arjuna's vision of the supernal form of Krishna in the eleventh chapter of the *Bhagavad Gītā* is an example:

> If the light of a thousand suns were to spring forth simultaneously in the sky it would be like the light of that great Being. . . . I see Thee, with many arms, stomachs, mouths, and eyes, everywhere infinite in form; I see no end nor middle nor beginning of Thee, O Lord of All. . . . I behold . . . Thy face as a shining fire, burning this universe with Thy radiance . . . Seeing Thy great form, of many mouths and eyes, O mighty-armed one, of many arms, thighs and feet, of many bellies, of many terrible tusks, the worlds tremble, and so do I. Seeing Thee . . . my inmost self is shaken and I find no strength nor peace, O Vishnu![51] Seeing Thy mouths, terrible with tusks, like time's devouring fire, I know not the directions of the sky and I find no security. Have mercy, O Lord of gods, Abode of the world. [I see kings and warriors] rushing into Thy mouths, dreadful with terrible tusks. . . . As the many water currents of rivers race headlong to the ocean, so these heros of the world of men enter into Thy flaming mouths. . . . Swallowing all the worlds from every side, Thou lickest them up with Thy flaming mouths; Thy fierce rays fill the whole world with radiance and scorch it, O Vishnu. . . . For whatever I said in rashness from negligence or even from affection thinking Thou art my friend, and not knowing Thy greatness . . . I pray forgiveness from Thee, the boundless one . . .

---

51   Krishna is an *avatara* ("descent") of Vishnu, the one Lord of heaven and earth.

Having seen what was never seen before, I am glad but my mind is distraught with fear. Show me, O Lord, that other [benign] form of Thine, O Lord of gods, be gracious, O refuge of the world.[52]

Or consider the story in Exodus 4 where "Yahweh came to meet [Moses] and tried to kill him." Or God's revealing to Job from the "heart of the tempest" that he is not only the author of the beneficent aspects of nature but the God who furnishes "a prey for the lioness," is the creator of the ostrich, who "leaves her eggs on the ground . . . forgetting that a foot may tread on them or a wild beast may crush them. Cruel to her chicks as if they were not hers . . . ," or Lord of the eagle, who "feeds her young on blood: whereever men fall dying, there she is." (Job 38–9) Or, again, consider Paul, who asserts that God has mercy on whom he will, and hardens whom he will (Romans 9: 18), or the author of Hebrews who says "it is a dreadful thing to fall into the hands of the living God," and "Our God is a consuming fire" (Hebrews 10: 31; 12: 29). Compare this with Luther: "For God is a fire, that consumeth, devoureth, rageth; verily He is your undoing, as fire consumeth a house and maketh it dust and ashes." Or again, "Yea, He is more terrible and frightful than the Devil. For he dealeth with us and bringeth us to ruin with power, smiteth and hammereth us and payeth no heed to us. . . . In His majesty He is a consuming fire. . . . For therefrom can no man refrain: if he thinketh on God aright, his heart in his body is struck with terror. . . . Yea, as soon as he heareth God named, he is filled with trepidation and fear."[53]

This theme resounds as well in aphophatic theology, and in the writings of major Christian mystics. Thus John Chrysostom, commenting on Psalm 139: 14, which the *Septuagint* translates, "I praise thee: for that Thou madest Thyself fearfully wondrous," says "we wonder at the greatness of the sea and its measureless expanse, but terror and 'fear' only seize upon us when we gaze down into its depths. So, too, here the Psalmist. When he gazes down into the immeasurable, yawning depth of the divine wisdom, dizziness comes upon him, and he recoils in terrified wonder and cries: . . . 'The knowledge is too wonderful for me; it is high, above my power'."[54] Meister Eckhart claims that the depth of the Godhead is beyond good and evil, and John of the Cross says that in mounting toward the deity, God "destroys, crushes and overwhelms the soul in such a deep darkness, that it feels as though melted and in its misery destroyed by a cruel death of the spirit. Even as though it were to feel it had been swallowed by some savage beast and buried in the darkness of his belly."[55]

---

52   Eliot Deutsch, *The Bhagavad Gītā, Translated with introduction and critical essays.* New York: Holt, Rinehart, and Wilson, 1968, chapter 11: 12, 16, 19, 23–5, 27–8, 30, 41–2, 45.

53   Quoted in Rudolph Otto, *The Idea of the Holy*, trans. John W. Harvey. New York: Oxford University Press, 1958, p. 99.

54   Quoted in ibid., p. 182.

55   *The Ascent of Mount Carmel*. Quoted in ibid., p. 106.

This is not the whole story, of course. The message of the *Gītā* is ultimately one of love and grace. Paul thinks that God sought us out when we were yet sinners, and exclaims that "no created thing can ever come between us and the love of God made visible in Christ Jesus our Lord" (Romans 8: 39) Luther believes that God is not only hidden and incomprehensible but revealed as gracious and loving in Jesus Christ. And John of the Cross tells us that in the final stage of her ascent, the mystic's soul is consumed in love.

The fact remains that important aspects of the *Gītā*'s God, or of Paul's or Luther's, or of the God of a number of major Christian mystics can't be easily assimilated by moral categories. Those of us who, like Otto, think that these are essential aspects of the "transcendent, in large measure incomprehensible God" of theism will resist attempts to sanitize the story of the binding of Isaac, or to deny that Abraham's dilemma is a real one. It may be true, as Evans says, that the Christian can be assured that whatever God may command, he is loving. It doesn't follow that *what* love commands may not be flatly contrary to what love *seems* to require or to the dictates of rational morality—that, as Johannes says, our "love to God may [not] cause" us "to give [our] love to [our] neighbor the opposite expression to that which, ethically speaking, is required by duty."[56]

---

56   Kierkegaard, *Fear and Trembling*, p. 80.

CHAPTER 11

Mysticism and Morality

Most of those who have studied mysticism believe that there is a significant relationship between mysticism and morality. Albert Schweitzer, Arthur Danto, and others think that mystical consciousness is incompatible with morality. The dominant view, however, is that mysticism supports it. Steven T. Katz is typical: "As an historical observation, it is difficult to find any major mystical figures, or mystical traditions, that can be said to preach moral indifference; and certainly none preach immorality."[1] But the evidence is actually much more ambiguous than Katz's remarks suggest.

As Jeffrey J. Kripal points out, mysticism's relation to morality has often been viewed as a problem within the mystical traditions themselves. Witness, for example, "traditional Christian heresiology's" attack on "the perceived ethical excesses and transgressions of various gnostic and mystical movements . . . ; medieval Christian debates about the respective benefits and virtues of the contemplative and active lives; . . . and the many Indic 'right-handed' attempts to tame, allegorize, or simply deny the explicit antinomianism and eroticism of 'left-handed' Tantra; Vaiṣṇava moral concerns about the love-trysts of Kriṣṇa with the married milk-maids (*gopīs*), . . . and the subsequent theological debates about whether the god's proper relationship to the women was adulterous or properly conjugal;[2] . . . Mahāyāna's ethical critiques of the Theravādin *arhat* and his solitary, allegedly selfish existence . . . ; Jain debates about the proper degrees of ascetic renunciation and social involvement and the subsequent split into . . . 'the Sky-Clad,' that is, naked, and 'White-clad' sects." Or consider the abuses and scandals that have accompanied the introduction of the "Asian institution of the guru into the west." (These include sexual exploitation, child molestation, abuses of power, and occasionally even murder.)[3] Kripal concludes that minimizing these phenomena is intellectually dishonest. They occur too frequently, and in connection with too

---

1   Steven T. Katz, "Ethics and Mysticism in Eastern Mystical Traditions," *Religious Studies* 28 (1992), p. 254.
2   The relevance of this to mysticism is that the *gopīs*, and especially Kriṣṇa's favorite *gopī*, Rādha, typify the soul in its relation to God (Kriṣṇa).
3   Jeffrey J. Kripal, "Debating the Mystical as Ethical: An Indological Map," in G. William Barnard and Jeffrey J. Kripal, eds, *Crossing Boundaries: Essays on the Ethical Status of Mysticism*. New York and London: Seven Bridges Press, 2002, p. 16. It is worth noting, however, that most (though not all) of the ethically suspect practices associated with some forms of mysticism involve breaches of conventional sexual morality, sexual exploitation, alcohol and drug abuse, and abuses of power. They do not typically include murder, theft, and the like.

many mystical traditions to be safely ignored. It is equally dishonest to simply "write them off as 'perversions,' 'abuses,' or 'exceptions.'" Dismissing all amoral or immoral mystics as fakes "flies in the face of overwhelming positive testimonial and textual evidence."[4] Although Kripal may overstate his case, enough has been said to suggest that the relations between mysticism and morality aren't as straight-forwardly benign as Katz, Henri Bergson, Aldous Huxley, Walter Stace, and many others have claimed.

Two questions must be distinguished. (1) Are there important empirical connec-tions between mysticism and morality? Does mysticism reinforce moral ideals and support moral activity in practice, or does it instead undermine the former and inhibit the latter? (2) Are there logical or epistemic connections between mystical consciousness and morality? Does mystical consciousness provide a backing or warrant for or against moral claims or, on the contrary, is mystical consciousness inconsistent with them?[5]

The first is a question for historians of religion and social scientists. The second is philosophical.

The first section of this chapter will consider several ideals of conduct that are closely associated with various forms of mysticism, attempt to determine whether they are *moral* ideals, and explore the relation of these ideals to mystical experi-ence. The chapter's second section examines attempts to show that mystical consciousness provides a backing or warrant for altruism, and arguments purport-ing to show that mysticism and morality are incompatible.

Although they are intimately connected, mystical experiences can be distin-guished from the religious traditions within which they are incorporated. If the argument of this chapter is sound, mystical experience is compatible with morality but provides less support for it than has often been supposed.

Moral Ideals and Mysticism

Ideals or models of human behavior are an integral part of most mystical traditions. This section examines several of the most important. I shall argue that some of

---

4   Ibid., pp. 54–5. Cf. p. 42f.

5   The two questions aren't unrelated. As Walter Stace has observed, it isn't particularly plausible to suppose that mystical consciousness provides a warrant for morality if it inhibits morality in practice. (Walter T. Stace, *Mysticism and Philosophy*. Philadelphia and New York: J. B. Lippincott, 1960, p. 333) The reason, I believe is this. Other things being equal, we expect people who are in a better epistemic position to perceive the grounds of morality to act at least as morally as those who are not. If the mystic's conduct and ideals are either immoral or amoral, then there is reason to suspect that mystical consciousness provides little or no epistemic support for morality. For similar reasons, that the mystic's conduct and ideals are exemplary provides indirect evidence that mysticism does not justify immoral or amoral activity.

them are nonmoral, and those which aren't may be expressions of beliefs and attitudes which are not specifically mystical. A person's picture of life at its best is an important part of his or her general moral outlook. If I am correct, the types of mystical experience we shall consider[6] support nonmoral ideals, or reinforce moral ideals whose principal roots lie partly elsewhere.

Christian Mysticism and the "Mixed Life"

Dom Cuthbert Butler's *Western Mysticism* examines the ideals of Augustine, Gregory, and Bernard.

According to Augustine, the contemplative life is to be preferred to the active life for three reasons. First, the contemplative life is the end of the active life. Moral action disciplines the soul and assists others. Its ultimate aim, though, is salvation, and salvation consists in the beatific vision, that is, in contemplation. Christ's words to Mary provide the second reason. Martha symbolizes the active life and Mary symbolizes the contemplative life, but Mary is said to have chosen the better part. The third reason is the conviction (perhaps ultimately inherited from Plato and Aristotle) that the life of theoretical reason is intrinsically the best life. Thus in *The Trinity* xii, 1, Augustine says that the most "excellent function" of the mind is the contemplation of "things eternal" which is "completed in cognition alone," and in *de Quantitate Animae* maintains that the intellectual grasp of "those things which truly and supremely are" is the "highest act" of the soul.[7]

Even so, the demands of charity sometimes require that one abandon a purely contemplative life. Thus, those who are fit for the government of the church and the discharge of ecclesiastical affairs "are often called upon, by the needs of the

---

6 I shall not discuss nature mysticism or "cosmic consciousness" (a perception of the unity or oneness of all natural phenomena) in this section. The moral effects of cosmic consciousness are ambiguous. They may occasionally be good, are sometimes bad, but are usually neither good nor bad. (There is little hard evidence that the feelings of empathy which *are* part of cosmic consciousness have significant effects upon a person's moral *behavior* in most cases.) In so far as cosmic consciousness *is* associated with a specific ideal, it is an ideal that embraces good *and* evil. Cosmic consciousness often expresses itself in "pantheism," the belief that nature, or the spirit which permeates it or animates it, is holy or divine. Because nature indifferently embraces both good and evil, ideals associated with pantheism tend to be amoral. (Though this should not be overstated. While the nature mystic or pantheist may say that everything is holy, the evil which he or she celebrates [along with the good] is usually natural evil such as suffering and destruction, unconventional social behavior, or deviant sexual behavior— not murder, theft, or betrayal.) There is therefore even less reason to believe that cosmic consciousness provides independent support for moral ideals than to believe that the other types of mystical experience do so.

7 Quoted in Edward Cuthbert Butler, *Western Mysticism, The Teaching of Augustine, Gregory and Bernard on Contemplation and the Contemplative Life*, 2nd edn with *Afterthoughts*. New York: Harper and Row, 1977, pp. 162–3. Henceforth Butler.

church, to undertake the works of the active life" (*Contra Faustum*, xxii, 58, Butler 160). For, as Augustine says in the *City of God* (xix, 19; Butler 165), "no one should be so at leisure as in his leisure not to think of his neighbor's welfare." (Plato speaks similarly of the return to the cave. The philosopher king turns his back on a life of pure contemplation—a life which is intrinsically better—in order to serve his community.)

There are similarities between Augustine's position and two which will be examined later in this chapter. Advaita Vedānta and Hīnayāna Buddhism, too, maintain that morality is a means to a higher end, namely, union with Brahman or enlightenment, although they too concede that the Brahman-knower or *arhat* may teach and administer to aid others. Yet there are also significant differences. (1) For Augustine, the essence of Christian virtue (morality) is *caritas*—the love of God for his own sake, and oneself and others in God. *Caritas* is also an integral part of the beatific vision and thus of the contemplative life. There is a continuity of content between morality and contemplation that is absent in Advaita and Hīnayāna. (2) The obligation to renounce contemplation in order to meet the needs of others is a vital part of Augustine's teaching (as it is of Plato's); far from being an afterthought, it is woven into the very fabric of Augustine's understanding of the best life. This is not so obviously true of either Advaita or Hīnayāna.

Although Gregory's position is essentially the same as Augustine's, he appears to place more weight on the active life.

The active life is defined as giving bread to the hungry, teaching the ignorant, correcting the erring, recalling "to the path of humility our neighbor when he waxes proud," tending the sick, dispensing "to all what they need," and providing "those entrusted to us with the means of subsistence" (*Homilies on Ezechiel* II, ii; Butler 171). Gregory calls our attention to the fact that contemplation reinforces morality and that, in spite of its superiority, the contemplative life is "by choice" whereas the active life is by necessity. The active life is necessary and sufficient for salvation. The contemplative life is neither necessary nor sufficient.

More significantly, Gregory suggests that contemplation is a gift that is at least partly given for the sake of others. "Whoever reaps benefit by seeing spiritual things, is bound by speaking to lay them before others. For he sees in order that he may announce, who, by the fact that he reaps benefit for himself, by preaching has a care also for the advance of his neighbor" (*Homilies on Ezechiel* II, ii, 4; Butler 176). And in the *Book on Pastoral Care* I, 5 (Butler 180), he insists that contemplatives have received their gifts "not for themselves only, but also for others."

Finally, Gregory implies that while the contemplative life is superior to the active life, the life that *combines* contemplation and action is better than either. "The excellence of preachers is far above that of the continent and silent, and the eminence of the continent outdistances greatly that of married people" (*Homilies on Ezechiel* II, iv, 6; Butler 180). The "continent" are those living a life of contemplation. As Butler points out, Gregory has already said that preachers must practice both lives. It would seem to follow that the "mixed life" that combines contemplation and action is the most perfect life. This evaluation is also implicit in Gregory's claim that Christ provides the model of both lives:

> Christ set forth in Himself patterns of both lives ... united together ... For when he wrought miracles in the city, and yet continued all night in prayer on the mountain, He gave His faithful ones an example not to neglect, through love of contemplation, the care of their neighbors; nor again to abandon contemplative pursuits through being too immoderately engaged in the care of their neighbors ... [but so to comport themselves] that the love of their neighbor may not interfere with the love of God; nor again the love of God cast out, because it transcends, the love of their neighbors. (*Morals*, xxiii, 33; Butler 176)

Or consider Bernard, who argues that even though the contemplative life is intrinsically better, our lives must include contemplation *and* action: first, because one cannot constantly maintain oneself in contemplation and should engage in works of charity rather than remain inactive during the intervals between contemplation; second, because even contemplatives are obliged to respond to the demands of their neighbor. "[W]ho doubts that a man when he is in prayer is speaking to God? And yet how often are we withdrawn from prayer, and that at the very dictate of charity, because of those who are in need of our assistance or our advice!" (Sermon on the *Song of Solomon* 50; Butler 192). In short, given the conditions of this life, where distractions and the weakness of the body make continuous contemplation impossible, and the needs of others make demands upon our charity, the "mixed life" is the best life.

This theme is echoed again and again. According to Richard of St Victor, the soul, in the fourth and highest degree of love, returns from the heights of contemplation and "goes forth on God's behalf and descends below herself ... she goes out by compassion."[8] In the last passage of the "Sparkling Stone," Jan van Ruysbroeck asserts that

> The man who is sent down by God from these heights into the world is full of truth and rich in all virtues. And he seeks not his own but the glory of Him Who has sent him. And hence he is just and truthful in all things, and he possesses a rich and generous ground, which is set in the richness of God: and therefore he must always spend himself on those who have need of him ... And by this he possesses a universal life, for he is ready alike for contemplation and for action, and is perfect in both of them.[9]

---

8   Richard of St Victor, "Four Degrees of Passionate Charity," in *Richard of Saint Victor: Selected Writings on Contemplation*, trans. Clare Kirchberger. London: Faber and Faber, 1957, p. 224.

9   Jan van Ruysbroeck, *The Adornment of the Spiritual Marriage, The Book of Truth, and the Sparkling Stone*, trans. C. A. Wynschenk Dom. London: John M. Watkins, 1916, pp. 220–21.

By the end of the Middle Ages, the mixed life was firmly enthroned as the ideal of the great Christian mystics.[10]

Advaita Vedānta, Hīnayāna Buddhism, and the Good of Enlightenment

Advaita Vedānta   Advaita Vedānta is a classical expression of a monistic mysticism which denies the reality of distinctions.[11] Eliot Deutsch describes its ethics as follows: the good is what leads to *mokṣa* (permanent release from the space-time world) and the bad is what hinders it. In general, truth and righteousness further self-realization while their opposites make self-realization more difficult. The Brahman itself, however, and a person who has recognized his identity with it, are beyond moral distinctions. "When the seer sees that person, . . . the Lord, as the womb of Brahman, then, shaking off the good and the bad, the wise man becomes spotless." (*Mundaka Upaniṣad*, chap. 3, 1, 3)[12] The Brahman-knower has no reason to refrain from deceit, theft, and murder because "conventional" moral reasons only apply within the world of *māyā* and he no longer dwells in *māyā*, and because, having already effectively attained *mokṣa*, righteousness need no longer be cultivated as a *means* to it. But even though a person who has transcended all distinctions has no *reason* to refrain from deceit, theft, and murder, he is psychologically unable to engage in them since unrighteous deeds are expressions of egoism, and the Brahman-knower is free from egocentricity.[13]

---

10   Butler maintains that John of the Cross departs from this tradition (Butler 211–12), and quotes from the prefatory remarks to stanza 29 of the *Spiritual Canticle*:

> Here it is noted that, for as long as the soul has not reached this estate of union of love, it must needs practice love, both in the active life and in the contemplative; but when it reaches that estate it befits it not to be occupied in other outward acts and exercises which might keep it back, however little, from that abiding in love with God, although they may greatly conduce to the service of God; for a very little of this pure love is more precious in the sight of God and the soul, and of greater profit to the Church, even though the soul appear to be doing nothing, than all these works together . . . Therefore if any should have aught of this degree of solitary love, great wrong would be done to it, and to the Church, if, even for a brief space, one should endeavor to busy it in active or outward affairs, of however great moment. (*Spiritual Canticle*, 3rd rev. edn, ed. and trans. E. Allison Peers, Garden City, New York: Image/Doubleday, 1961, pp. 416–17)

> It should be noted, though, that this passage is found only in the second redaction of the *Spiritual Canticle*, and that the second redaction may be spurious. (See Peers's introduction, ibid., pp. 36–7) Steven Payne, OCD, however, disagrees. See his *John of the Cross and the Cognitive Value of Mysticism*. Dordrecht: Kluwer, 1990, pp. 11–13.

11   Monistic mystical experiences are more or less identical with a state of pure consciousness in which the mind is empty of all contents and objects. One remains *conscious* but not conscious *of* anything.

12   *Upaniṣads*, trans. Patrick Olivelle. New York: Oxford University Press, 1996, p. 274.

13   Eliot Deutsch, *Advaita Vedānta: A Philosophical Reconstruction*. Honolulu: Univer-

I. C. Sharma maintains that Śaṃkara believed that the enlightened continue to work for the benefit of others, and as evidence appeals to his commentary on the *Bhagavad Gītā*.[14] But the great Advaitin's remarks are ambiguous. In iv, 20, Śaṃkara speaks of a person who has found the truth, but "who finding it impracticable to get away from action, engages in action as before with a view to set an example to the world or to avoid the displeasure of the orthodox."[15] Such a person, "having started with action, and having since obtained the right knowledge of the Self, really abandons action . . . but" finds "that for some reason he cannot abandon action." (iv, 19)[16]

Śaṃkara's remarks appear to refer to those who were committed to a social role *before* they achieved enlightenment, and cannot now divest themselves of it without failing in the duties which they have to others in virtue of that role. That Śaṃkara has this is mind is confirmed by another passage in which he says that a person who "thinks he has achieved his ends and has realized the Self, even he should work for the welfare of others, though for himself he may have nothing to do." (iii, 24)[17] The context of this passage makes it reasonably clear that Śaṃkara is referring to kṣatriyas, who because of their inherited role as rulers and warriors, have special obligations to others.

Śaṃkara's remarks may be usefully contrasted with the comments of Augustine, Gregory, and Bernard. According to the latter, the contemplative may be obliged to *assume* a role for the benefit of others (for example, that of a bishop), and is often obliged to perform acts of charity *irrespective* of his role. His obligations to others are not a function of commitments incurred prior to enlightenment or restricted to his special roles.

In any case, the circumstances to which Śaṃkara alludes in the quoted passages are clearly exceptional. The general thrust of his remarks is that action is only necessary for those who have not yet achieved enlightenment: "For the man who knows the Self there is nothing to do;" "For the man thus rejoicing in the Self no purpose is achieved by action;" "No evil whatever either by way of incurring sin, or by way of losing the Self, in this world arises from inaction." (iii, 17, 18) Not only are works unnecessary; they are not really appropriate. "Since the man who has realized the Self is free from illusory knowledge, *karma-yoga* [the path of works]

---

sity Press of Hawaii, 1973. Compare Richard H. Jones, "Must Enlightened Mystics be Moral?", in *Mysticism Examined: Philosophical Inquiries into Mysticism*. Albany: State University of New York Press, 1993, pp. 187–215. Enlightenment may eliminate the possibility of selfishness (in the usual sense) since it eliminates the sense of self, but it "does not compel any course of action . . . [Either] indifference or inaction can be opted for." (p. 193)

14   I. C. Sharma, *Ethical Philosophies of India*, New York: Harper Torchbooks, 1970.
15   *The Bhagavad Gītā with the commentary of Śrī Śankaracbāryā*, trans. A. Mahadeva Sastri. Madras: Samata Books, 1961, p. 136.
16   Ibid., p. 135.
17   Ibid., p. 107.

which is based upon illusion [the belief in "an active self"] must be impossible for him." (v, intro.)[18]

Modern neo-Advaitins like Vivekānanda do preach the "mixed life," the ideal of "disinterested *sannyāsins*, bent on doing good to others . . . disseminating education and seeking in various ways to better the condition of all, down to the *candala* (untouchable)."[19] But as R. C. Zaehner points out, it is important to remember that Vivekānanda had been educated at Calcutta's Mission College and, prior to his encounter with Rāmakrishna, was typical of a Westernized Indian middle class which had absorbed European social and ethical ideas.

Western thought has had relatively little impact upon Hindu metaphysics and spirituality. Only in the ethical and social sphere has the West had a significant impact upon Indian religious life and practice. This fusion of Western social and ethical ideals with Hindu thought and spirituality may be admirable. There may be elements within the Hindu tradition that lend themselves to this development. The fact remains that statements made by modern neo-Advaitin apologists concerning the intrinsic connection between monistic mysticism and the mixed life must be treated with caution. What is of interest for our purposes is not the view of modern neo-Advaitins, but the views of classical Advaita, that is, of an Advaita not yet familiar with Western ethical and social teachings. If the ideal of the mixed life is not found in classical Advaita, it is reasonable to infer that its inclusion in modern neo-Advaita is the result of extraneous influences.[20]

Hīnayāna Buddhism   Because of its reluctance to speculate on the nature of ultimate reality or draw metaphysical conclusions from its mystical experiences, Ninian Smart has suggested that Theravāda Buddhism many be the purest expression of

---

18   Eliot Deutsch and J. A. B. Van Buitenen, *A Source Book of Advaita Vedānta*. Honolulu: University Press of Hawaii, 1971, p. 219.

19   Quoted in R. C. Zaehner, *Hinduism*. New York: Oxford University Press, 1966, p. 167.

20   For a recent defense of these claims see Kripal, "Debating the Mystical as Ethical." One might object that classical Advaita assumes that, normally, one will already have fulfilled one's social obligations. (Ideally, one becomes a *sannyāsin* [an ascetic who has severed all ties to society] only after one has been a householder and discharged the duties of that stage.) But this misses the point, namely, that in classical Advaita, the *highest* stage of life does not involve any social obligations. By contrast, the mixed life *combines* contemplation and action *in the highest stage*. Note too that, in arguing that Advaita supports morality, Steven Katz misstates the content of their mystical vision. He says, for example, that it is an "existential awareness of the transcendental unity of all selves in which each is a part of the other," a perception "of the inter-relatedness of all being" (Katz, "Ethics and Mysticism," p. 257). But this is mistaken. The content of the Advaitin's mystical vision is, rather, that there is only *one* self, or that *all* distinctions are unreal. In either case, Advaita can't (as Katz claims) be consistently "other-directed" since there are no others to whom one *could* be directed. Nor is the *atman* or true or absolute self identical with the "particular self" (as Katz also claims on p. 258f.) because the former is real and the latter is not. Finally, since the self of Advaita does not really act, moral action turns out to be illusory.

monistic mystical consciousness.[21] Be this as it may, Hīnayāna Buddhism's attitude toward morality is very similar to that of a tradition in which monistic experiences clearly *are* central, namely, Advaita Vedānta. Four facts are especially telling.

First, *sīla* ("morality"), consisting in right speech, right action, and right occupation, constitutes the middle portion of the Noble Eight-Fold Path. "Morality" is a means to a nonmoral end, namely, the eradication of the *avijja* (ignorance) and *tanha* (craving) which bind us to a world characterized by *anicca* (impermanence) and *dukkha* ("unsatisfactoriness").[22]

Second, the *brahma vihāras*, which are associated with the eighth stage of the Path (namely, right meditation or *samādhi*) have moral overtones. *Mettā* ("friendliness") consists in wishing well to all creatures, pervading every quarter of the world with friendly thoughts. A person occupying this "station," says Buddhaghosa, identifies "all with his own self, without making the distinction that they are other beings." *Mettā* involves "bestowing benefits on others,[23] is based on the ability to see their pleasant side, and results in the stilling of ill-will and malice."[24] *Karunā* (compassion) consists in sharing the pain of all sentient beings, and cultivating the wish to remove it. *Muditā* (sympathetic joy) involves sharing the joy of all creatures. The fourth and highest station, however, is *upekkhā*. One is impartial, free from aversion to others and from any desire to win their approval—serene, calm, and unattached. *Upekkhā* results from the recognition that all beings are "nonexistent" (empty of self) and that, because of the law of karma, each individual most work out his or her own salvation. Edward Conze observes that "on reaching its perfection, the social attitude . . . seems to become distinctly a-social."[25] But while this is true, his remark is misleading: the *brahma vihāras as a whole* are not primarily instruments of moral discipline but ways of introducing order into our emotional life. Buddhaghosa's comment is significant. Their point is the elimination of malice and other disturbing emotions and feelings which make it difficult to achieve mental peace and equilibrium.[26] Their aim or point is not ultimately moral.

---

21 Ninian Smart, *A Dialogue of Religions*. London: SCM Press, 1960. Pure consciousness experiences *are* cultivated in Hīnayāna. Another experience seems to be more highly valued, however, namely, "cessation," the temporary absence or stopping of all thought and sensation—including, apparently, consciousness itself.

22 *Anatta* (no soul or self) is the third "mark of existence." But the nonexistence of a persisting ego or soul, or of any other permanent substance, is a logical consequence of the belief that *samsara* (the space-time world) is nothing but a flow of momentary constituents (*dhammas*).

23 Since the *brahma vihāras* are a method for disciplining our emotions, Buddhaghosa is presumably referring to the *wish* or *desire* to confer benefits, and not (except perhaps incidentally) to external behavior.

24 Quoted in Edward Conze, *Buddhist Thought in India*. Ann Arbor: University of Michigan Press, 1967, p. 82.

25 Ibid., p. 90.

26 The other tool that is closely associated with the eighth stage of the Path is the *jhānas*. The *jhānas* culminate in monistic mystical consciousness ("the sphere of neither

Third, the "virtue" or excellence which is most highly prized in Theravāda Buddhism isn't justice or compassion but *pannā* (wisdom), an insight into the "emptiness" of *samsāra* (that is, into its causal interrelatedness and lack of permanent substance) which has been so thoroughly appropriated that it pervades one's thought, feeling, and conduct. A combination of *pannā* and *samādhi* leads to Nibbāna.[27]

These considerations are reinforced by a fourth. Giving (*dāna*) is an important Theravādin virtue. But the primary *reason* for giving is to accumulate merit. The lowest motive is the "expectation of rebirth in a heavenly *deva*-world." The two highest are "to calm the giver's mind and to adorn the giver's mind." Others "include thinking 'It is good to give' and following custom." Giving for any of these reasons leads to "a heaven. But . . . none of the recognized motives are other-regarding: only self-centered benefits are mentioned."[28] Note, too, that "among contemporary Burmese Buddhists . . . the amount of merit depends" (among other things) "upon the sanctity of the *recipient*." Thus it is more meritorious to give to monks rather than to widows and orphans "regardless of their material needs."[29]

Taken together, these facts suggest that, like the Advaitins, Theravādins and other Hīnayāna Buddhists regard morality as a means to a private and nonmoral end, namely, their own enlightenment.

This may be something of an oversimplification, however. Richard H. Jones has argued that even though those who aren't yet enlightened may regard morality as a mere means, the enlightened do not. A person who has eradicated thirst and illusion is no longer governed by egocentric considerations and may, like the Buddha, elect to teach others. If he does, his actions can be regarded as altruistic since they are designed to benefit others and aren't expressions of self-interest.

While Jones is correct, it is important to note that altruistic behavior isn't an *intrinsic* feature of enlightenment. (Pacceka buddhas, for example, are solitary.) Nor are the enlightened *obliged* to teach others. In the Theravāda tradition, while Gotama in fact chooses to work for the enlightenment of everyone, he could have refrained from doing so without impairing or compromising his own enlighten-

---

perception nor nonperception") or, in some versions, "the attainment of cessation." There are usually said to be eight (or nine) *jhānas* but there is some reason to believe that the fourth *jhāna*—the state of equanimity, calm, or even-mindedness—is valued more highly than the last four (or five). For example, it is said that the Buddha, as he approached death, passed through all the *jhānas* but came to rest in the fourth. The *brahma vihāras* and the *jhānas* ultimately appear to have the same aim, namely, even-mindedness.

27   Of the two, modern Theravādins, at least, regard *pannā* as by far the most important.
28   With the exception of the fourth. Giving, thinking "It is good to give," may not be *other*- directed but it is not *self*-regarding either.
29   Richard H. Jones, "Theravada Buddhism and Morality," in *Mysticism Examined*, p. 229.

ment. Although the Buddha recommends the same choice to his disciples, the implication is that Buddhist enlightenment does not itself "spontaneously produce a life of other-regarding action."[30]

The ideal of enlightenment thus isn't *essentially* moral. Nevertheless, it *can* be developed in a moral direction. The principal model in Hīnayāna Buddhism is provided by the *arhat*, the successful disciple of the Buddha who has achieved enlightenment by putting the Buddha's teachings into practice in his or her own life. But the Buddha too provides an ideal which regulates Hīnayāna conduct, and enlightened monks sometimes do teach and direct others. Hīnayāna morality thus isn't entirely egoistic.[31] Still, the Hīnayāna ideal can't be regarded as altruistic in any fully developed or unqualified sense since the enlightened are not *obliged* to act altruistically nor is altruistic behavior an *instrinsic* feature of the best life. Morality is *binding* only in so far as it is a necessary condition for achieving one's own Nibbāna.

Advaita, Hīnayāna, and ethical egoism   Although the terms "moral" and "morality" are open textured, their meaning isn't entirely indeterminate. Morality is clearly concerned with actions, for example. Even though we may pay more attention to an agent's intentions and attitudes than to her behavior when we evaluate her actions, the intentions in question are intentions *to act*, and the relevant attitudes and dispositions are those expressing themselves *in action*. Morality is also concerned with our relations to other people. Whether we have moral obligations to ourselves is a moot question, but a code or way of life which recognized no obligations to others would not normally be called moral. Finally, actions we call moral are typically characterized by conscientiousness or a sense of duty, by a desire for justice and equity, or by a concern for the well-being of others.

That these features are part of what most people mean by "morality" has important implications. Ethical egoism is the position that an action is right or good or obligatory if and only if it (ultimately) promotes one's own well-being. There are different kinds of ethical egoism. In principle, ethical egoists might argue that benevolence and justice are expressions of weakness, and that the claims of others should be ignored when it is to one's advantage to do so. (Plato's Thrasymachus advocates a position of this sort.) Most would regard this position as amoral or (more probably) immoral. But in practice, most ethical egoists have acknowledged obligations to secure justice and promote the common good although they have attempted to justify them by showing how the promotion of justice and the common good ultimately serves one's own interests. Is this position moral or not? It

---

30   Ibid., p. 239.
31   How widely spread *is* this ideal? The fact that the Buddha's compassion is prized by those who aren't yet enlightened is inconclusive since one may prize it for self-regarding reasons. That a person values the Buddha's compassionate behavior because it benefits her is no evidence that she cherishes an altruistic ideal.

acknowledges that we have obligations to other persons, and enjoins us to be concerned about justice and the good of others. These obligations and concerns aren't ultimate, however, since they are a mere means to our own private good. A position of this type is neither clearly excluded by nor clearly satisfies our second and third criteria. It is thus unclear whether we should call it moral or not.

The situation is complicated by the fact that while most ethical egoists believe that virtue promotes one's own well-being, the relation between a virtue like justice and one's private good can be construed in different ways. Plato and Aristotle believed that justice and a concern for the public good are *part* of one's own private good. Epicurus and Hobbes thought that the moral virtues have only instrumental value but conceded that they are indispensable to human life. A third position is possible—that a person's private good can be secured at some point in his life but that, having secured it, he can then discard the moral virtues if he wishes to do so. I suggest that most of us would call the first position "moral" and regard the third as nonmoral or (possibly) immoral, but would be unsure as to whether to classify the second position as moral or not.

The relevance of these considerations is obvious. Advaitins and Hīnayāna Buddhists are essentially ethical egoists although the private good which they seek is neither pleasure (Epicurus) nor security and "commodious living" (Hobbes) but *mokṣa* or enlightenment.

But what *type* of ethical egoists are they? Moral behavior isn't *part* of *mokṣa* or enlightenment nor is it obligatory once one has achieved those goals. For classical Advaita, moral behavior is obligatory only in so far as it furthers one's pursuit of *mokṣa*, or is demanded by a role that one has assumed before one was enlightened and cannot now escape. For Hīnayāna Buddhists, moral behavior is only obligatory as a means to enlightenment. The enlightened *may* choose to aid others even though doing so doesn't further their own interests. Their behavior is an act of supererogation, however; it is not a duty. Classical Advaita and Hīnayāna Buddhism thus appear to be instances of the third type of ethical egoism. They are consequently nonmoral or possibly immoral. (Although this judgment should be qualified by the recognition that social obligations are still thought to hold in some cases [Advaita], and to the extent to which selfless behavior is either emulated by some enlightened monks or disinterestedly admired or praised by those not yet enlightened.[32])

---

32   The latter applies to Advaita as well as to Hīnayāna. Śaṃkara, for example, attempted to "pass the torch" to others. I have the impression, however, that admiration and emulation of selfless behavior is more pronounced in Hīnayāna than in classical Advaita. If this is correct, it is probably due to the fact that Advaita lacks anything comparable to the Buddha story. (The Buddha's selfless history lies at the core of Buddhism. Advaita has nothing quite like this.)

Mahāyāna Buddhism and the Bodhisattva Ideal

Mahāyāna Buddhism criticizes Theravāda and the other Hīnayāna schools precisely because of their insistence upon the pursuit of one's own "private Nirvāna." Although the richness and variety of Mahāyāna thought makes generalizations difficult, I would like to comment upon certain aspects of Zen and the bodhisattva ideal.

Arthur Koestler reports a Zen patriarch as saying, "Zen is . . . extremely flexible in adapting itself to almost any philosophy and moral doctrine as long as its intuitive teaching is not interfered with. It may be found wedded to anarchism or fascism, communism or democracy, atheism or idealism."[33] Or consider D. Z. Suzuki's remarks in Thomas Merton's *Zen and the Birds of Appetite*. According to Suzuki, even the "Zen man" is a social being who "cannot live outside society" or "ignore ethical values." The "field" (reality) is "open" or "empty," but the players on the field belong to a realm of distinctions that includes the distinction between good and evil. "Our actual life consists [that is, should consist] in the one supporting the other," or in their "inseparable" cooperation.[34] *Prajnā* (wisdom) and virtues like *dāna* (giving) reinforce each other. Giving "means anything going out of oneself, disseminating knowledge, helping people in difficulties of all kinds, creating arts, promoting industry or social welfare, sacrificing one's life for a worthy cause and so on. But this . . . is not enough as long as a man harbors the idea of giving . . . in the giving there must not be any thought of a giver or a receiver, and of an object going through this transaction." The giving must go "on thus in Emptiness," *dāna* "flowing out of prajnā."[35]

Koestler has argued that Zen presupposes the existence of a rigorous social code or ethics, for example, Confucian ethics. Zen's emphasis upon spontaneity and relaxation can best be understood as a reaction to the anxiety and mental cramps that are induced by the restrictions and demands of a code of this type.[36] Whether this is true or not, it does seem that, for Suzuki, "emptiness" and "no-mind" are not a *source* of ethics or ethical behavior, but something that enables the "Zen man" to engage in social and ethical action in a radically different manner from the rest of us. Its relation to ethics seems in principle no different from its relation to swordsmanship or archery or the tea ceremony. Familiar acts are performed in a new spirit or style.[37]

Moreover, Arthur Danto appears to be correct in asserting that the style in question is neither logically nor psychologically tied to any particular type of

---

33 Arthur Koestler, *The Lotus and the Robot*. New York: Macmillan, 1960, p. 270f.

34 Thomas Merton, *Zen and the Birds of Appetite*. New York: New Directions, 1968, p. 104. (Part II consists of a dialogue between Merton and Suzuki.)

35 Ibid., pp. 105–6.

36 Koestler, *The Lotus and the Robot*, pp. 271–2. Compare Arthur Danto on Taoism (*Mysticism and Morality*. New York: Harper Torchbooks, 1973, pp. 112f.).

37 Koestler, *The Lotus and the Robot*, pp. 80–82.

activity. This is less clearly true of the *"caritas"* style, in which love for God and one's neighbor in God forms the ambience within which action takes place. Some attitudes are logically and psychologically tied to certain types of behavior. Charity appears to be an example. (Charity typically expresses itself in support, relief of the needy, and the like, not theft, falsehood, and murder.) "Nonattachment," seeing into the "emptiness of things," on the other hand, does not, or at least not so clearly. If this is correct, then, even though the Zen ideal can be combined with moral activity, it is not intrinsically moral. As David R. Loy points out, *kensho*[38] (literally, "seeing into one's own nature") "does not automatically reveal the best way to really help people" with the result that, in practice, "we tend to find ourselves back within the normative ethical standards of our own group."[39] Japanese Zen's assimilation of, and assimilation by, the Samurai ethos is an example.

The bodhisattva ideal seems more clearly moral. The bodhisattva postpones his or her own final release until everyone has achieved enlightenment. Of the bodhisattva, the *Prajñāpāramitā* says, "they do not wish to obtain their own primate Nirvana . . . they have set out for the benefit of the world, for the ease of the world, out of pity for the world. They have resolved: 'we will become a shelter for the world, a refuge for the world, the world's place of rest, the final relief of the world, islands of the world, lights of the world, leaders of the world, the world's means of salvation.'"[40]

The bodhisattva ideal is contrasted with Hīnayāna's *arhat* ideal. Since the *arhat* is said to seek his own private Nirvāna, he is still affected by the distinction between mine and thine, and thus hasn't yet succeeded in entirely freeing himself from ignorance and self-attachment.

Whereas Theravāda and the other Hīnayāna schools place more value upon wisdom (*prajñā*) than compassion (*karunā*), Mahāyāna tends to equally emphasize both. They are, however, paradoxically related. In her compassion, the bodhisattva is cognizant of persons and vows to save them, but in her wisdom she recognizes that persons are unreal. (Persons are nothing but collections of momentary "dharmas" which, in the last analysis, themselves have no reality.) According to the *Diamond Sutra*, "a bodhisattva should think thus: As many beings as there are in the universe of beings . . . all these should be led by me into Nirvāna . . . And yet, although innumerable beings have thus been led to Nirvāna, no being at all has been led to Nirvāna. And why? If in a bodhisattva, the perception of 'a being' should take place, he would not be called 'an enlightenment-being' (= bodhi-sattva)."[41]

---

38   *"Kensho"* is often used interchangeably with *"satori."* See Philip Kapleau, *The Three Pillars of Zen*. Boston: Beacon Press, 1967, p. 335.

39   David R. Loy, "The Lack of Ethics and the Ethics of Lack in Buddhism," in Bernard and Kripal, *Crossing Boundaries*, p. 273.

40   Quoted in Edward Conze, *Buddhism: Its Essence and Development*. New York: Harper Torchbooks, 1959, p. 128.

41   Quoted in ibid., p. 130.

At first glance, the bodhisattva ideal appears quite similar to the Christian ideal of the mixed life. Just as the Christian mystic combines contemplation with active charity, so the bodhisattva combines wisdom with compassion. Neither ideal is exclusively moral, but both contain an important moral component. This similarity, however, may be deceptive.

In the first place, it isn't clear that Mahāyāna's criticism of the *arhat* ideal is primarily moral. The *arhat* believes that distinctions between persons *are* real[42] and that, because of the law of karma, each individual must work out his or her own salvation. All that a person *can* do is seek his own Nirvāna. If the *arhat* were right, it would be as unreasonable to condemn him for failing to seek another person's Nirvāna as to condemn someone for failing to resist another person's temptation. Mahāyāna thinks that the *arhat* is mistaken, however, since, in its view, persons aren't really separate and distinct.

The bodhisattva ideal appears, in part, to be a reflection of Mahāyāna beliefs in the unreality of distinctions and the mutual indwelling of all things, the interpenetration of every aspect and level of reality. According to this view, there are no hard and fast lines between one thing and another. Reality is fluid, and distinctions are arbitrary and conventional. It follows that persons too indwell or interpenetrate each other, and that distinctions between them are purely conventional. Against this background, it makes a certain amount of sense to speak of the transfer of merit, bearing one another's burdens, and working for universal enlightenment.

Mahāyāna's criticism is only partly moral. The *arhat* isn't so much morally imperfect as spiritually imperfect. He still recognizes distinctions, retains a kind of belief in the reality of his own self, and is not absolutely indifferent and nonattached. (He *distinguishes* between his *own* enlightenment and the enlightenment of others, and is *concerned* with his *own* well-being.) His basic flaw isn't lack of compassion but lack of wisdom, for his self-concern is rooted in a distorted way of viewing reality.

In the second place, a "love" or "compassion" that refuses to recognize the independent reality of persons may be only superficially similar to what we ordinarily regard as love or compassion. The latter is a relation between independently real persons. It is odd, for example, to speak of having compassion for oneself, or for a character whom one knows to be fictional. Of course, I might say that when I look back on my adolescence I feel compassion for the boy I once was, but in doing so I distinguish my present self from my past self, treating the latter as if it were another person. Again, while I can undoubtedly be moved by the misfortunes of fictional characters, an impulse to relieve their distress or a wish to remove their discomfort—which are part of the very concept of compassion—would indicate

---

42   More precisely, the *arhat* believes that there is a real distinction between the different causal chains of dharmas constituting the lives of different persons.

that I had forgotten that they *were* fictional characters.[43] Genuine love or compassion seems to presuppose a belief in the independence and reality of its object.

Attempts to evade this conclusion are unsuccessful. For example, Richard H. Jones objects that Mahāyāna doesn't deny the *reality* of other persons but merely their status as independent self-existent beings; that is, it only denies a certain *analysis* of them. But this isn't correct, for the dharmas into which a person and her states are analyzed are *also* regarded as constructs or mental fictions. Perhaps "there *is* something not totally unreal," as Jones says, but whatever it is, it isn't a person.[44]

The problem has long been recognized by Buddhists themselves. Thus Dharmakīrti suggests that there are two sorts of compassion. The first takes beings as its object. But the second, and superior, "takes as its object the particulars [dharmas] that constitute those beings," to which the commentator Śākyabuddhi adds that there is "an even more subtle kind of compassion . . . that has no object at all."[45] This merely states the problem, however; it does not resolve it. For how can compassion take (for example) a feeling of pain as its object,[46] or *nothing* as its object?

Or consider Candrakīrti, who argued that since a perfectly enlightened buddha has no cognitions (of beings), he is only compassionate in the following sense: the *dharmakāya causes* the *sambhogakāyas* and *nirmānakāyas* to teach because of the compassionately motivated vows undertaken by the buddha *before* reaching perfect enlightenment.[47] But, of course, this implies that perfectly enlightened buddhas are *not* (now) compassionate (although they *were* compassionate *before* they became perfectly enlightened). The problem of reconciling the simultaneous possession of *prajñā* and *karunā* has not been solved.

The mixed life combines contemplation and moral activity. Since there are reasons both for doubting that Mahāyāna's repudiation of the *arhat*'s self-seeking is primarily based on moral grounds, and for doubting that the bodhisattva's behavior is compassionate or moral in any standard sense, there are reasons for doubting that the bodhisattva ideal provides a genuine analogue of the mixed life of Bernard and other Christian mystics.

---

43   But can't I feel compassion for historical figures or deceased friends although I can do nothing to relieve their distress? I undoubtedly can, but if my compassion is genuine I *would* relieve their distress if I could do so, and *wish* that I were able to do so. Do I wish to relieve Anna Karenina's distress, however? And precisely what would it mean to say that I would relieve it if I could?

44   Jones, "Must Enlightened Mystics be Moral?," p. 198 (my emphasis).

45   John Dunne, "Thoughtless Buddha, Passionate Buddha," *Journal of the American Academy of Religion* 64 (1996), p. 539.

46   When I pity Mary for her suffering, I pity *Mary*. I don't pity her feelings.

47   Dunne, "Thoughtless Buddha," p. 548–50. The *dharmakāya* or "law body" is roughly equivalent to suchness (*tatāthā*) or emptiness (*śūyatā*), and is identical with the buddha in his fully enlightened state. The *sambhogakāya* or enjoyment body is the form the *dharmakāya* assumes in the various buddha realms or "pure lands." The *nirmānakāya* is (again, very roughly) a human body. The historical buddha, Gotama, had a *nirmānakāya*.

It should be noted that Mahāyāna incorporates what might be called "quasi-theistic elements." For example, the *dharmakāya* is emptiness or suchness thought of as an appropriate object of devotional attitudes. While the *dharmakāya* is some-times described impersonally, it is typically said to be an intelligent mind and a loving heart. Again, in Mahāyāna, buddhas and bodhisattvas assume the role of savior gods. With the possible exception of the Buddhism of Faith (Pure Land Buddhism) Mahāyāna is not theistic; reality is ultimately "emptiness" (*śūnyatā*). Nevertheless, from a certain point of view it is appropriate to think of reality *as if* it were personal.

It is difficult to believe that there isn't some connection between an outlook that places compassion at the heart of things (if only metaphorically) and an ideal or model of behavior which includes compassion as an essential ingredient. The presence of these quasi-theistic elements may partly explain why compassion is a constituent of the bodhisattva ideal. The fact that wisdom is at least as important as compassion, and that reality is ultimately empty or void, explains why that ideal is not fully moral.

These considerations lead to the following question: does the ideal of the mixed life ever *clearly* occur in contexts which are essentially "uncontaminated" by theistic notions and feelings?[48] The answer is uncertain, but our examination of the bodhisattva ideal suggests that it does not.

Theistic Mysticism and Morality

The ideal of the mixed life is closely associated with theistic mysticism but isn't peculiar to Christian mysticism. According to Reynold A. Nicholson, "to abide in God (*baqā*) after having passed away from selfhood (*fanā*) is the mark of the Perfect Man, who not only journeys *to* God, i.e., passes from plurality to unity, but *in* and *with* God, i.e., continuing in the unitive state, he returns with God to the phenomenal world . . . In this descent 'He makes the Law his upper garment/ And the mystic Path his inner garment'."[49] Afīfuddīn al-Tilamsānī maintained that there are four "journeys." The first involves unitive states of consciousness. The fourth is "associated with physical death." The second and third involve turning back towards creatures. Thus, "in the *third* journey, this Perfect Man

---

48 Compare Michael Stoeber, who suggests that at least a partial answer to the question, "How could . . . a positive orientation" to the spiritual well-being of others "be grounded . . . in a condition of absolute amoral nondualism," is that at least some nondualistic mystics speak of "other aspects or facets" of this nondual reality to which their concern with the well-being of others "can be coherently connected." These adepts tend to "integrate monistic and theistic elements into their mystical narrative." (Michael Stoeber, "Amoral Trickster or Mystic Saint?", in Barnard and Kripal, *Crossing Bounda-ries*, pp. 397–8)

49 Reynold A. Nicholson, *The Mystics of Islam*. London: Routledge and Kegan Paul, 1963, p. 163.

turns his attention to God's creatures, either as an Apostle or as a Spiritual Director (Sheykh)."[50]

Theism can't be identified with theistic mysticism. Ninian Smart has suggested that Jewish theism and the theism of primitive Islam are relatively pure expressions of numinous experience.[51] Christian theism, Sufism, and Indian theism weave the mystical and numinous strands together, but both Christian theism and Sufism have important nonmystical roots. Since the theism associated with the numinous strand tends to be preoccupied with questions of guilt, sin, righteousness, and atonement, we should consider the possibility that the moral concern of theistic mystics is to be attributed to their theism, and only incidentally to their mysticism.[52] On the other hand, theistic mysticism is a dualistic mysticism of love and grace. It incorporates a belief that souls are ontologically distinct from God, that God is love, and that God loves the unworthy. But beliefs concerning the nature of what is religiously ultimate, and thus most fundamental and valuable, tend to suggest patterns of action; the idea that human behavior should imitate divine behavior pervades religious thought and practice. (For example, the Taoist sage is himself an image of the Tao.) So it would be natural for a theistic mystic to infer that she too should love others in spite of their unworthiness. Thus, even though the ideal of the mixed life undoubtedly has many roots, there is nothing *intrinsically* implausible in supposing that it was created by theistic mystics at least partly on the basis of their own experience.

How can we test the hypothesis that theistic *mysticism* is an important source of the ideal of the mixed life? One way of doing so is by examining the theisms of India, since these appear to place relatively more weight on mystical consciousness that Western theisms do, and relatively less weight on numinous experience and themes of sin, guilt, righteousness, and atonement.

---

50   Ibid., p. 165.

51   Smart, *Dialogue of Religions*.

52   This hypothesis receives some confirmation from the following consideration. Although it strongly emphasized the affective side of religion, the Great Awakening was not a mystical movement. (The regenerate underwent a change of heart, but they were not extrovertive or introvertive mystics.) Nevertheless, in his *Religious Affections* (New Haven: Yale University Press, 1959), Jonathan Edwards maintained that genuine conversion involves a sense and relish of the "transcendently excellent and amiable nature of divine things, as they are in themselves" (p. 240), "a love to divine things for the beauty and sweetness of their moral excellency" (p. 253f.), an understanding of divine things and a conviction of their reality and certainty, "evangelical humiliation" (p. 311), "the lamblike, dovelike spirit and temper of Jesus Christ" (p. 344), and holy practice consisting "very much" in "all the duties of the second table of the law," that is, in moral behavior (p. 296). This ideal combines "experimental" (i.e., experiential) insight and practical activity, and is not that different from the ideal of the mixed life subscribed to by Christian mystics. This suggests that the primary source of both ideals is the (Christian?) theism which these evangelicals and mystics have in common (and/or their emotionally involved commitment to it), and not the specific nature of their rather different experiences.

The *Bhagavad Gītā* is, on the whole, a theistic work. One of its central teachings is the doctrine of karma yoga. The practitioner of karma yoga rejects inactivity. Instead of withdrawing from the world, he continues to discharge his social and moral obligations but does so in a spirit of nonattachment. He acts, but without regard for the effects that his actions have upon his own future. There is a certain similarity between karma yoga and the ideal of the mixed life for, for in both cases "contemplation" or "union" is combined with action.

Arthur Danto describes karma yoga in the following way. Suppose, for example, that one is a doctor. As a doctor, one *is* concerned with those consequences of one's actions that are *intrinsically* connected with the aim of one's profession, namely, health. The *Gītā* is not suggesting that a doctor who has been informed that she has administered the wrong medicine should reply that the consequences of her acts mean nothing to her; for *as* a doctor she wishes to do those things that produce health.[53] On the other hand, she should *not* be concerned with consequences like wealth, prestige, personal satisfaction, or a fortunate rebirth, which are only *extrinsically* connected with the aim of her profession. Nor should she be unduly elated by success or unduly grieved by failure. A person thus acts properly when she discharges the duties of her role well, but is not attached to the extrinsic consequences of her behavior, and when, having done her best, she accepts its results with equanimity.[54]

Danto believes that this ideal is morally defective. By merging with one's role in this way one becomes impersonal, and "we hold it against people who *are* utterly impersonal in their dealings, who identify with their offices: we say they are not human, are mere machines, or have no heart."[55]

Danto's objection isn't entirely convincing. In the first place, feelings, attitudes, and deep commitments are built into certain roles (citizen, priest, father, husband) but not others (garbage man, tennis player). I cannot perform my role as a father unless I love my children and am deeply committed to their well-being. By contrast, no special feelings or attitudes are needed to be a good garbage man.[56] Nor does this role involve commitments engaging the depths of one's being. The accusation of impersonality is usually directed against someone who identifies himself with the second type of role, or routinely discharges the external obligations associated with the first type of role while lacking the feelings and attitudes, the cares and concerns, that are also part of it. But it isn't clear that an accusation of impersonality would be justified if it were directed against a person who identified herself with *all* of her roles, displaying the inner attitudes and commitments, as well as the external behavior, appropriate to each.

---

53   That is, she is concerned with all those things that are *essentially* connected with being a good doctor, those things without which one can't *be* a good doctor.
54   Danto, *Mysticism and Morality*, pp. 92–3.
55   Ibid., p. 93.
56   Other than a desire to do the job well (which isn't peculiar to this role).

In the second place, no one who performs a function or role for an ulterior end identifies himself with that function or role since he has ends which do not belong to him in virtue of serving that function or playing that role. Danto's point appears to be that a person practicing karma yoga can't distinguish herself from her functions because karma yoga involves the renunciation of every end other than those defined by the roles she plays. But this is false, for a person practices karma yoga in order to achieve *mokṣa* (release), and *mokṣa* is an end that transcends all roles.[57]

Danto has another objection, though, which is potentially more damaging. The acts performed by a practitioner of karma yoga aren't really his: first, because they are performed by his "body," and he is distinct from his body, second, because the role with which he identifies is a kind of nature, and people aren't responsible for acts determined by their nature. Since the acts that the agent performs aren't really his, he is not really functioning as a moral agent and is consequently "exempted from any moral penalties in the karmic order."[58] This detachment is morally objectionable, however. "There is something chilling in the image that the *Gītā* creates as we approach the end: Krishna ... and Arjuna ... move through the battle with that half smile of the inturned face of Indian art as they slay their way dispassionately across the field of conflict." Their stand "is not a moral stand, but a stand outside morality."[59]

This objection, too, is inconclusive. As Danto himself recognizes, the *Gītā* presupposes that an agent can refuse to perform the duties associated with his role and thus act against his "nature." The *Gītā* doesn't argue that because one's acts are "determined" by one's "nature" (that is, defined by one's role) they are unavoidable, and that one is therefore not responsible for them.

It is true that one's "real I" or "true self" is distinct from the psycho-physical organism (that is, from the body together with sensation, vital forces [*prana*], and ordinary empirical consciousness). And the *Gītā* does tell us that it is not the Self but "nature," that is, "the whole of one's past experience conjoined with the energies that constitute the natural orders of the world," which is the "real doer:"[60] "All actions are performed by the gunas of prakriti alone."[61] Only "he who is deluded by

---

57   One might argue that *mokṣa* is an end associated with the role of *sannyāsin* or wandering ascetic. There is a sense in which this is true. The *sannyāsin*, having discharged his duties as citizen and father, is now in a position to devote himself exclusively to the achievement of *mokṣa*. In a more fundamental sense, it is false. *Mokṣa*, with its permanent release from life's ills, is the ultimate though often unrecognized aim of every conscious being *qua* conscious being; it is not an aim one has only in so far as one assumes a special role.

58   Danto, *Mysticism and Morality*, p. 98.

59   Ibid., pp. 94–5.

60   Eliot Deutsch, *The Bhagavad Gītā*. New York: Holt Rinehart Winston, 1968, p. 165.

61   *Prakriti*, which is composed of the *gunas*, is the "stuff" of which nature is composed. Nature comprises ordinary psychological realities and transactions as well as physical realities and transactions. It is distinct from the true self and distinct from the Lord.

egoism thinks, 'I am the doer.'" (*Gītā* III, 27)[62] In reality, the true self is "unaffected by empirical action and is a pure witness to this action."[63]

But the *Gītā* also contains another theme that counterbalances this one. The practitioner of karma yoga must achieve a higher *bhakti* (loving devotion) in which, united with the Lord, "he acts in the knowledge that all action is essentially the Divine's action. He becomes an instrument of the divine."[64] So in practicing karma yoga one *does* act although one's acts are (or are regarded as) God's own acts.

Still, while these considerations may blunt Danto's objection, they don't get to the heart of it. Suppose that someone wholeheartedly discharges the duties of his various roles but is otherwise detached from the consequences of his behavior, including its consequences for other people. Suppose, in particular, that as a soldier or policeman, he has correctly determined that he has an obligation to kill someone and does so in a spirit of detachment. Danto maintains that this is "chilling," and it may be. Is it morally objectionable, though? It would be if (1) empathy or compassion, a sympathetic participation in other people's joys and sufferings, is necessary for our acts to have moral value, and if (2) these attitudes are psychologically incompatible with detachment, a spiritual distance from one's own ordinary preoccupations and those of others. (1) isn't clearly true, however, (Kant denied it[65]) and (2) seems falsified by the lives of some of the great mystics, for example Bernard or Eckhart. (Their paradoxical combination of compassion and detachment isn't totally unintelligible. Consider, for example, the way we are capable of sharing in the joys and sorrows of a small child while at the same time recognizing their vanity.)

Even so, there may still be a problem here. As we have noted, feelings, attitudes, and commitments are built into certain roles. I can't properly perform my role as a father, for example, if I don't love my children, deeply care about their welfare, and enter into their joys and sorrows. But do I really share their sorrows if I am not genuinely distressed by them or regard them as vanity or am no more grieved by them than I would be by the sufferings of a total stranger? Not clearly. (Imagine my

---

62 Deutsch, *Bhagavad Gītā*, p. 50.

63 Ibid., p. 166.

64 Ibid., p. 169. R. C. Zaehner, though, argues that, in the *Gītā*, the purified soul is essentially inactive. It recognizes that its acts are not the expression of its own inner being but of the motions of *prakriti* which is activated by, or is in some way identical with, God's power and activity. It acquiesces in God's action, so to speak, but does not participate in it. (See Zaehner, *Concordant Discord*, Oxford: Clarendon Press, 1970, p. 134) However, it *may* be significant that in at least one important theistic development of the themes of the *Gītā* and *Upaniṣads* (namely, Viśiṣṭādvaita Vedānta), the Pure Self *is* regarded as a doer. According to Rāmānuja, the Pure Self is the agent in every action, and not merely (as it is for Śaṃkara) the consciousness in every act of awareness.

65 Natural feelings and attitudes aren't directly relevant to the moral value of our acts since we aren't responsible for them.

daughter's reaction if she were to discover that, at the core of my being, I remain untouched by her suffering, or if she were to learn that not only would I not be unduly grieved by her early death, I would be no more grieved by it than I would by the death of a person I hardly knew. Wouldn't she rightly think I wasn't a good father?)

Whether these considerations are sufficient to show that karma yoga is nonmoral, however, is another matter. As we have seen, Kant, among others, has denied that empathy or compassion is a necessary condition of our actions having moral value. Others have argued that the moral point of view is, by definition, disinterested and impartial. To adopt it, I must abstract from my interests, projects, and personal relationships, counting these as no more (though no less) important than those "of a man far beyond the seas" whom I have "never set eyes on."[66] If views like this are correct, then, while my detachment from my daughter's sorrows may be inhuman, it is not inconsistent with morality.

I conclude, then, that Danto has not shown that karma yoga is nonmoral.[67]

---

66   Meister Eckhart, *Meister Eckhart: German Sermons and Treatises*, 3 vols. London: Watkins, 1981, vol. 1, sermon 5(b), p. 182. Compare R. M. Hare, *Freedom and Reason* (Oxford: Clarendon Press, 1963), and elsewhere. And, arguably, the Christian love commandment demands just such impartiality. (See Chapter 8.)

67   Whether we have anything precisely corresponding to the mixed life is less clear. We would if karma yoga were an essential component of the most perfect life. I have already alluded to Viśiṣṭādvaita Vedānta. P. N. Srinivasachari (*The Philosophy of Viśiṣṭādvaita*, Adyar. Madras: Adyar Library and Research Center, 1943) characterizes its ethical position as follows: after having described karma yoga as "duty for duty's sake irrespective of inclination within and utility without" (p. 330), Srinivasachari concludes by asserting that it "is not really an end in itself, but is a means to mukti [release] through self-purification and self-knowledge" (p. 333)—which would imply that karma yoga is *not* part of the most perfect life. But he also maintains that "the *jhāni* [knower] realizes the kinship of all *jīvas* ["souls"] and regards the joys and sorrows of others as his own. Sympathy is not merely a feeling that impels the *yogin*, but is a spiritual motive that induces him to action . . . The monistic theory that abolishes individuality [Advaita Vedānta] affords no scope for such social love." (p. 345) "The mystic realizes that he is only an instrument of the divine will . . . His life is supra-moral in the sense that it is the crown and completion of the moral life. God is absolutely good and not morally indifferent, and the chief quality of God is transmitting His godliness to His *other* and making him perfect. Saintliness and unrighteousness can never co-exist." (p. 443) Mysticism is only amoral in the sense that whereas "morality is at best a struggle to reach the ideal of goodness," the saint "has no longer to seek the good but becomes goodness itself;" "spirituality is perfected in service." (p. 444) The Viśiṣṭādvaitin ideal thus appears to be the mixed life. These claims must be viewed with caution, however. In the first place, Srinivasachari is a modern Viśiṣṭādvaitin, a professor of philosophy familiar with Western thought. He is also heir to colonial (and postcolonial) developments in Hinduism which have tried to combine traditional Hindu spirituality with Western social consciousness. (On the latter see Jeffrey J. Kripal, "Seeing Inside and Outside the Goddess: The Mystical and the Ethical in the Teachings of Ramakrisna and Vivekananda," in Bernard and Kripal, *Crossing Bounda-*

Conclusions

If the argument of this section has been sound, we are entitled to draw the following conclusions. First, the ideal of the mixed life incorporates moral values. Second, Danto's moral objections to karma yoga are inconclusive. Third, the ideals of Advaita Vedānta and Hīnayāna Buddhism are essentially nonmoral. Since the ideal of the mixed life and karma yoga tend to be closely associated with theistic mysticism while Advaita Vedānta and (possibly) Hīnayāna Buddhism appear to be relatively pure expressions of monistic mystical consciousness, it seems reasonable to infer that theistic mysticism is implicitly moral whereas monistic mysticism is not. (Or perhaps more accurately, that theistic mysticism comports better with moral values, that there is less tension between them than between morality and monistic mysticism.) What is not clear is whether the theistic mystic's attitude toward moral values is determined by her theism or by her mystical experiences. I suspect that the former is the principal determinant, and that the theistic mystic's experiences affect her attitudes primarily by reinforcing her commitment to theism and its values.[68]

The force of these considerations would be diminished if it could be shown that the ideal of the mixed life is an important feature of one or more nontheistic traditions, and that the ideal's incorporation in those traditions is not due to theistic or quasi-theistic influences. (Further study of the bodhisattva ideal is needed in this connection.) To destroy the force of these considerations one would need to show that the ideal of the mixed life occurs as frequently within nontheistic as within theistic mystical traditions, and that its nonmoral alternatives occur as frequently within theistic mystical traditions as within those which aren't theistic. This is manifestly not the case.

---

ries, pp. 230–64.) The influence of Western thought can't be excluded. In the second place, Srinivasachari fails to cite classical texts which clearly take the position that he has articulated. As a result, we are not entitled to conclude that the mixed life was unambiguously recommended by pre-modern Viśiṣṭādvaita Vedānta. In spite of these reservations, however, it seems reasonable to conclude that the emphasis placed upon action in the *Gītā* and theistic Vedānta reflects a greater concern for moral and social values than is found in either Advaita or Hīnayāna Buddhism.

68 For some additional confirmation of the view that theistic mysticism tends to support morality see R. Blake Michael, "Work as Worship in Vīraśaiva Tradition," *Journal of the American Academy of Religion* 50 (1982), pp. 605–19. The Vīraśaivas have something like a Protestant notion of work as a vocation through which one serves God and one's neighbor.

Does Mysticism either Justify or Undermine Morality?

Many think that there are important logical or epistemic connections between mystical experience and morality.[69] I will examine two attempts to show that mystical consciousness provides a backing or warrant for altruistic behavior and two arguments purporting to show that mysticism and morality are incompatible. These arguments are paradigmatic. Most of the arguments that attempt to establish logical or epistemic connections between mysticism and morality are variants of those discussed in this section. My conclusion is that all four are unsound, and that there is thus reason to suspect that there are no significant epistemic or logical connections between them.

Does Mysticism Justify Morality?

Walter Stace believes that mystical consciousness provides a justification for altruism.[70] It does this in two ways.

First, mystical consciousness causally induces loving behavior by eliminating the egoism of ordinary consciousness, which is the major obstacle to altruism.[71] This thesis is empirical and some evidence supports it. Its truth is irrelevant to our present purposes, however. That there are causal connections between mystical consciousness and morality in no way implies that there are any logical or epistemic connections between them.

Second, mystical consciousness provides a justification or warrant for loving behavior. For consider the following argument:

1   We are all one—identical with one another or part of each other. There are no separate selves. (This proposition is directly warranted by mystical consciousness.)

---

69   Or, more accurately, between propositions which are directly warranted by mystical experience and moral propositions.

70   Stace, *Mysticism and Philosophy*, chapter 8.

71   Jonathan Shear ("Ethics and the Experience of Happiness," in Barnard and Kripal, *Crossing Boundaries*, pp. 361–80) argues that since the monistic mystic identifies herself with pure consciousness or pure joyous consciousness, and since pure consciousness or pure joyous consciousness is distinct from any and every social role and conditioned self-image, it should be "easier" for her "to recognize [her] common humanity with others;" "greater compassion and less confinement by concern for racial, class, religious, and other barriers ... seem to follow naturally" from the experience—or, more accurately, from one's identification with the self revealed in it. (p. 374) All that strictly follows, however, is that the experience weakens or destroys some of the more common *motives* for unethical behavior. It doesn't show that one *will or should be* concerned about others.

Therefore,

2   I should treat others as I (either do or should) treat myself, that is, I ought to care tenderly for them, benefit them, and the like.

This argument is suspect on three counts. First, the premise isn't clearly true and, in any case, is not directly warranted by most types of mystical consciousness. If it were, it would be difficult to explain why the claim that we are fundamentally identical with or part of one another is rejected by theistic mystics, Theravādins, and adherents of Sāṃkhya-Yoga. That they reject it suggests that it is an *interpretation* of mystical experience rather than a claim directly warranted by it.

Stace may think that *unitary* experiences at least (cosmic consciousness and monistic consciousness) *incorporate* the belief that all selves are one. But even this is doubtful. The impressions of intimate union and the dissolution of boundaries that are features of cosmic consciousness or nature mysticism are one thing; a belief that we are *literally* one entity is quite another. Only the latter would justify the conclusion that I should treat others as I treat myself because they really *are* myself.

Some think that the premise does immediately follow from a conviction that is directly warranted by *monistic* experience, however, namely, that all distinctions are unreal. That a belief in the unreality of all distinctions is an *intrinsic* feature of monistic consciousness isn't implausible. Nevertheless, it seems mistaken. Monistic mystics frequently distinguish aspects within (the object of) their experience (for example, being, consciousness, and bliss). More important, even if these experiences are cognitively valid, and even if the experience and/or its object is distinctionless, it doesn't follow that *all* distinctions are unreal, for the experience and/or its object may be something less than the whole of reality. The monistic experience, for example, might be an experience of the depth of one's own soul or of one's own ontologically distinct real self as Sāṃkhya-Yoga, Jains, and many theistic mystics have maintained.

Second, the argument suggests that we should care for others because they are identical with ourselves. Altruism is grounded in egoism and hence isn't real altruism. A love of this sort is like that of a parent who cares for his child because he views her as an extension of himself, or Aristotle's friends who love each other because each regards the other as an alter ego, another self. It involves a subtle self-centeredness.

Third, it has been argued (by Paul Tillich, Martin Buber, D. H. Lawrence, and others) that love at its best involves distance and difference as well as union. If so, and Stace's premise is true, then real love is impossible for the enlightened. Far from supporting the claim that we should care for others, Stace's premise makes love impossible for anyone who has succeeded in divesting herself of "illusions."

To sum up: since the premise of Stace's argument isn't directly warranted by nature mysticism or monistic mystical consciousness (let alone theistic mystical consciousness), we are not entitled to conclude that they justify altruism. We are at most entitled to conclude that a not unnatural *interpretation* of these experiences justifies altruism. Even this conclusion is unwarranted, however. Not only does the premise not justify altruism; it would, if true, make it impossible.

Don Browning has called our attention to the fact that in addition to arguments from union, there is a proof from "mysticisms of emptiness and void . . . Since in the final experience of nirvana, nirodh ["stopping"] or 'no mind' all vestiges of ego and self are abolished, it is argued by some that all egoism, selfishness, and self-centeredness vanish and only altruism and love remain."[72]

Up to a point, this makes a certain rough sense. The unreality of the self implies the unreality of its interests and concerns. "I am interested in (desire, hate, and so on) x" entails or presupposes "I exist." Hence, if the latter is false, so too is the former. Whether the experience of emptiness justifies altruistic behavior is another matter.

The argument would presumably go like this:

1   Reasons for acting egoistically are provided by one's interests, needs, concerns, and desires.
2   These interests, needs, concerns, and desires are real only if the self is real.
3   The self is unreal. (The emptiness experience provides the backing for this.)

Therefore,

4   A person's interests, needs, concerns, and desires are unreal. (From 2 and 3.)

Hence,

5   There are no good reasons for acting egoistically. (From 1 and 4, and the assumption that if an interest or need is unreal, it can't provide a good reason for action.)

Consequently,

6   There are good reasons for acting altruistically. (From 5.)

Several things are wrong with this argument.

First, (3) is a statement of the Buddhist no-ātman doctrine. But this doctrine appears to depend as much on metaphysical analysis as on mystical experience. (Remember that we are looking for logical or epistemic connections between

---

72   Don Browning, "William James' Philosophy of Mysticism," *Journal of Religion* 59 (1979), p. 58.

mystical *consciousness* and moral claims, not between moral claims and meta-physical statements which are more or less loosely *based* on mystical consciousness.)

Second, (5) does not entail (6). That there are no good reasons *for* acting egoistically doesn't entail that there are good reasons *against* acting egoistically. And even if there were, it would not follow that there are good reasons for *acting altruistically*. The wisest course of action might be to withdraw from society and its concerns, and doing so needn't be either egoistic or altruistic. (Those who withdraw from society *have* been accused of egoism. Confucians accused Buddhists of neglecting their social obligations, and Mahāyāna accuses Hīnayāna of a subtle self-seeking. But these charges are controversial. The Hīnayāna *arhat*, for instance, has succeeded in rooting out what we ordinarily regard as selfishness. He has extinguished thirst and neither injures others nor harbors ill will toward them. He no longer competes with them or sacrifices their interest to his own.)

There is also a third objection. The Buddhist school which developed the doctrine of emptiness with the most sophistication (namely, Mādhyamika) distinguished between *paramartha satya*, or absolute truth, the intuitive nonconceptual insight into the emptiness of reality, and *saṃvriti satya*, or conventional truth.[73] And this creates a problem, for on the conventional level the self is real. But if it is, the argument provides no reasons for thinking that ordinary motives for acting self-interestedly are suspended *at that level*. Ordinary prudential reasons may only apply at the level of mundane reality but, at that level, there is no reason to believe they aren't valid. (3) and (4) are only true at the level of absolute truth and hence (5) too is only true at that level. Therefore, unless we can assert that enlightened mystics no longer dwell in the conventional world at all,[74] we aren't justified in concluding that prudential considerations provide them with no reason for acting self-interestedly.[75]

---

73 Candrakīrti gives three definitions of "saṃvriti satya"—(1) "views," (2) the phenomenal world, and (3) "views in conformity with conventional ideas." False statements (for example, the statement of someone who, mistaking a rope for a snake, says "That's a snake") are subsumed under *saṃvriti satya*; and in this respect Mādhyamika differs from Advāita, which distinguishes between what might be called the absolutely true, the provisionally true, and the false. Even so, Mādhyamika does admit differences and degrees within the realm of *saṃvriti satya*; some claims are more deeply infected with falsehood than others. See T. R. V. Murti, *The Central Philosophy of Buddhism* (London: George Allen and Unwin, 1955), pp. 243–55.

74 And we can't. The enlightened mystic has the same reasons for eating rice and vegetables, rather than sawdust and sand, that we do. Furthermore, he acts on them.

75 It might be objected that this misses the point. Having achieved emptiness, the enlightened mystic has extinguished desires, and without them there can be no prudential reasons. (Prudential reasons are, as Kant saw, hypothetical imperatives resting on our desires. Their form is: "If you want so and so, do such and such.") Hence, enlightened mystics *can't* have reasons for acting egoistically. The trouble with this line of argument, however, is this: by parity of reasoning, the enlightened mystic can't have reasons for acting altruistically either—assuming (as seems reasonable) that these too are provided by, or presuppose, interests in, and desires for, other people's well-being.

Does Mysticism Undermine Morality?

We now turn to two arguments which purport to show that it does:

A(1) The divine (the absolute, the One, that which is truly real) embraces opposites or opposites coincide in the divine. (Mystical consciousness provides the backing for this statement.)
(2) These opposites include moral good and moral evil.

Therefore,

(3) The distinction between moral good and moral evil is unimportant or unreal. (It is unimportant if both moral good and moral evil manifest the divine. It is unreal if moral good and moral evil coincide.)[76]

B(1) The divine altogether transcends the phenomenal world and/or the phenomenal world is unreal or totally lacking in value. (Mystical consciousness provides the backing for this statement.)

Hence,

(2) Categories which apply within the phenomenal world, and distinctions between things within in it, are infected by illusion (or are at least unimportant).
(3) Moral categories apply within the phenomenal world, and the distinction between between moral good and moral evil is a distinction between phenomenal realities.

Therefore,

(4) Moral categories and distinctions are infected by illusion (or are at least unimportant).[77]

Several remarks are in order. First, some types of mystical consciousness do seem to suggest that moral values aren't the most important. One can respond to this in two ways. One might argue that because moral values are, by definition, the most important, the best life must include an unqualified respect for the moral law. If mysticism assigns a secondary role to morality, then mysticism undercuts it and is,

---

76   For an argument of this type see R. C. Zaehner, *Our Savage God* (London: William Collins Sons, 1974). Zaehner is critical of non-theistic mysticism precisely because he believes that it implicitly incorporates this type of reasoning.

77   Arthur Danto (*Mysticism and Morality*) argues that the "logic of mysticism" forces mystics to draw this conclusion.

for that very reason, flawed. Or one might argue that moral values are instrumental and, hence, logically posterior to those values (blessedness, happiness, self-realization, and the like) to which morally good things are means. If mystical consciousness is an end (or part of an end) to which moral values are means, then mystical consciousness is compatible with morality although it relegates moral values to a secondary position.

But the contention that moral values aren't the most important shouldn't be confused with the conclusions of the arguments we are presently discussing. If these arguments are sound, moral values don't merely play a secondary or instrumental role; they collapse altogether or are reduced to insignificance.

Second, premises A(1) and B(1) are based on cosmic consciousness and monistic consciousness, respectively. Since these aren't the only types of mystical consciousness, we can't conclude that mysticism as such is incompatible with morality. The most we can conclude is that cosmic and monistic consciousness are.

Third, the first argument appeals to cosmic consciousness and the second to monistic consciousness. Do these modes of consciousness really support the conclusion that moral values are illusory or unimportant? They would *if* the relevant experiences were veridical, and *if* the convictions articulated in A(1) and B(1) were directly warranted by those experiences. The second assumption seems false, however.

Nature mysticism includes a sense of the radical unity of all things, and nature mystics do sometimes speak of the identity of phenomenal objects. But it isn't clear that cosmic consciousness includes a sense of the coincidence of *all* distinctions, including those between truth and falsity, for instance, or reality and illusion. Nor is it clear that it normally involves a sense of the divinity of specifically *moral* (as distinguished from natural) evil.[78] If either of these intuitions *is* an intrinsic feature of cosmic consciousness, however, one can argue (with Zaehner) that, for that very reason, cosmic consciousness can't be veridical. If so, then if the second assumption is true, the first is false.

The unreality of the phenomenal world *would* follow from *monistic* experience if monistic experience were veridical and a belief in the unreality of all distinctions were built into it. As we have seen, however, a belief in the unreality of *all* distinctions does not appear to be a structural feature of monistic mystical consciousness. Nor do monistic mystics always conclude that the phenomenal world is unreal or lacking in value. (Monistic mystics like Plotinus and adherents of Sāṃkhya-Yoga believe in real distinctions and a real space-time world. Plotinus also believed that the world is good in so far as it reflects the One, and Sāṃkhya-Yoga ascribes value to it in so far as it serves the purposes of the true self or puruṣa.)

---

78 Thomas Traherne, for example, was a Christian nature mystic whose experiences involve nothing of the sort.

These considerations suggest that A(1) and B(1) are interpretations of cosmic consciousness and monistic consciousness, respectively, rather than claims directly warranted by them. We are, therefore, only entitled to conclude that some (extreme) *interpretations* of cosmic and monistic consciousness are incompatible with morality—not that they are *themselves* incompatible with it.

Fourth, the experience of "emptiness" would be incompatible with morality if it incorporated the conviction that *all* distinctions are equally invalid. For this would entail that all moral distinctions are invalid. But if it does, one can argue that because moral distinctions *are* valid, the experience is delusive. While it may not be clear precisely where the burden of proof lies, our moral experience is at least as compelling as our religious experience.

Finally, *theistic* mystical consciousness provides no support for the conclusion that moral values are illusory or unimportant.

In some contexts "x is more real than y" is equivalent to "x is more valuable than y, and y is dependent upon x while x is not dependent upon y."[79] Given that a sense of the dependence and comparative worthlessness of oneself and creatures generally is built into theistic consciousness,[80] that the world is less real, or only relatively real, or comparatively unreal does follow from theistic mystical consciousness. What does not follow is that moral values are less real, or only relatively real, or comparatively unreal. This does not follow because for theistic consciousness, the transcendent order is *itself* a realm of moral value. Indeed, the moral value exhibited in the phenomenal world is seen as no more than an image or reflection of God's archetypal moral goodness.

I conclude, then, that attempts to show that mystical consciousness is incompatible with morality are no more successful than attempts to show that it supports it.

Conclusion

Mysticism sometimes affects morality adversely. It does so when it makes someone indifferent to moral values and the importance of moral distinctions. On the other hand, mysticism seems to have positive and beneficial effects upon the moral lives of many of those touched by it. Mysticism strengthens morality by strengthening attitudes and dispositions, such as charity and humility, which are moral or have positive moral consequences, and by bringing home to us such morally relevant truths as the truth of the reality of the transcendent order and the fact that we

---

79 This usage may be contrasted with that of Advaita Vedānta, where "less real" is interpreted with the help of the concept of sublation (one perception or insight sublates another if it supersedes it and shows it to be in error), and with that of Mādhyamika, where "unreal" is interpreted as self-contradictory or incoherent.

80 It is clearly built into numinous experience. I believe that it is also built into theistic mystical consciousness.

belong to that order as well as to nature. What is not clear is that mysticism teaches any morally relevant truths which are unavailable to us apart from mystical experience,[81] or that any moral ideal or norm depends upon mystical consciousness for its validity.

Moreover, if my argument in the preceding section has been sound, neither cosmic consciousness, monistic consciousness, nor the emptiness experience is a necessary or sufficient condition of the truth or falsity of any moral proposition. Theistic mystical consciousness may include positive evaluations of love and holiness and a belief that these play an important part in the grand scheme of things. But even if it does, there is no reason to think that the conviction that love and holiness are morally valuable can't be adequately supported without appealing to mystical consciousness, or that mystical consciousness provides the most compelling grounds for this conviction.

I conclude, then, that while there may be significant psychological or social connections between mysticism and morality, there are few significant logical or epistemic connections between them. Morality is compatible with mysticism but does not depend upon it for its validity.

---

81 Mystical experience *might* have been the fountainhead of some of these insights. (It is conceivable that without mysticism they would never have occurred to anyone.) But, once discovered, we need not be mystics to discern their truth.

Bibliography

Adams, Robert M. 1987. *The Virtue of Faith and Other Essays in Philosophical Theology*. New York: Oxford University Press.
_____. 1990. 'The Knight of Faith.' *Faith and Philosophy* 7: 387-90.
_____. 1994. *Leibniz: Determinist, Theist, Idealist*. New York: Oxford University Press.
_____. 1999. *Finite and Infinite Goods*. New York: Oxford University Press.
_____. 2002. 'Reply to my Critics.' *Philosophy and Phenomenological Research* 64: 474-90.
Alston, William P. 1989. 'Some Suggestions for Divine Command Theorists.' In William P. Alston, *Divine Nature and Human Language: Essays in Philosophical Theology*. Ithaca, NY: Cornell University Press.
Anderson, Bernhard W. 1998. *Understanding the Old Testament*, 4th edn. Upper Saddle River, NJ: Prentice-Hall.
Aquinas, Thomas. 1947. *The Summa Theologica*. New York: Benziger Bros.
Aristotle. 1984. *The Complete Works of Aristotle*, ed. Jonathan Barnes. Princeton, NJ: Princeton University Press.
Augustine. 1948. *The City of God*, trans. Marcus Dods. New York: Hafner.
Baintain, Roland H. 1961. *Christian Attitudes Toward War and Peace*. London: Hodder and Stoughton.
Barnard, William G., and Jeffrey J. Kripal, eds. 2002. *Crossing Boundaries: Essays on the Ethical Status of Mysticism*. New York and London: Seven Bridges Press.
Boyd, Richard. 1988. 'How to be a Moral Realist.' In Geoffrey Sayre-McCord, ed., *Essays on Moral Realism*. Ithaca, NY: Cornell University Press.
Broad, C. D. 1959. *Five Types of Ethical Theory*. Paterson, NJ: Littlefield, Adams, and Co.
Browning, Don. 1979. 'William James' Philosophy of Mysticism.' *Journal of Religion* 59: 56-70.
Buber, Martin. 1955. *Between Man and Man*, trans. Ronald Gregor Smith. Boston: Beacon Press.
Byrne, Peter. 1998. *The Moral Interpretation of Religion*. Grand Rapids, MI: William B. Eerdmanns.
Chandler, John. 1985. 'Divine Command Theories and the Appeal to Love.' *American Philosophical Quarterly* 22: 231-39.
Conze, Edward. 1959. *Buddhism: Its Essence and Development*. New York: Harper Torchbooks.
_____. 1967. *Buddhist Thought in India*. Ann Arbor, MI: University of Michigan Press.
Cudworth, Ralph. 1731. *A Treatise Concerning True and Immutable Morality*. London: J. & J. Knapton. (Reprint, New York: Garland, 1976.)
Danto, Arthur. 1972. *Mysticism and Morality: Oriental Thought and Moral Philosophy*. New York: Harper Torchbooks.
Descartes, Rene. 1955. *Objections and Replies*. In Elizabeth S. Haldane and G. R. T. Ross, trans. *The Philosophical Works of Descartes*, vol. 2. New York: Dover Publications.
Deutsch, Eliot. 1968. *The Bhagavad Gītā, Translated with introduction and critical essays*. New York: Holt, Rinehart, and Wilson.
_____. 1977. *Advaita Vedānta: A Philosophical Reconstruction*. Honolulu: University Press of Hawaii.

_____, and J. A. B. Van Buitenen. 1971. *A Source Book of Advaita Vedānta*. Honolulu: University Press of Hawaii.

Dunne, John. 1996. 'Thoughtless Buddha, Passionate Buddha.' *Journal of the American Academy of Religion* 64: 525-56.

Eckhart, John. 1981. *Meister Eckhart: German Sermons and Treatises*, 3 vols. London: Watkins.

Edwards, Jonathan. 1959. *A Treatise Concerning Religious Affections*. (The Works of Jonathan Edwards, vol. 2.) New Haven: Yale University Press.

_____. 1989. *The Nature of True Virtue*. In Paul Ramsey, ed., *Ethical Writings*. (The Works of Jonathan Edwards, vol. 8.) New Haven: Yale University Press.

Ellul, Jacques. 1969. *Violence: Reflections from a Christian Perspective*, trans. Cecelia Gaul Kings. New York: Seabury Press.

England, F. E. 1929. *Kant's Conception of God*. London: George Allen and Unwin.

Evans, Stephen C. 1993. '*Faith as the Telos of Morality: A Reading of Fear and Trembling.*' In Robert L. Perkins, ed., *Fear and Trembling and Repetition*. (International Kierkegaard Commentary.) Macon, GA: Mercer University Press.

_____. 2004. *Kierkegaard's Ethic of Love: Divine Commands and Moral Obligations*. New York and London: Oxford University Press.

Ewing, A. C. 1961. 'The Autonomy of Ethics.' In Ian Ramsey, ed., *Prospect for Metaphysics*. London: George Allen and Unwin.

_____. 1973. *Value and Reality*. London: George Allen and Unwin.

Freud, Sigmund. 1958. *Civilization and its Discontents,* trans. Joan Riviere. Garden City, NY: Anchor Books.

Gauthier, David. 1986. *Morals by Agreement*. Oxford: Clarendon Press.

Gellman, Jerome I. 2003. *Abraham! Abraham!: Kierkegaard and the Hasidim on the Binding of Isaac*. Aldershot: Ashgate.

Grave, S. A. 1989. *Conscience in Newman's Thought*. Oxford. Clarendon Press.

Handy, Robert T. 1984. *A Christian America: Protestant Hopes and Historical Realities*, 2nd edn. New York: Oxford University Press.

Hare, John. 1996. *The Moral Gap*. Oxford: Clarendon Press.

_____. 2001. *God's Call: Moral Realism, God's Commands, and Human Autonomy*. Grand Rapids, MI: William B. Eerdmanns.

Hare, R. M. 1952. *The Language of Morals*. Oxford: Clarendon Press.

Hauerwas, Stanley. 1985. 'Pacifism: Some Philosophical Considerations.' *Faith and Philosophy* 2: 99-104.

Helgeland, John, Robert J. Daly, and J. Partout Burns. 1985. *Christians and the Military: The Early Experience*. Philadelphia: Fortress Press.

Hume, David. c.1947. *Dialogues Concerning Natural Religion*. Ed. with intro. by Norman Kemp Smith. Indianapolis: Bobbs-Merrill.

_____. 1955. *A Treatise of Human Nature*. Oxford: Clarendon Press.

Idziak, Janine Marie, ed. 1979. *Divine Command Morality: Historical and Contemporary Readings*. New York and Toronto: Edwin Mellon Press.

_____. 1989. 'In Search of "Good Positive Reasons" for an Ethics of Divine Commands: A Catalogue of Arguments.' *Faith and Philosophy* 6: 47-64.

_____. 1997. 'Divine Command Ethics.' In Philip Quinn and Charles Taliaferro, eds., *A Companion to the Philosophy of Religion*. Cambridge, MA and Oxford: Blackwell.

James, William. 1956. 'The Sentiment of Rationality.' In William James, *The Will to Believe and Other Essays on Popular Philosophy*. New York: Dover Publications.

John of the Cross. 1961. *Spiritual Canticle*, 3rd rev. edn, ed. and trans. E. Allison Peers. Garden City, NY: Image/Doubleday.

Jones, Richard H. 1993. 'Must Enlightened Mystics be Moral?' In Richard H. Jones, *Mysticism Examined: Philosophical Inquiries into Mysticism*. Albany: State University of New York Press.

Kant, Immanuel. 1956. *Critique of Practical Reason*. Trans. Lewis White Beck. New York: The Liberal Arts Press.

_____. 1956. *Critique of Pure Reason*. Trans. Norman Kemp Smith. London: Macmillan.

_____. 1959. *Foundations of the Metaphysics of Morals*. Trans. Lewis White Beck. Indianapolis: Bobbs-Merrill.

_____. 1960. *Reason Within the Limits of Reason Alone*. Trans. Theodore M. Greene and Hoyt H. Hudson. New York: Harper Torchbooks.

_____. 1964. *The Metaphysics of Morals, Part II: The Doctrine of Virtue*. Trans. Mary J. Gregor. New York: Harper Torchbooks.

_____. 1987. *Critique of Judgment*. Trans. Werner S. Pluhar. Indianapolis: Hackett.

Kapleau, Phillip. 1967. *The Three Pillars of Zen*. Boston: Beacon Press.

Katz, Steven T. 1992. 'Ethics and Mysticism in Eastern Mystical Traditions.' *Religious Studies* 28: 253-67.

Kierkegaard, Søren. 1954. *Fear and Trembling*. Trans. Walter Lowrie. Garden City, NY: Doubleday Anchor Books.

_____. 1962. *Works of Love*. Trans. Howard V. and Edna H. Hong. New York: Harper.

_____. 1997. *Christian Discourses; The Crisis and a Crisis in the Life of an Actress*. Ed. and trans., with intro. and notes by Howard V. and Edna H. Hong. Princeton, NJ: Princeton University Press.

King, Sallie B. 2002. 'Buddhism and War.' Delivered at the Annual Meeting of the American Academy of Religion, Toronto.

Koestler, Arthur. 1960. *The Lotus and the Robot*. New York: Macmillan.

Kørner, S. 1955. *Kant*. Middlesex: Penguin Books.

Korsgaard, Christine M. 1996. *The Sources of Normativity*. Cambridge: Cambridge University Press.

Kretzmann, Norman. 1991. 'A General Problem of Creation: Why Would God Create Anything at All?'. In Scott MacDonald, ed., *Being and Goodness*. Ithaca, NY: Cornell University Press.

Kripal, Jeffrey J. 2002. 'Debating the Mystical as Ethical: An Indological Map.' In Barnard and Kripal, eds., *Crossing Boundaries*.

_____. 2002. 'Seeing Inside and Outside the Goddess: The Mystical and the Ethical in the Teachings of Ramakrisna and Vivekananda.' In Barnard and Kripal, eds., *Crossing Boundaries*.

Kvanvig, Jonathan L. 1993. *The Problem of Hell*. New York: Oxford University Press.

Leibniz, G. W. 1951. *Theodicy*, trans. E. M. Huggard. London: Routledge and Kegan Paul.

Levenson, Jon D. 1993. *The Death and Resurrection of the Beloved Son*. New Haven: Yale University Press.

Lewis, C. S. 1947. *Miracles*. New York: Macmillan.

Loy, David R. 2002. 'The Lack of Ethics and the Ethics of Lack in Buddhism.' In Bernard and Kripal, *Crossing Boundaries*.

Luther, Martin. 1969. *The Bondage of the Will*. In E. Gordon Rupp and Philip S. Watson, eds., *Luther and Erasmus: Free Will and Salvation*. Philadelphia: Westminster.

Mackie, J. L. 1977. *Ethics: Inventing Right and Wrong*. Harmondsworth, Middlesex; Penguin Books.

_____. 1982. *The Miracle of Theism*. Oxford: Clarendon Press.

Maclagen, W. G. 1961. *The Theological Frontier of Ethics*. New York: Macmillan.

Mavrodes, George I. 1986. 'Religion and the Queerness of Morality.' In Robert Audi and William J. Wainwright, eds., *Rationality, Religious Belief, and Moral Commitment*. Ithaca, NY: Cornell University Press.

Mawson, T. J. 2002. 'God's Creation of Morality.' *Religious Studies* 38: 1-25.

Merton, Thomas. 1968. *Zen and the Birds of Appetite*. New York: New Directions.

Michael, R. Blake. 1982. 'Work as Worship in Viraśaiva Tradition.' *Journal of the American Academy of Religion* 50: 605-19.

Mill, John Stuart. 1958. *Considerations on Representative Government*. New York: Liberal Arts Press.

Miller, Caleb. 1999. 'Creation, Redemption, and Virtue.' *Faith and Philosophy* 16: 368-77.

_____. 2000. 'Character and Independent Duty: An Anabaptist Approach.' *Faith and Philosophy* 17: 293-305.

Mooney, Edward F. 1986. 'Abraham and Dilemma: Kierkegaard's Teleological Suspension Revisited.' *International Journal for Philosophy of Religion* 19: 23-41.

Moore, G. E. 1951. 'The Conception of Intrinsic Value.' in G. E. Moore, *Philosophical Studies*. New York: The Humanities Press.

Morris, Thomas V. 1987. 'Absolute Creation.' In Thomas V. Morris, *Anselmian Explorations*. Notre Dame, IN: University of Notre Dame Press.

Mouw, Richard J. 1985. 'Christianity and Pacifism.' *Faith and Philosophy* 2: 105-11.

Murphy, Mark C. 1998. 'Divine Command, Divine Will, and Moral Obligation.' *Faith and Philosophy* 15: 3-27.

_____. 2001. 'Divine Authority and Divine Perfection.' *International Journal for Philosophy of Religion* 49: 155-77.

_____. 2002. 'A Trilemma for Divine Command Theory.' *Faith and Philosophy* 19: 23-31.

_____. 2002. *An Essay on Divine Authority*. Ithaca, NY: Cornell University Press.

Murti, T. R. V. 1955. *The Central Philosophy of Buddhism*. London: George Allen and Unwin.

Newman, John Henry. 1859. 'Proof of Theism.' In Adrian J. Boekraad and Henry Tristam, *The Argument from Conscience to the Existence of God According to J. H. Newman*. Louvain: Editions Nauwelaerts, 1961.

_____. 1979. *An Essay in Aid of a Grammar of Assent*. Notre Dame, IN: University of Notre Dame Press.

Nicholson, Reynold A. 1963. *The Mystics of Islam*. London: Routledge and Kegan Paul.

Niebuhr, Reinhold. 1932. *Moral Man and Immoral Society*. New York: Charles Scribner's Sons.

_____. 1935. *An Interpretation of Christian Ethics*. New York and London: Harper.

_____. 1940. *Christianity and Power Politics*. New York: Charles Scribner's Sons.

Nuyen, R. T. 1998. 'Is Kant a Divine Command Theorist?' *History of Philosophy Quarterly* 15: 441-53.

O'Neill, Onora. 1989. *Constructions of Reason: Explorations of Kant's Moral Philosophy*. Cambridge: Cambridge University Press.

Otto, Rudolph. 1958. *The Idea of the Holy*. Trans. John W. Harvey. New York: Oxford University Press.

Outka, Gene. 1973. 'Religious and Moral Duty: Notes on *Fear and Trembling*.' In Gene Outka and John P. Reeder, eds., *Religion and Morality*. Garden City, NY: Anchor/ Doubleday.

Owen, H. P. 1965. *The Moral Argument for Christian Theism*. London: George Allen and Unwin.

Paley, William. 1819. *Principles of Moral and Political Philosophy*, 4th American ed. Boston: John West.

Paton, H. J. 1967. *The Categorical Imperative: A Study in Kant's Moral Philosophy*. New York: Harper Torchbooks.

Payne, Steven, OCD. 1990. *John of the Cross and the Cognitive Value of Mysticism*. Dortrecht: Kluwer.

Plantinga, Alvin. 1980. *Does God Have a Nature?* Marquette, WI: Marquette University Press.

Plato. 1937. *Euthyphro*. In Benjamin Jowett, trans., *The Dialogues of Plato*, vol. 1. New York: Random House.

Potter, R. Dennis. 2003. 'Moral Dilemmas and Inevitable Sin.' *Faith and Philosophy* 20: 63-71.

Price, Richard. 1974. *A Review of the Principle Questions in Morals*. Oxford: Clarendon Press.

Quinn, Philip L. 1978. *Divine Commands and Moral Requirements*. Oxford: Clarendon Press.

_____. 1979. 'Divine Command Ethics: A Causal Theory.' In Idziak, *Divine Command Morality*.

_____. 1986. 'Moral Obligation, Religious Demand, and Practical Conflict.' In Robert Audi and William J. Wainwright, eds., *Rationality, Religious Belief, and Moral Commitment*. Ithaca, NY: Cornell University Press.

_____. 1990. 'An Argument for Divine Command Ethics.' In Michael D. Beaty, ed. *Christian Theism and the Problems of Philosophy*. Notre Dame, IN: University of Notre Dame Press.

_____. 1990. 'The Recent Revival of Divine Command Ethics.' *Philosophy and Phenomenological Research* 50: 345-65.

_____.1990. 'Agamemnon and Abraham: The Tragic Dilemma of Kierkegaard's Knight of Faith.' *Journal of Literature and Theology* 4: 181-93.

_____. 1992. 'The Primacy of God's Will in Christian Ethics.' *Philosophical Perspectives* 6: 493-513.

_____. 2000. 'Divine Command Theory.' In Hugh La Follette, ed., *The Blackwell Guide to Ethical Theory*. Malden, MA: Blackwell.

_____. 2002. 'Obligation, Divine Commands, and Abrahams's Dilemma.' *Philosophy and Phenomenological Research* 64: 459-66.

_____. 2003. 'The Master Argument of *The Nature of True Virtue*.' In Paul Helm and Oliver D. Crisp, eds., *Jonathan Edwards: Philosophical Theologian*. Aldershot: Ashgate.

Rachels, James. 1971. 'God and Human Attitudes.' *Religious Studies* 7: 325-37.

Ramsey, Paul. 1950. *Basic Christian Ethics*. New York: Charles Scribner's Sons.

Rawls, John. 1971. *A Theory of Justice*. Cambridge: Harvard University Press.

_____. 1993. *Political Liberalism*. New York: Columbia University Press.

Richard of St. Victor. 1957. 'Four Degrees of Passionate Charity.' In *Richard of St. Victor: Selected Writings on Contemplation*, trans. Clare Kirchberger. London: Faber and Faber.

Ringgren, Helmut. 1966. *Israelite Religion*. Philadelphia: Fortress Press.

Ross, James. 1969. *Philosophical Theology*. Indianapolis: Bobbs-Merrill.

Ross, W. D. 1930. *The Right and the Good*. Oxford: Clarendon Press.

Rutenbar, Culbert G. 1957. *The Dagger and the Cross: An Examination of Christian Pacifism*. Nyack, NY: Fellowship Publications.

Ruysbroeck, Jan van. 1916. *The Adornment of the Spiritual Marriage, The Book of Truth, and the Sparkling Stone*, trans. C. A. Wynschenk Dom. London: John M. Watkins.

Samkara. 1961. *The Bhagavad Gītā with the commentary of Sri Sankaracharya*, trans. A. Mahadeva Sastri. Madras: Samata Books.

Schideler, Mary McDermott. *The Theology of Romantic Love: A Study of the Writings of Charles Williams*. Grand Rapids, MI: William B. Eerdmanns.

Sessions, William Lad. 1985. 'A New Look at Moral Arguments for Theism.' *International Journal for Philosophy of Religion* 18: 51-67.

Seung-Goo Lee. 1993. 'The Antithesis Between the Religious View of Ethics and the Rationalist View of Ethics in *Fear and Trembling*.' In Robert L. Perkins, ed., *Fear and Trembling and Repetition*. (International Kierkegaard Commentary.) Macon, GA: Mercer University Press.

Sharma, I. C. 1970. *Ethical Philosophies of India*. New York: Harper Torchbooks.

Shear, Jonathan. 2002. 'Ethics and the Experience of Happiness.' In Barnard and Kripal, *Crossing Boundaries*.

Sidgwick, Henry. 1913. *The Methods of Ethics*. London: Macmillan.

Sinnott-Armstrong, Walter. 1988. *Moral Dilemmas*. Oxford: Basil Blackwell.

Smart, Ninian. 1960. *A Dialogue of Religions*. London: SCM Press.

Sorley, W. R. 1918. *Moral Values and the Idea of God*. Cambridge: The University Press.

Srinivasachari, P. N. 1943. *The Philosophy of Viśiṣṭādavaita*. Adyar, Madras: Adyar Library and Research Center.

Stace, Walter T. 1960. *Mysticism and Philosophy*. Philadelphia: J. B. Lippincott.

Stearns, J. Brenton. 1978. 'A Moral Argument.' *Idealistic Studies* 8: 193-205.

Stoeber, Michael. 2002. 'Amoral Trickster or Mystic Saint?' In Barnard and Kripal, *Crossing Boundaries*.

Strong, Colin. 1963. 'Plato and the Third Man.' *Proceedings of the Aristotelian Society*, Supplementary vol. 37: 147-64.

Sullivan, Stephen J. 1993. 'Arbitrariness, Divine Commands, and Morality.' *International Journal for Philosophy of Religion* 33: 33-45.

_____. 1994. 'Why Adams Needs to Modify his Divine Command Theory One More Time.' *Faith and Philosophy* 11: 72-81.

Swinburne, Richard. 1979. *The Existence of God*. Oxford: Clarendon Press.

_____. 1986. *The Evolution of Soul*. Oxford: Clarendon Press.

Taylor, A. E. 1948. *Does God Exist?* London: Macmillan.

Talbott, Thomas. 1982. 'Quinn on Divine Commands and Moral Requirements.' *International Journal for Philosophy of Religion* 13: 193-208.

Thich Nhat Hanh. 1993. *For a Future to be Possible: Commentaries on the Five Wonderful Precepts*. Berkeley, CA: Parallax Press.

Upaniṣads. 1996. Trans. Patrick Olivelle. New York: Oxford University Press.

Wainwright, William J. 1996. 'Jonathan Edwards, William Rowe, and the Necessity of Creation.' In Jeff Jordan and Daniel Howard-Snyder, eds., *Faith, Freedom, and Rationality*. Lanham, MD: Rowman and Littlefield.

Weatherhead, Leslie Dixon. 1940. *Thinking Aloud in War-Time*. New York: Abingdon.

Westmoreland, Robert. 1996. 'Two Recent Metaphysical Divine Command Theories of Ethics.' *International Journal for Philosophy of Religion* 39: 15-31.

Wierenga, Edward. 1983. 'A Defensible Divine Command Theory.' *Nous* 17: 387-407.

_____. 1989. *The Nature of God: An Inquiry into Divine Attributes*. Ithaca, NY: Cornell University Press.

Wiley, Basil. 1949. *Nineteenth Century Studies: Coleridge to Matthew Arnold*. New York: Columbia University Press.

Williams, Bernard. 1981. 'Moral Luck.' In Bernard Williams, *Moral Luck*. Cambridge: Cambridge University Press.

_____. 1993. *Shame and Necessity*. Berkeley and Los Angeles: University of California Press.

Williams, Charles. 1959. *Witchcraft*. New York: Meridian Books.

Wood, Allen W. 1970. *Kant's Moral Religion*. Ithaca, NY: Cornell University Press.

Yoder, John H. n. d. *Reinhold Niebuhr and Christian Pacifism*. A Concern Reprint.

Zaehner, R. C. 1966. *Hinduism*. New York: Oxford University Press.

_____. 1970. *Concordant Discord, the Interdependence of Faiths, Being the Gifford Lectures on Natural Religion. Delivered at St Andrews in 1967-1969*. Oxford: Clarendon Press.

_____. 1974. *Our Savage God*. London: William Collins Sons.

Zagzebski, Linda T. 1990. 'What if the Impossible had been Actual?' In Michel D. Beaty, ed., *Christian Theism and the Problems of Philosophy*. Notre Dame, IN: University of Notre Dame Press.

_____. 1991. *The Dilemma of Freedom and Foreknowledge*. New York: Oxford University Press.

_____. 1997. 'Perfect Goodness and Divine Motivation Theory.' *Midwest Studies in Philosophy* 21: 296-309.

_____. 2004. 'Religion and Morality.' In William J. Wainwright, ed., *The Oxford Handbook for Philosophy of Religion*. New York: Oxford University Press.

_____. 2004. *Divine Motivation Theory*. Cambridge: Cambridge University Press.

Index